A
COLORFUL HISTORY
OF
POPULAR DELUSIONS

ALSO BY ROBERT E. BARTHOLOMEW

Hoaxes, Myths, and Manias
(with Benjamin Radford)

UFOs & Alien Contact
(with George S. Howard)

A
COLORFUL
HISTORY
OF
POPULAR
DELUSIONS

ROBERT E. BARTHOLOMEW
AND PETER HASSALL

 Prometheus Books

59 John Glenn Drive
Amherst, New York 14228

Published 2015 by Prometheus Books

Cover images © Bigstock
Cover design by Grace M. Conti-Zilsberger

Inquiries should be addressed to
Prometheus Books
59 John Glenn Drive
Amherst, New York 14228
VOICE: 716–691–0133
FAX: 716–691–0137
WWW.PROMETHEUSBOOKS.COM

19 18 17 16 15   5 4 3 2 1

Library of Congress Cataloging-in-Publication Data

Bartholomew, Robert E.
    A colorful history of popular delusions / by Robert E. Bartholomew and Peter Hassall.
        pages cm
    Includes bibliographical references and index.
    ISBN 978-1-63388-122-8 (paperback) — ISBN 978-1-63388-123-5 (e-book)
    1. Collective behavior—History. 2. Social psychology—History. 3. Delusions—Social aspects—History. 4. Fear—Social aspects—History. 5. Mobs—Psychological aspects— History. 6. Popular culture—Psychological aspects—History. I. Hassall, Peter. II. Title.
HM866.B36 2015
302'.13—dc23
                                                                    2015018990

Printed in the United States of America

To my brother, Paul Bartholomew.

—Robert E. Bartholomew

To my ever-supportive and loving wife, Sheila, and son, Jake.

—Peter Hassall

CONTENTS

INTRODUCTION

This book is a guide to recognizing and understanding the dynamics of collective obsessions and follies, from outlandish beliefs and baseless convictions, to short-term preoccupations with trivial objects or ideas such as fads. Nineteenth-century Scottish journalist Charles Mackay lumped these behaviors under the general heading of "popular delusions."[1] This survey is intended to entertain readers with its colorful stories and aid them in classifying an array of behaviors, some of which date back millennia. Social scientists refer to this as a typology: the classification and study of different types of behaviors and their underlying features. While many outbreaks may seem to have no obvious rhyme or reason, when we delve deeper, patterns do emerge.

Social delusions can be broken into two broad categories: social panics and enthusiasms. Both involve exaggerated reactions generated by extraordinary fear or excitement. Social panics are incubated in an atmosphere of anxiety and uncertainty, such as the appearance of urban legends about tainted imported products from undeveloped countries, reflecting a wider societal suspicion of foreigners. Examples also include the recent upsurge in Islamophobia and anti-Semitism in response to political tensions in Europe and the Middle East. These outbreaks have a long history and can be traced back to the Crusades and Jewish well-poisoning scares of the Middle Ages.

The second category, enthusiasms, involves a rush toward an esteemed object, person, or idea—as in fads, crazes, and manias. While fads are brief infatuations with trivial matters, crazes are often life-changing and may involve selling one's home to join a religious sect. Manias are collective wish fulfilments and include mass sightings of legendary creatures such as Bigfoot, reports of flying saucers, and collective perceptions of miraculous entities like the Virgin Mary. During episodes, prevailing beliefs shape what people see, as information patterns are perceived in the eye of the beholder; people tend to see what they expect or want to see. A classic example is the New Mexico mother who scorched a tortilla that was widely interpreted as representing the face of Jesus.

9

Psychiatric delusions refer to a range of psychotic conditions. Psychotics lose contact with reality and have difficulty distinguishing between the real world and a mental world of fantasy and hallucinations. Psychotic delusions include such conditions as schizophrenia and mood disorders like depression. In paranoid psychosis, patients may feel that they are being watched, or that others are conspiring against them. Social scientists use the term *social delusion* in a nonpsychiatric context to describe the spontaneous, temporary spread of false beliefs in a given population. In most cases, with the notable exception of some cult leaders, there is no sign of psychological disturbance. In fact, it could be argued that members are conforming to group norms. A word of caution is also in order as human behavior does not always fit neatly into unitary categories. Indeed, they often overlap. For instance, rumors commonly precede outbreaks of mass psychogenic illness; urban legends are often embedded within moral panics; a crowd stampede has been known to occur during a riot.

The ethnographic record of human behavior is truly remarkable and encompasses everything from altruism to Nazism. The influence of social, cultural, political, geographic, and religious forces has helped shape a vast array of beliefs that, while untrue, were or continue to be deemed as plausible by a group of people. For instance, during the late Middle Ages, the "Great Cat Massacres" erupted in France, as citizens scoured the countryside for felines, only to place them in large sacks that were burned at festive occasions. This reflected a popular belief that cats were familiars with the devil and should be exterminated. During the nineteenth-century Catholic Scare, many Americans came to despise adherents to the point of burning down convents and churches and refusing to hire followers. Near the height of the scare in 1844, thirteen people died in anti-Catholic rioting in Philadelphia. During the 1980s, the fear of contracting AIDS from casual contact resulted in people being barred from schools and shunned in public, despite the negligible risk to public health. A similar scare swept across the world in 2014, as governments began to isolate medical workers returning from treating Ebola patients in West Africa.

In chapter 1, we examine the dynamics of rumor and gossip, along with their causes and prevention, followed by several classic examples. Rumors have often been the driving force behind scares involving unpopular groups and social deviants. For instance, in parts of Europe during the Middle Ages, rumors were rife about the nefarious deeds perpetrated by Jews, resulting in many innocent people being tortured, executed, or deported. In 1630, a well-poisoning scare swept across Milan, Italy, after being fueled by rumors that foreigners from France and Spain were intentionally spreading the Black Plague. Rumors also preceded the East St. Louis Race Riots which broke out during the summer of 1917 in Missouri. The outbreak turned into one of the deadliest riots in American history. This tragedy unfolded after a series of unsubstantiated claims of evil deeds perpetrated by African Americans on whites and vice versa.

Occasionally rumors pervade entire countries. In 1789, fear and uncertainty preceding the French Revolution fostered a series of false alarms that swept through the countryside accompanied by rumors that the antirevolutionary nobility had dispatched small armies intent on terrorizing the common folk. Between 1915 and 1916, as World War I raged in Europe, rumors circulated across Canada that German-Americans sympathetic to the Kaiser were planning to launch surprise aerial bombing raids in a bid to destabilize the country. In 1996, hatred and distrust between Israel and its Arab neighbors fueled rumors near Cairo, Egypt, that Jewish agents had dispensed chewing gum spiked with an aphrodisiac in an effort to corrupt the morals of Palestinian women.

Each rumor has a unique social and cultural context that must be understood, no matter how strange the content may appear to outside observers. Southern Africa was the scene of many food-contamination rumors during the twentieth century—rumors that were supposedly perpetrated by their colonial masters, involving everything from claims of poisoned margarine to assertions that stores were selling cooking fat made from human babies. Over the past century, head-hunting scares have plagued parts of Indonesia, driven by rumors that a head was needed to ensure a strong foundation for a local government construction project. In 1969, near the peak of the popularity of the British rock group the Beatles, stories circulated that lead singer Paul McCartney had died and had been secretly replaced by a look-alike. While unfounded, these stories did not appear out of thin air, they occurred at a time when the band was breaking up.

We also examine gossip. During October and November 1998, a sorcerer scare broke out in Indonesia, resulting in the deaths of many residents who had been falsely accused of dabbling in the black arts. An anthropologist who was conducting fieldwork in the area at the time identified local gossip as a major instigator. Other studies point to positive aspects of gossip. In 2011, two Dutch psychologists published the results of a study dubbed, "How the Grapevine Keeps You in Line." They concluded that contrary to popular opinion, gossip can benefit groups. A more recent study conducted at Stanford University also found that gossiping behind people's backs and excluding them from the group can actually be a good thing.

Fads, popular enthusiasms on trivial matters, are explored in chapter 2. We discuss the four phases of a fad and theories behind their sudden popularity and equally sudden waning. For economies, distinguishing between a fad and a long-term trend can translate into the loss or gain of millions of dollars in sales.

Fads often involve sports. For instance, gambling on how many squirrels one could kill within a set time became a national pastime in parts of the southeastern United States during the 1790s. Occasionally, teams of hunters killed thousands of the furry creatures in a single day, and the tallies were printed in newspapers. A new version of golf suddenly gained popularity in 1929 when Garnet Carter built hundreds of miniature golf courses in Florida. The idea quickly caught on, and by autumn 1930, miniature golf had become nothing short of a national obsession, with four million people a day playing on any one of forty thousand courses. However, the fad quickly lost favor and most establishments went bankrupt. Sometimes the subject of a fad is not a sport but a game. Diabolo—a novelty toy made up of two hollow cones twirled on a string, became a popular obsession during the early 1900s. At one point, a Boston reporter observed that it was being performed on nearly every street corner.

Fads often appear suddenly and unexpectedly and involve unanticipated acts such as goldfish swallowing and streaking. The goldfish swallowing fad began in 1939 with a bet between two Harvard students. Before ending three months later, some college students were gulping down over two hundred live fish in a single sitting, prompting complaints from animal-rights advocates. The practice of streaking, stripping naked and running in public, swept through college campuses for a short time between 1973 and 1974. The brief infatuation with streaking has not been seen since, but studies have identified a pattern to these seemingly random events.

Perhaps the most bizarre fad was the popularity of the "pet rock" during the mid-1970s. The brainchild of California advertising executive Gary Dahl who became a millionaire by selling them, this odd "pet" rage collapsed by the end of 1976 as numerous imitators saturated the market.

In chapter 3, we survey crazes: short-term preoccupations or obsessions with a person, idea, or object. More intense and life-changing than fads, common types of crazes include get-rich-quick schemes and religious movements that advocate radical change for both their members and society at large.

An early religious craze was self-flagellation—the practice of flogging oneself with sharp objects—which swept across many European Christian monasteries during the Middle Ages. People engaged in the practice as a form of self-punishment for their sins in the hope of attaining a heavenly reward in the afterlife. A famous American example involved the Kentucky Revivals that appeared at the turn of the nineteenth century, where congregants were whipped into emotional frenzies by traveling preachers and rendered suggestible to imitating the behaviors of those around them. One of the most fascinating religious examples is the strange case of Kondrath Maliovanny who started a Russian religious sect in which he claimed that through intense prayer and singing, he could detect unearthly odors that indicated the presence of the Holy Spirit. In 1892, the movement began to lose supporters after he was judged to have been insane and was committed to the mental asylum. The Native American utopian movement known as the Ghost Dance was active during the late 1800s. It featured a ritual that reenacted a series of visions by a medicine man who foretold of a time when Native Americans would unify and wrest back control of their lands. Perhaps the most notorious modern-day craze is that of the Heaven's Gate group suicide in San Diego, California, in 1994. Thirty-nine members of the group died after taking a cocktail of alcohol and pills under the misguided notion that they would be beamed up to a spaceship.

Manias are the subject of chapter 4 and represent a form of collective wish fulfillment involving great enthusiasm for an esteemed object or agent. Classic examples include sightings of legendary creatures such as Bigfoot, lake monsters, and miraculous entities.

A common theme involves purported appearances of religious figures. In 1953, a team of sociologists converged on the small community of Rincón on the island of Puerto Rico to observe the prophesized appearance of the Virgin Mary. While many claimed to have witnessed miraculous sights, others in the audience saw or felt nothing out of the ordinary. The experiences of those present seemed to be guided by their religious convictions, or lack thereof. Another "appearance" was reported between April 1968 and May 1971, as throngs of onlookers claimed to witness the Virgin hover above a church in Egypt. A psychologist has concluded that the "visions" were electromagnetic discharges from nearby earthquake fault lines.

Arguably the most humorous incident of collective wish fulfillment took place in 1977 when a New Mexico housewife was cooking burritos and realized that the scorch marks on one of the tortillas resembled the face of Jesus. She soon turned her house into a religious shrine that drew the faithful—that is until a relative brought it to school one day for show-and-tell and accidentally dropped it!

In 1995, Hindu idols appeared to drink milk that had been offered by worshippers. Soon, millions of Hindus flocked to temples to experience the reported miracles. In some places, milk was selling for exorbitant prices due to high demand as residents rushed to buy some in order to make an offering. Scientists concluded that the episode had stemmed from an illusion created by the statues absorbing the liquid through the well-known "capillary effect."

Urban legends are the focus of chapter 5. Folklorists commonly refer to these accounts as FOAF tales, or "friend-of-a-friend" stories. While virtually impossible to prevent, these enduring stories typically circulate by word of mouth and are believed by the teller to be of recent origin. From accounts of vanishing hitchhikers to alligators roaming the city sewers, these stories have long captivated listeners.

Since the nineteenth century, there have been many press reports of alligators slithering through the sewers of major cities. However, despite such claims, there has yet to be a single verifiable instance. Another popular tale that has appeared around the world is that of drivers picking up a hitchhiker—usually a young woman—who suddenly vanishes. Like all urban legends, these are cautionary tales; folklorists believe that they serve as a warning about the possible consequences of accepting rides from strangers and what can happen when young ladies act recklessly. In this regard, they can be considered to be a form of living folklore.

Urban legends often speak to our busy, modern lifestyles. Stories about a mother who drops dead after unknowingly nibbling on a fried rat at KFC have appeared around the world and appear to be cautionary tales aimed at the changing role of women. By choosing to take the family to KFC instead of preparing a home-cooked meal, the moral in this tale is clear: if you fail to stick with tradition, bad things may happen.

The tragic circumstances surrounding flight panics (when people flee from an area) and stampedes (which typically involve flight from a more enclosed space) are examined in chapter 6. Stampedes are commonly reported among Islamic pilgrims in the holy city of Mecca in Saudi Arabia. One of the worst incidents occurred on July 2, 1990, when 1,426 worshippers were either trampled to death or suffocated. In 1902, panic in Birmingham, Alabama, claimed the lives of 120 people who had gathered at the Shiloh Negro Baptist Church to hear a talk by George Washington Carver. When two men began fighting over a seat, a woman suddenly cried out, "There's a fight!" Some people mistook the word "fight" for "fire," triggering a mass exodus. Carver was unhurt. The following year, stage curtains caught fire at Chicago's Iroquois Theater, sending 1,900 patrons stampeding for the exits. Within minutes, hundreds of patrons were dead. Remarkably, the fire was quickly extinguished, and no one died from the flames or smoke; every death was attributed to the crush of the crowd. Had they remained calm, everyone would have survived.

Episodes in theatres and nightclubs continue to be a common occurrence. In 2003, patrons mistakenly believed that the E2 nightclub in Chicago was under attack by terrorists, prompting upward of 1,500 people to race down a narrow stairway, resulting in bodies being piled over six feet high.

Anxiety hysteria, short-lived outbreaks of transient illness symptoms triggered by the perceived threat from a harmful agent, is the subject of chapter 7. Common symptoms include fainting, headaches, dizziness, nausea, and breathing difficulties. Most incidents subside within a day. In 1944, for example, a group of high-school students near Philadelphia, Pennsylvania, began acting strangely after watching a hypnosis demonstration. Authorities concluded that their actions were the result of mass suggestion as they believed they were still under a hypnotic spell.

One of the most fascinating episodes occurred during a pitched battle between rival high-school football teams at Natchez, Mississippi, in 1952, when 165 cheerleaders suddenly fainted. A remarkably similar incident occurred in Alabama during a football game in 1973, when 123 members of a marching band collapsed—one after the other. And one of the largest incidents on record happened in 1959, when five hundred chorus members attending a festival at Oklahoma State University were rushed to area hospitals after being felled by a mysterious odor. The odor was later identified as relatively harmless and should not have caused anyone to faint.

During the summer of 1999, nearly one thousand residents of Belgium and France reported feeling ill after drinking Coca-Cola and other company soft drinks. It was later determined that the soda was harmless but had more fizz than normal and an unusual smell. The incident reportedly cost the Coca-Cola Company a quarter of a billion dollars in lost sales.

In chapter 8, we describe classic outbreaks of mass hysteria triggered by repressed and oppressed people. Episodes are typified by bouts of twitching, shaking, and trance-like states, as the stress results in disruptions to the nerves and neurons that send messages to the brain.

One of the more remarkable episodes took place at the Louviers Convent in

Normandy, France, between 1642 and 1647, when a group of nuns fell into hysterical seizures after being forced to worship in the nude. The tension, guilt, and sexual escapades that ensued triggered an array of bizarre behaviors that took years to quell. An outbreak of trance states and barking like dogs occurred in a Dutch orphanage in 1673, after the orphans were placed under great stress and forced to endure monotonous religious instruction and prayer. At the time, dogs were considered familiars with the devil, and people who were supposedly possessed would commonly bark and howl.

Arguably one of the most infamous outbreaks of repression-based mass hysteria occurred during the Salem witch scare of 1691 to 1693, when hysterical fits in a group of young Puritan girls were interpreted as demonic possession. This diagnosis prompted the girls to accuse others of having bewitched them in an effort to deflect possible blame on themselves. Twenty residents lost their lives after accusations of being in cahoots with Satan. They were let down by a legal system where the accused were presumed guilty until proven innocent.

Repression-based outbreaks of mass hysteria are not confined to the distant past. In 1962, a ghost scare at an Islamic school in Johor Bahru, Malaysia, was triggered by a belief that a fruit tree in the schoolyard was harboring the nest of a mother ghost and her forty-four children. That same year, a high school in Welch, Louisiana, was the scene of a wave of hysterical fits among a group of sexually active students after rumors that the girls would be given pregnancy tests. A more recent example of traditional mass hysteria involved the appearance of Tourette's-like symptoms at a high school in LeRoy, in western New York State between 2011 and 2012. Neurologists investigating the incident concluded that the key trigger was the use of social media by the victims.

In chapter 9, we scrutinize immediate community threats: the sudden appearance of exaggerated or imaginary threats to entire communities or regions. We shine light on an obscure historical incident that occurred in England between March 1788 and June 1790 in which nearly sixty women were reportedly assaulted by a supposed maniac who became known as the London Monster. A subsequent investigation revealed that the attacks may have resulted from a combination of hoaxes and imagination. A remarkably similar scare occurred in 1938, near Halifax in England, when a crazed slasher was reportedly stalking victims in the streets. After a spate of hoax confessions by attention-seeking young women, police concluded that the episode had resulted from a combination of fabrications and innocent encounters that had been interpreted as slasher-related.

A famous North American episode involves the case of the Jersey Devil. During January 1909, the Pine Barrens region of New Jersey was overwhelmed with reports of a devilish creature or its footprints. The episode culminated in vigilante groups roaming the countryside in an effort to kill or capture the creature. The flap is a classic example of a community scare grounded in a long-standing regional urban legend that primed residents to experience the scare.

In 1910, sensational newspaper coverage about the presence of toxic gas in the tail of Halley's Comet triggered a global panic that the flyby in May could snuff out all human life. Some worried residents refused to work immediately prior to the comet's closest appearance to Earth, while others held prayer vigils. In several instances, people hoarded oxygen tanks and stuffed rags in keyholes to protect themselves.

During the late 1950s and early 60s, the rise of rock 'n' roll music was widely viewed as portending the moral decline of Western civilization. The media carried sensational reports on the harm from this new evil that was supposedly corrupting youth.

More recently, during the summer of 2014, sensational media reports about the fear of an Ebola pandemic spread across the United States and Europe. The fear spread despite the difficulty in transmitting the disease and the fact that 99 percent of cases were confined to just a few West African countries that had experienced widespread, intense transmission.

Moral panics are examined in chapter 10, as we recount exaggerated threats to the social order and the creation of moral deviants and scapegoats. One of the most remarkable incidents happened between 1830 and 1860 in the United States and involved fear and suspicion of Catholics, many of whom were immigrants with unfamiliar customs. The scare culminated in the anti-Catholic riots of 1844, which left thirteen people dead in Philadelphia.

A fear of foreigners and the unfamiliar have a long history in the United States and include the anti-German scare of 1914–1918. At the time, the mass media and politicians fanned the flames of fear until it was widely reported that German spies were lurking in every town and had infiltrated government posts. In the wake of World War II, the Communist Red Scare swept across the United States amid rumors of communist sympathizers in Hollywood, resulting in many actors, producers, and writers losing their jobs and being placed on "do not hire" blacklists after being suspected of supporting communists.

There are many contemporary examples of moral panics, such as the ongoing scare over the possibility of trick-or-treaters being poisoned or injured by nefarious deviants tampering with candy and apples. Surprisingly, an analysis of these stories finds that they are mythical.

The "knockout game" is another relatively recent scare that has supposedly been played by gangs of wayward youth who approach innocent people and knock them out with a single punch. While such claims have been the subject of numerous Western media reports, a closer examination reveals that such incidents are extremely rare and are not part of an organized game or gang initiation. A more recent scare, the great hoodie fear in Great Britain, took place between 2005 and 2006 when the local media and politicians began to warn against the dangerous acts perpetrated by corrupt youths wearing hooded sweatshirts and the need to ban their clothing items.

In chapter 11, we look at different types of riots, their key features, and their triggers. Riots often highlight inequalities in societies and prompt political action to rectify such discrepancies. On March 3, 1863, Congress passed the Conscription Act, which required able-bodied men between twenty and forty-five to join the military if called upon. Anger and rioting soon broke out in New York City over the stipulation that one could legally avoid the draft by paying $300 to the government, who would then use the money to hire someone to fight in their place. Many of those who could not afford to pay were furious at the inequity. Before it was over, at least seventy people lay dead.

Often riots serve as a pivotal event in civil rights movements. The Stonewall riots during the summer of 1969 in New York City are credited with marking a turning point in the fight for gay rights after violence broke out following a police raid on a popular gay and transvestite bar which led to claims of harassment.

Riots are also commonly fueled by racial tensions. During the summer of 2011, large-scale rioting and looting broke out across several major cities in Great Britain. The violence appeared after relations between local communities and the police had reached a low point. This was blamed on the lack of minority ethnic groups serving on the police force and these same groups being unfairly targeted by police who were carrying out the controversial 'stop and search' law. Another outbreak of racial tension took place in Ferguson, Missouri, in 2014 after an unarmed African American youth was shot by a white police officer.

Chapter 12 is the subject of a little-studied phenomenon involving people who panic in small groups after being exposed to a perceived threat that is imaginary in origin. One of the most famous examples occurred near the height of the Salem witch trials at Salem Village in 1692, when locals, fearing an attack by French and Indian raiders, reported a series of encounters with phantom attackers. The tense times and atmosphere of great suspicion almost certainly resulted in overactive imaginations. A more humorous incident took place near Windham, Connecticut, in 1758. After hearing what sounded like French and Indian intruders massing for an attack, locals grabbed their muskets and waited anxiously throughout the night for the attack that never came. The noises were later identified as the sounds of croaking frogs from a nearby pond.

Phantom attacks are often grounded in the belief in imaginary or legendary creatures such as Bigfoot and space aliens. During the summer of 1924, a group of mining prospectors in a remote part of Washington State reported being attacked by several hulking apelike creatures with long, black hair. A closer investigation reveals that pranksters, coupled with the vivid imagination of one miner, likely spooked the entire group of prospectors into believing that their cabin was under attack by Bigfoot-like creatures. Another Bigfoot siege was reported to have occurred over several months during the early 1980s in Rome, Ohio, after a family claimed to have been attacked by two-legged monsters. When police failed to spot the creatures, a group of Bigfoot researchers moved in and managed to work the family into such a fragile emotional state that they lived in constant fear of an attack from the imaginary creatures.

Perhaps the most serious repercussions to stem from a phantom attack occurred in 1964, when US warships off the coast of North Vietnam in the Gulf of Tonkin were reportedly fired on by Viet Cong warships. The encounter was used as the pretext for America to escalate its involvement in the Vietnam War. However, it is now clear that the attack never happened and that nervous American naval forces were firing at phantom radar images.

CHAPTER 1

RUMOR AND GOSSIP: "PSSSST"

Rumors are unverified stories of perceived importance that lack substantiating evidence. They occur within a backdrop of anxiety and ambiguity, and they must contain an element of plausibility, otherwise they would be dismissed as lacking credibility and would not be passed on. Rumors are always "making the rounds," but are most common during times of crisis and uncertainty. The topic is challenging for social scientists to study because rumors are dynamic and constantly changing, giving rise to a myriad of variations. They are both frustrating to track down and complex to interpret, because while they may be true or false, they often fall somewhere in between.

While many rumors are predominantly false, they typically contain elements of truth. For instance, in 1750, when a kidnapping scare swept through Paris, it had a foundation in reality. Authorities, in an effort to clear the streets of beggars and other undesirables, had enacted a series of ordinances to address the issue, but police exceeded their authority and temporarily placed a number of children in houses of detention before they were reclaimed by their worried parents. The "missing" children fostered claims that King Louis XV was suffering from leprosy and was having children kidnapped in order to cure his condition by bathing in their blood. The scare triggered riots and angry scenes as mobs began chasing suspected kidnappers through the streets.[1]

American sociologist Tamotsu Shibutani describes rumors as "improvised news" that spreads rapidly when demand for information exceeds the supply.[2] This is why rumors flourish during periods of war and crises. Hence, the greater the importance and uncertainty, the more likely rumors are to appear and thrive. Shortly after the Japanese attack on Pearl Harbor in 1941, and the destruction of the World Trade Center in 2001, amid conflicting reports and claims, rumors of imminent terrorist attacks on US targets swirled across the United States.

Conversely, the less interest and importance in a topic, the less likely it is to generate rumors. Thus, if just prior to the world yo-yo championships, a rumor spread that the reigning champ had sprained his index finger, it is unlikely to spread like wildfire across the country, as most people would have little interest in the outcome of the competition. Yet, if your daughter was the second ranked yo-yo player in the world, lived in a yo-yo "mad" community, and was competing for a hefty cash prize, the likelihood of rumors spreading through her hometown, and the yo-yo fraternity in general, would be high.

The more likely a rumor is deemed to be true, the more likely it is to be passed on.[3] Rumors typically last from a few days or weeks to several months. On rare occasions they can endure for years. Contrary to popular belief, the appearances of most rumors are not deliberate, malicious attempts to spread uncomplimentary information about a person or organization. In reality, the content is impossible to control and often branches in unexpected directions. Most rumors are unconsciously generated in ambiguous situations of perceived importance as people construct stories in an effort to gain certainty and reduce fear and anxiety.

Some researchers have cleverly tried to plant rumors in hopes of influencing consumer decisions to buy their product. Such attempts usually fail. For example, sociologist Richard LaPiere reports that during the Great Depression in the United States, an advertising agency paid actors to spread rumors about certain products, believing it would increase sales.[4] In one instance, two actors would board a busy commuter train, posing as a rich businessman and his chauffeur. The pair proceeded to engage in a loud conversation about the quality of tires, with the chauffeur vigorously recommending a certain brand. Such elaborate advertising campaigns were destined to fail as the story either did not spread, or the passengers got the brands confused. Such efforts highlight the fluid, spontaneous nature of rumors and the means by which they spread—the content is difficult to influence as they tend to have "a mind of their own."[5]

Traditionally, rumors have spread by word of mouth during face-to-face interaction. In modern times, telephones, the mass media, and Internet-based social networks have been the primary mode of spread. Rumors thrive on controversy and confusion and tend to swarm around a few key issues. Sociologist Gary Fine notes that several issues are especially rife with rumors: race and ethnicity, migration, globalization, corporate misconduct, and government corruption.[6] Racial rumors commonly precede riots and social unrest, with their content typically reflecting popular stereotypes and mistrust between the groups involved. Rumors alleging misconduct by governments and corporations are common and often portray them as deceptive, greedy, and evil. Nowadays, these entities often have public-relations specialists who attempt to refute claims. One common, recurring rumor holds that large corporations such as McDonald's and Procter & Gamble are fronts for religious cults.[7]

In 1947, Harvard psychologists Gordon Allport and Leo Postman published *The Psychology of Rumor*, the first scientific study of the field.[8] Their pioneering work examined the origin and spread of rumors. The pair monitored rumor formation by conducting a series of controlled laboratory experiments, noting that as they are passed on with retelling, rumors become simpler and more easily understood. In observing how rumors change with retelling, they identified three processes: leveling, sharpening, and assimilation. The process of leveling refers to the tendency to either leave out certain details or eliminate them altogether. In doing so, stories tend to become shorter and more concise with retelling. Sharpening occurs when the remaining details are accentuated and made more prominent while other key information becomes more specific. The final process, assimilation, is the tendency for people to shape the emerging rumor in such a way that it is sharpened and leveled as a reflection of social and cultural stereotypes and biases.[9] In other words, as a rumor is passed on, the content tends to increasingly reflect the expectations and beliefs of those retelling it.[10]

A classic example of assimilation took place in the hours and days following the Japanese bombing of Pearl Harbor on December 7, 1941, as rumors questioning the loyalty of Japanese-Americans, spread quickly across the Hawaiian Islands. Such fears, while unfounded, had long been the subject of concern on the Islands as 160,000 Hawaiians had Japanese ancestry. Shibutani recounts some of the rumors, which included claims that a ring from a local high school (McKinley High) "was found on the body of a Japanese flier shot down over Honolulu; the water supply had been poisoned by the local Japanese; Japanese plantation workers had cut arrows pointing to Pearl Harbor in the cane field of Oahu; the local Japanese had been notified of the attack by an advertisement in a Honolulu newspaper on December 6; . . . automobiles driven by local Japanese blocked the roads from Honolulu to Pearl Harbor; Japanese residents waved their kimonos at the pilots and signaled to them; [and] some local men were dressed in Japanese Army uniforms during the attack."[11] Despite failing to be verified, these stories continued to persist long after the attack, especially in the mainland press. When a rumor persisted that the Pacific fleet had been destroyed in the attack, and continued to circulate across the US mainland for several months, President Franklin

D. Roosevelt felt the need to give a national radio address to dispel the claims and restore public confidence.[12]

Contemporary research on rumors has identified other key elements in their formation, not noted by Allport and Postman, including anxiety relief,[13] and their use as a form of entertainment which elevates the teller's status.[14] Folklorist David Samper observes that rumors also serve as a social barometer. As rumors pass from person to person, the ability to reshape the content over and over "transforms it into a collective representation of fears and anxieties."[15] In this sense, French rumor expert Jean-Noël Kapferer views rumors as a collective problem-solving exercise through which "in the course of successive exchanges, the group tries to reconstruct the puzzle made up of scattered pieces gathered here and there. The fewer the pieces they have, the greater a role the group's unconscious plays in their interpretation; the more pieces they have, the closer their interpretation is to reality."[16]

Social scientists have identified different types of rumors. *Bogy rumors* make reference to an imminent disaster such as a tsunami or flood. On February 8, 1761, minor earth tremors struck London, followed by another quake a month later, prompting rumors that a great earthquake was to strike the city on April 5 after a "psychic" predicted the calamity. Much of the city's population left for the day.[17]

Pipe-dream rumors (sometimes referred to as magical- or wishful-thinking rumors) are stories that people hope are true. For instance, once the US bombing of the Taliban in Afghanistan began in response to the September 11, 2001, terror attacks on the United States, rumors spread that Osama bin Laden had been killed in an American-led bombing raid. Another story held that he had died of kidney failure. Yet another series of rumors had him succumbing to a lung ailment. In reality, bin Laden was alive, in reasonably good health, and eventually found living in Pakistan. There were even rumors that bin Laden was hiding in the United States.

Scapegoating rumors blame an innocent person or group for allegedly perpetrating a nefarious deed. Throughout history, Jews have often been the subject of poisoning claims. For instance, in 1321, Jews in Guienne, France, were rumored to have poisoned local wells, resulting in an estimated five thousand people being burned alive for their alleged involvement. During the Black Death which spread through Europe during the latter Middle Ages, thousands of Jews were executed following rumors that Satan was protecting them in exchange for their poisoning the wells of Christians.[18] Shortly after September 11, 2001, there were widespread scapegoating rumors in the Arab-Islamic world that the World Trade Center attacks had been orchestrated by the Mossad (the Israeli secret service) in a cunning attempt to foul pro-Muslim sentiment for Middle Eastern countries.

Some researchers refer to *diving rumors*, which recur periodically, suddenly appearing and disappearing.[19] Claims that headhunters are active in Southeast Asia are a classic example, and have waxed and waned for centuries among indigenous tribes.[20]

Product rumors are another common type and focus on stories about popular consumer goods. In the 1950s, it was rumored that an employee at a Coca-Cola plant had suddenly disappeared under mysterious circumstances. It was eventually determined, so the account goes, that he had fallen into a large vat of Coke, and the acid dissolved his body.[21]

Atrocity rumors are common during wartime and civil unrest and focus on the "other group" as evil-doers. When race riots exploded in Detroit during 1943, rumors spread among the African American community that several white sailors had pushed a black woman off the Belle Isle Bridge. To make matters even more incendiary, it was said that she was clutching her baby as she went over the side. Meanwhile, in the white community, a rumor spread that a black man had raped and murdered a white woman at Belle Island.[22]

While rumors are difficult to prevent and control, psychologist Nicholas DiFonzo reports that governments and businesses can take certain steps to manage their damage. The first step is to practice "regular, rapid, and reliable communication."[23] Rumors should not be ignored, and if they are true, they should be confirmed quickly, along with a factual description of the situation or incident. In squelching false rumors, he considers it important to avoid remarks such as "no comment," which tends to fuel uncertainly and speculation. DiFonzo states that effective refutations reduce uncertainty by offering "a clear point-by-point refutation with solid evidence." He also recommends that the authority doing the refuting should ideally be a "trusted, neutral, third party" and explain the context for why it is being issued.

The financial impact of rumors can be exceedingly costly. On April 23, 2013, a bogus tweet from a hacked Twitter account at the Associated Press claimed that US President Barack Obama had been injured after explosions had rocked the White House. This single fake tweet caused instability on the financial markets and led to a sudden plunge in the Standard and Poor's 500 Index, which lost $130 billion in a short period, although it quickly recovered.[24]

GOSSIP

Joseph Epstein once wrote: "Listening to gossip can be likened to receiving stolen goods; it puts you in immediate collusion with the person conveying the gossip to you."[25] Gossip comes from the Old English word *godsibb* (God akin) and refers to one who sponsors another in baptism or "a sponsor in God."[26] Gossip and rumors are two distinct phenomena, although the former can lead to the latter. These separate entities are often confused by the lay public. Epstein writes that "gossip is particular, told to a carefully chosen audience, and is specifically information about other people."[27] While gossip was once thought to have been trivial, there is now a consensus within the field that it serves important uses in everyday social life.

Gossip typically involves a moral judgement and has a variety of functions: it can entertain; help to maintain group cohesiveness; and can serve to establish, maintain, and change the norms of a group, its group power structure, and its membership.[28] Rather humorously, Epstein observes that all people "seem to enjoy that conspiratorial atmosphere of intimacy in which two or three people talk about another person who isn't in the room. Usually they say things about this person that he would prefer not to have said. They might talk about his misbehaviour in any number of realms (sexual, financial, domestic, hygienic, or any other that allows for moral disapprobation) or about his . . . hypocrisy, tastelessness, immodesty, [or] neuroses."[29] Some researchers refer to proximate gossip about people we know, as opposed to distal gossip about people who we are unlikely to have met such as celebrities. Researchers have identified two fundamental types of gossip: positive and negative. These have been referred to by a variety of terms including good and bad, information sharing versus judgmental, blame versus praise, and critical versus uncritical.[30]

Alexander Cowan offers historical insight into the shifting views of gossip over time and how it has been used to put down females. In early modern Europe, "gossip" was a negative term used by men to describe conversations among women—the content over which men had little control. "The content of these conversations was belittled in order to give greater value to the purposeful exchanges between men. These value-loaded associations persist to the present day in terms such as *commérage* (French) or *pettegolezze* (Italian), the one drawing attention to the exclusive participation of women, the other to the potentially scandalous subject matter of gossip." More recently, the study of gossip has become an acceptable topic of serious scholarly study and is no longer viewed as a predominately female phenomenon.[31]

Rumors come from an anonymous source—hence they are unable to be veri-fied—and help people to resolve the uncertainty by making sense of the world and better managing the risk. The spread of rumors typically occurs informally from person to person, but later may be spread through more formal communication channels such as television, radio, newspapers, or the Internet.[32] Rumors usually reflect collective hopes and fears, and involve factual claims about people, groups, institutions, and events. They tend to be more general, more diffuse, and less per-sonal than gossip.

Human beings possess an inherent need to belong to a group, which is a key motivation for engaging in gossip. Gossip researchers Nicholas DiFonzo and Prashant Bordia have reviewed the key functions of gossip. First, they observe that gossip enables people to learn key pieces of social information about others in a group, often without having met those people. For example, "The newcomer is quietly informed: 'Oh yes, be sure that you do not interrupt Harry—he is very touchy,' Or 'Have you met Sally? She is quite amiable.' This is rather useful infor-mation in forming my social network: I'll avoid Harry and approach Sally. More broadly, gossip enables one to 'keep tabs' on a much larger number of people than if one were required to have contact with them personally."[33] Given that people have a finite amount of time and energy for interpersonal relationships, gossip allows us to have larger social groups and awareness.

A second function of gossip is to help people to build social networks through interpersonal bonding. DiFonzo and Bordia observe: "We know we are accepted by another when they share a tidbit of gossip with us. Gossiping thus gains us friend-ship and alliances."[34] Third, the formation of bonds may also involve breaking old ties and forming new ones. In this regard, it occurs through engaging in nega-tive gossip about a third party. Thus, such statements as "Brittany wears way too much make-up!" or "Agnes is a stuck-up snob!" are typically viewed as pejorative remarks and can be seen as a form of indirect aggression.[35] Gossip also functions to enhance the social status, prestige, and power of the participants. This is reflected in the old adage that people often tear others down in order to build themselves up. Gossiping can be empowering and make people feel popular.

Last, gossip lets people know the rules of admittance into specific social networks. Through gossip, we learn fundamental group norms by listening to comments about people you know, or about people we are unlikely to associate with, such as movie stars. DiFonzo and Bordia provide examples of how this process works: "'Cheri is so hot!' (be slim and attractive). 'Jeremy 'brownnoses' his teachers' (don't flatter your professors). 'Madonna is a slut' (don't be promiscuous). . . . 'Jacques is lazy' (do your fair share of the work)."[36]

Some researchers observe that gossip is a form of cheap entertainment, either by listening to or engaging in such behaviors. Eric Foster contends "that gossip can exist solely for the entertainment or recreational value of the gossipers."[37] He writes that while the mass media produces gossip about public figures such as film stars, sports figures, and politicians, and this differs from private gossiping, "the entertainment value of gossip is clearly the basis of this enormous cultural and economic enterprise."

Not all researchers agree on the usefulness of gossip. Some have argued that gossip is a form of covert hostile conflict which alienates people from interacting and reduces solidarity. Sociologist Tim Hallett and his colleagues outline this perspective: "Since the critical evaluations typical in gossip serve the interests of particular groups by putting (and keeping) others 'in their place' . . . gossip can be a form of punishment and control. . . . It is also part of power struggles."[38]

MEMORABLE EXAMPLES OF RUMOR AND GOSSIP

Anti-Jewish Rumors, Middle Ages (Europe)

During the Middle Ages, rumors about nefarious deeds perpetrated by Jews were rife. In 1285, 180 Jews were burned to death in Munich after rumors arose that they had conducted a blood sacrifice involving a child as part of a religious ceremony.[39] Nine years later, in Bern, Switzerland, rumors that a group of Jews were involved in a ritual murder resulted in some being put to death or deported. Most of the Jews residing in Trent, Italy, were tortured and burned in 1475 following the spread of a rumor that they had murdered a young boy. In 1348, as the Black Death (Bubonic Plague) swept across Europe killing upward of half the population, rumors spread that the Jews were responsible for poisoning wells. Some communities expelled the Jews, while in other locations they were massacred.[40] An influx of Jewish physicians at this time cast suspicion that Jews possessed the know-how to poison wells. During May 1348, stories of Jewish wellpoisoning led to widespread rioting in southeastern France. In some places, entire Jewish settlements were burned to the ground. The next year at Bradenburg, in what is modern-day Germany, city leaders passed a law denouncing Jews for poisoning wells.[41] The appearance of anti-Jewish rumors throughout history can be explained by several factors. These include Jews holding powerful positions in business and banking which made them unpopular and convenient scapegoats for events such as disease or severe conditions.

Well-Poisoning Scare, 1630 (Milan, Italy)

In 1630, Milan was the scene of the "Great Poisoning Scare."[42] Italian writer Count Alessandro Manzoni offers a detailed account of the events as they had unfolded. At the time, Europe was gripped by fears that certain people—namely social deviants and the unpopular—were determined to spread the Black Plague across Europe, either through sorcery or "contagious poisons." In 1629, the governor of Milan received a message from King Philip IV warning that four Frenchmen were heading to the city, intent on spreading the plague with "poisonous and pestilential ointments." The warning passed without incident, but in May 1630, fears of an attack were rekindled as the plague erupted in the city. Rumors soon spread that it had resulted from a plot by Jews to poison the water supply.[43]

The crisis began on the night of May 17 after some people were observed placing what appeared to be poison at the city cathedral. Several members of the city health board went to the cathedral and had a number of suspicious items removed and piled up outside. While no evidence of poison was uncovered, the mere fact that the items had been piled outside of the cathedral, lent credence to the rumors. Manzoni writes: "This mass of piled-up furniture produced a strong impression of consternation among the multitude, to whom any object so readily became an argument. It was said, and generally believed, that all the benches, walls, and even the bell-ropes in the cathedral, had been rubbed over with unctuous matter."[44] The next day, fears were stoked further when mysterious stains appeared. "In every part of the city they saw the doors and walls of the houses stained and daubed with long streaks of I know not what filthiness, something yellowish and whitish, spread over them as if with a sponge."[45]

Instead of interpreting this event as a type of graffiti or a mischievous act, in some quarters it was believed to have been a sign that the poisoning was imminent. It seemed that the entire city was on the lookout for the poisoners. During the scare that followed, many of those suspected were either beaten, thrown into prison, or killed. Two eyewitness accounts of the chaos that followed are provided by Josephi Ripamontii. In one case, an elderly man was in church and began to wipe off a bench that he was about to sit on. Suddenly he was accused of rubbing poison on the seat. Ripamontii writes that "an old man . . . was observed, after kneeling in prayer, to sit down, first, however, dusting the bench with his cloak. 'That old man is anointing the benches!' exclaimed with one voice some women, who witnessed the act. The people who happened to be in church fell upon the old man; they tore his gray locks, heaped upon him blows and kicks, and dragged him out half dead, to convey him to prison, to the judges, to torture. 'I beheld him dragged along in this way,' says Ripamontii, 'nor could I learn anything further about his end; but, indeed, I think he could not have survived many moments.'"[46]

Amid the fear and tension that accompanied the plague, Ripamontii recounts the harrowing tale of three young Frenchmen who were visiting the city and admiring the architecture of the Milan cathedral. "One, two, or more passers-by, stopped, and formed a little group, to contemplate and keep their eye on these visitors, whom their costume, their headdress, and their wallets, proclaimed to be strangers, and, what was worse, Frenchmen. As if to assure themselves that it was marble, they stretched out their hands to touch it. This was enough. They were surrounded, seized, tormented, and urged by blows to prison. Fortunately, the hall of justice was not far from the cathedral, and by still greater good fortune, they were found innocent, and set at liberty."[47] The episode coincided with a fear in the district of foreigners, especially the Spanish and French, in addition to bitter feuds between leading families in Milan, Florence, and elsewhere, keeping the populace in a state of chronic tension and fear.

The Great Fear, 1789 (France)

Amidst the fear and uncertainty that preceded the French Revolution, wild rumors and false alarms were the order of the day. Starting in July 1789, panic swept through the French countryside following rumors that the antirevolutionary nobility had sent out armies of brigands intent on terrorizing the common people. Brigands are robbers operating in mountain and forest regions, who ambush their victims. The events have been studied in-depth by historian Georges Lefebvre who writes: "*le peuple se faisait peur à lui-même*" (the populace scared themselves).[48]

During the first half of the year, unrest among the peasants broke out across the country. In the wake of political uncertainty, central government authority became nonexistent, and local leaders were required to maintain regional law and order. To complicate matters, food shortages brought about by rising prices led to riots and attacks on hoarders. These outbreaks reached panic levels just before harvest period, when farmers feared that their crops would be stolen by gangs directed by the aristocrats.

Distant lights and mundane sounds were assumed to have been evidence of the brigands, so the enemy was soon sighted by farmers on the lookout. A typical incident occurred on July 24, near Troyes, when a group of brigands were spotted entering a wooded area: "The alarm bell was sounded and three thousand men gathered to give chase to these supposed brigands. But they turned out to be no more than a herd of cattle."[49]

When a government soldier, who defected to side with the people, fell ill on a Paris street, rumors quickly spread that his entire regime had been poisoned on orders of the aristocrats.[50] They had not. These and other rumors were fueled by the widespread belief that the nobility would stop at nothing to retain their privileges and lands.

France's economic collapse at this time led to the existence of large groups of migrants traveling the countryside looking for work, and some, no doubt, engaged in robbery. These groups were prone to becoming identified as brigands. Provincial towns and villages formed militias, and soon most communities had a defensive force of some kind. Instead of reducing anxieties, such forces actually stoked fears by heightening the sense of emergency. Peasants reasoned that if a militia had been formed, surely it must be for good reason.

When a community believed it was under attack, messengers were sent to alert neighboring towns and villages. Unfortunately, this pattern generated more fear, with false alarm after false alarm. At Sarlat, a messenger ran to report that Limeuil had been burnt to the ground during the night. The report proved to be untrue. At Lubersac, the vicar of Saint-Cyr-le-Champagnes announced that brigands were active in the community. Another untrue claim. Lefebvre writes: "Anything could set off the alarm. A band went to protect a village, and saw lights burning on the other side of the village. They found it was another band of defenders . . . from another district. At Clermont-en-Beauvais, as happened elsewhere, a troop of peasants marching against the enemy was mistaken for the enemy themselves. The lights from chalk furnaces, bonfires of weeds, even the reflection of the setting sun in windows, gave alarm that brigands were setting fire to crops or grain stores. A monsieur de Tersac, hearing that the enemy was approaching with drums and trumpets, decided to look for himself: he found a group of harvesters, working by moonlight, singing at their work."[51] The Great

Fear eventually died down as the continual false alarms and waxing and waning tensions could not be sustained. The very next year near harvest time, similar fears flared up, but to a lesser extent, once again driven by rumors.

American Invasion of Canada Rumors, 1915–1916 (Canada)

While Canada entered World War I in 1914, the United States did not declare war until April 1917. During much of the period prior to the United States joining the war, rumors circulated across Canada that German-Americans sympathetic to the kaiser were planning to launch surprise bombing raids or espionage missions. At the time, there were nearly ten million German-Americans living in the United States. As residents speculated on the flimsiest of evidence, there were scores of false accusations about scheming Germans on both sides of the border.[52] British consul-general Sir Courtney Bennett, stationed in New York, held top honors for being the worst offender. During the war, in the early months of 1915, Bennett made several sensational claims about a plan in which as many as eighty thousand well-armed, highly trained Germans who had been drilling in Niagara Falls and Buffalo, New York, were planning to invade Canada from northwestern New York State.[53] Despite the incredulity of his assertions, it was a testament to the deep anxiety and suspicion of the period, that Prime Minister Sir Robert Borden requested a report on the invasion stories, which Canadian Police Commissioner Percy Sherwood assessed to be without any foundation.[54]

Race Riots, 1917 (East St. Louis, Missouri, USA)

One of the deadliest riots in US history took place in July 1917, after being fueled by a series of rumors that inflamed tensions. The episode can be traced back to February, when hundreds of white workers at the local Aluminum Ore Company went on strike and were replaced with African American workers. In the years leading up to the violence, East St. Louis had experienced an influx of southern blacks who were anxious to escape the blatant racism in the Deep South. The riots broke out in late May and again in early July, resulting in the deaths of thirty-nine African Americans, nine whites, and the destruction of about three hundred buildings.

On May 28, a union delegation representing the white workers met with the mayor in a bid to stop any further migration of blacks to the city. As they were leaving City Hall, the workers learned that a black man had shot a white man during a robbery. Within minutes, other anti-black rumors swept through the white community, triggering several days of violence. Sociologist Terry Ann Knopf examined the riot and noted that before the riot broke out, there were widespread stories "that blacks were forcing whites from their neighborhood, that they were planning to assault white women, and that employers were to blame for the influx of blacks."[55] Knopf also found that different versions of the same rumor would occasionally circulate. For instance, throughout June, "whites charged that blacks were secretly arming and planning a massacre on July 4, in retaliation for the May riots." It came as no surprise then, that during the July riots, police "relayed false reports of reprisal attacks by blacks on the outskirts of the city," a move that inadvertently diverted manpower from the city when it was needed most.[56]

Headhunting Rumor Panics, 1937–1981 (Indonesia)

In March 1937, the man who would later become Indonesia's first prime minister, Sutan Sjahrir, was on the Moluccan island of Banda, when headhunting rumors swept through his village.[57] According to the rumors, a *tjoelik* (a government-sanctioned headhunter) was searching for a head to place near a local jetty construction project. It is widely believed among the locals, that such heads are necessary to ensure that the structure remains strong. Without such an offering, it is thought to crumble. Sjahrir said that "people have been living in fear" and were "talking and whispering about it everywhere" and that the streets were nearly deserted by 7:00 p.m.[58] There were many reports of strange noises and sightings. Sjahrir stated: "Every morning there are new stories, generally about footsteps or voices, or a house that was bombarded with stones, or an attack on somebody by a tjoelik with a noose, or a cowboy lasso. Naturally, the person who was attacked got away from the tjoelik in a nick of time!"[59]

Over several weeks in 1979, headhunter kidnapping rumors appeared in Indonesian Borneo. Anthropologist Richard Drake was living among the Mualang peoples at the time and noted that guards were placed around the village, a local school shut down, and some workers stayed home. The scare was sparked by rumors that government headhunters were looking for a head to ensure that a new government bridge project would have a firm foundation. Drake believes that the scare was a reflection of the tense relationship between distant tribes and the state: a relationship that is typified by suspicion and distrust of a far-off central government that has the ultimate say over their lives. He believes that episodes represent fears by "primitive" peoples of losing political control to a distant, central government.[60]

A similar scare occurred during the spring of 1981 in southern Borneo, when anthropologist Anna Lowenhaupt Tsing was living among the Meratus Dayak in the Meratus Mountains. The episode coincided with reports that nearby government-operated oil fields were having problems with malfunctioning equipment. According to the rumors, the government had sent out headhunters because the magical power provided by securing human heads would be able to stabilize the equipment. It was also claimed that both the police and the Indonesian military had been ordered to turn a blind eye to the raids. During the scare, everyday life was transformed as people were fearful of working in the fields. Tsing writes: "Everyone was terrified. Hiking from one community to another, even from one house to another, became treacherous and frightening. Several times my hiking companions smelled cigarette smoke on the trail and heard suspicious rustling noises in the bushes . . . others we knew had glimpsed unknown men huddled under the trees."[61] In non-Western settings, rumors of impending threats are closely associated with cultural traditions, as in the case of the headhunting rumor-fueled panics that have occurred for centuries in remote parts of Malaysia and Indonesia.[62]

Paul McCartney Is Dead, 1969 (Worldwide)

Near the peak of the popularity of the British rock group the Beatles, stories circulated around the world that one of the band members—singer and musician Paul McCartney—had died and the information was being kept secret. One strain of rumors held that McCartney had been dead for three years following an auto accident in November 1966. Soon after, record-company executives decided that it was necessary to replace him with a look-alike, worried that if the truth got out, their record sales would plummet. Writing in the *Journal of Contemporary Ethnography*, sociologist Barbara Suczek summarizes key elements of the story: "Paul McCartney was allegedly killed in an automobile accident in England in November 1966. The remaining Beatles, fearing that public reaction to the news would adversely affect the fortunes of the group, agreed among themselves to keep the matter a secret. Since it was obvious that Paul could not simply disappear from their midst without rousing a storm of embarrassing questions, they hit upon the idea of hiring a double to play his part in public."[63] That role was supposedly filled perfectly by a man who had won a McCartney look-alike contest—an Edinburgh orphan, William Campbell. "By an astonishing stroke of good luck, it turned out that Campbell not only bore a striking physical resemblance to McCartney, but was also endowed with similar musical abilities so that, with a bit of practice, he was able to sustain a performance that completely deceived an attentive and discriminating audience for almost three years." However, the situation became awkward when Campbell had an affair with Linda Eastman (McCartney's first wife) and later married her. It is noteworthy that, in real life, many Beatles fans were surprised by McCartney's marriage to Eastman. It was widely anticipated that he would take British actress Jane Asher as his wife. According to the story, Asher was paid a large amount of money to keep quiet about the imposter Paul.

The first known published account of the rumor appeared in the Illinois University campus newspaper on September 23, 1969. The *Northern Star* reported that "there has been much conjecturing on the present state of the Beatle Paul McCartney."[64] On October 12, a man phoned radio station WKNR-FM in Detroit, Michigan, and told disc jockey Russ Gibb that he could explain why there had been so few recent public appearances by McCartney, claiming that he was actually dead and had been replaced by a double. The man said there were hidden clues to support his theory in several of McCartney's songs. For instance, in the song "Revolution Number 9," a voice repeats the words "number nine, number nine." Coincidentally, the word "McCartney" has nine letters.[65] What's more, when the song was played backward, some overenthusiastic listeners with too much time on their hands claimed that it sounded like "turn me on, dead man, turn me on, dead man." Further, when the entire track was played in reverse, some said it resembled a collision (Paul's fatal car crash). Also, at the end of "Strawberry Fields Forever," it sounded like someone was saying, "I buried Paul."[66] Shortly after these claims were discussed on the air, the news director of the radio station received a phone call from McCartney who was adamant that he was still alive![67]

Two days later, the student newspaper at the University of Michigan, the *Michigan Daily*, published the article, "McCartney Dead." The author, Fred LaBour, claimed that McCartney had died in a car mishap in November 1966, "after leaving the EMI studios tired, sad, and depressed."[68] LaBour also claimed that a double had assumed McCartney's place. The story was given further credence when in late October, numerous newspapers and magazines reported on the rumors.[69] Over the next two months, people began to scrutinize the Beatles and pointed out more and more coincidences. For instance, McCartney wears an armband on the *Sgt. Pepper* album with the letters OPD—interpreted by some to mean "Officially Pronounced Dead." On the *Magical Mystery Tour* album, McCartney wore a black carnation—another symbol of death. On the *Abbey Road* album, someone noticed a car in the background with the plate "28IF." This was interpreted to signify that if McCarthy had not died, he would have been twenty-eight years old. The same album cover showed the Beatles crossing a road, single file. Some said it resembled a funeral procession with John Lennon—dressed in white and resembling a priest—leading the pack. He was followed by drummer Ringo Starr dressed in black—resembling an undertaker. McCartney, who was third, was walking barefoot—the corpse, while bringing up the rear was George Harrison wearing street clothes—the grave digger.[70]

Once the rumors spread across the country, they became difficult to dispel. For instance, on November 2, the *New York Times* reported that a journalist was flown to London to dig up information on the story in order to confirm or deny the claims. Alec Bennett said that the only definitive solution to the persistent rumors was to develop "a set of fingerprints from a 1965 passport which can be compared to his present prints."[71] A few days later, *Life* magazine published a cover story on the mystery titled: "The Case of the Missing Beatle."

Even McCartney's denial of the rumor in a face-to-face interview in *Life* magazine—an interview that even included photos of McCartney—left some fans suspicious, noting that "on the back of the page upon which McCartney's picture appeared, there was an advertisement for a car –if one looked through the page, the car could be seen cutting McCartney's head off."[72] In denying his death, McCartney stated: "It is all bloody stupid. I picked up that O.P.D. badge in Canada. It was a police badge. . . . Perhaps it means Ontario Police Department. I was wearing a black flower because they ran out of red ones. It is John, not me, dressed in black on the cover and inside of *Magical Mystery Tour*. On *Abbey Road* we were wearing our ordinary clothes. I was walking barefoot because it was a hot day. The Volkswagen just happened to be parked there."[73] When a representative of McCartney was contacted in London and was asked about some of the claims, the band's agent Derek Taylor observed that the voice at the end of "Strawberry Fields Forever," was not saying, "I buried Paul." It said, "I'm very bored."[74]

Suczek has identified different factors that may have contributed to the spread of these rumors. For instance, in retrospect, the Beatles had undergone several changes that may have given rise to speculation about the band and may have incubated rumors. The first change involved their decreasing number of personal appearances. Suczek states: "Due to the increasing complexity of their music, requiring the use of elaborate technical equipment and the manpower to manipulate it, the Beatles had reportedly been experiencing difficulty in presenting concerts that would satisfy the rising expectations of their record-listening public and, at the same time, uphold their image as a self-reliant, spontaneous group of four."[75] A second factor appeared to be their diminishing public visibility as band members were gravitating away from the limelight, toward a more private lifestyle. Two other key factors centered on Paul McCartney, who was involved in a dispute with other members of the Beatles and, as result, had withdrawn from several of the band's activities. Finally, there was McCartney's surprise marriage to Linda Eastman.[76]

During the episode, at least one professor took the side of the conspiracy theorists. Dr. Henry Truby at the University of Miami had compared sonograms of McCartney singing "Hey Jude" with one taken using an early recording of "Yesterday." He announced that the voices were from two different people, supporting the notion that there was an imposter Paul.[77] Some of the claims surrounding the rumor bordered on the ridiculous and were hilariously far-fetched. In his study of the rumor, R. Gary Patterson observes that on the cover of the *Sgt. Pepper* album, an obvious clue to some was McCartney's back being turned away from the camera while the other Beatles were fronting the camera with stern facial expressions. People singled out McCarthy for being different. "Some of the more overzealous fans believed that the imposter had to turn his back to the camera simply to avoid being recognized as a fake. Those same fans noticed that the McCartney likeness appeared unnaturally stiff. Was this but a three dimensional cutout?"[78] Some noted that McCartney was holding a black instrument, with three fingers from his left hand placed at the base. Some believe that this was a hint that there were three original Beatles left.

Tainted-Chewing-Gum Rumors, 1996–1997 (Middle East)

In July 1996, alarming rumors swept through Mansoura, a town northeast of Cairo, Egypt. Stories circulated that chewing gum had been deliberately spiked with an aphrodisiac. These rumors gave rise to claims that students in the town's university had been taking part in orgies and were having indiscriminate sex with strangers. A local member of Parliament, Fathy Mansour, claimed that the gum had been distributed by agents of the Israeli government in an effort to bring about the demise of Egyptian youth. *New York Times* journalist Douglas Jehl reported that in response to the perceived crisis, mosques in the town began using loudspeakers to warn community members of the tainted gum. The Ministry of Health soon got involved by examining the gum, but could find nothing suspicious. Egyptian authorities also investigated the dramatic claim by Mr. Mansour that fifteen female students had been attacked and sexually assaulted by their male classmates after they chewed the gum. The offending gum had supposedly been peddled under the names "Aroma" or "Splay." While authorities went so far as to close down some shops and made several arrests, all turned out to have been unfounded.[79]

The following year another tainted gum scare swept through the region. This time it was said to have been packages of strawberry-flavored gum, supposedly sold at discount prices near schools on the Gaza Strip and along the West Bank. The gum was rumored to come in packages that had such stickers as "Thunder in Paradise," "The Legend of Pocahontas," and "Aladdin and the Magic Lamp." The gum had reportedly been infused with sex hormones and gave women uncontrollable sexual urges before rendering them sterile. While Palestinian Supply Minister Abdel Aziz Shaheen claimed the gum was harmful, *Washington Post* reporter Barton Gellman observed how the tale grew with retelling. Shaheen said the "(Palestinian) authority seized 154 pieces of the suspect gum. By the time the story reached Hebron in the West Bank, local health official Mahmoud Batarna was saying he had captured 200 tons of the stuff in his city alone. His theory about the gum differed from Shaheen's: Rather than ruining children, he said, Israel sought to turn Palestinian women into prostitutes, with the goal of making them easier to enlist as informants for its Shin Bet security service."[80]

The Palestinian Authority was reported to have ordered tests on the gum at the Food Technology and Research Institute of Cairo and detected progesterone. A Supply Ministry official, Salah Waheedi, stated: "This chewing gum causes sterility and stimulates sex. This is proved. This is scientifically proved." The *Washington Post* obtained pieces of the supposedly contaminated gum from Palestinian health authorities. It was given to Professor Dan Gibson, a chemist at Hebrew University. While there were widespread claims that the gum contained progesterone, he found no trace of the hormone.[81]

Sorcerer Gossip Murders, 1998 (East Java, Indonesia)

During October and November 1998, a sorcerer scare broke out and resulted in the deaths of many residents who had been falsely accused of dabbling in the black arts. Anthropologist Nicholas Herriman had conducted fieldwork in the region soon after the episode and noted that people commonly received most of their information from the outside world through gossip—and that gossip appeared to have been a key factor in the deaths. He said that the primary means of communication was face-to-face and that where he resided in Tegalgaring village, there were no newspapers, telephones were uncommon, and mobile phones were useless as there was no reception. Further, radio and television stations were devoid of any local news. He said that virtually all local knowledge was *kabar angin* (news spread by the wind). Locals also appeared to place a high reliability to such communication. Alarmingly, he reports that the information learned through gossip served as the basis for many killings. "On the basis of gossip, one could be identified as a 'sorcerer' and be killed for that reason."[82]

In 1998, at a time when the national government was considered weak, residents in rural Banyuwangi watched protests in many major cities. Some took this as an opportunity to correct perceived past injustices perpetrated by sorcerers. In an effort to stop the potential for such acts, the head of the Banyuwangi district ordered local officials to move suspected sorcerers to a safe location before they could be relocated as their safety could not be guaranteed. This process included a visit to a police station where, according to rumor, they would have their photos taken. Visits to a police station were used to confirm the suspicion that someone was a sorcerer. Herriman says that as the killing of these "sorcerers" began, "gossip played a crucial role." For instance, in the village of Watukebo two residents, Sikin and Yasin were both murdered on the suspicion of being sorcerers. Herriman interviewed the former head of the village, Idris, who was involved in the killing. He claimed that Yasin had made nine of his neighbors fall sick.

Herriman said that the information used to identify Yasin as a sorcerer was gossip and suspicion, which had little supporting evidence. "For example, following the directive from the district head, Yasin's sorcery was discussed at a village meeting. Mahmud admitted, 'I was not present,' at the village meeting . . . [but] 'I know.'" He was also sure that the police had taken Yasin's photo and knew he was a sorcerer. Herriman writes: "Local residents had killed this 'sorcerer' because they 'knew' he was a sorcerer, and this 'knowledge' had been spread and reinforced through face-to-face gossip. . . . Local people became convinced that one among them was a sorcerer, and then took it upon themselves to kill that person. Despite the national or district-level events that are part of the background to the 1998 killings, each of the many killings that I researched originated in local, face-to-face gossip."[83]

"How the Grapevine Keeps You in Line" Gossip Study, circa 2011 (Holland)

In 2011, two Dutch psychologists published the results of a study that showed how gossip can have a positive benefit on a group. Bianca Beersma and Gerben Van Kleef devised a study that demonstrated that gossip can be used to prevent someone from taking advantage of others. Beersma and Kleef took 147 students at a large university in the Netherlands—forty-seven were male; one hundred were female—and informed them that they had been randomly selected to receive one hundred lottery tickets, each with a potential cash prize of seventy-five euros. "Participants were told that they were free to contribute as many tickets as they wanted into two accounts: A group account and a personal account. The total number of tickets contributed to the group account would be split equally among the members of the group."[84] Part of the time, the participants were told that their decision to either keep or distribute their tickets would be private. Other times they were told that group members would know of their decision. There was also an added twist. On some occasions, participants were told that there was a likelihood of group members gossiping about the tickets. The results of the study found that the higher the likelihood of gossip, the more generous people were in dispensing the tickets into the group account.

Beersma and Van Kleef concluded that gossip serves to keep members of a group "in line" as "knowing that one may become the subject of gossip when one has to make a decision concerning how much to contribute to one's group and knowing that group members will learn about this decision heightens group opinion concerns, and thereby increases contributions to the group."[85] As to why people behaved in this manner, Beersma and Van Kleef write that "when the threat of gossip is high, participants realized that a selfish choice could be used by their gossiping group members as a basis to construe a negative social reputation that could have severe consequences for them in the future. Interestingly, in our experiment, participants in the high tendency to gossip condition may even have considered the possibility that group members could tell negative things about them to people not involved in the study, such as fellow students, friends, and family members. This strengthens the explanation that gossip constrains undesired behavior because it is seen as a social sanction."[86] This study shows just how powerful gossip is in controlling behavior. Beersma and Van Kleef suggest that while gossip is often viewed in a negative light, such portrayals are undeserved, and that gossip can also be seen as an essential component of group survival.

The Stanford University Gossip Study, circa 2014 (California, USA)

A study led by Stanford University researchers Matthew Feinberg and Robb Willer published in 2014, found that gossiping behind people's backs and ostracizing them (that is, excluding them from the group), can be beneficial. The 216 people who took part in the study were broken up into nine groups of twenty-four. Their research showed that using gossip and ostracism can have beneficial effects on a group by encouraging cooperation among members, reforming bullies, and stopping exploitative actions. Each of the groups took part in a public-goods game which looks at social dilemmas. Before moving to the next round with a new group, participants had the opportunity to gossip about the members of their previous group. Future members received this information and could exclude a suspect individual from their group prior to making their next financial choices. The participants used the gossip about potential group members to align themselves with members that were viewed as likely to be more cooperative. As a result, selfish behavior could result in exclusion from group activities due to gossip.

Clifton Parker, a journalist who reviewed the findings, observed that the gossip process "serves the group's greater good, for selfish types are known to exploit more cooperative people for their own gains."[87] Feinberg remarked: "Groups that allow their members to gossip . . . sustain cooperation and deter selfishness better than those that don't. And groups do even better if they can gossip and ostracize untrustworthy members. While both of these behaviors can be misused, our findings suggest that they also serve very important functions for groups and society."[88]

According to Willer, "Those who do not reform their behavior . . . behaving selfishly despite the risk of gossip and ostracism, tended to be targeted by other group members who took pains to tell future group members about the person's untrustworthy behavior. These future groups could then detect and exclude more selfish individuals, ensuring they could avoid being taken advantage of."[89] The threat of excluding people from the group often served to counter selfish behavior.

For instance, members who had been kicked out of the group but were later let back in, tended to show a marked improvement in what they could contribute to the group after they returned. The researchers believe that the process of gossip alone appears sufficient to promote cooperation as "gossiping and knowing that others could gossip about you makes reputation salient, which tends to foster pro-sociality . . . and because defecting when future partners will know what you did will lead these partners to not cooperate with you, which reduces the incentive to defect in the first place."[90]

Rumor and gossip are the building blocks of collective behavior and social delusions. They are often responsible for the rapid spread of false or exaggerated information. They have the power to trigger riots, topple political leaders, or lead to the outbreak of war. While the content of these stories is unverified, people often act on them as if they were real. Hence, regardless of their truth or falsity, they become real in their consequences. Rumor and gossip are powerful forces that contribute to the formation of many social delusions. They do not occur willy-nilly; they have a structure that governs their appearance and spread. Rumors thrive in ambiguous situations of perceived importance as people try to make sense of the world around them and reduce tensions. Gossip is a double-edge sword. It has the power to sanction and punish those of us who are different or outsiders. As we have seen, it has even resulted in the deaths of innocent people. But overlooked until relatively recently, is the good side to gossip; it has the power to bind people together and serves as a clear indicator of how one should behave in any given group.

In chapter 2, we look at fads. Like rumor and gossip, fads operate in the short-term. While not directly related to rumor and gossip, they too contain fundamental elements of social delusions, namely, preoccupations with objects, ideas, or people. While arguably the least destructive form of collective behavior, fads can also be classified as a social delusion in that participants typically consider them to be enduring aspects of the social landscape, while in reality, they quickly fade into relative obscurity.

CHAPTER 2

FADS: THE NEXT BIG THING

F ads are intense, popular enthusiasms on trivial or frivolous matters. While the origin of the word is uncertain, one school of thought holds that it is a shortening of *faddle* from the sixteenth-century term *fiddle-faddle* (to play with).[1] It may also have its origin from the French *fadaise*, meaning trifle or nonsense. Fads involve large numbers of people who exhibit short-term interest in a trivial object or activity. Fads can involve words, ideas, people, and habits. While fads may be intense, those involved do not become obsessive and it does not become the central feature of everyday life. That is, while of great interest, people do not typically quit their jobs or sell their homes to participate in fads, although fads may take up much of their spare time over the few weeks or months that they are in vogue.

Fads often originate as symbols of prestige that are engaged in by people of high status such as professional athletes and film stars, only to quickly wane as the novelty wears off and "everyone" seems to be doing it. Sometimes youngsters will take up a fad to rebel against authority. In other instances it is a way of gaining attention. Some experts believe that fads are more popular among young people because their identities are less developed.[2] Others suggest that fads become more common in times of crisis as a way of diverting attention from more serious issues of the day.[3]

The biggest fad of the twentieth century was a molded tube of circular polyethylene that became popularly known as the Hula-Hoop. Thirty million hoops were sold in the United States over a four-month span in 1958.[4] Other classic fads include Cabbage Patch Kids dolls, CB radios, goldfish swallowing, Davy Crockett coonskin hats, and the phrases "far out," "no-brainer," and "where's the beef?" Fads are "a flash in the pan" that once were "the flavor of the month." A fad may appear silly in hindsight, once it has faded into obscurity. Pet rocks, ant farms, virtual pets, hair ironing, and the coughing ashtray spring to mind as examples. Diets are notoriously faddish. One of the most bizarre diet fads was advocated during the early twentieth century by Wilbur Voliva, who expected to reach the ripe old age of 120 by consuming buttermilk and Brazil nuts. He died in 1942 at the age of seventy-two.[5]

It is difficult to control or predict what fad will temporarily capture the public's imagination or how long it will endure. In 1959, after twenty-five school students in South Africa crammed into a single phone booth, "phone booth stuffing" became all the rage on US campuses. Of course, not all booths were the same size. *Life* magazine documented the various strategies, which included the "limbs-in" and "sardine" methods. There seemed to at least be agreement on the single best method: use undersized undergraduates.[6] The fad was soon over, replaced by the year's end with a variation: Volkswagen stuffing.

A study of 735 fads by California sociologist Emory Bogardus identified several broad categories: female dress and decoration (73 percent), male dress and decoration (11 percent), recreation and amusements (6 percent), and language (4 percent). The remaining 6 percent involve education, architecture, cars, and culture.[7] The typical fad remains popular for three months or less. Few fads are able to captivate the public interest for more than six months.[8] However, due to their spontaneous nature, it is difficult to predict the next fad.

The study of fads falls under the domain of sociology, psychology, and economics. Social scientists have identified the four phases of a fad.[9] First is the latent period when the fad emerges but lies relatively dormant. Some writers contend that most, if not all fads, are recycled from existing social and cultural themes that are later rediscovered and only give the appearance of being the latest rage. For instance, the tree- and flagpole-sitting fads of the late 1920s and early '30s can be traced to "pillar hermits" in early Christian Europe.[10] While a string attached to a spool spiked in popularity during the early 1930s and again in the 1960s, the yo-yo was not new. Similar devices were used as either toys or weapons in a variety of cultures dating back to ancient Greece. Even bungee jumping has long been practiced in the jungles of Papua New Guinea and the Solomon Islands, where natives continue to leap off wooden towers with only a vine tied to one ankle in order to prove one's manhood. Occasionally, jumpers unfortunately miscalculate.

Before the Hula-Hoop exploded in popularity, it was experiencing an obscure existence as a bamboo hoop in Australian gym classes, who in turn had gotten the idea from Pacific islanders. Yet, in 1958 when it was marketed by the Wham-O Company in the United States, tens of millions of tubes were sold in a single year, before the market for the hoops suddenly collapsed. In fact, bamboo hoops have long been in use as a toy in many cultures dating back millennia, but instead of being gyrated with the body, they were often rolled with a stick or the hand. The Ojibway Indians, in what is now Canada, have long practiced a sacred hoop dance using up to fifty wooden hoops to create shapes such as butterflies, eagles, snakes, and flowers.[11]

During the breakout phase, the item or activity is adopted by people other than those who used it in the latent period, spreading mainly by word-of-mouth and the media. The spread is boosted when those who use it during the period, actively promote it. Until the early 1970s, Citizen Band radios led a relatively obscure existence among truckers and were sold at a few specialty locations such as select truck stops, truck garages, and in little-known mail-order catalogues. Once CBs started to catch on outside the trucker community, they soon found a wider audience and eventually wound up on department store shelves. The plastic throwing disc was marketed in 1955 under the name "Pluto Platter" and renamed the following year as the Frisbee. A similar game had long been popular at Yale University where students had a tradition of tossing pie plates, made by Frisbie's Pies of Bridgeport, Connecticut, across the campus lawns. Frisbees gained initial popularity on several eastern US college campuses where Wham-O recruited students to sell them.[12]

The third stage is the peaking period, characterized by a rapid, dramatic increase in appearance, coinciding with frequent media coverage. During this phase, if a fad doesn't already have a readily identifiable name, the media coins one, such as the slicked-back "D.A." (duck's ass) hair style of the 1950s. During the roaring '20s, a relatively small number of sassy young women defied the conservative mores of the period: they drank alcohol during the government Prohibition that forbade its manufacture and social use; smoked cigarettes when it was considered unladylike; and wore bold, revealing dresses that flaunted their sexuality. They quickly gained the label of "flappers." Soon, older, more traditional women began adopting some of their habits such as short skirts, haircuts, and makeup. Some fads come ready-made, such as the Hula-Hoop; others, like the flappers, are soon given a label.

In September 1930, the US Department of Commerce estimated that there were an astounding thirty thousand mini-golf courses.[13] During the peak period, it seems as though everyone is either doing it or talking about it, has one or has to have one. This saturation effect seems to portend the inevitable decline, as once fads peak, the excitement and novelty have worn off, and they are unable to maintain their intensity.

Occasionally fads endure due to new marketing strategies. Between 1956 and 1966, Milton Levine sold over twelve million ant farms. A major reason for the longevity of the ant farm was that Levine gave away fancy versions made of mahogany to TV personalities, such as Dick Clark, who placed them on their TV sets with other knick-knacks. Levine once noted: "Ants work day and night, they look out for the common good and never procrastinate. . . . Humanity can learn a lot from the ant."[14]

The decline phase begins when excitement and interest rapidly wane. The meteoric rise of a fad is inevitably met with a steep decline in interest. Sociologist David Miller observes that during this stage, the once "hot" item is typically discarded or stored in closets and garages to gather dust, never to be used again. If traces linger, it is because the fad has remained only with the few original users from the dormant or latent phase.[15] In the case of activities, the goldfish swallowing rage that swept across college campuses in the spring of 1939, lasted only two months before the novelty wore off. Not only did goldfish swallowing become unpopular, it was viewed in a negative light. What was initially a hilarious fad was soon being condemned as cruelty to fish, and public health officials were warning of the dangers of getting tapeworms. Some communities even passed ordinances making it illegal to gulp the critters, and colleges threatened to expel swallowers.

Sometimes a fad will die out, only to be revived in a different form. A classic example is the 1959 penchant for phone booth stuffing that petered out but was rekindled years later in the form of Volkswagen stuffing.

Occasionally fads become part of the establishment, though their popularity and the fever-pitch of desire has waned. These include Frisbees, skateboards, yo-yos, and miniature golf. There was an explosive interest in miniature or Tom Thumb golf during the early 1930s, but soon people grew disinterested and most outlets went bankrupt.[16] Fads sometimes also decline due to supply and demand. During World War II, for example, the availability of silk from Japan was interrupted after the Japanese attack of Pearl Harbor, prompting the US Government to ban silk stockings as silk was vital in the production of parachutes. As a result, a new fad was born: newly marketed leg makeup exploded in popularity as women on the home front applied liquid foundation to simulate the appearance of hose. Many ladies would then also use an eyebrow pencil to give the appearance of a black "seam."[17]

Fad words gain rapid acceptance as local or regional slang for short periods. Language expert Jack Hart says they are identifiable by their vagueness. He gives the example of "no-brainer" which became chic in 1994, replacing such words as "apparent," "simple," "straightforward," "logical," "evident," and "clear."[18] British writer Charles Mackay describes a variety of fad words and phrases that spread through London during the nineteenth century. Words and phrases such as "flare up," "quoz," and "Does your mother know you're out?" were evoked to describe almost any act or situation, only to suddenly lose vogue. In America between 1900 and 1910, the word "go-getter" was seemingly on everyone's lips, followed by "doughboy"—a US soldier fighting in Europe near the end of World War I. "Lounge lizard" was used to describe a womanizer in the 1920s; a "hepcat" was 1930s lingo for someone who was hip, while a "drugstore cowboy" was a 1940s teen who hung out at the local soda fountain.

In his book on effective writing, William Noble urges authors to avoid fad words like the plague, as their currency is usually limited to a specific time and place, and just a few years later many people may not recall or understand their meaning. While decades later, phrases like "Let's split the scene" may still be understood, other phrases such as "Here comes the fuzz" may be unrecognizable. Few teenagers today are likely to know that "fuzz" was 1960s lingo to describe the police.[19] A short-lived fad in 1947 was to talk in rhymes. For instance, a girl might ask a guy, "What's cookin' good lookin'?" To which he may reply, "Got no story, mornin' glory."[20]

FADS, FASHIONS, AND TRENDS

The words *fad* and *fashion* are often used interchangeably, but social scientists disagree as to the exact difference between the two terms. Sociologist Joel Best states that unlike fads, fashions are systematic and a form of institutionalized change. A classic example is the clothing industry. Best writes that high-end fashion designers traditionally work "on a seasonable timetable to prepare new creations for the upcoming shows that would attract the fashion press and buyers. This world—in spite of all the hype about the designers' genius and originality and spontaneity, consisted of established businesses producing goods within a fixed routine. No one in the haute couture [French for "high fashion"] world imagined that the upcoming show's fashions would remain fashionable forever— the new designs were intended to be popular only for a season, before losing favor to the next scheduled inspiration."[21] The annual changes in the fashion industry are far from unique. Other popular examples include the music, film, and book publishing industries, where the popularity of certain genres waxes and wanes and trends are the order of the day. Despite their systematic, institutionalized nature, these industries do share a key feature with fads: their unpredictability. Best observes: "Nobody expects this week's number one best seller, top box-office draw, or chart-topping song to stay on top forever—or even for all that long. These are all fashion industries that depend on people's continually shifting tastes."[22]

Fashions, such as wearing the latest dress design from Paris or New York, serve functions for the wearer. In addition to providing protection from the elements and concealment of their bodies, wearing the latest style helps to differentiate people from others and to identify them with a particular group. The popularity of certain brands among youths, such as Tommy Hilfiger clothes or Nike sneakers, signifies that they belong to a certain group and social class. It is an image that we wish to project to others. In giving the wearer an identity, it helps the group members to stand out in society.

In America near the turn of the twentieth century, technological progress and industrialization created a new wealthy class of people, at a time when dress and personal adornment were a way to make others aware of their new social economic status. Economist Thorstein Veblen coined the term *conspicuous consumption* to describe how some people buy certain goods in order to show off their wealth and status.[23] According to sociologists Margaret Andersen and Howard Taylor, the fashion industry often adopts the fads of marginalized subcultures that are, in turn, marketed to elite groups as a new clothing trend. "Hip-hop fashion first emerged as a style among inner-city, low-income Black youth and was captured by the fashion industry, which then marketed wide, baggy jeans, caps, and oversized shorts to elite and middle-class markets. A cycle of fashion develops when the style of low-status groups, trickles up to high-status groups. The style then becomes a status symbol and is sold widely to the middle class. Marginalized subcultures then may develop new styles that, if appropriated by high-status groups, create another cycle of fashion." They cite as an example, the fashion trend in the first decade of the twenty-first century of women wearing low-cut jeans, animal-skin prints, and high-heel boots—a style originally associated with prostitutes.[24] Of course, fashions can also trickle down from people of higher status and become adopted by the lower classes.

While fads by definition involve trivial things, understanding them can be important to businesses. Telling the difference between a fad and a long-term trend can translate into big money. Business executives can grow rich by marketing fad products as they initially sell like hotcakes, then bailing out just before interest plummets. However, knowing when the market has peaked is notoriously difficult to determine, and to use a fad cliché, if one is not careful, they could "lose their shirt" by being stuck with thousands of units of an item that no one wants. Businesses hoping for stability by selling more enduring products may wish to avoid fad items altogether due to their unpredictable nature. For instance, near the end of 1958, some companies that had jumped on the Hula-Hoop bandwagon were left with warehouses filled with millions of unsold hoops that could not be sold for any price. The challenge for the seller is to be able to differentiate between a fad and a trend.

Consumer researcher Martin Letscher identifies several ways to tell a fad from a trend.[25] A key distinguishing feature of a product or action is whether it fits with changes in lifestyles. Since most Americans lead busy lives, gourmet foods that take a long time to prepare would not be likely to endure. Another important element involves the benefits of a product or action. Selling tofu burgers and raw nuts may coincide with the trend toward healthier living and also has the added benefit of showing your family that you care for them. It is hard to imagine Rubik's Cube solving or goldfish swallowing offering comparable health or monetary benefits. Yes, during their fleeting periods of vogue, Rubik's Cube contests, dance marathons, and yo-yo competitions often offered prize money, though it was a pittance by the standards of the time, and certainly few people have ever managed to eke out a living as a Rubik's Cube or yo-yo professional!

Letscher also considers it important to determine whether the product is a trend or a side effect. He observes that while exercising is a long-term trend with a solid foundation, some related activities lack staying power, such as new types of exercises. Line dancing and exercise gadgets that target your buttocks or promise "six pack" abdominal muscles are notoriously fleeting. Another strategy is to look for related trends, such as the marketing of vitamin and mineral supplements to the health conscious. Some fads and trends have carry-over effects, such as the popularity of the miniskirt during the 1960s, which led to a steep rise in the sales of pantyhose and tights.

MEMORABLE FADS

Squirrel Barking, 1790s (Kentucky, USA)

Kentucky frontiersman Daniel Boone helped to popularize the local custom of "barking off squirrels" when he began to wager his fellow marksmen as to who could "bark off" the most squirrels within an allotted time. The object was to kill the furry creatures without hitting them directly, by targeting a piece of nearby bark. At the time, parts of Kentucky were teeming with so many squirrels that shooting them by conventional means, posed little challenge. Naturalist John James Audubon was an eyewitness: "Judge to my surprise, when I perceived that the ball had hit the piece of the bark immediately beneath the squirrel, and shivered into splinters, the concussion produced by which had killed the animal, and sent it whirling through the air, as if it had been blown up by explosion of a powder magazine."[26] The practice grew so popular that Kentucky newspapers even published regular columns detailing the outcomes of "barking" contests. Skilled marksmanship was a necessity on the frontier in colonial Kentucky. This state of affairs, coupled with the affinity for gambling and Boone's popularity, led to the temporary, widespread emulation of squirrel barking. The practice became so popular that Audubon wrote that gambling on squirrel barking seemed to be taking place "on every tree around us."[27]

Diabolo, 1906–1909 (Europe and North America)

A diabolo is a novelty toy made up of two hollow cups joined base-to-base. The diabolo is quickly rolled back and forth along a string attached to two sticks and can be tossed, twirled, and caught. Skilled practitioners are able to fling the bobbin more than sixty feet into the air and still catch it with the string. If the diabolo's spin slows too much, it falls off the string. In 1906, Frenchman Gustave Philippart created a metal diabolo that was lighter and more durable than the wooden ones used until then. This created an explosion of interest in France, rapidly followed by England, and later the world, with the diabolo being a popular toy for both children and adults.[28] While Philippart claimed the invention for himself, it was actually a new version of an age-old toy. Similar devices were first made out of bamboo in China about four thousand years ago. The Parker Brothers of game and toy fame secured the US patent for the diabolo in 1906;

within two years, it had swept across the country.[29] Most people would throw and catch the double cones on the string as many times as possible without missing it. Others vied to catch the bobbin in unusual positions, such as over the shoulder or behind their head. Sets ranged in price from $1 to $8.

At the height of its popularity, two teenage boys in Boston, one French and one American, were paid by the Henry Siegel Company to demonstrate various diabolo throws and tricks to the public, enthralling passersby. According to the *Boston Evening Transcript* of December 3, 1907, the boys were so proficient they seemingly defied the laws of gravity. "Before the play had been in progress twenty minutes, the walks on all sides of the playground were dotted with persons who had stopped to watch. . . . As these persons came nearer, amusement turned to wonder and finally to open applause. . . . Hurried shoppers forgot their errands and stood cooling their heels on the walks, always waiting to see one more throw."[30]

By 1910, the sales of the diabolo took a sudden, precipitous decline, as the market had become flooded with cheap imitations. Game historian Philip Orbanes notes that while these cheap "knock-offs" were sold under different names, "poor quality stopped the fad dead in its tracks."[31] While Parker Brothers used steel bobbins and placed rubber on each end, competitors tended to use poor quality lathed wood which spun more slowly and could not be tossed as high. In an attempt to counter these shoddy imitations, Parker Brothers came out with an inexpensive, wooden version of their own, dubbed the "Whirling Wizard," but by this time it was unable to rekindle interest.[32] For the better part of a century, diabolos were only seen in variety stage shows. Today, jugglers can often be seen doing dozens of varied tricks using up to three lightweight, plastic diabolos on a single cord while either busking in the street or juggling at conventions.

Miniature Golf, 1929–1930 (USA)

In 1929, Garnet Carter of Chattanooga, Tennessee, built hundreds of miniature golf courses in Florida to boost the popularity of his hotels there. It quickly caught on, and soon tiny courses began popping up like mushrooms across the country. By the fall of 1930, miniature golf had become nothing short of a national obsession as four million people a day were playing on any one of forty thousand courses employing two hundred thousand people and generating profits of $225 million.[33] Known by such names as "midget," "pigmy," and "Tom Thumb golf," some neighborhoods protested their appearance due to the rowdy crowds that were sometimes associated with them. With money in short supply, the "half pint" golf boom grew from the ashes of the Great Depression. At a time when most people were hurting financially and could not afford to play a game that was associated with the rich and famous, "mini golf" typically cost a mere thirty cents. For less than a dollar extra, you could even hire a caddie to carry your clubs. Peter Skolnik observes that miniature golf was novel, inexpensive, and coed—an attractive combination.

But the fad began to fade by year's end, and most establishments soon went bankrupt. As a remarkable testament to its spectacular rise and sudden collapse, by the winter of 1931, it was reported that not one miniature golf course in California had turned a profit for the year.[34] While miniature golf continues today, its popularity is a shadow of its former self. During a brief surge in popularity in 1989, there were an estimated 1,800 courses in the United States,[35] while during another peak in 2001, there were six thousand courses: far fewer than in its glory days following the Depression.[36]

Goldfish Swallowing, March–May 1939 (USA)

One day while showing off his aquarium, Harvard student Lothrop Withington Jr. casually boasted to a classmate that he could eat a live fish. The pair agreed to a $10 bet. The stage was set for one of the most improbable fads of the twentieth century. Word of the dare quickly circulated across campus and throughout the city of Boston, prompting several major newspapers to send reporters to cover the story and take photos. Sure enough, at the appointed time—Friday evening, March 3, 1939—Withington appeared and a scrum of students and reporters gathered around as the freshman dipped his hand into a small bowl. He then pulled out a three-inch goldfish, tipped his head back, let the fish go, and began to chew, followed by a hard gulp. He then cheekily pulled out his toothbrush to clean his teeth, before sitting down to dine on the meal of the night: fillet of sole.[37] When later asked about the feat, Withington remarked: "It was purely a case of mind over matter. I didn't mind, and the fish didn't matter."[38]

As reports of Withington's exploits spread across the country, it inspired a series of one-upmanship among college students. At Franklin and Marshall College, Frank Pope won a $5 bet after swallowing three goldfish whole after sprinkling them with salt and pepper and proclaiming Withington to be "a sissy."[39] Donald Mulcahy of Boston College then took the lead by swallowing twenty-eight goldfish with a glass of milk as a chaser, amid protests by animal rights advocates.[40] At the University of Michigan, a student also gulped down twenty-eight fish. The record eventually reached 210, although there were unverified claims of over three hundred fish.

Just before goldfish swallowing's sharp decline, students were branching out for more exotic quarry and began swallowing and eating everything from earthworms to phonograph records. One student was even reported to have bitten the head from a live snake. At Oregon State College, a student slid down 139 earthworms. At Lafayette College in Pennsylvania, an undergraduate student ate an entire issue of the *New Yorker* magazine. While at the University of Illinois, John Poppelreiter appeared to trump everyone after eating five white mice![41] These increasingly outrageous antics seemed to portend the fad's demise, which came in the spring with the end-of-school-year exams.[42] Near the end of the fad, there was a flurry of warnings by health officials about the dangers of goldfish swallowing, which included choking to death or getting tapeworms from eating raw fish.[43]

The origin of goldfish swallowing seems to have begun with a chance event that received widespread publicity and followed a classic fad pattern, beginning with a person of high status (from Harvard University), who spread a new act to other students who copied these behaviors and set new records. In doing so, they raised the prestige and status of the swallowers. But the novelty and excitement soon wore off, to the point where students began seeking out new, more thrilling and bizarre variations on the theme. In the end, the growing list of increasingly outlandish feats proved too difficult to top. After all, swallowing over two hundred live goldfish in one sitting or eating a live mouse are tough feats to surpass. What had started out as a humorous novelty was eventually viewed in a widely negative light. Near the end of the fad, animal rights groups were complaining, universities were suspending students, health authorities were warning against the consumption of animals, and politicians even tried to legislate against such acts.[44] In the latter instance, State Senator George Krapf proposed a bill to the Massachusetts legislature that would prevent cruelty to goldfish.[45]

The Hula-Hoop, 1958 (Worldwide)

The greatest fad of the twentieth century, the Hula-Hoop, took the United States by storm in 1958. The bamboo hoop had long been in use by Australian grade-schoolers as a fun way to exercise in physical education classes. When the popularity of the hoop in Australia caught the eye of Arthur "Spud" Melin of the US–based Wham-O toy company, he and co-owner Richard Knerr set out to market the product using polyethylene plastic. They named the new toy after the Hawaiian hip-gyrating hula dance. That spring, Melin traveled to schools and other venues across Southern California, in a systematic effort to drum up interest. The media quickly picked up on the local hoopla, and it quickly spread to the East Coast. Knerr later observed: "First we tried it on our own children and then we took it into the neighborhood, the best testing laboratory there is for toys. Well, the kids just wouldn't put the hoop down. It had the longest 'play-value' we had ever seen on any toy we produced so we put it out on a test basis."[46]

At its peak, it seemed as though every psychologist had a pet theory for the Hula-Hoops phenomenal popularity. Explanations ranged from a subconscious eroticism evoked by gyrating the hips, to the encirclement offering a sense of comfort and security. It was even postulated that the hoop was the symbolic equivalent of a vagina. It may have been that the Hula-Hoop allowed people of all ages the ability to gyrate their hips in public, under the guise of playing with a toy. Two years earlier in 1956, when Elvis Presley performed live on the popular Ed Sullivan Show, the cameramen were careful not to show his gyrating hips as it was seen as too sexually provocative. In fact, when Spud Melin's wife first heard of her husband's idea to market the hoop, she discouraged him, noting the fuss created by Elvis's dance moves. At $1.98 and easy to use, it may have simply been cheap, fun, and novel—and a way to gyrate one's hips in public. It cost a mere fifty cents to manufacture.[47]

Some communist countries initially banned use of the Hoop, viewing it as the epitome of Western capitalist emptiness. In Jakarta, Indonesia, the police destroyed thousands of hoops seized from shops. Ironically, it was pointed out that long before the Western plastic Hula-Hoops appeared on the scene, a similar rattan hoop was used as a physical-education aid there.[48]

Scores of companies quickly offered spin-offs, selling them for between one and two dollars. It is estimated that over 100,000 million hoops were sold worldwide by the end of 1958, comprising no less than forty-seven varieties of hoops. By November, Americans seemed to be all hooped-out as sales plunged and the fad faded away almost overnight. Despite several carefully planned attempts to rekindle public interest in the Hula-Hoop—complete with expensive promotional campaigns—none have come even remotely close to the phenomenal success of 1958. Perhaps the most fascinating aspect of the Hula-Hoop is that social scientists are still uncertain as to the factors behind its sudden rise and its equally sudden decline.[49] Now, few Hula-Hoops are seen outside specialist circus performance acts. One impressive exception was when sixty-four-year-old singer Grace Jones twirled a hoop nonstop for four minutes while she sang "Slave to the Rhythm" at the Queen of England's Diamond Jubilee Concert in 2012.

Streaking, 1973–1974 (Worldwide)

Imagine sitting in a crowded lecture theater busily writing notes in your math class when suddenly, several naked students dash down the aisle and exit through a side door. Similar scenes were repeated on college campuses across the United States in 1973, when the sudden appearance of streaking began raising eyebrows. Within a few weeks, streaking had spread to all aspects of American life and was gaining popularity around the world.

At its peak, people streaked on bicycles, roller skates, ice skates, and in their bare feet. There were reports of streakers on motorcycles and skis. Five adventurous students streaked with parachutes above the campus of the University of Georgia. No place was free of streakers, from state legislatures to shopping malls. In some instances, streakers wore only tennis shoes, ski masks, or just a smile. From Wall Street in New York to St. Peter's Square in Rome, people took off their clothes and bared all. While the culprits were comprised mostly of college students, streaking was reported among those as young as eleven and as old as sixty-five. Sociologist Ben Aguirre conducted a study on streaking and found that of 1,016 schools surveyed, 78 percent had reported at least one event.

Then in May 1974, just a few months after the trickle of reports began in January, the streaking fad ended as suddenly as it had started. Occasional incidents at sporting events, where streaking has become an institution, still occur, but outside of its heyday, this behavior is discouraged and typically results in boos from disgruntled fans, arrests, and fines. During the fad, few were arrested and most authorities looked upon it as humorous and harmless.[50]

A study of streaking on college campuses by sociologists Robert Evans and Jerry Miller uncovered a pattern. Incidents typically began on a small scale with one or a few bold students streaking at night. The following day, news of these exploits spread quickly across campus by word of mouth and the local media. A flurry of streaks would quickly follow and culminate in an advertised public event attracting a large audience including journalists. During these large-scale public exhibitions (known as "streak-ins"), streakers would often engage in innovations such as donning rolling skates or performing stripteases. Within a few days, a second streak-in would be held, but by the third cycle, students had typically lost interest and were all "streaked out."

Sociologist Jack Levin notes that the timing and social backdrop of fads are essential to their success, as prevailing values set limits as to what is acceptable at any given time. For instance, he writes that during the streaking fad, the tolerance of taking off one's clothes and running nude in public was rendered acceptable as a result of the 1960s' sexual revolution. "The same act would undoubtedly have received quite a different reception if it had occurred during the 1950s. Any student who had dared run naked through a college campus then would, in all likelihood, have been quickly locked away as a sexual pervert and a menace to society. In 1954, streaking could hardly have gained the popularity of a fad."[51]

Sociologist William Anderson noted that the act of streaking posed a challenge for university campuses because unlike past fads such as swallowing goldfish or phone booth stuffing, the act of running naked in public was widely viewed by administrators as a more serious deviation. Furthermore, it could be considered illegal if people filed complaints. Anderson viewed streaking as representing a new morality that posed a challenge to existing traditional values. Based on an analysis of streaking on his home campus of Arizona State University, Anderson found that the emergence and decline of this fad was regulated by several factors.

Milling is seen as an essential factor in prompting the emergence of streaking. As students heard media reports and read posters promoting streaking, people milled together to define the situation—a process that also led to the spread of streaking-related rumors.[52] A second factor was the involvement of *core activists* who were influential in helping to organize the streaks and got people excited about joining in. While it was not viewed as essential that these activists emerged from preexisting groups, the presence of such groups provided a convenient advantage. Fraternities were one such key group at ASU. Anderson writes: "Like fraternities elsewhere, it was traditional for them to be among the first to adopt innovative antics. Also, the fact that fraternity members were linked by their common group membership made it easier for them to plan their collective participation in the fad and coordinate their actions once the crowds actually formed and the streaking began."[53]

Another factor identified in the spread of streaking was the support that the participants received. Anderson notes that there was widespread campus support for the fad, although three ASU students did file complaints with police after being offended by specific acts. However, these students later withdrew their complaints. The positive tone of articles in the campus newspaper appeared to spur on the behavior, as did cheering crowds that "left little doubt that activists had the backing of many persons on campus."[54] At the same time, *weak social control* was pivotal at the beginning of the fad on the part of campus security and the dean of students. This was due in part to the lack of a clear policy on streaking. There was some initial uncertainly as to whether briefly running naked on campus constituted a crime. Furthermore, Anderson observed that university officials "made no attempt to interfere with the crowds during the mass streaking episodes."[55] This gave many students the impression that they could join in without having to worry about negative consequences.

On the other hand, stronger social control as the fad wore on appeared to have contributed to its abrupt decline. Just before the fad ended, campus officials and security placed pressure on students not to streak.[56] The student dean and the head of campus security met with the fraternity leaders and issued a stern warning that further incidents would not be tolerated. "The fraternity presidents were warned that streaking was against the law (although these officials were far from sure that this was true) and prohibited by the university's code of conduct, and that those who could be later identified as having participated in it could be charged with indecent exposure, under state law"—violations that could stop them from entering graduate school and cause problems in getting a job.[57]

Anderson also identified adverse situational conditions as another factor in the streaking fad. For instance, on those days when the fad was exhibiting popularity, the weather was mainly fine. Conversely, coinciding with the rapid decline in incidents was cool, rainy weather. As for other possible factors—the sudden decline coincided with the advent of the school's spring break. Anderson noted that after the break, just one streaking incident was reported involving a lone student.[58] One cannot underestimate the extent to which streaking had entered the public consciousness in 1974. In March, Ray Stevens reached the Billboard Hot 100 with his song "The Streak," and a streaker even appeared live on national television during the 46th Academy Awards ceremony on April 2 of that year.

As for an explanation for the sudden appearance and decline of interest in streaking, social scientists are still unsure. Psychologist Philip Zimbardo postulates that it may have been "an attack on dominant social values," while another psychologist, Dorothy Hochreich, suggests that it was "a form of escapism" and a way of "letting off steam."[59] It may have been no coincidence that the fad came to a close with end-of-year exams and returning home for the summer.

Kung Fu Mania, 1973–1978 (USA and Worldwide)

Prior to their sudden rise in popularity during the 1970s, kung fu movies had enjoyed limited success and distribution outside Asia. That changed with the popularity of Bruce Lee. Until this time, audiences had only seen martial arts in a few notable films: James Cagney using judo in *Blood on the Sun* (1945), Spencer Tracy's jujitsu moves in *Bad Day at Black Rock* (1955), and the karate fight between Frank Sinatra and Henry Silva in *The Manchurian Candidate* (1962). These cinematic examples involved Japanese martial arts, whereas kung fu is of Chinese origin.

Bruce Lee was born in San Francisco in 1940 but was raised in Hong Kong. During his teenage years, he became involved in street fights, and his parents encouraged him to train in wing chun style kung fu so he could defend himself. Lee returned to the United States when he was eighteen. It was only a matter of time before he made it onto American screens after gaining small acting roles as a martial arts instructor in television shows like *Ironside* (1967) and *Longstreet* (1971). In the movie *Marlowe* (1969), Lee's character demolished James Garner's office before being ridiculously tricked into doing a flying kick out the window while falling to his death. The role that gained Lee the greatest publicity was as Kato, the title character's sidekick in the television series *The Green Hornet* (1966–1967).

After losing the lead Asian martial artist part in the series *Kung Fu* (1972–1975) to the non-Asian, non-martial-artist David Carradine, a disillusioned Lee returned to Hong Kong. There he starred in three successful movies: *Fists of Fury* (1971), *The Chinese Connection* (1972), and *The Way of the Dragon* (1972). All three films showcased his charismatic personality, muscular physique, and lightning-fast fight moves. In 1973, Hollywood finally took notice of his talents, and Lee was given the lead role in *Enter the Dragon*. Tragically, he collapsed and died on July 20, 1973—a week before the film's release. Lee had eaten a hashish cookie and then, after complaining of a headache, taken a single Equagesic pill for pain relief. An adverse reaction to this combination of drugs caused brain swelling.[60] *Enter the Dragon*, made for an estimated $850,000 US, grossed $90 million worldwide.[61]

Spurred by the success of the film and the television series *Kung Fu*, there was a hunger in America for the next five years for everything kung fu. In late 1974, the Carl Douglas song "Kung Fu Fighting" went to number one on the charts in the United States. The song was done in a rush as it was originally intended as the B-side of a single. "So I went over the top on the 'huhs' and the 'hahs' and the chopping sounds. It was a B-side: who was going to listen?" says writer and producer Biddu. "We thought it would sell about 20,000—it sold 11 million records around the world."[62]

The hit song was followed by a new kung fu dance style. The basic steps were easy: "one shifts the arms back and forth while clenching the fists, then spins and kicks the feet."[63] By the end of 1974, *Kung-Fu Monthly* (a slim British magazine that folded out into a poster) had a circulation of 200,000.[64] There was even a highly successful Marvel comic called *Master of Kung Fu* that was published for nearly a decade from 1974.

At least five hundred kung fu movies were made in the 1970s. After Lee's untimely death, a number of look-alike actors assumed similar names (Bruce Li, Dragon Lee, etc.) and produced shoddy imitations of his fighting style in dozens of dreadful films with cash-in titles like *Bruce Lee Strikes Back*, *The Clones of Bruce Lee*, *Re-Enter the Dragon*, etc. Using editing tricks, old footage, and body doubles, Bruce Lee appeared posthumously in two of the so-called Bruceploitation films: *Game of Death* in 1978 and *Game of Death II* in 1981.

Lee's funeral in Hong Kong was accompanied by an emotional outpouring that had not been seen since the death of actor Rudolph Valentino in 1926. This was a testament to Lee's huge following in Asia. His enduring legacy is that he was able to inspire hundreds of thousands to better themselves through martial-arts training, while at the same time destroying the stereotypes that were then prevalent in Hollywood and Western countries. This included caricatures of Asians as foolish foreigners, elderly wise men, nerdy asexual wimps, cooks, and comedic sidekicks.[65]

Citizen Band Radios, 1973–1980 (USA)

The Citizen Band (CB) radio fad burst onto the American scene during the early 1970s after getting a massive boost from two unlikely sources: the shortage of oil and gas, and a national truckers strike. In 1958, the US government approved the use of CB radios among the public. Most early CB users were delivery companies and taxicab operators, but that changed dramatically with the 1973 Arab oil embargo and the imposition of fuel rationing as long-distance truckers began using CBs to locate service stations that sold diesel fuel. Prior to this time, the growth in radio sales and the number of licenses issued was holding steady at around 100,000 annually. Up until this point, few people used CBs for recreational purposes.

In that watershed year for CB radios—1973—sales suddenly jumped twentyfold. That same year, the government issued nearly two million licenses, most to long-haul truck drivers looking for diesel fuel, as most big rigs could not operate on gasoline.[66] The second major cause of the rise in CB popularity was the effect of a nationwide strike by independent truckers that occurred between December 1973 and January 1974. During this time, media outlets reported on how truckers were able to disrupt traffic during protests by sharing information about police movements over their radios.[67]

As the use of CBs quickly spread among the trucking community, it was found to have additional benefits such as relaying information about road conditions, accidents, and other emergencies. The CB also allowed truckers to engage in conversations during their long-distance trips. While the broadcast distance of the average CB radio was between ten and thirty miles depending on terrain, time of day, and weather conditions, truckers traveling along the same roadway in close proximity could stay in communication for hundreds, and sometimes thousands, of miles. For many truckers, it was also used to tip off their traveling companions of the presence of police speed traps. Soon CB users developed their own jargon such as referring to the police as "smokies," while a person's "handle" was their CB nickname.[68] Before long, commuters and sales representatives began installing CB radios in their vehicles.

The CB fad peaked in 1976 when an astounding eleven million radios were sold. This translated to an estimated 1.5 billion US dollars in sales. This may have been a result of the national fifty-five-mile-per-hour speed limit that was imposed that year. As a result, many motorists wanted to go over the speed limit without getting caught, so they used the radios to avoid police speed checks. They sometimes teamed up with truckers and drove together on roadways in what they called "convoys" and were able to reduce their risk of being caught speeding as oncoming CB-equipped vehicles could alert them to the presence of police on the road ahead and they could then reduce their speed to "double nickels" or fifty-five miles per hour. One survey of CB users found that only about ten percent had bought their radio to avoid speeding fines. Most said it was to communicate with friends and talk with strangers.[69]

By 1977, the demand for CBs was so great that the government expanded the limited number of channels from twenty-three to forty.[70] CB radios were suddenly popping up everywhere, from farm tractors to golf carts. Books outlining the definitions of CB jargon appeared, as did several popular films that featured CB radios as an important element. The CB was not only a novelty, it was also practical and useful, although that would soon change. At the height of its popularity, the CB became an icon of American culture, and in November 1975, Bill Fries released a song about a group of cars and truckers evading police, under the stage name of C. W. McCall. "Convoy" spent several weeks in the number-one position on the American Country Music Chart.[71] One of the most popular films of 1977 was *Smokey and the Bandit*, featuring truckers who evaded police by using their CB radios.

At this time, many groups popped up that centered on the use of CBs. CB clubs were formed allowing people who only talked with each other on the radio to meet in person and exchange information about their radios and buy and sell CB-related items. Local emergency groups were created, and some operators took turns monitoring the CB emergency channel in order to relay information on accidents to the local police. Other groups formed to relay road conditions during winter storms.

Sociologist David Miller describes some of the jargon of the time. "CB jargon invaded popular speech. Tractor-trailer rigs became 'eighteen-wheelers,' state police became 'smokies,' and exceeding the speed limit became 'putting the pedal to the metal.' The term 10-4 was often substituted for saying yes. . . . People adopted 'handles' like the truck drivers, calling themselves such names as Vitro, Big Red, Hot Shot, The Professor, Rubber Duck, Ditch Witch, and Squirrelly Shirley." QSL cards, essentially postcards used by CB radio operators, became common. Originally intended to be exchanged with other CB operators to confirm reception, these cards began to include elaborate designs and logos and became collector's items.[72]

The interest in CBs soon waned. What had once been a useful tool to obtain the latest road conditions was soon rendered obsolete during the late 1970s when many radio stations began broadcasting local traffic reports. CB users also faced other problems: channels became cluttered, and transmissions often interfered with television and radio reception, causing family disputes and irate neighbors to complain. Also, if your car had a CB, it was a target for a break-in. In short, the CB was not as practical as originally thought so the novelty wore off, and by 1978, sales tumbled. By 1980, the market for recreational CB users had crashed. Unlike some fads, CBs have not disappeared altogether. They continue to be used by a relatively small group of hard-core users—most of whom were using CBs before they became widely popular—such as taxicab drivers, police and emergency personnel, and some truckers.[73]

Sociologist Harold Kerbo and his research team observe that for some users, having a CB radio afforded people the opportunity to have a loose association of contacts across the United States, allowing them to occasionally meet through CB clubs or on their own initiative. In one sense, they believe that the widespread use of CB radios among enthusiasts was a way of countering the impact of an increasingly isolated and impersonal society. "The CB 'subculture' maintains a tightly knit, in-group structure. It possesses its own language (as shown in the many new CB dictionaries) and identifying symbols (such as 'handles,' badges, and club jackets with the club name and person's 'handle' on the back). The 'subculture' even maintains its own system of social control. At the 'breakers' (club meetings) observed by the authors, for example, one of the main events was the awarding of 'prizes.' The 'channel hog' was awarded for obvious reasons, and the 'bucket mouth' award went to the person reported using objectionable language on the air."[74] In addition, this group, like so many similar ones at the time, would engage in local volunteer work, the most important being to monitor CB channel nine—for emergencies.

Of course, one of the greatest benefits of CB use—expanding the area of mobile communication, soon lost its applicability. Kerbo observed that "unlike the telephone, individuals can be contacted at almost any time with a CB radio, especially when the individual has both a base station and a mobile unit."[75] The rise of the CB was always destined to decline with the widespread use of cellular phones in the 1980s and the subsequent proliferation of mobile-phone technology.

Pet Rocks, 1975–1976 (USA)

Arguably the oddest pet fad ever hit America in April 1975. Inspired by complaints made by some friends about their pet cats and dogs misbehaving, leaving behind a mess, and costing too much too feed, California advertising executive Gary Dahl came up with the idea of the Pet Rock. The whimsical gift was a smooth egg-sized pebble nestled on a bed of hay inside a cardboard box with air holes. Also included was a tongue-in-cheek instruction manual explaining how to train your rock to do such tricks as how to sit, roll over, and play dead.

By October, Dahl was shipping an astounding ten thousand rocks daily. In the three months leading up to Christmas 1975, more than one million Pet Rocks were sold at $4 each, making Dahl a millionaire.[76] Accessories could also be purchased, including such "must have" items as pet rock food and pet rock shampoo.[77] In Michigan there was an All-Breed Pet Rock Show. For those wishing to properly get rid of their "pets," entrepreneurs in California and Colorado set up Pet Rock cemeteries. Plots cost between $2.50 and $7.00, with "Rock of Ages" sung at a service as part of the premium funeral package. In Nashville, Chuck McCabe released a song titled "That Old Pet Rock of Mine."[78] By the end of 1976 the craze had ended, spurred on by numerous imitators that saturated the market, and Dahl gifted his remaining inventory of 100,000 rocks to children.[79] Pet Rocks were the ideal pet: they were always well-behaved, made no noise, and never had to be cleaned up after. They were a humorous fad, perhaps appealing because they were so silly and impractical, but once millions of Americans had acquired them, Pet Rocks ceased to be novel and lost their attraction.

While fads are notoriously difficult to predict, once they emerge, they follow a predictable pattern, starting with the dormant period, followed by the breakout phase, the peak, and finally the rapid decline. While they may involve trivial objects and activities, understanding fads is important because being able to differentiate between fads and trends can spell the difference between a company thriving or going bust.

Fads are the antithesis of crazes, which are the subject of chapter 3. Crazes are far more intense and serious, and they have a greater potential to be life-changing. Crazes typically involve something that seems too good to be true such as get-rich-quick schemes. Religious movements and cults are other common forms. Here we must tread carefully as most religious groups are not cults, which by their definition are coercive.

CHAPTER 3

CRAZES: GOING OVERBOARD

Crazes are widespread, short-lived preoccupations or obsessions.[1] While some writers use the word interchangeably with fad, we make a clear distinction. If fads are short-lived infatuations—be it with a Hula-Hoop, a Frisbee, or a book series such as Harry Potter—a sort of "puppy love" that soon wanes, crazes are more serious love affairs where a person falls "head over heels" for an object, idea, or person. Crazes involve fewer people, persist longer, and are more intense than fads; they often have life-altering consequences. Crazes require a greater commitment than fads and may result in participants quitting their jobs, selling their homes, or divorcing their spouses. Due to the level of commitment required, it is hard to imagine someone having a life-changing experience by engaging in the yo-yo fad. Even if they were so proficient as to win international yo-yo competitions, the social and financial rewards of such an accomplishment are likely to be muted.

Prior to the sixteenth century, "craze" meant to shatter into small pieces, as in broken shards of pottery. After that time, it changed to mean a breakdown in health, because if one's physical well-being is poor, it could be described as shattered. Soon "craze" was also being used to describe a state of mental breakdown, and the word became synonymous with "deranged."[2] We use the term in this sense, which is best described in *The Century Dictionary* of 1902 as "an unreasoning or capricious liking or affectation of liking, more or less sudden and temporary, and usually shared by a number of persons, especially in society, for something particular, uncommon, peculiar, or curious."[3] This definition also captures the common view that during crazes, participants have become so enthused as to appear to others to have temporarily lost their sense of reason or judgment.

For example, the Great American Revival of 1832 was especially intense in Madison and Oneida counties of Western New York. With the apocalypse believed to be near, some became convinced that man should "find his Paradise and his

[Adam or] Eve," and so many sought new relationships. "Old rules did not bind people together anymore; old obligations were eliminated. Men and women were choosing heavenly friends without respecting spousal relationships."[4] While such unions were supposed to have been purely spiritual and platonic, some yielded to temptation and engaged in sexual unions. Before long, many individuals returned to their legal spouses. After a relatively short period, the religious excitement began to fade as many men and women went back to their original partners.

Get-rich-quick schemes are one of the most common types of crazes, where those who join in are blinded by the prospect of amassing fast wealth. Crazes are also notoriously associated with financial bubbles. The term "bubble" came into popular use in the early eighteenth century to describe property and share market booms.[5] In 1711, the South Sea Stock Company was formed with the promise of reducing huge debts that the British government had accrued during the War of Spanish Succession between 1702 and 1713. An investment frenzy was soon underway as people expecting to get-rich-quick, rushed to buy real estate in several South Sea Islands. The speculative bubble suddenly burst in October 1720, and vast sums of money were lost. As a result, England was plunged into a recession that lasted for years.[6]

The stock market collapse of 1929, which helped to usher in the Great Depression, is another example of an unsustainable boom that was artificially created on the back of easy credit and the lure of "easy money." Sociologist Richard LaPiere writes that between 1927 and 1929, business magazines and newspapers painted a rosy picture of a golden era where share prices "were to continue indefinitely upward at an accelerative rate. The few writers who ventured to express doubt were quickly shouldered out of print by those who had caught the spirit of the new age."[7] Many investors bought up shares at a fraction of the cost by buying on margin. A common down payment was 10 percent of the full price. When the sell-off began, investors were unable to pay their creditors. The Dutch Tulip Mania of 1634–1637, saw the price of some tulip bulbs exceeded their weight in gold.

During crazes, people rush toward something that offers a solution to a problem. Unfortunately, those promises are usually too good to be true and fail to materialize. Between 1897 and 1898, upward of 100,000 Americans left their jobs and sold their belongings to join the great Klondike gold rush in the Yukon region of northwest Canada. The mass exodus was triggered by sensational, exaggerated accounts in the US press of unspoiled riches just waiting for the taking.

Excited by stories of easy wealth that awaited those who were adventurous enough to make the trek, people from across the country headed for Seattle by train, where they boarded steamships north to make their fortunes. It did not take long before most grew disillusioned by the inhospitable conditions, where the average monthly high temperature in January is often below zero degrees Fahrenheit. The lure of riches was so great that entire mills and factories in Washington State were left abandoned after the workers were smitten by the "gold bug."[8]

Crazes may also take the form of social movements: an organized effort by a group of people with a shared identity, who are dissatisfied with the existing state of society, and who band together to effect change, either within their group or society as a whole. Members of *reformist movements* are satisfied with the overall system but are intent on changing certain parts of society. *Resistance movements* are comprised of conservative members who oppose change and desire to retain traditional values. They would typically view same-sex marriage as a moral perversion and abortion as murder. Some resistance movements are insular and introspective and focus on the condition or state of group members as opposed to society at-large. For example, Jehovah's Witnesses will not pledge allegiance to the flag of any country, do not run for political office, and do not vote in public elections. By comparison, revolutionary groups seek radical change and may even advocate overthrowing governments, as in the case of the American Revolutionary War. At the very least, they desire dramatic, sweeping transformations of society.

Messianic movements feature members who excitedly anticipate the appearance of a messiah or religious savior and can be viewed as a type of craze. Hence, social psychologist E. A. Ross includes early Christianity, the Crusades, and prophecies of the end of the world as types of crazes.[9] Influential sociologist Neil Smelser also lists religious revivals and enthusiasms as forms of crazes.[10]

Some escapist or utopian movements seek radical change by withdrawing from what they view as an unjust or corrupt system of government and limit contact with the outside world. In 1974, members of the American-based People's Temple movement, led by the Reverend Jim Jones, fled to the tiny South American country of Guyana in order to live a "pure" life by following Jones's teachings. On November 18, 1978, 918 members died in a mass suicide undertaken on the orders of their leader. Some members were forced to drink cyanide-laced Kool-Aid and several were shot while attempting to flee, but most people died willingly. Investigators sifting through the compound found literature describing how members expressed their unwillingness to remain in the existing immoral system and had been promised a new utopian life for believers who kept the faith.

MEMORABLE CRAZES

Dutch Tulip Mania, 1634–1637 (Holland)

During the mid-1630s, an affection for tulips swept across Holland as people paid fantastically exorbitant prices for certain types of tulip bulbs. Charles Mackay studied the event and wrote: "In 1634, the rage among the Dutch to possess them was so great that the ordinary industry of the country was neglected, and the population, even to its lowest dregs, embarked in the tulip trade. As the mania increased [by] 1635, many persons were known to invest a fortune of 100,000 florins in the purchase of forty roots."[11] However, he writes that by 1637, the price of bulbs plummeted and many merchants lost fortunes.[12] One account tells of a sailor who had been overseas during the craze, only to return and find a *Semper augustus* bulb which he mistook for an onion and made into relish for a dish of herring. It turned out to be worth three thousand florins. "Little did he dream that he had been eating a breakfast whose cost might have regaled a whole ship's crew for a twelvemonth," Mackay wrote.[13]

While the Tulip Mania remains synonymous with large share market swings, economist Peter Garber has challenged this perception, believing that the episode was exaggerated. He found that while the prices for some tulip varieties did skyrocket then tumble, the economic fallout was far from the devastating effects claimed by Mackay. Garber says that extreme prices were paid for very rare bulbs, but that these prices were destined to decline due to supply and demand as they proliferated and became more common. He also notes that rare bulbs could be used to produce expensive hybrids that often made good business sense as they yielded lucrative returns.[14] Garber found that once prices fell, many rare bulbs continued to sell for high prices—a trend that continues to modern times.[15] Despite his dispelling of the Tulip Mania myth, Garber thinks that it will continue to be widely believed due to its appeal. "The wonderful tales from the tulip-mania are catnip irresistible to those with a taste for crying bubble, even when the stories are so obviously untrue."[16]

Self-Flogging, twelfth through fifteenth centuries (Europe)

Self-flagellation—the practice of flogging oneself with sharp objects—swept across many Christian monasteries in Europe in the Middle Ages. People engaged in the practice as a form of self-punishment for their sins in hopes of attaining a heavenly reward in the afterlife. In 1266, an extraordinary outbreak of self-flogging began in Italy and spread across Europe as people became preoccupied with the fear of Christ and how to atone for one's sins. Russian psychiatrist Vladimir Bekhterev observes that both young and old were swept up in the fervor. "Everybody had a whip of leather straps with which they so cruelly lashed their own limbs, with tears and sighs, such that blood was running from their wounds."[17] Historian Norman Cohn cites a graphic account of a fourteenth-century flagellant: "[He] shut himself up in his cell and stripped himself naked . . . and took his scourge with the sharp spikes, and beat himself on the body and on the arms and on the legs, till blood poured. . . . One of the spikes was bent crooked, like a hook, and whatever flesh it caught it tore off. He beat himself so hard that the scourge broke into three bits and the points flew against the wall."[18] Similar scenes were repeated across the continent. Cohn writes that the man "stood there bleeding and gazed at himself. It was such a wretched sight that he was reminded in many ways of the appearance of the beloved Christ, when he was fearfully beaten. Out of pity for himself he began to weep bitterly. And he knelt down, naked and covered in blood, in the frosty air, and prayed to God to wipe out his sins from before his gentle eyes."

Slow Poisoning, sixteenth and seventeenth centuries (Italy and France)

Scottish journalist Charles Mackay writes that in parts of Europe, many citizens engaged in death-by-slow-poisoning as a means of righting perceived wrongs, either real or imagined. Husbands accused of marital infidelity were reported to be favorite targets. A network of poison vendors emerged to meet the black-market demand. Mackay believes that poisoning became fashionable as a result of a few high-profile cases among the upper class, which spread to the masses through a herd mentality. "Italians of the sixteenth and seventeenth centuries poisoned their opponents with as little compunction as an Englishman of the present day brings an action at law against any one who has done him injury."[19] At least one group of wives held regular meetings to plot their crimes, but they were eventually arrested after a women, posing as a disgruntled wife, expressed a desire to punish her husband for cheating on her and treating her poorly.

The leader of the group, a woman named Hieronyma La Spara, had given her victims several drops of a clear, tasteless liquid. La Spara and several other women were hanged in Rome, while about thirty more "were whipped publicly through the streets; and several, whose high rank screened them from more degrading punishment, were banished from the country and mulcted in heavy fines. In a few months afterwards, nine women were hanged for poisoning; and another bevy, including many young and beautiful girls, were whipped half naked through the streets of Rome."[20] In spite of these actions, slow poisoning remained popular. "This severity did not put a stop to the practice, and jealous women and avaricious men, anxious to step into the inheritance of fathers, uncles or brothers, resorted to poison. As it was quite free from taste, colour, and smell, it was administered without exciting suspicion. The vendors compounded it of different degrees of strength, so that the poisoners had only to say whether they wanted their victims to die in a week, a month, or six months. . . . The vendors were chiefly women, of whom the most celebrated . . . was in this way accessory to the death of upwards of six hundred persons."[21]

During the latter 1600s, a similar penchant for poisoning became popular in France, where two women, identified as Lavoisin and Lavigoreux, were thought to have been responsible for hundreds of deaths, after serving as dealers in slow poisons. As in Italy, most customers were women seeking to use the substances on their husbands. In a few instances, their customers were husbands, intent on killing their wives. The slow poisoners masked their activities by claiming to be midwives or fortune-tellers. In late 1679, Lavoisin and Lavigoreux were caught, and both women were burned alive on February 22, 1680. Authorities found a list of clients kept by Lavoisin and were able to track down many others who were apparently involved in the slow poisoning. At about this time, upward of fifty women were arrested across France and were hanged.[22]

One of those whose name was on the list was the Duchess of Bouillon who was arrested and put on trial by the Chambre Ardente (a special French court of justice). It appeared that she had innocently come into contact with the poisoners while seeking the services of a fortune-teller and wishing to know what the face of the devil looked like. One of the prosecutors, an elderly man named La Reynie, sought to exploit this claim and asked her if she indeed had seen the devil's face. She is reported to have looked at him and replied: "Oh, yes! I see him now. He is in the form of a little ugly old man, exceedingly ill-natured, and is dressed in the robes of a Counsellor of State." He was said to have asked no further questions. The duchess served the next several months in the Bastille and was eventually released. Mackay wrote that slow poisoning "continued to rage" for the next two years, after upward of one hundred people were either burned at the stake or hanged.[23]

Kentucky Revival, 1795–1805 (Eastern USA)

The "Great Revival" began amid emotional religious gatherings in Logan County, Kentucky, and quickly spread to Tennessee, Ohio, Virginia, and North and South Carolina. During the Kentucky Revival, congregants were whipped into an emotional frenzy rendering many of those in the crowd hypersuggestible and prone to imitating the behaviors of those around them. Some would roll on the ground until exhausted. This "rolling exercise" prompted their nickname—"Holy Rollers." Some of the behaviors reported are remarkable by any standard. Historian Ronald Knox writes that at one gathering, no less than a thousand persons collapsed to the ground in various states of mind. The 'rolling exercise' involved participants joining the feet and head together and rolling over like a hoop, while 'the jerks' consisted of powerful twitching and contortions affecting every part of the body. When affected with 'the jerks,' victims sometimes leaped into the air like frogs and displayed grotesque facial gestures and contortions of the limbs. During 'the barks,' people would get on all fours and behave like a dog—barking, growling, and snapping their teeth. "Sometimes numbers of the people squatted down, and looking in the face of the minister, continued demurely barking at him while he preached to them. These last were particularly gifted in prophecies, trances, dreams, rhapsodies, visions of angels, of heaven, and of the holy city."[24]

Another systematic form of worship that developed during the Kentucky Revival was "the Holy Laugh" in which first one, and then scores of participants, would exhibit uncontrollable laughter. Even today, the central feature of the Toronto Blessing movement involves intense, collective laughter. It is viewed as a form of "intoxication" of the Holy Spirit. It is important to understand the context of these behaviors. For instance, medical historian George Rosen provides insight into the seemingly nonsensical behavior of barking like dogs. He observes that barking was an acceptable and well-known reaction of the period in these revivals, and served as "a means of chastisement for sins" as adherents would often get on all fours, surround a tree and start barking in an effort to "tree the devil." Such behavior was considered to be an act of piety.[25]

Séances, 1840s–1930s (USA and Europe)

Beginning in the 1840s and enduring for nearly a century, Spiritualism gained widespread acceptance throughout North America and Europe. This movement was premised on the belief that certain people could communicate with the souls of the dead—and that the dead were both interested and able to send messages back from "the other side." The alleged spirits of the deceased would purportedly manifest in different ways including rapping sounds, levitating objects, and even materializing in person. Many people took these events as proof of life after death. Some skeptics believed that mediums through whom the alleged spirits supposedly spoke, wrote, or materialized were engaging in outright fraud. However, some paranormal researchers were more sympathetic and believed that mediums may have been subconsciously using telepathy, telekinesis, and other "psychic powers" that were being misinterpreted as messages from and appearances of the dead. Historian Hilary Evans describes the sad modern state of Spiritualism by observing that "after more than a century, a hypothesis is all that the Spiritualists' beliefs remain. The conditions under which evidence has been obtained, the inconsistency of the phenomena, the undoubted prevalence of conscious fraud on a very wide scale, and an incalculable amount of unconscious fraud and self-deception besides—these and many other factors work against the ready acceptance of the Spiritualist hypothesis."[26]

In 1848, Kate and Margaret Fox (ages twelve and fifteen) made their older sister, their parents, and other adults think their home was haunted. They supposedly communicated with spirits using a system of rappings. In later life, they recanted their claims and even demonstrated how they did it. Inspired by the Fox sisters, soon the search was on for other ways to communicate with the deceased. The movement soon graduated to verbal and written messages that were supposedly from the spirit world, including those that were received when attempting to contact "the other side" using Ouija boards.

Before long, some mediums were claiming to act as intermediaries by relaying messages from the spirit world. "Thus came about the whole range of séance-room physical phenomena—the levitated trumpets and other articles, the tambourines played in mid-air by unseen hands, the levitation of the medium and of furniture, slate writing and so on."[27] The range of effects produced during séances was extensive. Believers came away from these sessions convinced that they had communicated with dead relatives or friends. There was even contact of various kinds with Martians! It sounded too good to be true—and of course, it was. We now know there are no Martians, so any alleged contact with them by mediums had to be faked.

One of the more prominent mediums was a young woman named Helene Smith, a late-nineteenth-century French medium who regularly fell into a trance state and channeled messages from those as diverse as Native Americans and Martians. A skeptical journalist, who read what Smith had supposedly written in Sanskrit, was not impressed. "The rest of Miss Smith's Sanskrit is mainly two or three words for 'My dear, my good fellow,' with a deal of Sanskrit-sounding babble. This is pronounced, not as a Sanskritist pronounces it, but as a French person would do who had only seen the words in print."[28] Smith's written Martian was apparently no better, described as "merely a distortion of French, like the languages which many children invent and use as cryptic methods of discourse."[29]

During the late nineteenth and early twentieth centuries, many mediums claimed to communicate with extraterrestrials—mostly from Mars. In 1897, a British medium named Mr. West said that he had communicated with Martians and produced photos of two Martian men as evidence. They looked exactly like normal men of the time, but were wearing robes to try and lend them an exotic air.[30] Perhaps the most remarkable claim of Martian contact came during the 1930s when a female medium, Madame Marxa, disrobed and was then securely bound to a chair (precautions such as this were often taken in séances to try and prevent fraud). Reporter Joseph Dunninger was an eye-witness: "Suddenly a chill swept the séance room and the manager declared that a Martian spirit, accustomed to polar temperature, had provided it in order to survive its brief visit. The outer curtains stirred, and from the cabinet came the most outlandish creature I have ever viewed anywhere. . . . The thing from Mars was round and squatty, with a head that seemed a bulbous protuberance of its body. . . . Women screamed and men shoved backward as the living horror hopped about the circle."[31] Dunninger, a mentalist and magician, was not fooled. He tripped the Martian with a rope and called for the lights to be turned on. At that point it was revealed that Marxa—a contortionist and acrobat—had slipped her ropes and masqueraded as a Martian in the dim light of the séance room![32]

Many skeptics attended séances to expose the methods of mediums. The greatest skeptic of all was Harry Houdini, the most famous escapologist and magician in history. Magician and author John Cannell observed that Houdini's vast knowledge of fraud and trickery made him both feared and hated by many mediums. "He attended hundreds of séances to obtain his evidence and observed what he believed to be the conjuring methods of certain mediums. He claimed to have discovered a large number of trick methods used at séances, and devised what he called improvements upon them. Both on the stage, and in private, he gave many mock séances at which remarkable results were obtained."[33] Any control exerted on the medium to prevent fraud was often easily worked around. Cannell notes that controls often consisted of the participants linking arms. Many sitters would not use controls as they had implicit faith in the medium. "This leaves him free to do anything he wishes, and as most séances are held in the dark the possibilities of cheating are great. The way of the fraudulent mediums is made easier by the fact that sitters usually give a solemn undertaking not to touch anything during the proceedings."[34] The tilting, moving, and levitation of tables could be done by various methods. Houdini favored two metal pegs disguised as part of a design on the table top. These would pop out of place so he could grip them and appear to levitate the table while only his fingertips touched it. He also used a lever strapped to his arm.[35]

The famous English mentalist and "thought-reader" Stuart Cumberland once saw a table chase a medium around a room. Cumberland never claimed to possess psychic powers and was skeptical of matters of mediums. He soon discovered that the woman had tied a strong invisible silk thread to it. A bent pin at one end was connected to the table and at the other end another bent pin connected to one of her shoes. Small castors were at the bottom of the table legs to aid movement.[36] Houdini once called out a fraudulent medium in an ingenious manner. In a darkened séance room, the medium levitated a trumpet. Different voices were heard coming from the trumpet as it floated around the room like a stray balloon. Suddenly, Houdini jumped to his feet and shone an electric torch on the medium, denouncing him. To the astonishment of all but Houdini, the medium's face and hands were covered with a finely powdered soot that Houdini had secretly applied to the trumpet before the medium—entirely dressed in black—could pick it up. Cannell wrote: "The medium claimed that the trumpet floated about the room by psychic power, but had that claim been true there would have been no stains of lamp-black on his face and hands. He had himself been holding the trumpet and speaking through it."[37]

Magician David Abbott warned of another method to levitate objects. It was a telescopic aluminum rod that was only as long as a pencil when hidden but could extend to a length of six feet. A small hook on the end could be used to hang objects off it so that they appeared to be floating in the air.[38] The effect of a floating, disembodied spirit hand could be achieved by being completely dressed in black from head to toe except for one hand and the lower part of one arm that had been covered in a powdered form of luminous paint. This could be done either by the medium or an accomplice who came out of hiding when the lights went off.[39]

Eventually public belief expanded to the viewpoint that a gifted medium was not needed to communicate with the spirits of the dead. Anybody could do it with a Ouija board or even a homemade setup. The Ouija board was invented by Baltimore brothers and toy makers William and Isaac Fuld. It consisted of a breakfast-tray-sized board covered with all the letters of the alphabet, the numbers one to ten, and the words "yes", "no," and "goodbye." The exotic-sounding word "Ouija" is a combination of the French and German words for yes. A tiny triangle-shaped pointer called a planchette was touched with the fingertips of the séance participants and would move around the board to spell out alleged spirit messages. The game was especially popular in times of crisis when many loved family members were killed, such as during the World War I era.[40] Believers thought the spirits of the deceased moved the planchette. Skeptics said it was unconscious (or sometimes deliberate) muscle movements in the participants that really moved the planchette around to spell out messages. If you could not afford to buy a professional Ouija board, messages could be obtained by using an upturned glass on a piece of cardboard with letters, words, and numbers handwritten on it.

Professional spirit mediums are still around, long after the decline of Spiritualism. However, their job is much easier in the modern era. They do not have to materialize apparitions or levitate objects. All they need to do is verbally deliver vague messages (supposedly from dead relatives) that consist of lucky guesses and general statements that could apply to almost anyone. So-called mediums, such as Colin Fry, Georgia O'Connor, and Tony Stockwell, excel at this trickery and prey off the gullible.

The Ghost Dance, 1889–1891 (USA)

During the late 1800s, Native American societies in the Great Plains were disintegrating after demoralizing defeats at the hands of the US Army; many were further humiliated after being forced from their traditional lands. The European settlers had also killed off most of their precious buffalo. Efforts were soon underway to "civilize" their "savage lifestyle" by converting them to Christianity, and by the 1880s, large numbers of Native Americans were being converted to their oppressor's god.[41] It was within this background of emotional turmoil and cultural devastation that a utopian movement known as the Ghost Dance was born. The dance was a reenactment of smallpox-induced visions that were experienced by Wovoka, a medicine man from a tribe in Nevada. The visions foretold of a time when Native Americans would unify and wrest back control of the lands. The key to success was to perform the ritual, along with singing certain songs and wearing "ghost shirts."[42] The dance was believed to bring about a new era of harmony between Native Americans and non–Native Americans.

The frenzied nightlong dance had to be performed over five successive nights and repeated at six-week intervals. Dancers trembled, fainted, wandered aimlessly in a trance-like state, and reported seeing visions that included being taken to the happy hunting ground and meeting dead ancestors.[43] Widespread support for the movement quickly waned under tragic circumstances as many settlers misinterpreted their dance rituals as a prelude for war and decided it necessary to strike first. On December 29, 1890, nearly three hundred Native Americans were massacred at Wounded Knee Creek, South Dakota, ending a sad chapter in American history.[44] The Ghost Dance was a revitalization movement involving an attempt to recreate an earlier golden age that could only be restored if the ways of the Native American ancestors were respected and followed.

Florida Land Boom, 1924–1926 (USA)

During the prosperous 1920s, investors across the country became preoccupied with buying land in Florida, only to then sell it for a quick profit as the price of real estate continued to spiral upward. At the height of the boom, many investors bought land sight unseen; occasionally it turned out to be swampland. Interest peaked in 1925, when a single edition of the *Miami Daily Herald* totaled 504 pages, most of which was devoted to real estate advertising.[45] Newspapers and magazines fueled the boom by publishing "rags to riches" stories of people who had amassed fabulous wealth virtually overnight by purchasing property in Florida. At this time, Miami alone had an estimated two thousand real estate offices as thousands of agents swarmed the city. Historian Frederick Allen, who lived through the event, wrote that by 1925, people "were buying anything, any-where, so long as it was in Florida. One had only to announce a new development, be it honest or fraudulent, be it on the Atlantic Ocean or deep in the wasteland of the interior, to set people scrambling for house lots. . . . The stories of prodigious profits made in Florida land were sufficient bait."[46] The boom took off when spec-ulators entered the market, intent on selling for a quick profit. One investment property, "Manhattan Estates," was promoted as being situated within "a mile from the prosperous and fast-growing city of Nettie." The problem was, Nettie was a deserted turpentine camp. Another site, "Melbourne Gardens," was virtu-ally inaccessible as the access road was mired in mud and "prairie muck land."[47]

The real estate market in Florida began to decline in early 1926 and collapsed that September with the arrival of the Great Miami Hurricane, which devastated the region between Miami and Fort Lauderdale, causing $100 million in damages—the modern-day equivalent of billions of dollars.[48] In 1928, one writer quipped that Miami had gone from the wealthiest place to live—to the cheapest. Economist John Kenneth Galbraith observed that the land boom was based more in fantasy than reality: "This is a world inhabited not by people who have to be persuaded to believe but by people who want an excuse to believe. In the case of Florida, they wanted to believe that the whole peninsula would soon be populated by the holiday-makers and sun-worshippers of a new and remarkably indolent era."[49]

Free Love "Cult," 1944-1951 (New Hebrides, Melanesia)

Near the end of World War II, on the South Pacific island of Espiritu Santo, a thirty-five-year-old native man, Tesk, began preaching about a coming utopian lifestyle. If only locals would rekindle their original way of life, they could live in a world without shame, war, or jealousy. His message resonated with the locals. Tesk's movement was likely inspired by contact with Christian missionaries, and in 1945, he instructed thirty people to spread his message as the apostles had done. As property disputes were common, he proposed that the islanders live a harmonious commune existence. In an effort to rid the island of jealousy, he relaxed marriage restrictions and ordered the people to live naked and practice free love. All men and women were to be open to the sexual advances of others. Tesk urged his people to copulate freely and publicly—just like the creatures from the animal kingdom.[50]

People were also ordered to burn down their homes and build two large community houses per village: one for women, the other for men. Tesk also predicted that a group of Americans would soon arrive and bring them a variety of goods—and once this happened, the islanders would live forever.[51] Following Tesk's death in 1951—which must have come as a shock to many after he had predicted his eternal existence—followers were prompted to question his claims, and the movement quickly declined.[52]

Prince Philip Cult, 1950s and ongoing (Tanna Island, South Pacific)

During the second half of the nineteenth century, a large number of religious movements took root among native peoples in islands across the Pacific, especially Melanesia. Anthropologists referred to them as "cargo cults," a term that comes from the word *kago*, which is pidgin English for material wealth that originated from Western countries. Pidgin refers to a local language that has been derived from English. Cargo cults are typified by the emergence of a local prophet who announces the future arrival or return of a great messiah-like leader who will usher in a new era of spiritual and material prosperity. Theologian Gottfried Oosterwal describes the new world that is typical of these movements: "He is not expected to come empty-handed, but with a shipload (cargo) full of western articles such as clothing, axes, guns, tobacco, outboard motors, cars, etc. The 'messiah' will be accompanied by a cloud of ancestors. All the dead will return and start a new life together with the living. This is the 'Golden Age.' Henceforth there will be no more sickness no more death; there will be an abundance of food and comfortable houses for all. The 'redeemer' will rule the people in righteousness, without oppression or injustice. In colonial areas these ideas have often given rise to strong anti-foreign attitudes and movements for independence."[53] The messiah's arrival may be preceded by signs, often cataclysmic in nature, such as an earthquake, volcanic eruption, flood or eclipse. While cargo cults follow this general theme, no two are exactly alike.

One such movement developed on the remote Pacific island of Tanna, in Vanuatu, sometime after the end of World War II. The origin is unclear, but it centered on the belief that the husband of Queen Elizabeth II—Prince Philip—was immortal and a god whose spirt remained with the people on the island.[54] During World War II, many "cargo cults" proliferated in Oceania (the Pacific Islands) with the arrival of Allied troops, especially from America, Australia, and Britain. The natives had made their possessions on the island, usually by hand, and did not have a good understanding of factories and how goods were mass produced, so many believed that the foreigners possessed a magic power to produce cargo that appeared on their islands with the arrival of ships and planes. As many of the soldiers were dark-skinned like them, it encouraged the native's to believe that they, too, could share in the magic. Social and political unrest broke out on the island during the 1950s, as natives raided European storage facilities. The British resident commissioner in Port Vila (about a one hour flight away) was able to quell the trouble—not through force but appeasement. Fearing that using force could make martyrs out of the natives, the resident commissioner is reported to have offered them a special relationship with Prince Philip, who, in exchange for their allegiance, would offer them magical protection. The islanders were given a signed picture of the prince in an oak frame, they began to worship him as a god, and the rest is history.[55]

In 1983, journalist John Hamilton of the *Sydney Morning Herald* visited the island of Tanna to see the worshippers firsthand. Once there, he traveled to the village of Iounhanan situated at the base of a volcano, where he interviewed the chief, Jack Navia, of the Yaohnanen tribe. He asked, "I understand you and your people worship Prince Philip, Duke of Edinburgh?" The chief replied, "Yes. Would you like to see him?" He went to his hut and came out carefully holding with two hands his prized possession: a personally autographed portrait of the prince in an oak frame. He held it up and gazed at it with great affection and proclaimed, "He is my special friend." Villagers standing around responded by repeating the word "Amen." It was estimated that about 3,500 residents of the island believed in Philip's deity status.[56]

When Hamilton inquired further about Prince Philip, the chief showed him a well-worn letter in an envelope with the Royal Coat of Arms. Written by the Major Andrew Wigram, the letter was dated September 7, 1982, and read: "Dear Chief Jack, The Duke of Edinburgh has asked me to thank you for his letter. His Royal Highness was pleased to hear from you and is delighted that you and all members of the village of Iounhanan are well. Prince Philip has asked me to give you his very best wishes. Yours sincerely, Andrew Wigram." Excited and encouraged by the letter, and unhappy with the tax demands on the islanders by the government, the chief wrote back asking for help. Chief Jack pulled out a second letter dated July 27, 1983. It read: "Thank you for your letter. I am afraid that all I can do is to offer you my sympathy. I know it will not be any consolation but there are a great many communities in the world with exactly the same complaint as yours. The problem of taxation can only be resolved between the people and the Government of each country. I am glad to say that all the family is in good health. Please give my best wishes to all the people of Iounhanan village. Yours sincerely, Philip."[57]

In the early 2000s, journalist Matthew Baylis spent a month on the island interviewing the villagers about their relationship with Prince Philip. He noted one of Chief Jack's favorite sayings: "They've been waiting 2,000 years for a sign from Jesus, but our Philip sends us photographs! And one day he will come." Chief Jack is reported to have died in 2009, although the worship of Philip continues.[58]

Heaven's Gate Group Suicide, 1994 (San Diego, California, USA)

On March 26, 1994, the San Diego County Sheriff's Office received an emergency phone call about a mass suicide. When officers arrived, they were stunned by what they found: thirty-nine bodies—all members of a group that called themselves "Heaven's Gate." Even more surprising was that these people seemed to have been prospering financially and were living in a mansion in a suburb of San Diego. As authorities pieced together the circumstances of their deaths, they soon learned that members believed that their spirits would be taken on a spaceship that was traveling behind the Hale-Bopp comet. In November of 1993, rumors began circulating that a spaceship was flying alongside the comet, out of human sight. Then, as the comet made its closest approach to earth on Friday March 21, the group's website was updated one last time. It read: "Red Alert, Hale-Bopp Brings Closure to Heaven's Gate."[59] Religious scholar Phillip Lucas said that group's like Heaven's Gate often view the world as tainted, and the solution is to leave it. "They believe the Earth is impure. Therefore it is a rational decision to try to escape from it. By killing themselves physically, they're not entering oblivion, they're making their transit."[60]

Members of the group ranged in age from twenty-six to seventy-two. As investigators probed the suicides, more and more bizarre details were uncovered. Group members had not taken drugs or engaged in sex. In fact, some celibate members had gone to extreme lengths to ensure that they would remain celibate: they had castrated themselves.[61] In the hours before they died, they dressed in long black pants and wore shirts and Nike sneakers with the shoe manufacturer's comet-like "swoosh" insignia. Police found a note that read: "Take the little package of pudding or applesauce and eat a couple of tablespoons. Pour the medicine in and stir it up. Eat it fairly quickly and then drink the vodka beverage. Then lay back and rest quietly."[62]

Social psychologist Frederick Pope views the incident as a form of *folie à deux* (French for "double insanity" or "madness between two"). Psychiatrists commonly refer to it as socially shared psychosis. Pope refers to the incident as a shared psychosis involving thirty-nine people. He views the episode as an example of a person with a strong personality who is able to sway others to accept their beliefs.[63] Martin Gardner concurs with this view, contending that normal people would never engage in such acts unless they had been "brainwashed." "To me the saddest aspect of this insane event was the firm belief, expressed on the incredible videotapes, that cult members were killing themselves of their own free will. Nothing could have been more false."[64] Gardner admits that group members had not been physically coerced—rather the coercion had taken place on a psychological level. "Although Bo [Marshall Applewhite] always told his robots they were free to go at any time—and hundreds had done just that—so powerful was his control over the minds of those who stayed that they believed anything he said, obeyed every order."[65]

Some researchers reject labels of mental illness in explaining the mass suicide. James Rosenfield argues that the episode was predictable and culturally logical. "Our culture's heavens flutter with angels and UFOs. They represent the same longing for apocalyptic intervention and delivery. And they highlight the fact that in our fin de siècle, religiosity substitutes for religion. Religion forces us to deal with gods. Religiosity is a cheaper thrill, and angels and UFOs are less disquieting forces."[66] Rosenfield points out that the famous psychoanalyst Carl Jung had long ago described UFOs as "technological angels." He also believes that Heaven's Gate was made possible, in part, because of the Internet age in which they lived. He observes that "cultists referred to their bodies as 'containers,' an image very close to the cyberdelic idea of 'meat cages.' Denunciation of the body, followed by its mortification, is an end-time theme that pops up predictably in decades that precede the turn of a century. It was in the 1490s, for example, when Savonarola and his friends threw Florence into an orgy of self-flagellation."

Benjamin Zeller notes that Heaven's Gate followed a common belief within the UFO subculture about the existence of ancient astronauts having been described in the Bible. Books such as Erich von Däniken's *Chariots of the Gods?* and *Gods from Outer Space* appeared just prior to the founding of what would eventually become Heaven's Gate, foreshadowing many of their views. "Von Däniken proposed that the sacred texts of the world's ancient religions, including both Old and New Testaments, describe alien visitation, utilizing language appropriate to their own time and place. Space ships became chariots and clouds, since the biblical authors could only understand extraterrestrial technology with reference to nature or primitive vehicles."[67]

The leaders of Heaven's Gate, Marshall Applewhite and his partner Bonnie Lu Nettles, interpreted the Bible as a record of human-extraterrestrial contact with the purpose of helping humans to reach a higher plane of existence or transformation. Zeller states that if potential followers wanted to join them on their trip, they had to leave their earthly attachments behind and be exclusively dedicated to overcoming the frailties of the human condition. "Those dedicated to the message of Nettles and Applewhite, who rechristened themselves 'the Two,' would rise into the heavens and achieve eternal salvation. This process, the Two declared, was entirely materialistic, requiring a metamorphosis of the biological and chemical makeup of the human body, resulting in a transformation into an ideal extraterrestrial creature. The Two believed that extraterrestrials visited Earth in order to teach this process."[68]

Historian Ronald Steel also considers the importance of interpreting the actions of group members within the greater historical and cultural context. He found that the key views held by group members include ideas about peace, community, and celibacy that are rarely reflected in mainstream Christianity. Steel points out that religions are supposed to "[offer followers] solace, explain mysteries, provide standards of behavior and offer the promise of escape to a better world. The Heaven's Gate group would appear to be particularly benign, and even praiseworthy, in that its members were gentle, industrious, supportive and kind to one another. They did not try to coerce others into joining them. All they asked was to be left alone."[69] Steel finds many parallels between the Shakers and Heaven's Gate as both went to great lengths to avoid confrontation with government officials by trying to separate themselves from what was viewed as the corruption that pervaded mainstream society. Both groups also practiced celibacy, communal ownership, sexual equality, and the freedom to leave the group.

Religious scholar Mark Muesse warns against viewing members of Heaven's Gate as having been all that deviant from mainstream society, despite some of their seemingly bizarre beliefs and practices. For instance, he says that there was no parallel with most past group suicides. "We saw no indication of struggle, coercion, or second thoughts. No federal authorities were threatening the group. Members of Heaven's Gate seemed to welcome their deaths. . . . Indeed, the rational way in which they approached their deaths made them seem even more irrational."[70] In addition, the group tended to be asexual. "Instead of a sex-crazed leader who abused his disciples, as Jim Jones and David Koresh did, Marshall Applewhite . . . emphasized sexual negation rather than sexual expression. Sexuality, he taught, was merely an aspect of the bodily container that would be sloughed off as believers passed to the next level 'above human.'"[71] What may have appeared to many as their strangest convictions, which were based on a science-fiction mythology, had not been plucked from the mind of a madman, but rather were "blended with elements of Christianity and astrological divination. As the Heaven's Gate page on the World Wide Web explained, the appearance of the Hale-Bopp comet signaled the advent of extraterrestrials, whose starship in the comet's wake would rescue the faithful from Planet Earth. Yet the members of Heaven's Gate saw themselves as following the same pattern established 2,000 years ago, when Jesus of Nazareth discarded his physical vessel in exchange for a spiritual one. There was surely significance in the group's decision to exit this planet during the Christian Holy Week."[72]

Like fads, crazes are difficult to predict, but often have a religious or spiritual theme. As we have seen, individuals and small groups tend to join crazes, whereas manias are experienced and typically involve significant portions of a particular population. The fallibility of human perception and the desire to believe in something greater than ourselves are the driving forces behind manias as people start to redefine ambiguous stimuli as verifying the existence of the esteemed object or person. During outbreaks of collective wish fulfillment, people often interpret information patterns that reflect their hopes and expectations: seeing what they want and expect to see.

CHAPTER 4

MANIAS:
"WHAT ARDENTLY WE WISH,
WE SOON BELIEVE"

In psychiatry, "mania" refers to an unstable mental state typified by great excitement, euphoria, and hyperactivity. It is commonly associated with such conditions as bipolar disorder and schizophrenia. Hence, mania is derived from the Greek word for madness and is a derivative of the word maniac. Sociologists use the word to describe typically short-lived, nonpsychotic behaviors involving great enthusiasm of an extreme nature.

A wish mania is a form of collective wish fulfillment that is characterized by the rapid spread of false or exaggerated beliefs within a given population about an esteemed object or agent that satisfies psychological needs. They are comprised of events involving extraordinary but unsubstantiated claims, often about rumored inventions or the existence of legendary creatures or beings. Edward Young's quote about the tendency for people to see what they ardently wish, aptly describes this category.[1]

These events are forms of collective wish fulfillment and are experienced, whereas crazes are joined. During a craze, one can disown their family to join a religious sect or invest their life savings in what turns out to be Florida swamp land. One cannot join a UFO, but you experience a sighting or encounter. Examples of wish manias include appearances of the Virgin Mary and sightings of legendary creatures such as Bigfoot and the Loch Ness Monster. To take root, the belief must be plausible. During episodes participants become preoccupied with the possible existence of the rumor-related object or agent. Cases typically persist from a few weeks to several months and recur periodically in clusters.

Many outbreaks have religious overtones. But how is a sighting of Bigfoot or the Loch Ness Monster even remotely related to religion? Persistent reports of legendary creatures can be viewed as antiscientific symbols during an increasingly secular age where the belief in a supreme being is declining. In the absence of absolute proof, science is skeptical of the existence of these extraordinary creatures or beings. Yet each year, credible people report them. A report of Bigfoot is not simply a sighting of a potentially unclassified creature, it also suggests that science has gotten it wrong; and if it is wrong about Bigfoot, it may be wrong about religion as well.

Sightings of UFOs since 1947 also possess religious qualities. UFOs are objects in the sky that are unidentified, and there remains no proof of their carrying extraterrestrials. Since the mid-1950s, numerous books and documentaries have speculated as to there being alien spacecraft, conditioning the populace to believe in their possible, if not likely, existence. Some social scientists view UFOs as a substitute for God in terms of their technology, which if shared with humanity, would have magical qualities. Psychoanalyst Carl Jung referred to flying saucers as "technological angels," carrying saviors from the sky, for this very reason.[2] For Jung, flying saucers are just a new variation of an old theme: the salvation myth.

Accounts of fairies, once prevalent in Europe, parallel the UFO experience as they depict godlike beings capable of transcending natural laws. Similar beings can be found in mythology and folklore around the world. As folklorist Thomas Bullard observes: "Science may have evicted ghosts and witches from our beliefs, but just as quickly filled the vacancy with aliens having the same functions. Only the extraterrestrial outer trappings are new."[3]

Even observations of phantom animals, that science would consider to be imaginary or extinct, have grown powerful. The capabilities of Bigfoot now rival those of extraterrestrials and fairies in terms of their power and function. The creature has been reported to vanish or materialize, become transparent, communicate telepathically, alter shape, and even withstand motor vehicle impacts and bullets.[4]

A key factor driving most wish manias is the fallible nature of perception, specifically what psychologists refer to as the "autokinetic effect." A classic example took place in 1985, when a flurry of reports involving "moving statues" swept across Ireland.[5] The incidents almost always occurred near dusk and involved outdoor statues that appeared to be moving to an audience of Christian followers who had been staring at them for long periods in expectation of a "miracle." Following a sensational initial report that appeared in the media, people began to scrutinize statues in their own area. Soon, more and more people were flocking to local church grottos to confirm or deny the event for themselves. Many were not disappointed and reported that the statues were indeed moving. These new reports generated even more press coverage which resulted in even more excited faithful turning out to witness the spectacle.

A key factor in this outbreak was the "autokinetic effect"—a visual illusion that can give the appearance that an object is moving when it is not. Psychologist Jurek Kirakowski of Cork University studied the episode and observed that as audience members stared at the statues for long periods, their neck muscles would begin to tire and sway, giving the appearance of movement as "the image in your eye of the statue will move. If you have no idea you are moving you are likely to attribute the movement to the lighted portion of the statue rather than to yourself . . . Since it is yourself that's really moving, you will tend to see the entire lighted portion of the statue moving as a solid mass, rosary and all."[6] The effect is most prominent at dusk—hence the cluster of sightings at that time.

A similar effect has been identified in triggering UFO sighting waves. Most people do not stare for long periods at the night sky, but during periods of high UFO sightings, people who learn about the reports either by word of mouth or in the media, will often scan the sky at night in order to confirm or deny these claims. Yet, because there are no familiar frames of references with which to base visual judgments (like cars, trees, or houses), stars often appear to move.[7] In fact, if one stares at almost any object under the right conditions—be it a statue or a rock—especially at dusk, it will appear to move.

This effect was first demonstrated in 1936 by psychologist Muzafer Sherif.[8] As people view a common pinpoint of light, in the absence of stable perceptual anchorages, they soon feel uneasy and feel a need to either define the light or make sense of it. It is an anxiety-reducing strategy. Sociologist Richard Beeson describes the power of this effect: "A viewer in a completely dark room seeing one pinpoint of light experiences a visual stimulus without its normal attendant visual context. Up, down, back, forward, far and near, exist in relation to other stimuli and when this frame of reference is missing, the light is free to roam in one's perceptual field. It is for this reason that considerable random motion will be experienced by anyone viewing the light."[9]

Nonreligious examples of mass wish-fulfillment involve extraordinary inventions or abilities. In the late nineteenth century, rumors swirled across the United States about a new contraption invented by Thomas Edison. He had supposedly developed an "electric balloon" that on a clear night, could be seen for vast distances. Before long, people started misidentifying Venus and other bright astronomical objects in the night sky, thinking it was Edison's new invention.[10] During the New England airship wave of 1909–1910, thousands of residents across New England, read newspaper stories about a Worcester inventor who claimed to be secretly perfecting an airship. Within days, residents were redefining stars and planets as airship-related.[11]

Perhaps the most humorous example of a wish mania involved the remarkable abilities attributed to horses during the Great Horse Calculating enthusiasm of the early 1900s. During this episode, horses that were incapable of even recognizing numbers on a blackboard were supposedly performing complex calculations such as the square root of 256, with little trouble. It sounded incredible—and it was—and it took scientists a while to figure out how it was being done. It began with a horse named Clever Hans, who could supposedly solve complex math problems posed to him on a chalkboard. Incredulous scientists looked on in amazement and could detect no trickery as the horse gave the correct answers. Soon other horses were being exhibited around the United States and Europe, their owners claiming that they, too, could solve complex problems. Eventually it was noticed that whenever the questioner asked for the right answer and Hans began tapping his foot in reply, the questioner always looked down at the horse's foot as Hans reached the correct number of taps. This was Hans's cue to stop, and he usually did. Unbeknownst to the owner, his horse was conditioned to stop when he saw the questioner lower his or her head. Many people had overlooked this simple process because they were hoping so much that it was true.

MEMORABLE WISH MANIAS

Lake Champlain "Monster," 1818 to present
(Northeastern USA and Southern Canada)

Sightings of a large snakelike creature, as thick as a barrel and measuring between fifteen and forty feet long, have captivated residents living in the vicinity of Lake Champlain for centuries. The lake, which borders Upstate New York, Vermont, and Canada, has 587 miles of shoreline and can reach depths of over four hundred feet. Local residents affectionately refer to the creature as "Champ" or "Champy."

Despite an absence of any concrete evidence to support the creature's existence other than eyewitness testimony and dubious photos, many people continue to believe that a prehistoric creature once thought to have been extinct—or a species entirely new to science—resides in the lake. Five major forces appear to drive this belief: the fallibility of eyewitness testimony, reports that Native Americans had legends about the creature, the influence of the mass media, scientific ignorance, and our evolutionary heritage that may preprogram us to see monsters. As the fallible nature of human perception has been outlined at the beginning of this chapter, we will focus on the other four factors. Before doing so, let us look at the early history of the creature.

There are many Native American legends that have been interpreted as supporting the existence of Champ. For instance, the Abenaki, who occupied the land that is now southern Quebec and northern Vermont, referred to a "great snake" that was believed to live in the lake.[12] While to some this is proof of Champ, tales of giant serpents were part of Indian folklore across much of the continent. The Abenaki also told of *makwaaskadamôd,* a giant snake that lived in ponds, lakes, and bogs that made off with young women. These stories may be Native American versions of urban legends intended to remind young women that they should not venture too far from the safety of the tribe on their own.[13] It is known that when the Native Americans found mastodon bones and tusks, they "identified them as underwater horned monsters."[14] In this regard, the discovery of dinosaur fossils may have fueled Champ myths among Native Americans in the region.

The first known report of the Lake Champlain monster appeared on May 18, 1808, when a New York newspaper, the *Public Advertiser,* stated: "Lake Champlain—A monster has lately made its appearance on the waters of the lake."[15] Since the nineteenth century, there have been hundreds of documented sightings.[16] In 1871, passengers on the steamship *Curlew* spotted a mysterious creature north of Crown Point, New York. It was described as moving "at railroad speed" while the water was "strongly agitated for thirty or forty feet from the erected head of the monster when in motion."[17] Two years later, railroad workers constructing the New York and Canadian Railroad line that hugged the shore of the lake, reported a dramatic encounter. The *Whitehall Times* of July 9 reported: "From his nostrils he would occasionally spurt streams of water above his head to an altitude of about 20 feet. The appearance of his head was round and flat, with a hood spreading out from the lower part of it like a rubber cap often worn by mariners with a cape to keep the rain from running down the neck. His eyes were small and piercing, his mouth broad and provided with two rows of teeth, which he displayed to his beholders. As he moved off at a rate of ten miles an hour, portions of his body appeared above the surface of the water, while his tail, which resembled that of a fish, was thrown out of the water quite often."[18] This very vivid report may seem like strong evidence for the creature, but the *Whitehall Times* is also known to have published a hoax story on the creature soon after, so the original account must be viewed with great skepticism. Furthermore, no specific witness names are given.

Some believers point to extraordinary reports of Champ ramming boats as positive proof of the creature's existence. On the afternoon of September 2, 1937, for instance, a respected couple from Rouses Point, New York—Mr. and Mrs. Charles J. Langlois—were fishing in a sixteen-foot motor boat when ripples appeared in the water. According to the local paper, "Thirty feet in front [of them] a giant form emerged from the water [moving] toward the little craft. Mrs. Langlois screamed; her husband jerked the tiller [motor] and the form struck the side of the boat, swerved sharply and disappeared under the water."[19] The couple quickly motored to the safety of shore. Mrs. Langlois later said: "What we saw was the back . . . It was traveling toward us and was looped out of the water at least 15 feet long. It was black, without scales, as thick through as a large telephone post, and it traveled through the water in loops like a snake. We didn't see a head or tail. When it hit the boat it jarred it considerably and swerved it from its course. I judged it was making between four and six miles an hour. It churned the water and left a wake like that made by a small boat."[20] While scientists are not certain as to why, there have been numerous reports around the world of sturgeon ramming boats, with their ribbed backs being mistaken for humps.[21]

The media has played a major role in perpetrating the Champ myth. It has been widely claimed in books and press articles that the first Champ sighting was by French cartographer Samuel de Champlain.[22] This myth can be traced to 1970 and the appearance of an article in *Vermont Life* magazine by New York historian Marjorie Porter. Porter stated that in 1609, Champlain saw "a serpent-like creature about twenty-feet long, as thick through as a barrel and with a head shaped like a horse."[23] Yet Champlain never wrote this in his log, as Porter claimed. In his log, he wrote about having seen creatures that were five feet long and "as large as my thigh." The head was "as big as my two fists."[24] Porter also claimed that the encounter happened on Lake Champlain, which is also untrue. In July 1609, Champlain was actually in the St. Lawrence River estuary, a body of water that feeds into the lake, not in Lake Champlain itself, as was commonly reported.

While historians now agree that Champlain never saw his creature in the lake,[25] the claim that the lake's namesake had the first known sighting continues to be reported in books and in the press. Champlain said the creature had "jaws two feet and a half long, and a double set of very sharp and dangerous teeth. The form of the body resembles that of the pike, and it is armed with scales that a thrust of a poniard [dagger] cannot pierce; and is of a silver grey colour. The point of the snout is like that of a hog. This fish makes war on all others in the lakes and rivers."[26] His description is identical to that of an adult gar pike, or *Lepisosteus osseus*, which continue to flourish in the lake today. These strange looking fish are gray, possess razor sharp teeth, and sport a distinctive piglike snout.

Another key factor in the propagation of the Champ myth is the failure of people to either understand or accept basic scientific facts. For instance, Lake Champlain as we know it today did not become landlocked until about ten thousand years ago. Prior to this time it was part of the Champlain Sea. The creature certainly could not have adapted from living in saltwater to living in the fresh-water lake in such a short time span. University of Vermont biologist Ellen Marsden also observes that for Champ to exist, there would have to be a breeding population of at least fifty creatures. If so, why are there not more sightings or carcasses washing on shore?[27] Supporters of Champ's reality claim that based on the descriptions of witnesses, the most likely candidates are a Zeuglodon—a snake-like primitive whale—or a Plesiosaur, a creature with flippers and a long neck, believed to have gone extinct about sixty-five millions of years ago. However, both were air breathers. How would they be able to survive when the lake freezes over? Because air breathers must continually surface—like modern-day whales—and as there must be a community of Champs, there should be many more sightings. In fact, some years there have been no sightings at all, while during other years, there are many reports. This appears to be more a function of media reports than any creature in the lake.

Harvard biologist Edward Wilson believes that the human fascination with fearsome "monsters," such as sharks and snakes, may lie in evolutionary biology, and that we are preprogramed to see predators lurking in the water or in the woods at night. Humans have always had to fend off predators waiting to have us as a meal, and this tendency to redefine a piece of floating wood as a shark, or some rustling in the bushes as Bigfoot, may have significantly contributed to our very survival as a species.[28]

The widespread belief in Champ may be a form of mass wish-fulfilment that serves a variety of functions. The Lake Champlain monster is a story that offers something for everyone. As one of the authors (RB) has written: "To some biologists it is part of our evolutionary heritage which pre-programs us to see mythical beasts. To environmentalists it is a green symbol. To sports lovers it is a baseball mascot. Local politicians and shopkeepers view it as a symbol of economic revival. For parents it is a cautionary tale and a way to scare children ('Don't go to the lake alone or Champ will get you!'). For children it is a comforting stuffed toy, a friendly monster and a dead set certainty. For believers, it is an anti-scientific symbol epitomising the view that science does not have all the answers, while for skeptics, depending on their temperament, it is either a humorous legend or an annoying myth."[29] Champ can be viewed as a symbol of what may lie undiscovered as it is scientifically plausible.

Great Moon Hoax, 1835 (USA and Worldwide)

During late August 1835, the *New York Sun* published details about extraordinary lunar discoveries made by Sir John Herschel using a gigantic new telescope at a South African observatory. Many people were soon fooled into believing that the moon was inhabited with intelligent life after reading a series of stories created by journalist Richard Adams Locke who was in cahoots with *Sun* publisher Benjamin Day.

The first inkling of the great discovery took place on Friday, August 21, when the *Sun* published a brief account on page two under the heading, "Celestial Discovery." The article was brief but set the stage for what was to follow. It read: "The Edinburgh Courant says—'We have just learnt from an eminent publisher in this city that Sir John Herschel at the Cape of Good Hope, has made some astronomical discoveries of the most wonderful description, by means of an immense telescope of an entirely new principle.'" Over the next four days there was silence. Then on Tuesday, August 25, the *Sun* published a description of the telescope, which served the purpose of establishing credibility with its readers. The telescope reportedly weighed 14,826 pounds (6,731 kg) and could magnify objects 42,000 times.[30] Written in scientific language that in parts were almost incomprehensible to the layperson, the articles that would follow were said to have been excerpts from the prestigious *Edinburgh Journal of Science*. Unbeknownst to most readers, the journal became defunct years earlier.

The August 26 installment carried news of amazing discoveries: the moon was reportedly teeming with strange animal life including bisontine creatures and many colorful birds. "In the shade of the woods on the south-eastern side, we beheld continuous herds of brown quadrupeds, having all the external characteristics of the bison, but more diminutive than any species of the *Bos genus* in our natural history. Its tail is like that of our *Bos grunniens*; but in its semi-circular horns, the hump on its shoulders, and the depth of its dewlap, and the length of its shaggy hair."[31]

The following day, it was reported that Herschel had classified nine types of mammals including a two-legged beaver-like creature. "The last resembles the beaver of the earth in every other respect than in its destitution of a tail, and its invariable habit of walking upon only two feet. It carries its young in its arms like a human being, and moves with an easy gliding motion. Its huts are constructed better and higher than those of many tribes of human savages, and from the appearance of smoke in nearly all of them, there is no doubt of its being acquainted with the use of fire. Still its head and body differ only in the points stated from that of the beaver, and it was never seen except on the borders of lakes and rivers [where it] has been seen to immerse for a period of several seconds."[32]

The greatest discovery came on the fourth day—flying, intelligent humanoids—that he referred to as *Vespertilio homo*, or bat-man. These creatures were described in scientific terms. "We could then perceive that they possessed wings of great expansion, and were similar in structure to this of the bat, being a semi-transparent membrane expanded in curvilineal divisions by means of straight radii, united at the back by the dorsal integuments."[33] The final article describing these discoveries appeared on Monday, August 31, informing readers that the reflection chamber of the telescope was damaged, making any further observations impossible.[34]

In her book, *A Glance at New York*, which was published just two years after the event, Asa Greene wrote: "The sensation, among the people of New York, during the publication of the great lunar discoveries—which occupied something like a week—was wonderful."[35] She observed that while some were skeptical, the majority believed the story until the hoax was revealed. "The credulity was general. All New York rang with the wonderful discoveries of Sir John Herschel. Every body read the *Sun* and every body commented on its surprising contents. There were, indeed, a few sceptics; but to venture to express a doubt of the genuineness of the great lunar discoveries, was considered almost as heinous a sin as to question the truth of revelation."[36] The moon hoax caused the *Sun*'s circulation to soar to 19,360.[37] This made it the largest circulating daily in the world at the time.[38]

The hoax was reprinted in other New York newspapers, then around the United States and eventually in Europe and the rest of the world. Papers of the period commonly reprinted stories from other papers, so long as they were credited. The practice was a major factor in spreading the hoax beyond the confines of the *Sun*, although the accounts were typically brief snippets of no more than a few lines. In reprinting the story, the *Albany Daily Advertiser* carried the headline: "Stupendous Discovery in Astronomy." It stated: "We have read with unspeakable emotions of pleasure and astonishment, an article from the last *Edinburgh Scientific Journal*, containing an account of the recent discoveries of Sir John Herschel at the Cape of Good Hope."[39] The August 28 edition of the *New York Daily Advertiser* was equally brief, but no less subdued: "No article, we believe, has appeared for years, that will command so general a perusal and publication. Sir John has added a stock of knowledge to the present age that will immortalize his name, and place it high on the page of science."[40] On August 29, the *New York Transcript*, while more cautious, considered the story plausible, observing that although marvelous, it was certainly possible.

At the time it seemed plausible that there might be life on the moon. This was long before any unmanned probes had landed there and proved it was an airless, lifeless world. The moon hoax was a product of its time, in the absence of an intercontinental telegraph cable which was not in operation until 1858. If a similar hoax about life discovered on an extrasolar planet was perpetrated today, the spread of the news would take mere hours through the Internet, social media, television, etc. The collapse of the hoax would come equally as quick once the truth was revealed. The moon hoax was eventually unmasked by the New York–based *Journal of Commerce* newspaper after Locke admitted to fabricating the articles, although the *Sun*'s editor, Benjamin Day, refused to admit it. The hoax spread as other papers reproduced the claims made by the *Sun*. After having a drink at a hotel, Locke reportedly warned a fellow journalist not to reprint the story as he had written it himself.[41]

While Locke sold sixty thousand copies of a pamphlet within a month in order to meet demand for the story, it may have been more of a novelty.[42] Journalism historian Brian Thornton has examined editorials and letters to New York newspapers during the affair. He concludes that the excitement about the bogus discoveries were met with much greater skepticism than has previously been realized, although it is apparent that many readers did accept the accounts as factual.[43] Consistent with Thornton's analysis, it is notable that many papers also rejected the claims, such as the *New York American*, who's editor saw the hoax for what it was. Under the title, "News from the Moon," the article began in mocking fashion: "The news from this planet, received through the *Sun*, is truly astonishing." It ended by recommending that the articles be republished and bound "with Gulliver's Travels, and the Voyages of Peter Wilkins, and that the editor of the *Sun* should secure a copy-right."[44]

The Edison Star, 1880–1910 (USA)

During the last two decades of the nineteenth century, inventor Thomas Edison began to experiment with a wireless telegraph in his hometown of Menlo Park, New Jersey. As part of his experiments, he tried to communicate between tethered balloons. Edison soon noticed that he got better results at night, so he continued his experiments with tethered illuminated balloons. It was within this backdrop that rumors spread across the United States and Canada that Edison was experimenting with a giant arc lamp which he had attached to a balloon that was suspended several miles aloft, in hopes that it could be seen across the continent. The rumors were aided by press speculation about the existence of the supposed lamp. Before long, people started spotting what was dubbed the "Edison Star," or "electric balloon." From the mid-1880s until the turn of the century, observers from across the country claimed that they could see the balloon tethered to a rope, or that they could distinguish the outline of a balloon.

One intense wave of sightings occurred across the United States between March and mid-April 1897. Most of the reports corresponded with the appearance of Venus. On March 29, a crowd had assembled in Iron Mountain, Michigan, hoping to glimpse the lamp, after rumors circulated that a bright light in the evening sky "was an electric light hoisted two miles over St. Paul" in the nearby state of Minnesota.[45] In Portland, Maine, the light was spotted for several consecutive days in early April. In the city of Bangor, one witness was certain that he saw "by the light of the balloon, a faint outline of the frame which sustained the machinery." While the sightings in Maine corresponded with Venus, many residents rejected the possibility.[46] The situation was aptly summed up by the editor of the *Bangor Daily Commercial*, who used the headline: "See that Balloon? Everybody is staring at Venus and Venus is Fooling Everybody . . ."[47] In commenting on the observations, the editor of the *Augusta Chronicle* wrote: ". . . just think of the people of New England, the cultured east, in the state of Massachusetts where Boston is, taking the planet Venus for an electric light swung in the sky by Mr. Edison."[48]

The sightings were preceded by unprecedented technological changes that dramatically altered lifestyles, as Americans became infatuated with popular literature on science and inventions, fostering an exaggerated optimism that almost any invention was possible. Historian Ivan Clarke writes that "the Frank Reade Library [was] . . . designed to meet the insatiable demand for tales of mechanical novelty by concentrating on a nonstop run of invention stories . . . and every issue throbbed with the dynamism of coming things—robots, submarines, flying machines . . . and the rest of the imaginative bric-a-brac of an age that was in love with the great wonders of science."[49] In his biography of Edison, Matthew Josephson wrote that many people living in the vicinity of Menlo Park "gossiped about his having machines that could overhear farmers talking or even cows munching the grass in the fields a mile away."[50] The Edison Star sightings reflected the popular fascination with inventions, the appearance of plausible rumors, and the fallible nature of human perception.

Virgin Mary Appearance, May 1953 (Sabana Grande, Puerto Rico)

In May 1953, a miracle was reported to have taken place near Sabana Grande, a small town on the island of Puerto Rico, a territory of the United States. The foundation for the "miracle" was laid on a hot day during the previous month when four children decided to get a drink of water from a spring near a sugar cane field. They said they saw a beautiful woman standing next to the spring and had felt an instant attraction to her. The children claimed that the woman was the Virgin Mary, and that she spoke to them. The children told others about several more encounters with the woman, but she would only appear to them. The Virgin supposedly told the children that she had blessed the spring with special healing properties, and she would make her presence known by performing a miracle at eleven o'clock on the morning of May 25.[51]

A media frenzy preceded the event, and a local mayor enthusiastically organized the visionaries to lead throngs of pilgrims in mass prayers and processions. There was tension and excitement in the air in the hours before the anointed time as estimates of between 100,000 and 150,000 people encircled the spring. At 10:45 a.m., it began to rain, and umbrellas started popping up. They were put down almost as quickly as word spread through the crowd that the children said there should be no open umbrellas.[52] When the time came, some reported miraculous healings; others said they could discern strange colored rings encircling the sun; still others claimed to see a form resembling the Virgin Mary in the clouds. Shortly after eleven, people cried out, believing that the Virgin had materialized to the crowd, wearing black attire and walking down the western hill in the direction of the spring. It turned out to have been an elderly woman. Soon after, another wave of excitement swept through the crowd as it was claimed that the Virgin was walking up the eastern hillside, dressed in white. It soon became apparent that the figure was an elderly man donning a white shirt. By noon the crowd was dwindling, and by 5:00 p.m. there was a mass exodus.[53]

Many people in the crowd claim to have been healed or saw miraculous happenings. A representative for radio station WAPA in San Juan, Pedro Vazquez, signed a statement testifying to what he saw. For instance, he claimed that at one point when it was raining, the children's hands appeared to be dry. A man, standing by the altar where the children were, noticed that his white shirt had a gold stain. This was taken as a heavenly sign as he had no recollection of it having been there.[54] At least two physicians signed statements attesting miraculous healings. Dr. J. Ramirez Ledesma from Mayaguez, Puerto Rico, wrote: "I certify that (on) the 25th of May 1953 I examined the lower extremities of Mrs. Nora Freyre de Del Valle and that she did not present evidence of any muscular atrophy. When she walked I observed perfect coordination. The neurological reflexes were intact. . . . I know Mrs. Freyre de Del Valle was disabled with a paralysis due to a brain hemorrhage (derrame cerebral) for a period of eight years. It is undoubtable that in that period of time muscular atrophy and stiffness of the joints had to occur."[55] He concluded that the only possible explanation for the change in her condition was through a miracle or supernatural occurrence.

Princeton University sociologist Melvin Tumin led a group of researchers who mingled with the crowd over the next six hours, conducting interviews. Tumin and his team found that most of the people in the crowd were believers in the children's claims and had made the trek to seek cures for incurable illnesses, for either themselves, members of their family, or their friends. As for the visual signs of a miracle, they concluded that hopefuls saw what they wanted to see by redefining ambiguous events and atmospheric phenomena as being Virgin-related. Despite the many seemingly extraordinary happenings, many saw or experienced nothing extraordinary.[56] Portions of the "miracle" appear to have been inadvertently scripted by the children. For instance, when Mr. Vazquez was near the altar shortly after eleven, broadcasting the event over the radio, he said that many people were looking at the spot where the children claimed they could see the Virgin. "Some people claimed that they were seeing her. I also looked to that place, and all I saw on top of the hill was the silhouette of a nun, with dark dress and white coif, no hands, no face, apparently moving what appeared to be her head. Even though some people said that it was a tree with that shape . . . moments later the image I had seen disappeared."[57]

Miracle Tortilla, 1977 (New Mexico, USA)

On a hot autumn day in October 1977, Maria Rubio was cooking burritos for her husband Eduardo at their home in Lake Arthur, New Mexico. What happened in the kitchen that day would transform her life. She suddenly noticed skillet burns forming an unusual pattern on one of the tortillas. Mrs. Rubio gasped and cried out: "It is Jesus Christ!" She ran to find her daughter Rosie and showed her the tortilla. "It is Jesus," Rosie said. Mrs. Rubio then took it to her sister Margarita Porras, who affirmed her suspicions: "I think it's Jesus, too." She then showed her husband, who carefully examined the tortilla. "It's Jesus, all right," he said.

Mrs. Rubio decided to have a priest bless the tortilla, so she and her husband walked across the street to the Our Lady of Guadalupe Church, taking great care as they went so as not to break the fragile piece of crispy corn. The pastor was not there, so they piled into their 1968 Chevy and drove seventeen miles to the nearby community of Dexter, New Mexico, to have the tortilla blessed. While the priest thought the image was a coincidence, Mrs. Rubio was adamant: "It's not a coincidence. I have been rolling burritos for twenty-one years, and this is the first time the face of Jesus ever appeared in a tortilla."[58]

Mrs. Rubio then placed the tortilla under glass resting on a bed of cotton, giving the appearance that it was floating among the clouds, and built a shrine around it. Believing that the appearance of Jesus was a miracle, she quit her job as a maid and decided to oversee the tortilla full-time. She told her friends: "This is a miracle. It is meant to change my life." She placed a sign in front of her house announcing the existence of the tortilla and allowed people to view the sacred object at no charge. Visitors came and lit candles in front of it and left flowers. Some left photos of sick family members, hoping that the tortilla would be able to cure them. "Since this miracle happened, I am no longer impatient. I do not know why this has happened to me, but God has come into my life through this tortilla. . . . I see happiness come into the faces of the people who visit the tortilla. That is enough for me."[59] Each night Mrs. Rubio knelt in front of the tortilla and prayed.

Mrs. Rubio believed that she witnessed a miracle that day, as indeed, the skillet burn did bear a remarkable resemblance to Jesus. The problem is, no one knows what Jesus actually looked like, assuming that he was an historical figure. All we have to go on are idealized images based on artist's interpretations. Maria Rubio's granddaughter is reported to have later taken the tortilla to school for show-and-tell—and dropped it![60]

Images said to resemble Jesus have been reported over the years on a grilled cheese sandwich, a frozen fish stick, and a pancake. There are many historical examples of people seeing miraculous objects. In 1986, for example, Rita Ratchen was driving near a water tower in Fostoria, Ohio, and reported seeing the image of Jesus on a soybean-oil tank. When the story appeared in the media, scores of people went to the tank—many convinced that it was a miracle. In August 1986, United Press International reported that hundreds of people were visiting the tank after sunset, when the image was visible. Many believed it depicted the "image of a long-haired, bearded man, clothed in a white robe" standing next to the outline of a young child on the side of the thirty foot high tank.[61] Officials representing the owners of the tank attributed the images "to a combination of shadows, light and steam vapors from the soybean processing plant." One of the believers, Deana Minard said, "I believe it is Him. You can't see facial features, but you can see the white robe. The farther back you go, the more clear it gets."[62]

Psychologists Leonard Zusne and Warren Jones observe that Mrs. Rubio's experience with the scorched tortilla is referred to by social scientists as a *pareidolia*—the perception of a pattern or meaning where one does not exist. Such interpretations of ambiguous objects have formed the basis of divination practices for centuries, "be it tea leaves, smoke, patterns formed by randomly falling objects, or the shapes assumed by molten wax or metal poured into water."[63] Once people do interpret random patterns within a specific framework, it can be difficult to convince them that the image is a mere coincide. According to Zusne and Jones: "If two cloud puffs are seen as the cheeks of Santa Claus, it becomes more difficult to see them as the two humps of a camel, and vice versa. Patterns that are attributed religious or supernatural meaning are particularly powerful in this respect, whether they are seen in tortilla burns, the walls of rusty water tanks, or wood grain patterns."[64]

Hindu Milk Miracle, September–October 1995 (Worldwide)

In 1995, millions of Hindus flocked to temples around the world after reports that idols of the elephant god Lord Ganesh were reportedly drinking milk that was offered by worshippers. As the excitement of the "miracle" spread, it was soon reported that milk was being drunk by other idols including those of Lord Shiva and the bull deity Nandi. According to reports, the affair began after a worshipper in India visited a temple and offered a spoon of milk to Ganesh by emptying it on the statute, which, to his astonishment, drank it. Within twenty-four hours, temples were being deluged with the faithful, who either were making their own milk offerings by placing the spoon in contact with the trunk of Ganesh or wanted to witness the miracle for themselves.[65] On September 22, the *Statesman* described the excitement caused by the event: "Mass hysteria gripped Calcutta, Delhi, Bombay, Bangalore and several other parts of the country today, as word spread that idols of Ganesh Parvati, Shiva and even His Bull were 'sipping' milk out of the hands of their devotees. Thousands flocked to temples to give offerings of milk to the deities. The nation was obsessed with the milk 'miracle,' and people talked of nothing other . . . It all started at 2:30 a.m. . . . Telephone lines were kept busy with people calling friends and relatives . . . The Gods were particular about how they were to be fed, large utensils or tumblers would not do. Only spoonfuls, were acceptable."

The "miracle" was an illusion created by the statues absorbing the liquid referred to by scientists as the capillary effect. This process was demonstrated by a group of scientists who had placed red dye in a spoon of milk before making an offering. The liquid was "sucked in by capillary action dripping from the idol's body."[66] London chemist Julia Higgins offered an example of the process: "Break a flowerpot, dip it in water, and the water disappears like mad."[67] While many of the statues were glazed, Joe Nickell observed that "only a bit of the glaze need be absent . . . for capillary attraction to work."[68] This helped to explain why, in many of the statues, instead of disappearing in a miraculous fashion, the milk was found to be pooling at the bottom of the idols. The absorption effect can be rather startling as many people were not pouring the milk out of the spoon, but placing the spoon in the statue, only to have the milk seemingly disappear. Chemists say that through surface tension, the molecules of milk are "pulled from the spoon by the texture of the statues."[69] At the height of the excitement, milk prices in India rose as much as twentyfold, and police had to be called in to maintain order.[70] According to media reports, the milk-drinking "miracles" began around September 21 and quickly tapered off during early October.

The episode had a powerful effect on many people. The experience of the former general secretary of the Hindu Council in the United Kingdom, Anil Bhanot, illustrates how many people were affected. After receiving a phone call from his mother-in-law to go to the temple and offer milk, Bhanot did so and found himself standing in a line with four or five people in front of him. "They were all offering milk in a spoon to the Deity Nandi—a marble idol of the bull that is supposed to be Lord Shiva's vehicle and his foremost devotee and is worshipped as a family member of Lord Shiva . . . I was not thinking of Lord Shiva or Ganesh or Parvati at the time but just offered a spoon full of milk to Nandi as directed by the priest."[71] Bhanot then had a profoundly spiritual experience. "As I raised the spoon to Nandi's mouth and the milk touched the idol, very slightly, the level of milk in the spoon started to go down as if someone was actually drinking it, quite evenly . . . I was shaking with awe." Bhanot said that before the incident, he saw Hinduism as a theory, but after, it crystalized his faith and that of his wife, after each offered milk and it appeared to be taken.

Social manias affirm our hopes and expectations—whether in the form of the existence of imaginary creatures such as Bigfoot and the Loch Ness Monster, or in the appearances of supernatural beings who offer the potential for spiritual immortality, like the Virgin Mary. Urban legends on the other hand, confirm our worst fears and serve as cautionary tales about the dangers of modern life. Each tale has a clear and meaningful moral or message.

In chapter 5, we will learn that urban legends serve as powerful, behavior-changing stories that highlight old fears and new dangers. They are often effective because they prey on preexisting stereotypes and prejudices.

CHAPTER 5
URBAN LEGENDS: LIVING FOLKLORE

Thomas Craughwell once observed that urban legends feed both our fears and our fantasies as they reflect popular hopes and anxieties.[1] The term *urban legend* is not easily defined, and many scholars disagree as to an exact definition.[2] For instance, many of these stories are neither urban nor legends, although the backdrop of the account is often a metropolitan environment. The term became popular in the early 1980s after the publication and success of *The Vanishing Hitchhiker* by folklorist Jan Harold Brunvand.[3] The term even gave rise to the 1999 slasher film *Urban Legend*, which was followed by *Urban Legends: Final Cut* the following year and *Urban Legends: Bloody Mary* in 2005.

People do not sit around thinking of urban legends and spread them; such tales occur spontaneously. Urban legends are usually studied by sociologists, social psychologists, and folklorists. Also known as contemporary legends, or urban myths, they can be viewed as enduring rumors that are usually passed on by word of mouth and are believed to be of recent origin. More recently, this definition has changed with the popularity of e-mail, which has become increasingly notorious for passing on chain letters of dubious authenticity. According to Brunvand, urban legends involve improbable happenings that are repeated as true and embellished during retelling. It is common for different versions of a story to appear in different places and time periods. The sources of these accounts are often attributed to the media, such as the news or popular talk shows. Another commonly attributed source are what folklorists refer to as FOAFS (friend-of-a-friend stories) in reference to the often-attributed anonymous source of many urban legends, sources that are usually impossible to verify.

Urban legends have been traced back centuries. Brunvand believes that their persistence is a reflection of their important function in society as these stories have hidden meanings that fill psychological needs. He identifies three key components of these accounts: they must be interesting, believable, and offer lessons. He describes them as "living narrative folklore."[4] Nicholas DiFonzo and Prashant Bordia have conducted extensive research into urban legends, stating that they "stem from the human need for meaning and arise in contexts where stories are told to yield meaning. Urban legends therefore function to convey mores and values, and they do so in an entertaining fashion. As a result, the contents of urban legends are funny, horrible and humorous events, woven into narratives that adapt to various locales and times."[5]

Seven factors necessary for the spread of urban legends have been identified by sociologist Erich Goode.[6] These are a *dramatic story* that reflects *current fears*, contains an *element of truth*, and has a *moral or message*. Such stories are attributed to a *credible source* such as scientists or journalists, contain *local content*, and are often *repeated by the news media* lending further factual credence. Often, if people see something reported on television or printed in a newspaper, they assume it to be accurate.

It would seem that urban legends are part of human nature and are impossible to eradicate. However, their impact can be reduced through critical-thinking, education, and familiarization with their key features so as to be able to identify these stories when they appear. One strategy to determine their validity is to contact those allegedly involved to confirm or deny the story's truthfulness. As a general rule, if you are not able to contact the original source or person involved, it is probably not true.

Urban legends often function as "cautionary tales" that alert the listener to something that is commonly viewed as a threat. A good illustration of this is a story known to folklorists as "the snake in the blanket" that has appeared in different forms over the years in many Western industrialized countries. It goes something like this: A shopper in a big chain department store is looking for a new coat, rug, blanket, or mattress. After inspecting the particular item (or in the case of the coat—trying it on), the shopper suddenly winces in pain, collapses to the floor, and dies. It is later discovered that the item in question is infested with venomous baby snakes that had hatched on the long journey from overseas. Sometimes it's poison spiders or other deadly creatures. While the details (such as the country or the name of the store) vary depending on the location of the teller, the item is always of foreign origin. The lesson is unmistakable: do not buy foreign products.[7]

It is common for urban legends to reflect prevalent societal fears and involve popular products or services. Between about 1983 and the early 1990s, many stories circulated in Western countries warning of the existence of a network of satanic cultists who were kidnapping and murdering children in ritual sacrifices. According to sociologist Jeffrey Victor, at least sixty rumor-panics were triggered in various sections of the United States during this period. The cultists were never found because they did not exist. They were part of a major urban legend that was often situated in daycare facilities.[8]

Another common urban legend around this time was of the Kentucky Fried Rat. While there are many different variants, one involves a housewife who decides to take her family to KFC instead of eating at home. When she opens the chicken, she sees the fried rat and is so horrified and distraught that she drops dead from fright. While these stories of fried rats and Satanists may seem unrelated, Victor and most folklorists view their origins as similar. They coincide with the breakdown of the traditional family and serve as a metaphor for concerns over the weakened family and its capacity to protect children. The message is clear: by taking one's family to a fast-food restaurant instead of preparing a home-cooked meal, the mother seemingly got what she deserved. Mothers should not cut corners; they should stick with tradition.

As for the Satanic cult scare, Victor believes it reflects the guilt of many parents of placing their children in daycare. The message: parents should raise their own children and not trust their care to strangers. Victor writes: "There is a great deal of parental guilt today; many parents feel guilty about leaving their children at daycare centers or about having little time to spend with them or about being reluctant to use their authority to guide their children's choice of entertainments and friends or about feeling unable to guide the moral values of their children."[9]

Folklorist Gary Fine observes that with the decline of small-town life in the rural United States, many people have grown fearful of the anonymity of urban life that includes fleeting brushes with strangers and transients. He writes: "What could better serve as a metaphor for the city as a jungle than the belief that the New York sewer system is filled with albino alligators, which swim through toilet pipes and bite victims in public washrooms?"[10] These accounts remind us that urban legends are not deliberately contrived stories, they are created by people, in a spontaneous, unconscious process that reflects prevailing fears at a particular time and place.

Contemporary legends have also been viewed as cautionary tales about the consequences of human greed. Writing in the *Journal of Consumer Market*, Todd Donovan and his colleagues note that a majority of urban legends involve characters who are trying "to gain something, such as money or a good time, while acting against dominant norms. In the process of achieving an illicit goal, an ironic twist occurs, in which something negative happens to the characters. In sum, the characters portrayed in the urban legend pay a price for their greed, lust, drunkenness, or other human imperfections"[11]

Urban legends also evolve as cultures and societies change over time. For instance, a popular urban legend during the 1950s involved teenagers who were murdered by an escaped prisoner. The incident took place while the youths were necking in a car. New variants of this legend are closely tied to rapid social and technological changes. For example, in one version a teen meets for a date using the Internet. Her partner turns out to be her father. Both the necking-couple tale and the story of the girl who ended up dating her father revolve around a similar theme: the dangers posed by new technologies. In the case of the necking teens, the technology was the car, while in the latter instance it was cyber technology. This constant changing of urban legends to reflect current issues serves to support their credibility.[12]

Folklorist Donna Wyckoff believes that urban legends are essentially collective community responses to crises that reinforce the importance of upholding community standards. Hence, the message is overwhelmingly traditional and conservative and essentially says, "don't drive alone on highways or park in dark places; don't buy foreign products; don't put something in your mouth if you don't know where it came from; don't neglect basic hygiene; and don't dabble with forces (supernatural, sexual, technological, social) you might not be able to control. The more subtle message of the legend is 'be traditional': don't stray beyond any of the established limits—behavioral or ideological; mind set and behavior are intricately interrelated. But such legends arise specifically because boundaries have been transgressed."[13]

It is also important to make the distinction between rumors and hoaxes. As Pamela Donovan observes that hoaxes are spread intentionally with the knowledge that they are false, while are typically "complicated by the sincerity of the promulgators. Some rumors may of course begin their lives as lies, that is to say, knowingly inaccurate information passed along with the aim of deception. Most who study such forms have observed that the vast majority of dissemination is done sincerely: the promulgator believes that what they are saying is true."[14]

One of the most well-known folklorists of the twenty-first century is Jan Harold Brunvand, who has perhaps done more to popularize the subject than anyone else. His books, such as *The Vanishing Hitchhiker* and *The Choking Doberman*, have been met with widespread praise for both their scholarly nature and readability.[15] His tales of housewives dropping dead after munching on a Kentucky Fried Rat or of someone's pet exploding in a microwave highlight a key theme. As Pamela Donovan observes: "these stories reflected anxiety about our transition to a fully modern life—urban legend in the sense of urbanized and urbane."[16] Donovan believes that these accounts appear to highlight our shift toward an increasingly depersonalized world and the loss of *gemeinschaft*—the German word for the strong bonds between one's community and people—even for those who may never have encountered it.

MEMORABLE URBAN LEGENDS

The Vanishing Hitchhiker, early 1900s to present (Worldwide)

Stories about drivers who pick up hitchhikers who then vanish are told in many countries around the world. Folklorist Jan Harold Brunvand has collected an example from a Romanian novel where the driver had coffee in the apartment of two women after he had given them a lift. During the visit, the driver washed his hands. The following day, he discovered he had forgotten to put his wrist watch back on. "After work that day he returned to the apartment, but the doorman for the building said that the two women he had sought no longer lived there, having been killed in an automobile accident three weeks earlier. . . . The man protested that he had been with the women the night before in their apartment, but the doorman said this was impossible and showed him the seals that had been placed on their front door by a lawyer, pending the settlement of their estate. Later, with the attorney's help, the man was allowed to break the seals and open the apartment door. He found his watch just where he had left it in the bathroom."[17] In a Japanese version of the tale, a pond near the hitchhiker's destination is thought to be the ghost's final resting place after the car's backseat is left wet where she sat.[18]

The most extensive modern study of vanishing hitchhikers is written by Michael Goss. He distinguishes between several versions of hitchhikers (ghost, prophet, godly being, etc.) and notes distinct differences between the urban legend/ghost-story varieties and the allegedly true reports of phantom hitchhikers. One difference is the lack of a purpose for the ghost in the real accounts.

Most interesting of all, Goss interviewed one witness firsthand. In 1979, Roy Fulton picked up a male hitchhiker who never spoke. "So I was driving up the road, I suppose I was driving for—what, four, five or six minutes, I suppose, doing a speed of about 40 [miles per hour] minimum. I turned around to offer him a cigarette and the bloke had disappeared, I braked, had a quick look in the back to see if he was there. He wasn't and I just gripped the wheel and drove like hell. And that's all—you know . . ."[19]

One of the authors (PH) is a veteran stunt performer and knows that even the most skilled professional in his field would not jump from a car traveling at that high a speed. Furthermore, a real passenger could not have jumped from Fulton's car without the interior light automatically coming on (as it did when the passenger opened the door to get in the car). There are only three possibilities: Fulton made up his experience, he had some type of vivid hallucination, or he experienced something unexplained. As individuals, we will interpret this case in light of our own beliefs.

Folklorist Elizabeth Tucker collected a number of vanishing-hitchhiker stories from the Binghamton, New York, region that reflect accounts found all over the world. The following is a sample: "Many, many years ago, a young girl was walking down the road near Devil's Bend. This was before there were many cars. She lived on the road and liked to go walking by herself. Even though it was getting dark, she kept walking down the road. Just as she got to the curve a wagon came rumbling around from the other side. Something spooked the horses, and they ran wild. It's her ghost that now walks the road there and that people see. If you pick her up, she disappears before the car stops. And she leaves her white scarf and calling card on the seat. If you go up to the house they say you see her picture hanging inside the living room, and the people there tell you she used to live there and explain what happened to her."[20]

This vanishing-hitchhiker legend became popular around 1900 as motor vehicles overtook horses and carriages as the preferred means of travel and a more efficient means of attaining freedom from elders. The story suggests that the woman was killed by the out-of-control horses. Tucker believes that such accounts are cautionary tales that hold that "girls who go out walking by themselves at dusk may get into terrible trouble. Tokens of the ghost's presence—her scarf and her calling card—serve as reminder that young women should not go out by themselves and throw caution to the wind."[21] She observes that the wild horses represent dangerous deviations "from safe and proper behavior, while the white scarf and calling card symbolize the innocent demeanor that young ladies should follow."

One of the most common modern-day versions of the story involves a ghostly woman in a prom dress or wedding gown, who is picked up on a lonely road and asks to be dropped off at a house several miles away. When they arrive and the driver turns toward her, she has vanished. The driver then knocks on the door and is met by an elderly woman who says that her daughter was killed on her prom night when she was picked up while hitchhiking home at the same spot he had picked her up. The story appears to be an updated version of the turn-of-the-century tale of the woman who had failed to exercise proper caution and was killed by runaway horses. The modern variant contains a warning about the possible consequences of accepting rides from strangers and what can happen when young ladies act recklessly.[22]

Vanishing-hitchhiker accounts vary distinctly depending on culture and values. For instance, Gail de Vos recounts a story from Israel. One rainy night, a driver stops to give a ride to a female soldier and, owing to the poor conditions, insists on dropping her off at her home. Upon arriving, he turns to her, only to find that she has vanished. All that is left is her military coat. The bewildered man knocks on the door of the house and is met by a woman. After telling her what happened, she explains that three years earlier her daughter, a soldier, died in a road accident on the same highway and that ever since, on rainy nights, drivers come to the house with items of her daughter's clothing.[23] De Vos says the power of the story is that it highlights the inequity between male and female soldiers. She notes that male soldiers who die "in the line of duty, especially a son," are dotted over with public ceremonies, but in this instance, the woman receives a quiet funeral."[24] She writes that the story highlights "the guilt about hapless female victims whose death goes unremarked."

While folklorist Alan Dundes is in agreement with most of his colleagues that the tale of the vanishing hitchhiker is a cautionary tale, he takes the analysis one step further and adds a psychoanalytical twist about teen morality and dating. He writes: "A girl who hitch-hikes, that is, allows herself to be 'picked up' by a perfect (male) stranger, runs the risk of losing her virtue" as cars to teens are akin to a "mobile bedroom."[25] He contends that "a girl who allows herself to be picked up in this way can never go home again. In more explicit terms, a girl who has once lost her chastity is punished for all eternity by trying desperately though to no avail to return to the sanctity of home with all its associations of family values."

Dundes says that the influence of these stories lie in their subconscious power. He believes that some informants may be skeptical of the moral because they do not think about it on a conscious level. He observes: "If individuals . . . consciously knew, what they were doing when they participated in symbolic rituals, or told jokes, or sang folk songs, etc., they could not perform such."

Sewer Alligators, eighteenth century and ongoing (USA)

On February 10, 1935, a remarkable and alarming headline appeared in the *New York Times*: "Alligator Found in Uptown Sewer."[26] It was reported that sixteen-year-old Salvatore Condulucci had been shoveling snow into an open manhole with a group of friends when the gator was spotted. When the hole became clogged, he began to move away the snow and spotted the creature. He and his companions grabbed a clothesline, fashioned a knot, and Condulucci lowered the noose into the sewer. After several near misses, he finally managed to secure the rope around its neck and yanked back—snaring it. His friends joined in and they all heaved together, yanking the creature from the murky depths of the city underworld. They promptly clubbed the critter to death with their shovels as it thrashed about in the snow. The account states that the boys brought the gator's remains to the Lehigh Stove and Repair Shop, where it weighed in at 125 pounds and measured nearly eight feet in length. "It became at once the greatest attraction the store ever had had. The whole neighborhood milled about, and finally, a call for the police reached a nearby station . . . But there was little for the hurrying policemen to do. The strange visitor was quite dead; and no charge could be preferred against it or against its slayers. The neighbors were calmed with little trouble and speculation as to where the 'gator had come from was rife." As there were no area pet shops, it was hypothesized that the creature may have been a passenger on a steam ship from the Florida Everglades that had fallen overboard. The account states that about 9:00 p.m., a Sanitation Department truck pulled up to the store and drove the carcass to Barren Island where it was incinerated.

Despite many details in the report, including specific names and addresses, the story has never been verified and is likely an urban myth. The United States has a long history of reporting this urban legend, and despite the many claims, not a single case has been confirmed. The *Times* article contains several red flags. For instance, it is clear that the reporter did not observe the creature firsthand and was relying on the claims of others. It is highly suspicious that no one took a photo of it and it was promptly incinerated, destroying any potential confirming evidence.

Since the nineteenth century, stories have circulated in newspapers across the United States of alligators making their home in the sewer systems of major cities, especially New York. A typical version of this story claims that tourists from Florida or local carnival goers on Coney Island had purchased a baby gator and brought it home. Before long, these cute babies outgrew their welcome and were flushed down the toilet. Some of them reportedly survived in the sewers beneath the city and grew to full size. Some variations of the legend hold that the alligators are albino and sometimes also blind due to the lack of light underground. Despite numerous news reports about sewer alligators, to date none of the claims have been verified.

One of the earliest press reports of sewer alligators appeared on page three of the *Atlanta Constitution* on August 5, 1873.

THE NEW SENSATION.

Alligator in the Heart of the City—Great Commotion.

Although Atlanta is situated about 1100 feet above the level of the sea, and has neither the climate of Florida or the waters of the Nile, yet, to-day she is convulsed from "center to circumference," by the fact that a live alligator is "circulating around" in the very heart of the city.

It is said to float at ease in the sewer running from the American Hotel down by the residence of Postmaster Denning. At night it is said his deep bass voice can be heard making the welkin ring, and little negro children shake with terror, for every now and then if one gets out of sight, it is generally believed that his alligatorship has had a good meal.

Like the sea-serpent, the length of his alligatorship is variously stated from six to ten feet.

That such a dreadful monster should make his incursions into the heart of a city like Atlanta, is passing strange. How it came there and how it exists, is a conundrum we can't now answer. It is supposed he escaped a museum. But until the animal is captured and brought before the Recorder for trial for "high crimes and misdemeanors," we would advise parents to keep children away from the branch, and married men to stay at home at nights.

Similar press accounts of sewer alligators—claimed to be fact—have been reported in 1886 in Dallas, Texas, and Newark, New Jersey,[27] in Detroit, Michigan, in 1913,[28] and in Dayton, Ohio, in 1919.[29] These are just a few of many reports. In 1982, the *New York Times* published an interview with the design chief in the New York City Bureau of Sewers, John T. Flaherty, noting that for years his department had been haunted by alligator stories. Flaherty said that each year several people from all over the country wrote the department to ask about the alligator claims. A Denver woman wanted to know if sewer employees were given guns for protection. A resident of Celoron, New York, wanted Flaherty to settle a disagreement with his coworker as to whether the creatures changed color after being out of the sun for so long. It was suggested that they turned white over time. The good-humored and tactful Flaherty wrote in reply: "I could cite you many cogent, logical reasons why the sewer system is not a fit habitat for an alligator, but suffice it to say that, in the 28 years I have been in the sewer game, neither I nor any of the thousands of men who have worked to build, maintain or repair the sewer system has ever seen one, and a 10-foot, 800-pound alligator would be hard to miss."[30] During his interview, Flaherty did admit that there were fierce creatures living under the streets of New York. He said they were called sewer rats!

Mark Barber notes that claims over the years that alligators were breeding in the sewers of New York are physically impossible as the sex of offspring is determined by the temperature of the nest. Male alligators require a temperature over ninety-three degrees Fahrenheit. Since the temperature in the sewers is well below this, there would be no male alligators born to reproduce. He suggests that the story continues to flourish due to our "deep fascination and fear of what might be lurking underneath our cities."[31] Folklorist Jean-Noel Kapferer concurs and suggests that the proliferation of sewer-alligator tales and kindred accounts may be a commentary on modern city life. He asked: "Is it a metaphor that means under a thin gloss of civilization (the city), a world of violence, instinct and aggression lives on (the jungle is just under the black top)?"[32]

While the origin of the legend is unknown, accounts of pigs living under the streets of London during the nineteenth century, may be a historical precursor, reflecting similar fears of life in the big city.[33] Toshers, or shoremen, were people who routinely trekked through the London sewers looking for lost items such as coins, jewelry, and scrap metal. In his book, *London Lore*, Steve Roud noted that this group had a vibrant folklore of "black swine" slouching through the sewers in the vicinity of the suburb of Hampstead. According to the story, a young sow accidentally got trapped in the system and reared her young, who in turn, reared more and more sewer pigs who flourished by feeding on the garbage.[34] These unsubstantiated accounts were common at the time. For instance, on October 10, 1859, the *Daily Telegraph* recounted the tale, but without any supporting evidence besides word of mouth. "It has been said that . . . Hampstead sewers shelter a monstrous breed of black swine, which have propagated and run wild among the slimy feculence, and whose ferocious snouts will one day uproot Highgate archway . . ."

The legend of sewer alligators in major cities has been further spread through modern popular culture. In his 1963 novel *V*, Thomas Pynchon described two-man alligator patrols hunting the creatures with shotguns. How the alligators got there closely follows the urban legend—after being purchased as souvenirs in Florida, they were later discarded. The 1980 John Sayles movie *Alligator* stars a monster gator that emerges from the sewers to terrorize a Midwestern town by feasting, in *Jaws*-like fashion, on human prey. But perhaps most of all, more than any other medium, the legend of sewer alligators had been spread by the press, giving legitimation to the myth despite the absence of supporting evidence. For many people assume that because it appears in print, it is likely to be true.

The Baby in the Microwave, 1950s to present (USA)

In 1946, Percy Spencer was granted US Patent 2,408,235 for a high-efficiency magnetron that was eventually refined and mass produced as the microwave oven, which became commercially available the following year. It would take twenty years and a series of refinements for it to become popular as the first prototypes weighed 750 pounds and stood five-and-a-half-feet high.[35] Spencer's invention would soon give rise to one of the most enduring urban legends of modern times. In the microwaved-baby story, also known as "The Hippie Babysitter," two parents asked that at the designated time, their new babysitter place a turkey in the microwave and put the baby to bed. After they left, the babysitter became high on drugs after either smoking marijuana or tripping on the hallucinogenic drug LSD. In a confused state, the babysitter is said to have put the turkey in the cot and cooked the baby in the microwave. Upon their return, the parents went to check on the baby and discovered the terrible result of the babysitter having taken drugs.

Microwaved-baby stories appear to serve multiple functions that reflect widespread popular fears. The first centers on concerns over new technology and its impact on our daily lives. When microwave ovens first appeared, like all new products, most people did not have a good understanding as to how they functioned, prompting widespread safety concerns. The legend also appears to be a warning to parents not to entrust the safety of their child to a relative stranger.

A variant of the microwaved-baby story is "The Poodle in the Microwave." According to this variation, a woman had a miniature pet poodle. She liked to knit outfits for the dog to wear during cold weather. The woman felt terrible after giving her dog a bath each week because it was impossible to completely dry it's coat, and the small animal would tremble violently from the cold. While she tried using a hairdryer, the noise frightened the dog, and the hot air resulted in severely dried skin. The frustrated woman then had an idea: dry the poodle in the microwave. On shampoo day, after the dog had been rinsed, the woman placed the dog in the microwave chamber, set it for eight minutes, and went back to clean up the mess in the bathroom. The microwave soon exploded, and upon rushing to the kitchen, the woman was shocked to find bits of cooked poodle everywhere.[36] The story of the pet cooked inside a microwave serves as a cautionary tale about the dangers of new technology in a world undergoing changes that are often viewed as progress, but may have unintended consequences.

While the baby in the microwave story is a popular urban legend, it is worth noting that there have been several verified cases where babies have been placed inside microwave units and they were turned on. In 1987, the journal *Pediatrics* published two cases of suspected child abuse where infants suffered microwave burns, although both survived and appeared to avoid serious long-term damage.[37] In 2005, a woman in Dayton, Ohio, was indicted on murder charges for placing her month-old baby in a microwave and turning it on. Montgomery County prosecutor Mathias H. Heck Jr. stated that the county coroner concluded "that the injuries sustained by this baby could have only been caused by being placed into a microwave oven and having that oven turned on and (cooking) the baby to death."[38] In 2000, a Virginia woman, Renee Otte, was given a five-year prison term for putting her month-old baby into a microwave. While the woman had stopped taking her seizure medication and claimed to have no recall of the event, experts concluded that she had cooked the infant for about ten minutes.[39]

The Hook, 1950s to present (USA)

One urban legend/horror tale is about a narrow escape from a fugitive psychopath. The November 8, 1960, edition of the famous "Dear Abby" newspaper column carried a typical version of the story about "The Hook" that was sent in by a reader: "A fellow and his date pulled into their favorite 'lovers' lane' to listen to the radio and do a little necking. The music was interrupted by an announcer who said there was an escaped convict in the area who had served time for rape and robbery. He was described as having a hook instead of a right hand. The couple became frightened and drove away. When the boy took his girl home, he went around to open the car door for her. Then he saw—a hook on the door handle! I don't think I will ever park to make out as long as I live. I hope this does the same for other kids."[40]

The tale of the hook has entered popular culture and has been repeated by characters in such movies as *Meatballs* (1979), *Stand By Me* (1986), and *I Know What You Did Last Summer* (1997). In *Meatballs*, Bill Murray's character scares a group of children by telling the tale around the campfire at night and then whipping out his sleeved arm from behind him with a hook where his hand should be.

The hook narrative highlights the potential dangers of casual sexual relationships and shows what could happen when we do not heed our parents' advice and hold to our values. In many versions of this story, the boy insists on staying and continuing their amorous encounter, but the girl insists that she be driven home promptly. The boy protests but the girl refuses to engage in any further necking. The frustrated boy reluctantly agrees and speeds off. When they discover the hook stuck in the handle (in some versions, it's covered in blood), it becomes apparent that that the girl's restraint and moral fortitude had saved their lives.

The Dead Boyfriend, 1964 and ongoing (USA)

Sometimes referred to as "The Boyfriend's Death," these stories have circulated, usually on college campuses. In them, two romantically involved university students drove to a remote location and parked under a tree. When it came time for them to return to the dorm, their car wouldn't start, so the boyfriend decided to walk to a nearby motel to summon assistance. He fails to return and the girlfriend soon hears scratching on the roof. Finally, near daybreak, a group of people wander by and help her from the car. When she looks up, she is horrified to see her boyfriend hanging from the tree, his feet scraping against the roof. Later versions have the police finding the woman and asking her to step out of the car, but not to look back.[41] Folklorist Jan Harold Brunvand notes that urban legends are powerful influences in society because they have a strong story appeal, may be plausible, and have a meaningful moral or message. In the case of the "Dead Boyfriend," he believes that it "warns young people to avoid situations in which they may be endangered, but at a more symbolic level the story reveals society's broader fears of people, especially women and the young, being alone and among strangers in the darkened world outside the security of their own home or car."[42] He believes that it is no coincidence that in many versions of the story, the woman is dressed in an evening gown and high heels, and cowers under a blanket until help arrives. Such elements appear to imply that she is passive, helpless, and requires rescuing by men.

Simon Bronner observes that while this tale appears to be a warning to women not to take unnecessary risks, there is also a clear male message: do not be foolishly macho to the point of endangering your life.[43] Folklorist Linda Dégh believes that this legend, like that of the kindred story of the hook, represent a wake-up call for youth in a modern society to be more aware of potential dangers, especially if they violate norms. "In both legends, the connecting link is the sober warning of law enforcement conveyed through the car radio, interrupting the pleasant music that has been a prelude to a sexual adventure. The news of the lunatic killer's escape from a nearby asylum comes as a turning point that changes the tone of the story. Having violated community norms and left the safety of their hometown, the dating couple must face life-threatening conditions in the isolation of the nocturnal forest."[44]

Kentucky Fried Rat, 1970s to present (USA)

This urban legend strikes at a basic human worry about contamination of our food, as well as the increasing reliance on restaurant and fast-food outlets. In a 1971 version collected by folklorist George Carey, two couples were sitting in a car munching on chicken from a fast food outlet. One of the women remarked that the chicken tasted "funny," but she continued to eat it. She soon realized that she had been eating a fried rodent and was rushed to the hospital in shock.[45] It is left up to the listener's imagination to decide whether the rat was deliberately deep fried and added with her chicken pieces (either by a disgruntled employee or as a cost cutting measure by a cheap meat supplier) or if it accidentally got into the system due to poor hygiene practices in factories or stores. Although the brand of fast-food chain store in not mentioned in this example, it is commonly stated as Kentucky Fried Chicken (KFC). Often, the consumer dies from the shock.

This legend highlights the nature of urban legends as dynamic. Far from being static and uniform, they vary with the time and place, even within countries and cultures, to reflect changes in local values and beliefs. It is noteworthy that prior to the placement of the fried rat in local fast-food outlets, earlier versions of the tale had the incident happening at an ethnic restaurant. In more recent times, the "foreigner" to be feared is now the large corporation.

Some variants of the fast-food-rat story address the growing concern over the impersonal way in which many people now get their food and our lack of control over these outlets, which are usually operated by multinational corporations. Gary Fine believes that one of the reasons for the popularity of the fried-rat legend is the growing dominance of fast-food chains and their mechanical, impersonal nature. Customers at fast-food establishments such as KFC often feel like a number. Employees also must adhere to a strict set of guidelines for everything from how the food is prepared to interacting with customers with preset responses (e.g., "May I take your order?" and "Have a nice day."). Fine writes that this contrived strategy of personalizing service by staff at fast-food outlets actually has a reverse effect and "can be understood as representing a lack of concern—and other symbolic indications of a lack of concern—such as serving rats instead of chicken." It is within this context that the story of the fried rat becomes believable.[46]

Another key message or moral from the fried-rat tale is in what it says about the changing nature of female roles and the dangers posed by eating food prepared by strangers. In noting that the overwhelming majority of victims in the fried-rat narrative are female, the story is a commentary on contemporary life in American society. If, as most folklorists believe, these accounts represent a longing for a lost way of life where people did most things for themselves and knew who was making their food, it is only fitting the woman is made the victim after shirking her familial responsibilities. Fine observes: "The woman by neglecting her traditional role as food preparer helps to destroy the family by permitting the transfer of control from the home to amoral profit-making corporations. Thus, the receipt of a rat is appropriate symbolic punishment."[47]

It should be pointed out that there have been alleged real-life instances of similar food contamination. In November 2000, Mrs. Katherine Ortega allegedly found a fried chicken head in a box of fried chicken wings bought at a local McDonald's. According to an ABC News report, the head, complete with the beak, comb, and eyes, had been breaded and fried and served to the customer in a box with wings. Katherine Ortega said: "I noticed that it had a beak and it had eyes . . . I screamed."[48] The incident happened in the state of Virginia. Ironically,

Mrs. Ortega told the local press: "I will probably cook at home from now on." While this was clearly no urban myth as the woman posed for pictures with the head, it was also not a rat.

In some cases of alleged food contamination, customers have actually added the contaminant themselves in an attempt to make money through a lawsuit filed for emotional distress. In other cases, a piece of plastic, plaster, or a similar contaminant is accidentally or deliberately introduced into the food. Even if one were to confirm an incident of someone being given a fried rat at a fast-food establishment, it would not alter the power or popularity of these stories, which reflect prevailing anxieties about the health and safety of eating food made by strangers.

Disneyland Kidnappings, 1980s to present (Worldwide)

There are numerous urban legends about Disneyland but one of the most enduring is that children have been kidnapped from the bathrooms there. A child goes to the toilet alone and, in the space of ten minutes or less, they are disguised with a wig and a change of clothes and taken away. In most versions of the story, the child is saved when their distinctive sneakers are noticed by park security or their parents after the kidnappers failed to switch them. There is no explanation as to how an uncooperative child is forcibly disguised either in the cramped confines of a cubicle or in plain view of anyone entering the toilet. Occasionally, the kidnapping is said to have taken place at a major store such as Kmart, Target, or Toys"R"Us or in a large shopping mall.

In 1987, a journalist for the Salt Lake City–based newspaper the *Desert News* noted that he had collected hundreds of similar stories about attempted abductions from around the world. The reporter—Jan Brunvand—would go on to become a famous American folklorist. He wrote: "Missing children are no joke, of course: children really do disappear. But so far, I haven't found authenticated instances of them disappearing in this fashion. Obviously, this legend feeds on people's fears in an age when missing youngsters stare out at us from milk cartons and posters. The many versions of the story—all essentially the same, yet all slightly different— mark it as a prime example of any apocryphal story that warns of real danger."[49]

In 1989, Dr. Michel Snyder, a dermatologist from Leesburg, Florida, was stopped on the street by concerned residents after hearing a story that his children had been kidnapped at Disneyland. People also phoned his office to see how he was holding up and if his children (ages one and two) had recovered from the terrible ordeal. "It was particularly strange because the rumors began before we'd ever been to Disney with our kids . . . I haven't the foggiest notion how this got started," said Snyder.[50] Orange County Chief Deputy Comptroller Jim Moye expressed concern over the story, saying that "Disney does not like incidents at the park to go public. With the amount of control and privacy that Disney has, and the potential damage to the park, it would seem that they would want to keep something like that quiet."[51] Disney spokesman Charlie Ridgway fired back: "Come off it. You're telling me Disney is going to cover up a kidnapping? The rumor is so groundless it's ridiculous."[52]

More recent versions of this urban legend have surfaced in Hong Kong, where in March 2010, it was claimed that there had been an attempted kidnapping of a Caucasian boy at the popular Ocean Park amusement complex. Worried parents contacted the *South China Morning Post* and posted messages on Internet discussion boards. While stories about a kidnapping at the park were not uncommon, this account received major media coverage. An anthropologist at the Chinese University of Hong Kong, Joseph Bosco, said the rumor was unusual because the origin of most rumors is never determined, but in this instance, it was possible to determine the origin, which was a single e-mail.[53] Bosco wrote: "The original poster simply wrote a message to three friends. Several individuals helped the message reach the tipping point: a woman who sent it to her entire book club, a kindergarten headmistress who sent it to all the children's parents, and a bank director who sent it to her employees. Each contributed to the spread of the rumor, albeit not maliciously, since they believed it might be true. As usually happens with such stories, the Ocean Park kidnapping rumor slowly died and was forgotten, perhaps to be resurrected in a new form."[54] As for the meaning behind the Disney kidnappings and other child-abduction stories, it would appear to be a warning about the perils of not keeping a close eye on your children in public places. While this may be good advice, many folklorists point out that the vast majority of kidnapping victims are snatched by relatives.

Sociologist Pamela Donovan contends that the Disneyland and shopping-mall kidnapping panic has its roots in the British and American white-slavery scare dating from the 1880s when women were allegedly tricked or drugged into engaging in prostitution. The legend flared up again in Orleans, France, in 1969, with claims that women were being kidnapped from theme parks, shopping malls, and boutiques in order to serve in prostitution rings. It popped up again during the 1970s in North America when "the legend attached itself to shopping mall restrooms and the alleged victims were also teenage girls. The narrative varied little from the one at the turn of the century, which fretted over the fate of women lured out of theaters and candy stores. From the 1980s onward the legend shifted again: from young women as victims to one in which children are the prey." [55] While these modern variants of the story involve children, they "often fail to specify an ultimate nefarious purpose for the elaborate abduction," which "opens up a great deal of leeway to the creative hearer and reteller." This ambiguity gives the story plausibility because it allows the teller to include recent trappings. Donovan writes: "One may believe the abduction story without believing that a kidnapping and prostitution ring was operating; perhaps, to fill in the blanks, one might imagine black market adoption or sexual abuse at the hands of the perpetrator himself. That is, one may substitute a more plausible ending for the tale than the traditional one as a way to support the overall plausibility of the bathroom abduction, without changing the story itself."[56]

Spinach and the Misplaced Decimal Point: An Academic Urban Legend, twentieth century (Worldwide)

While academics are typically the ones who identify and analyze urban legends in society, according to Norwegian health instructor Ole Rekdal, the academic community has also occasionally been the source of urban legends. His example involves the high iron content in spinach. Writing in the prestigious journal *Social Studies of Science*, Rekdal observes that while the myth of spinach being high in iron is widespread among health professionals, it is in reality a myth that continues to flourish. While generations of parents have nagged their child to eat more spinach in order to boost their iron content, spinach should be avoided if one has an iron deficiency. Rekdal states: "Truth be told, there is iron in spinach, but not significantly more than in other greens, and few people can consume spinach in large quantities. A larger problem with the idea of spinach as a good source of iron, however, is that it also contains substances that strongly inhibit the intestinal absorption of iron . . . Simply put, spinach should not at all be the first food choice of those suffering from iron deficiency."[57]

But the story does not end here. Rekdal also found that many academics are not only aware that spinach is low in iron, they attribute the myth that it is high in iron (for human consumption) to a typographical error decades ago. When Rekdal attempted to trace the claim of the misplaced decimal point, he found that earlier researchers had cited secondhand references that were in turn, repeated. While spinach is indeed low in absorbable iron for human consumption, the widespread belief that the myth is the result of a decimal point error has never been verified, yet it has been peddled by academics for decades. He states that the decimal-point myth has become so commonly accepted among academia that it is often repeated without any citation. "In the past 30 years, a large number of apparently independent sources have mutually confirmed the 'fact' that a decimal point error was made, whether it was in 1870, in the 1890s, or in the 1930s. Nothing indicates that the decimal point error ever was made, but the account about it will most likely live a long and colorful life, just like its parent myth, the belief that spinach is a good source of iron."[58]

Rekdal views the digital age as being a double-edged sword in both generating and extinguishing urban legends among academics. While digital technology has made it easier to expose myths, he worries that more scholars may be tempted to take shortcuts and cite sources without having consulted the source. That is, they may have seen a source cited in another source and used the cited source as their own, assuming that it is correct. In the rare instances where errors have been made by the original author, there is a risk of other authors also repeating the erroneous claim. Rekdal states: "Some academic urban legends may perish in the new digital academic environment, but others will thrive and have ideal conditions for explosive growth."[59]

"Lights Out" Gang Initiation, 1993 to present (USA and Worldwide)

Picture yourself driving down a nearly deserted highway late at night. In the gloom, you suddenly realize that a car driving toward you in the opposite lane has no lights on. As a courtesy, you flash your lights to alert the other driver. With a squeal of tires, the other car does a 180-degree turn and speeds up to tailgate you. Riding just behind your car's bumper, the other car is close enough for you to see several gang members in it. The high beams of the gang car suddenly turn on, blinding you. Then your car is rammed from behind, forcing you to swerve off the road. You desperately try to restart the engine as the gang, armed with knives and guns, walk toward you . . .

This nightmare scenario has been popularly believed to be a real one by people worldwide for just over two decades. The "Lights Out" urban legend gained widespread publicity in the second half of 1993. Before the prevalent use of email and social media, the story was most commonly circulated by fax machine, leaving some folklorists to describe it as an example of "faxlore." It was commonly placed as a hardcopy notice pinned up in shop windows and on business notice boards.[60] The warning was also publicized through newspaper reports although the majority of these included statements from police discrediting it. One police chief wittily commented: "I'd rather deal with the gangs than talk to any more hysterical people on the phone."[61]

Urban legends warn us about dangers that are unlikely to happen. The likelihood that a man is hiding underneath your car in a shopping-mall parking lot, waiting to slash your ankles when you return with your arms full of packages, while possible, is highly remote. However there is no real harm if the urban legend causes you to have a heightened sense of your surroundings in order to stay safe. However, believing that you should not alert another driver that their lights are off at night in case they chase you down and kill you could have potential adverse effects. How would you feel if a crash happened due to your inaction out of fear that was based on an urban myth?

Urban legends are powerful social forces that take many forms, from tales of alligators in the sewers to the "Kentucky Fried Rat." A key factor is that while often outlandish, these stories remain plausible. The messages they convey—often on a subconscious level—are enduring cautionary tales that have been repeated over millennia. While the message varies little, the form these stories take may change with the times. For instance, accounts of phantom hitchhikers can be traced all the way back to horse-and-buggy days. But the message is no less topical or relevant; accepting rides from strangers and acting recklessly have been concerns for generations.

In chapter 6, we will shift focus to a very different form of social delusion—the stampede, or panic. The great irony of these forms of collective behavior is that while urban legends are not real but can scare people into acting more responsibly, stampedes and panics are typically triggered by a false alarm. In most instances, if the participants had remained calm and not attempted to flee, they would have likely survived.

CHAPTER 6
STAMPEDES AND PANICS

Mass panics, sometimes referred to as "flights," occur when a group of people react to what they believe is an immediate or imminent threat. In order to qualify as a true panic, members must not only exhibit fear of an object or event but also try to flee from the perceived threat. Immediate threats usually begin and end quickly and last from a few seconds to several minutes. Imminent threats typically have a longer build-up period and are more orderly. For a panic to occur there needs to be a perception of an immediate or impending personal threat to one's physical well-being. At the same time, escape routes are limited or perceived to be limited, which quickly fosters fear, uncertainty, an adrenaline rush, and confusion. Other factors can include fatigue, the degree of plausibility of the perceived threat, and the mass media spreading and often exaggerating the threat.

There are three common types of panics. *Enclosed-space panics* involve such events as yelling "Fire!" in a crowded theater. During such panics, people start moving faster than normal and soon begin pushing and shoving in an uncoordinated manner; a bottleneck develops that clogs exits, dangerous pressure builds up on both people and buildings, and escape is either further slowed or prevented by fallen or injured people who become obstacles.[1] In 2013, a fire at a garment factory in Bangladesh killed over one hundred workers as they jammed a stairwell in a frantic bid to escape.[2] A calm, orderly exit would have almost certainly resulted in far fewer deaths and injuries. This case underscores findings by some researchers that the faster one tries to escape, the longer it takes them to get out (known as the "faster is slower effect").[3]

During enclosed-space panics, some participants are believed to think egocentrically ("every man for himself") and be overcome by fear and a desire to flee the perceived danger. However, a consensus has emerged among researchers that in the overwhelming number of cases in a variety of disaster events, most participants maintain self-control. Lee Clarke observes: "When the ground shakes, sometimes dwellings crumble, fires rage, and people are crushed. Yet people do not run screaming through the streets in a wild attempt to escape the terror, even though they are undoubtedly feeling terror. Earthquakes and tornadoes wreak havoc on entire communities. Yet people do not usually turn against their neighbors or suddenly forget personal ties and moral commitments. Instead the more consistent pattern is that people bind together in the aftermath of disasters, working together to restore their physical environment and their culture to recognizable shapes."[4] However, it must also be said that in many instances (of stampedes, in particular), if the participants had left the premises in a calm, orderly manner, the loss of life would certainly have been far less, and in some instances, perhaps none at all.

Rumors occasionally trigger such panics, such as in August 2005, when thousands of Shiites were crossing a bridge to a sacred shrine in Baghdad. In the wake of a series of recent suicide bombings, the crowd was tense. When a rumor spread that a suicide bomber was among them, a stampede ensued. At least 960 people were killed, either from the crush of the crowd or by drowning in the Tigris River after the bridge railing collapsed.[5]

Diffuse panics affect a wider area, such as a community, region, or country, and are often fueled by mass-media speculation. They can be short-term and last a few hours, or they can endure for weeks or months. One of many contemporary examples of a diffuse panic involves apocalyptic prophecies and occurred in Adelaide, Australia, in the month leading up to January 19, 1976. Many people fled the city and some even sold their homes after "psychic" John Nash predicted that an earthquake and tidal wave would strike on that date at midday. When the designated hour came, nothing happened. In examining the circumstances, many of those who sold their homes or just left to the hills for the day were first-generation Greeks and Italians. Both countries have a long history of devastating earthquakes, and the belief in clairvoyants is generally taken very seriously.[6] Historical examples of diffuse panics include spontaneous mass flights from the city of London that have occurred over the centuries in response to prophecies of the city's destruction by a great flood in 1524, by the Day of Judgment in 1736, and by an earthquake in 1761.

The third type of panics, *small-group panics*, often involve people in cars or houses in isolated areas at night. These people commonly believe that a UFO or monster is stalking them. The 1988 case involving a family who believed they were being chased by a UFO in the remote Nullarbor Desert of South Australia, is one example. Another classic involves a family in Kelly, Kentucky, who on one night in 1955, reported seeing 3-foot-tall space aliens with elephant-like ears prowling outside of their remote farmhouse. Frightened, household members grabbed rifles and began firing indiscriminately at anything that moved for several hours before piling into their car and dashing for help (they didn't have a phone). After a thorough police investigation of the scene, there was no evidence of aliens, only a house pocked with bullet holes and full of jittery family members.

MEMORABLE PANICS

London Earthquake Panic, 1761 (London, England)

Many residents of London became fearful of the city's imminent demise after hearing a prophecy of destruction following two minor earthquakes. The first quake was felt on February 8, 1761 and knocked down several chimneys in the vicinity of Poplar and Limehouse. On March 8, a second quake struck, primarily affecting northern London in the vicinity of Highgate and Hampstead. When citizens began to remark on the coincidence that the two quakes had been exactly one month apart, a soldier named Bell predicted a third quake on April 5. Journalist Charles Mackay wrote that thousands of people believed in the impending disaster. "As the awful day approached, the excitement became intense, and great numbers of credulous people resorted to all the villages within a circuit of twenty miles, awaiting the doom of London."[7] People flocked to the suburbs of Blackheath, Harrow, Highgate, and Islington to secure temporary accommodation and were charged exorbitant fees for their lodgings. Those too poor to pay remained in the city until two or three days prior to the appointed time then left for the relative safety of the surrounding fields where they camped and waited. As the time neared, Mackay stated that "the fear became contagious, and hundreds who had laughed at the prediction a week before, packed up their goods, when they saw others doing so, and hastened away. The river was thought to be a place of great security, and all the merchant vessels in the port were filled with people who passed the night between the 4th and 5th on board, expecting every instant to see St. Paul's totter, and the towers of Westminster Abby rock in the wind and fall amid a cloud of dust."[8] Most people returned to London the following day, but some jittery residents stayed away for another week. Despite his unsuccessful prediction, Bell made a series of other failed predictions, and within several months, he was committed to a mental institution.

Church Stampede, 1902 (Birmingham, Alabama, USA)

On the evening of September 19, 1902, Booker T. Washington was one of the most acclaimed African Americans in the United States. When he was invited to address the annual meeting of the National Baptist Convention, people packed into the Shiloh Negro Baptist Church to hear him speak. The church was cavernous and had a capacity of three thousand. As the aisles and stairwells became jammed beyond capacity, the church pastor, Reverend T. W. Walker, asked police to stop admitting people. But the police, positioned at the front of the church, could not stop the masses from filing in. Washington gave his speech, despite the stifling heat, and as he finished, he received a rousing ovation. What happened next would go down as one of the worst stampedes in American history.[9]

Two men appeared to begin arguing over a seat on stage, when a woman near cried out, "There's a fight!" In the crowded, noisy church, some people mistook the word "fight" for "fire," causing people at the back of the building to begin scrambling for the doors. While there were six exits in the building, most of the crowd pushed for the main entrance. A quick-thinking minister then mounted the rostrum and called out for people to be quiet—repeating the word several times while motioning for everyone to be seated. According to a report in the *Boston Evening Transcript* published the following day, a second misunderstanding took place, making matters worse. "The excited congregation mistook the word 'quiet' for a second alarm of fire and again rushed to the door. Men and women crawled over benches and fought their way into the aisles, and those who had fallen were trampled upon."[10]

Contributing to the crush were those in the overflowing crowd—the hundreds of people that were outside the building and on the front steps. Upon hearing the cries from inside the church, many tried to push inside to see what was happening. At the same time, people inside were desperately trying to push their way out. Usher John Bunn was positioned near the front door when the panic started and called to another usher to try and calm the crowd. He then waded into the mass of humanity and was trampled. "Bunn climbed onto a table and shouted into the mayhem that there was no fire, but he was knocked off the table by people rushing by. He saw a little girl who was 'being squeezed to death' and pushed into the crowd to try and save her."[11] Bunn survived the ordeal and later said: "My last glance saw her in the crowd, wedged as tight as wax."

The panic spread with shouts of fire passing from person to person. Washington was at the front of the church and was unharmed. The church floor was fifteen feet above ground level, with steep steps leading to the sidewalk from the main lobby. The brick walls extending on both sides of the steps turned into death traps. A reporter wrote that those "who had reached the top of the steps were pushed violently forward, and many fell. Before they could move others fell upon them, and in a few moments persons were piled on each other to a height of ten feet where they struggled vainly to extricate themselves. This wall of struggling humanity blocked the entrance, and the weight of 1500 persons in the body of the church was pushed against it."[12] The final death toll was 120: all were African Americans.[13]

The head archivist for the city of Birmingham, James Baggett, described the aftermath. "Within ten minutes the panic was over. Dead bodies lay in the aisles of the church. In the entranceway and around the steps outside, survivors found a massive pile of human beings, some dead, some alive. Two men who had climbed out a window summoned the fire department, and fire wagons quickly responded. More police officers arrived, and a call went out for every available doctor. Survivors and people from the neighborhood helped pull bodies from the piles and bring water to the injured."[14] Baggett also recounts the remarkable story of one of the survivors: Annie Bradford had been trapped beneath a pile of bodies, petrified but alive. She was in a sitting position, but her legs were pinned, and she was unable to move. He recalled that "she waited thirty minutes as doctors examined those on top of her, pronounced them dead, and had them taken away." Within a week, Bradford had recovered.

Baggett described the eerie scene as rescuers laid bodies in a nearby florist garden. "Worried family members looking for relatives stumbled among the bodies in the darkness, holding lanterns or matches to the dead faces. Some faces bore heel marks from being stepped on in the rush. Others who died inside the church were laid on pews. The city's ambulances were overwhelmed by the number of dead and injured."[15]

Some blamed the episode on the two men who were seen to be fighting at the front of the church. The two men were a Baltimore lawyer named Judge Ballou and a choir member, Will Hicks. Ballou claimed that Hicks had ordered him and a friend to move from their seats, verbally abused him, and grabbed him by his coat. Hicks fled Birmingham on the night of the tragedy. No person or agency accepted blame for the tragedy. A statement issued by the Birmingham Fire Department read that the disaster was unforeseeable, noting that they were "sorry to acknowledge that the unfortunate circumstances were entirely beyond the control of human power."[16] The police also weighed in and said that "every precaution was taken to prevent any possible damage to life and property."

In the sad days of mourning that followed, there was one bright note. John Bunn, the usher who had valiantly tried to save the little girl but had failed, was greeted on the street by a woman who called out: "Mr. Bunn, you saved my daughter." Bunn was resigned to the fact that the little girl had perished, but she had somehow survived. It was a small sliver of light in an otherwise dark and gloomy episode.[17]

Iroquois Theater Fire, December 30, 1903 (Chicago, Illinois, USA)

Less than a month after the Grand Theater's opening in 1903, tragedy struck during an afternoon performance of the musical *Mr. Bluebeard, Jr.* A hot light ignited part of the stage set, and the fire quickly began spreading. Despite pleas made by an actor to keep calm and stay in their seats, the capacity audience of 1,900 patrons—mostly women and children—soon stampeded for the exits. Within fifteen minutes, 602 people were dead.[18] Ironically, the fire department had extinguished the blaze within thirty minutes, and most people did not die from smoke or flames, but rather from having been trampled to death. If audience members had remained calm and stayed in their seats, perhaps no one would have lost their life. People panicked and were unable to open the exit doors that were frozen shut from below-zero temperatures, setting the backdrop for the brutal crush.

According to one description of the events, those in the balcony were particularly at risk. "The fire escape ladders could not accommodate the crowd, and many fell or jumped to death on the pavement below. Some were not killed, only because they landed on the cushion of bodies of those who had gone before."[19] In some stairways, "particularly where a turn caused a jam, bodies were piled seven or eight feet deep. An occasional living person was found in the heap, but most of these were terribly injured. The heel prints on the dead faces mutely testified to the cruel fact that human animals stricken by terror are as mad and ruthless as stampeding cattle. Many bodies had the clothes torn from them, and some had the flesh trodden from their bones." According to disaster expert Angus Gunn, the incident was made even more ironic by claims made before the tragedy that the building was fireproof. However, regardless of whether or not the building was actually fireproof, it should be remembered that it was the reaction to the fire rather than the fire itself that had caused the large loss of life.[20]

Invasion Panic and Riot, 1949 (Quito, Ecuador)

On Saturday evening, February 12, 1949, one of the most remarkable panics in modern history took place in Quito, Ecuador. The incident, which involved a massive panic over what was widely believed to have been an invasion from Martians, made headlines around the world. On February 14, the *New York Times* published the following front-page headline: "Mars Raiders Caused Quito Panic; Mob Burns Radio Plant, Kills 15."[21] The tragic events unfolded after a radio station broadcast a realistic drama that was based on the famous science-fiction novel by H. G. Wells, *The War of the Worlds*, in which Martians invade earth. At the time, Quito had a population of 175,000. According to a journalist on the scene, when people listened to the program and became frightened, it "drove most of the population of Quito into the streets" in a desperate effort to escape what they had been led to believe were Martian "gas raids."[22] Fake news reports claimed that the Martians approached the city after landing twenty miles away in the community of Latacunga, leaving it a wasteland.

Broadcast in Spanish on Radio Quito, the drama was highly realistic and included impersonations of government leaders, local officials, and even journalists. The names of actual places were also mentioned as reporters offered vivid descriptions of the scene. Fear turned to anger as many residents became enraged after learning the true nature of the broadcast. Crowds formed and began to march toward the radio station while chanting, "Down with the radio." Some people were still donning their nightgowns. One group surrounded the building that housed the radio station—the La Previsora Tower and hurled stones through windows, forcing those who had not already escaped to move to the third floor.[23] Wads of paper were set alight and tossed into the building, As the smoke and fire reached the third floor, the people trapped there became desperate. Some leaped to their deaths in an effort to escape the advancing flames. Others saved themselves by forming a human chain with their arms and legs down the side of the building. Some people lost their grip and plunged to the ground.[24] One of the survivors was the radio station's director of programing, Leonardo Páez. Faced with almost certain death, Páez used quick thinking to survive. He wrapped his body in paper from the massive rolls used in the printing presses from the newspaper that was also housed in the same building. He then leaped out of a window and landed on several people in the street, which helped to break his fall. He survived the jump, but he did suffer serious injuries.[25]

Authorities were slow in responding to the attack on the building as the majority of police and soldiers had been dispatched to the countryside to repel the Martians. By the time order was restored with tanks and tear gas, twenty people had died and upward of fifty were hurt.[26] At least four security guards received head wounds, while police and firefighters were also injured.[27] The nation's largest newspaper, *El Comercio*—which owned the radio station and was housed in the same building—was also destroyed along with the daily paper *Ultimas Noticias*.[28]

The drama sounded like a typical radio broadcast that was interspersed with news reports, and it began when a special bulletin interrupted regular programing: "Here is an urgent piece of late news."[29] Kenneth MacHarg describes how the program slowly drew listeners into believing that they were being invaded. "Two popular singers began what appeared to be a program of live music, but were soon interrupted with the news that an observatory in the United States had noted strange, unidentified objects flying toward the earth. During a second song, the announcer again interrupted to report that objects had now been sighted over the Galapagos Islands, off the coast of Ecuador. The third song had barely begun when reports were broadcast that a saucer had landed in the Quito suburb of Cotocollao."[30]

The report continued: "The airbase at Mariscal Sucre has been taken by the enemy and it is being destroyed. There are many dead and wounded. It is about to be wiped out."[31] The epicenter of the invasion was reported to have been the town of Cotocollao, an outer suburb of Quito to the northwest. A voice resembling the mayor of Quito urged residents to evacuate before the attackers reached the city. "People of Quito, let us defend our city. Our women and children must go out into the surrounding heights to leave the men free for action and combat."[32] A reporter later wrote that residents then "began fleeing from their homes and running through the streets. Many were clad only in night clothing."[33] After the radio station was flooded with phone calls from frightened listeners, station employees realized that they had a serious situation on their hands, but they failed to discontinue the drama. Instead, they broke in at intervals with disclaimers, announcing that what listeners were hearing was just a drama. Ironically, many listeners never heard the disclaimers as they had already fled for their lives. While panic was reported nationwide, it was worst in Quito given its proximity to the supposed attack. Hundreds of people in the countryside were reported to have sought refuge by fleeing into the mountains.[34] Police arrested at least sixteen people for their alleged role in the broadcast or for rioting.[35]

Lima Soccer Panic and Riot, 1964 (Peru)

The worst soccer riot in sporting history took place at a stadium in Lima, Peru, during an Olympic qualifying match between Peru and Argentina on May 24, 1964. The violence broke out near the end of the game before a crowd of forty-five thousand people. Argentina was leading one to nil with two minutes remaining when suddenly Peru scored, sending fans in the stands into joyous celebrations— until the goal was disallowed. A man well-known to fans, jumped onto the pitch and ran after the referee. He was subdued by police with batons. As spectators moved toward the pitch, police reportedly fired canisters of tear gas in a vain attempt to disperse the crowd. At the same time, police also tried to guide the fans toward exits using Alsatian dogs, but the move backfired because the gates had been locked to keep people from trying to gain illegal entry.[36]

According to sports historian John Nauright, firing tear gas into the stands triggered a stampede as people fled to get away from the fumes. Hundreds of people died in the stairwells due to the locked gates, and several police officers were killed as riots spread across the city. Many of those who managed to get out of the stadium formed angry mobs that vandalized cars and busses. Order was only restored after the government called out the military and imposed a curfew.[37] Police Commander Jorge de Asumbuja later denied that he ordered tear gas to be fired into the stands. He blamed the mass trampling and suffocation of victims on the locked gates.[38] While estimates of the number of deaths vary, later reports agree that more than three hundred people died and at least five hundred were injured. The tension before the match had been high due to the stakes: Peru needed only to attain a draw for the team to advance and qualify to play at the Tokyo Olympics. The referee, Ángel Eduardo Pazos initially ordered the match to be suspended as objects were being tossed onto the pitch, and the two teams were escorted to safety. Soon after, the pitch was invaded.

Hajj Stampede, July 2, 1990 (Mecca, Saudi Arabia)

The Hajj (Arabic for pilgrimage) is the fifth pillar of Islam, and according to the Muslim holy book, the Koran, any follower who is healthy enough and can afford to, has a duty to make the trek to Mecca to pay homage to Allah. The exact dates vary from year to year but always occur during the last month of the Islamic calendar. On July 2, 1990, five thousand followers were in a pedestrian tunnel leading to a series of Holy sites. The tunnel was five hundred yards long and designed to hold only one thousand people. As pilgrims began pushing forward, several fell at the entrance, blocking their path. As crowd members turned back and began moving in the opposite direction, they collided with other pilgrims. Suddenly, the electricity failed, plunging the tunnel into darkness and cutting off the air conditioning system. During the ensuing panic, 1,426 worshippers were either trampled to death or suffocated.[39] Access to clearly marked emergency exists, backup generators, and the use of more guides familiar with evacuation procedures could have prevented the tragedy. Stampede experts have analyzed several Mecca stampedes and suggest creating "pressure release valves" where structures can open in the event of a crush, and having smaller entry points and larger exit areas. Some experts also recommend that intersecting crowds (cross flows), should be minimized by creating lanes like on a roadway.[40]

E2 Nightclub Panic, February 17, 2003 (Chicago, Illinois, USA)

Chicago's Epitome restaurant and its E2 nightclub directly above on the second floor were popular gathering spots in 2003. But in the early morning hours of February 17—ladies' night, where women were allowed free admission—a crowd crush would develop, leaving twenty-one people dead from compressional asphyxiation. Fifty-seven others were injured. The tragedy began at about 2:00 a.m. after a fight erupted and poorly trained security personnel used pepper spray to quell the disturbance. The spray reached the overhead fans and was dispersed over a wide area. As people in the vicinity of the spray were choking, and some even vomited, excited patrons made matters worse by yelling that the spray was from a chemical attack by terrorists. The event took place less than a year and a half after the September 11 attacks on the United States. Pandemonium ensued as an estimated 1,100 to 1,500 people raced down a narrow second-floor stairway and began piling up. Alcohol impairment, dim lighting, and a smoky haze further contributed to the state of panic and confusion.[41] Most people died after being crushed in a small lobby at the top of the stairs; others were crushed at the bottom of the stairs. One security guard, who was over six feet tall, said that bodies were piled higher than he was, while another person caught in the crush told of being trapped in the doorway for forty-five minutes until people and bodies could be removed.[42] An analysis of the incident revealed that the primary exits on the second floor of the club were inadequate and that some secondary exits were locked. According to one report, the manager had ordered "that the two back exit doors be locked to stop staff from freelancing cover charges and letting people inside."[43] Local fire officials had recently obtained a court order stopping the second floor of the club from being used.

Russian Invasion Panic, 2010 (Republic of Georgia)

On Saturday evening, March 13, 2010, fear and panic swept through parts of the former Soviet Republic of Georgia following a half-hour television report that claimed Russian troops had crossed the border and were invading. The timing of the scare was critical in creating widespread fear as political tensions between the two countries were high. Just two years earlier, in August 2008, Russian troops actually had invaded Georgia. The realistic broadcast included archival film footage from 2008, including that of Russian troops and tanks crossing the border and planes shelling the capital. Also included was earlier footage of US President Barack Obama urging the Russians to cease hostilities and remarks by Prime Minister Vladimir Putin and Russian President Dmitry Medvedev. Archival footage of Georgian citizens fleeing the fighting in 2008 also fueled fears.

The program included a disclaimer at the beginning and end of the broadcast, but many viewers did not notice that the events they were viewing had happened two years earlier. Station officials later billed the program as a "simulation" of what could happen if the Russians were to invade again. An announcer also claimed that the Georgian president had been assassinated and the opposition leaders had formed a new government that was pro-Russian. During the program, a news anchor provided regular "updates" on the latest known positions of the Russian forces who had reportedly bombed the main airport in the city of Tbilisi.

The broadcast began at eight o'clock with the following statement: "Good evening. This is a breaking-news edition of 'The Chronicle.' In a few minutes, President Saakashvili is expected to make a special statement on the situation in the country. We don't know if it's going to be a recorded or a written message. It's being reported that the Russian troops deployed at Leningor have been put on combat alert."[44]

Georgian president Mikheil Saakashvili, who claimed to have been distressed over the broadcast, said he was "very concerned and alarmed of what he saw on TV. I understand the position of the journalists. I understand that it is possible to make such projects, but it mustn't impact the population of the country. No one must pour oil on the fire and cause alarm among the people. This is a very sensitive topic."[45] The president apologized for the show in a nationwide broadcast, but claimed he was not responsible. Critics were skeptical of these claims given the government's strict control of state-run television.[46]

The Reuters news agency described the fake broadcast as "a barely disguised swipe at opponents of Saakashvili who recently met Russian Prime Minister Vladimir Putin in Moscow and called for the countries to restore ties."[47] This view was bolstered the very next day when Saakashvili shied away from his earlier apology and identified the Russian government as the true enemy of the people. "But the major unpleasant thing about yesterday's report—and I want everyone to realize it well—was that this report is maximally close to reality and maximally close to what may really happen, or to what Georgia's enemy keeps in mind."[48]

Sarah Marcus, a journalist for the United Kingdom-based *Telegraph*, said that news of the "attack" spread rapidly. "I heard when my neighbour, in a state of distress, knocked on my door to tell me about it, someone else saw people on the street begin to run in panic, the mobile phone networks crashed as everyone tried to contact friends and family. The emergency services reported a peak in calls from people who'd suffered heart attacks." She observed that during the scare, friends with parents in the city of Gori, which had been significantly affected by the real invasion in 2008, were frantic at what they believed to be a Russian takeover. Her brother and a friend even "tried to work out how to gather enough money to get their parents out of the city by taxi—presuming taxis would already be charging rack rates to go in and out of Gori, as they did during the real war."[49]

Journalist Matthew Collin was in the capital when the scare occurred. He described the scene: "People rushed out of cinemas. They rushed out of theaters. The mobile phone networks briefly crashed. Some people in the region where the war actually happened actually got ready to flee their homes yet again, and there were several reports of people having a heart attack."[50] The editor of the Georgian *Messenger* newspaper, Zaza Gachechiladze said: "People were completely shocked. I was driving to my friend's party when I got a phone call telling me to turn on the TV." He immediately raced home. "I rushed upstairs. There was Dmitry Medvedev saying that Russia was intervening in Georgia. I didn't notice this was old footage from August 2008. I immediately started looking for my children."[51] Gachechiladze was infuriated by the hoax. "It was a very cruel simulation. One lady whose son was in the army had a heart attack and died. Another pregnant lady lost her baby. Many children were taken to hospital suffering from stress. It was horrible what happened, actually. It is a criminal act that should be punished."

A Russian Foreign Ministry spokesman, Andrei Nesterenko, was scathing in his criticism of the program, characterizing it as "irresponsible and immoral primarily with regard to the Georgian public as it provoked quite understandable panic."[52] He expressed suspicion that the broadcast was approved without the knowledge of President Saakashvili. "The opinion is widely spread in Georgia that the provocation on Imedi [TV] could not have been aired without approval from the authorities," and noted that "The Georgian president does not conceal his supportive attitude to the scandal-making program describing its scenario as realistic to the utmost."

Stampedes and panics may be the shortest-lived forms of social delusions, but they are arguably the most destructive, tragic, and preventable.

In chapter 7, we will look at one form of conversion disorder: anxiety hysteria, which involves a short-lived collective stress reaction to the sudden appearance of a perceived threat. Unlike motor hysteria, there is no preexisting tension. The symptoms soon subside and most commonly involve headache, dizziness, fainting, abdominal pain, and shortness of breath.

CHAPTER 7

ANXIETY HYSTERIA: THE POWER OF SUDDEN FEAR

Mass hysteria is the rapid spread of "conversion hysteria," a term coined by psychoanalyst Sigmund Freud, where illness symptoms appear with no physical cause. Known today as conversion disorder, this well-documented condition involves the converting of psychological conflict into involuntary physical symptoms without a corresponding organic basis. Psychiatrists have identified two common types of conversion disorder: anxiety hysteria and motor hysteria. Motor hysteria appears gradually over time and usually takes weeks or months to subside. It appears in settings where people are repressed and have no way to channel their emotions. Twitching, shaking, and trance states are common. While in this chapter we will focus on anxiety hysteria, both anxiety and motor hysteria share distinct features, the presence of which are reliable indicators of an outbreak. In both forms, there is no plausible organic basis for the physical complaints. Symptoms are transient and benign—in other words they come and go rapidly and are relatively harmless. Episodes most often occur in a segregated group which is undergoing extreme stress. Symptoms tend to spread by sight or sound and commonly begin in older or higher-status persons.

Anxiety hysteria is of shorter duration, usually lasting no more than a few days, and is triggered by the sudden perception of a threatening agent, most commonly a strange odor. Symptoms typically include headache, dizziness, nausea, breathlessness, and general weakness. Outbreaks were rarely reported prior to the twentieth century but have dramatically increased in Western and other developed countries. Incidents occur with little prior warning, so there is usually not much preexisting group tension. Most reported episodes are in schools or factories.

Outbreaks of anxiety hysteria usually begin with illness symptoms in a single student or factory worker and spread rapidly to others nearby who experience a variety of stress-related complaints. Symptoms of the first person to be affected (the index case) are often dramatic, giving rise to sudden fear among workers or classmates. Often the first person affected has a medical condition such as an epileptic fit, schizophrenia, tonsillitis, or heat stroke. The rest of the group is usually not aware of this. Information about the specific cause of the symptoms is typically unknown and is only learned later. Soon after the appearance of the index case, others begin to attribute the cause to a strange odor that is assumed to represent a toxic gas or an agent such as a communicable illness, both of which are believed to pose an immediate personal threat to the other workers or students. Commonly, food poisoning from the school or factory cafeteria is indicted. Rumors often spread like wild fire. Television and newspaper reports, recent events, local traditions, and superstitious beliefs exacerbate the situation.

In non-Western countries such as Malaysia, odors or food poisoning are rarely suspected. Instead, suspicion falls on an array of diminutive supernatural entities. In such settings, the index case typically exhibits screaming, crying, and overbreathing after seeing what is believed to be such spirits. Fellow pupils assume that the index subject is hexed or charmed, or that a ghost is roaming the school, triggering sudden, extreme anxiety as it is assumed that they may be the next victims. The search for potential explanations among pupils is limited only by plausibility, as the lack of educational and life experiences can foster hypotheses that are potentially fantastic to adults or individuals living outside of the culture or subcultural milieu. Students who are in the closest spatial, visual, or social contact with the index case and subsequent fallen cohorts are most susceptible to developing symptoms. In the majority of cases, investigators identify a downward spread of symptoms along the age scale, with the oldest students affected first, followed by younger classmates. In Kenya, anxiety hysteria outbreaks are common and usually blamed on ghosts who are believed to strangle students, who are, in actuality, simply hyperventilating.

Most outbreaks of anxiety hysteria last a single day and rarely more than a week. Lengthier cases or episodes involving relapses appear related to the inability of medical, school, and community leaders to convince the affected workers, or students and their parents, of the psychogenic nature of the symptoms. In rare instances where the imaginary agent is believed to persist, or authorities are not perceived to have thoroughly examined the premises, cases can endure sporadically for several weeks or months. Episodes of mass anxiety hysteria cease rapidly once the students are reassured that the phantom threat, most typically a harmless odor, has been eliminated or never existed.

Since the early twentieth century, anxiety hysteria episodes have been dominated by environmental concerns over food, air, and water quality, especially exaggerated or imaginary fears involving mysterious smells. Outbreaks have a rapid onset and recovery and involve the symptoms of anxiety. Unsubstantiated claims of strange odors and gassings were a common contemporary trigger of hysteria outbreaks in schools. A typical incident occurred in 1985, at a Singaporean secondary school when pupils were suddenly stricken with chills, headaches, nausea, and breathlessness. Tests of the school and the students all came back negative. The episode began when several pupils noticed a strange smell and occurred amid a preexisting rumor that a gas had infiltrated the school from a nearby building site.[1] This incident is similar to a mystery gas at a Hong Kong school a few years earlier affecting more than 355 students ages six to fourteen. Before the outbreak, there were rumors of a recent toxic-gas scare at a nearby school. Several teachers had even discussed the incident with their pupils—some to the point of advising them on what action to take if it should hit their school.[2]

On July 8, 1972, stench from a pigsty may have triggered an outbreak of stomach pains, nausea, faintness, and headaches at an English schoolchildren's gala.[3] That same year, headaches and overbreathing affecting sixteen pupils at a school in Tokyo, Japan, was traced to smog. A 1994 episode of breathing problems among twenty-three students in a female dormitory at an Arab school in the United Arab Emirates was triggered by a "toxic fire" that turned out to be the harmless smell of incense.[4] The perceived threatening agent must be seen as credible to the affected group. On any given school day, a fainting student would not be expected to trigger anxiety hysteria. Yet, if this occurred during the 1991 Persian Gulf War, and it coincided with the detection of a strange odor in the building, many of the naive schoolchildren might exhibit sudden, extreme anxiety after assuming that it was an Iraqi poison-gas attack. This is just what happened at a Rhode Island elementary school during the Gulf War, coinciding with intense publicity about chemical weapons attacks on Israel and the possibility of US terrorist attacks.[5]

Since the early twentieth century, strange odors have been a common trigger of anxiety hysteria in job settings, with environmental pollutant fears leading to lost productivity time. An outbreak of breathing problems in male military recruits at their California army barracks in 1988 happened when the air was laden with a heavy odor from brush fires that was mistaken for toxic fumes. A chance event combined to worsen the situation. Some recruits were "resuscitated" in the early confusion as medics had wrongly assessed their conditions to have been grave. These factors created more anxiety and further breathing problems. A study of the incident showed that those who saw the "resuscitations" or witnessed others exhibiting symptoms were three times more likely to report symptoms themselves.

What is the best way to handle short-lived outbreaks of anxiety hysteria? School and factory administrators should seek the cooperation of staff leaders, medical authorities, and respected community members to reassure those affected and the community at large that the agent believed to pose a threat was either imaginary or no longer exists. In non-Western countries, the services of witch-doctors or native healers are often rendered and may provide reassurance, although, on occasion, they may make things worse.

MEMORABLE EXAMPLES OF ANXIETY HYSTERIA

Hypnosis Hysteria, October 1944 (Philadelphia, Pennsylvania, USA)

A group of students from Springfield High School near Philadelphia took a field trip to see a hypnosis demonstration in the city in October 1944. During the show, the hypnotist, E. K. Ernst, asked thirty-five students (thirty-four of whom were girls) to focus on a spot on the ceiling above the stage, then waved his hands, compelling thirty-one of them to collapse. Many students were crying or laughing, and they continued to be excited and agitated for the next two hours. The examining physician, Dr. James Ellzey, worked with the school nurse to calm those affected. He was convinced that the students were not experiencing mass hypnosis, but were instead suffering from mass suggestion, apparently believing they were still in a trance.[6]

Curiously, several similar incidents have been recorded over the years. At Ipswich High School in Massachusetts on January 16, 1953, at least two dozen pupils, fearing they were under the hypnotist's control, reported "drowsiness and emotional upset," although medical exams were unremarkable and the students soon recovered.[7] In June 2012, a private girls' school in Quebec, Canada, was the scene of an end-of–the-school-year activity that appeared to go horribly wrong. Twenty-year-old hypnotist Maxime Nadeau was performing at the Collège du Sacré-Coeur in Sherbooke before an audience of twelve- and thirteen-year-olds. All seemed well until the show ended and several audience members appeared to be still in trances. One girl reported feeling "spaced out," while another said it was as if she was having an "out-of-body experience."[8] The girls continued to feel strange, so later that day, another hypnotist, Richard Whitbread, was brought to the school. Whitbread reportedly "went through the process of making the girls think they were being re-hypnotized and then brought them out using a stern voice." Whitbread noted that the original hypnotist was young and handsome, which may have influenced the impressionable girls to follow his instructions. Once again, it would appear to have been an example of mass suggestion rather than "mass hypnosis."

The Thanksgiving Song Festival, November 23, 1959 (Stillwater, Oklahoma, USA)

On Monday evening, November 23, 1959, 5,400 high-school chorus members from across Oklahoma, converged on the field house of Oklahoma State University to attend the annual Thanksgiving Song Festival. An estimated two hundred buses were parked outside the stadium, waiting for their students. The weather was typical for November—cool. As a result, about halfway through the program, as the temperatures dropped, many of the bus drivers started their engines so the busses would be warm by the time the event was over and the students arrived back to the vehicles for the ride home. At this juncture, diesel fumes were sucked into the stadium's air intake fans causing a smell to permeate the stadium. The strange odor frightened many students, who began fainting, and the stadium was evacuated. Observers noted that many students appeared to have been unaffected by the fumes and calmly left the stadium, only to feel ill once they got outside after seeing their friends ill. Over five hundred students who were taken to area hospitals were examined and quickly released, except for a few who were kept for observation overnight. The chorus director for Stillwater High School, G. C. Epperly, attributed the episode to "a combination of too many hot dogs, a little carbon monoxide and a lot of mass hysteria."[9]

Merphos Poisoning Scare, 1973 (New Zealand)

On January 26, 1973, the cargo ship *Good Navigator* left a port in Mexico, bound for Sydney, Australia, with a consignment of fifty drums of the chemical Merphos, a commonly used pesticide and defoliant. On February 10, some of the drums were damaged when the vessel was buffeted by strong winds and heavy seas. The ship was diverted to Auckland, New Zealand, where it arrived on February 26. Wharf workers immediately noticed a sickly sweet odor onboard and refused to unload the cargo, fearing possible exposure to harmful chemicals. After being promised two dollars extra per hour plus protective respirators and clothing, workers went ahead with the job. The drums were loaded on two trucks and taken to a temporary storage place near the waterfront edge of the inner-city suburb of Parnell. At this juncture, there was confusion as to exactly what chemicals were in the drums and how harmful they were, but it was widely reported that the chemicals were toxic, and correspondingly, hundreds of residents reported feeling ill.[10]

As the sickly sweet smell spread as far as Grafton Bridge in the inner city, and people reported feeling ill, the decision was made to evacuate a four-block area of Parnell. By early afternoon on February 27, an extended area was sealed off. Parnell had effectively become a ghost town. Some residents and office workers insisted they were not in any danger. "We've been smelling that for hours," said one.[11] Police, fire, and ambulance staff were only allowed in the area for a maximum of one hour at a time. "That's about all they can stand," said another resident.

On the morning of February 28, the Parnell fumes scare dominated the news with dramatic headlines. Four thousand people had been evacuated. Hundreds had been treated for symptoms—half at Auckland City Hospital and half on-site by ambulance staff. In all, twenty-three streets were evacuated, and many residents of nearby streets had chosen to leave and stay with relatives or friends.[12] Evacuees from young children to the elderly were temporarily housed at the Pitt Street Ambulance Station in central Auckland City. The feelings of most were probably summed up by ninety-five-year-old Mrs. N. A. Ha'ul: "All I want to do is to get back to my room, but they won't let us yet. It is not safe."[13] An elderly couple—a Mr. and Mrs. Carlton, were the first locals affected. Many people, including police and firemen, felt ill and were rushed to the hospital.[14]

As the evacuation spread and shops closed, more and more people began to complain of symptoms, most prominently headaches, nausea, chest tightness, weakness, vomiting, fatigue, and sore eyes. Mrs. Carlton observed: "They deposited the tanks right outside our place. I could have thought of better presents [it was their fiftieth wedding anniversary]. Right away we noticed the peculiar smell. Next thing the place was bedlam with fire trucks and policemen all over. . . . more policemen came around and told us we had to clear out. It was all terribly confusing. So when I told them my friend, Mrs. Kath Williams, was still in her house opposite. They tried to tell me Mrs. Williams wasn't there but we went over and there she was with all the windows closed, almost out on the floor. They gave her oxygen and I was feeling sick and giddy and so they sent us both off to hospital."[15]

Auckland University psychiatrist R. W. McLeod would later conclude that the outbreak was an episode of mass hysteria fueled by confusion over exactly what was in the containers. Evidence that the contents of the containers was relatively harmless has been noted by McLeod who later wrote that before the ship docked in Parnell, "The captain knew the drums were leaking because of the smell which came over the ship. It should be noted that the chemical leaking from the drums and the fumes from the chemicals did not appear to produce any untoward effects amongst the crew," despite that they were continuously subjected to the fumes over two weeks![16]

Further evidence of the harmless nature of the chemicals can be found in the reaction by animals. In the rush to evacuate, many people left their pets behind. Owners asked the Society for the Prevention of Cruelty to Animals (SPCA) to collect them. "We have received numerous calls and the ambulance vehicle is coming and going all the time. We will stay on duty as long as we are required. Of course it is very difficult to find cats which are running around outside," said Mr. A. G. Hill, SPCA secretary.[17] The SPCA was looking after twenty pets—cats, dogs, and birds. "None of the animals appeared to be suffering from any ill effects," stated Mr. Hill.[18] "I was collecting animals until 10:30 last night and I have been doing the same all day today," said SPCA chief inspector Mr. J. G. Doughty.[19]

It is surely significant that Mr. Doughty repeatedly went into and out of the evacuated area but never fell ill. Also, there were no reports at any time during the four-day crisis or afterward of pets left behind having died or becoming sick. If the chemical fumes were real, it would be expected that they would have a significant effect on the pets that stayed in the area, as they have a smaller body mass than humans. The alleged poisonous fumes were curiously selective.

Ten people collapsed in the central city (outside the Parnell cordon), but thousands of others around them were not affected.[20] Some firemen were taken to the hospital. One, Trevor Dowdy, attended a callout to a rugby-club fire. He collapsed at the scene. He had been on duty for a long time. Maurice Doughty worked from 10:00 a.m. to 6:00 p.m. and then was back working after only two hours sleep. "I got the odd sit-down yesterday, but by the evening I was tired out. I saw a number of men affected—they just seemed to change, losing all energy," he said.[21] Clearly exhaustion was a major factor in the firemen who apparently fell sick from the alleged fumes.

Between February 27 and March 4, 643 supposed victims of the fumes were treated at Auckland City Hospital. Forty-nine were diagnosed as having organophosphorus poisoning symptoms (excessive salivation and sweating, muscle weakness and fatigue, nausea, vomiting, diarrhea, blurring of vision with constricted pupils). Another 192 were diagnosed with butyl mercaptan poisoning (headache, dizziness, dry mouth, and throat constriction). Significantly, it was not possible to be specific about the symptoms of the remaining 402 patients.[22]

In stark contrast to the hundreds of Aucklanders up to a mile away from the leaking drums who were reportedly struck down by the fumes, the crew of the ship were totally unharmed and unconcerned. "We have been living with the leaking drums for 17 days and it has hurt no one," said Captain A. Karantis.[23] The fact that the unconcerned crew were in close proximity to the leaking drums for an extended time and were unaffected, while people in Parnell much farther away from the drums for a much shorter time felt sick and had varied illness symptoms after sensing the smell, strongly indicates mass suggestion was the true cause.

One article in particular must have alarmed many in the community. One of several stories about the fumes crisis to make the front page of the morning newspapers appeared in the *New Zealand Herald* and was titled "Launched by the Nazis." It stated that DEF, the defoliant mistakenly blamed for the fumes, is "one of the organophosphorus group of compounds developed from the German nerve gas formulations of the Second World War."[24] The article then detailed the symptoms that could be expected of DEF poisoning: "Mild exposure causes headache, loss of appetite, nausea, weakness, dizziness, blurred vision and a decrease in the size of the pupils of the eyes. A moderate attack will cause vomiting, abdominal cramps and diarrhoea, increased production of saliva, running eyes, sweating, shortness of breath, tightness across the chest, slow pulse, tremors and cramps in the muscles, and staggering."[25]

By March 1 the crisis was largely over. The drums had been removed. Despite the odd whiff of fumes in the air, most residents were allowed to return to their homes. Only five streets were still cordoned off. Food that was suspected to have been contaminated was left out on the pavement for collection. Not everyone was convinced it was safe. "I don't think I would bring my wife and children back here. Some say the smell is stronger than before," said a young policeman.[26] Contaminated concrete and soil from the site where the drums had been originally dumped were to be removed and taken to the local garbage dump. Civil Defence coordinator Mr. G. O. Sims said none of the material would be removed until it was determined to be harmless after testing. "Samples were taken at various depths and then taken to the [Department of Scientific and Industrial Research] laboratory for testing," he said.[27]

By March 3, the last remaining evacuated residents were told they could return. Although Red Cross workers were still in the area, the Civil Defence emergency operation was scaled down.[28] Concerns about long-term health impacts were downplayed by Dr. R. F. Moody of Auckland City Hospital who said there was "no evidence of any harm resulting to anyone . . . or of nerve damage and none is expected. There is also no evidence of nerve damage from any who had physical contact with the chemical."[29]

At midnight on March 4, the state of emergency was lifted by the Civil Defence minister.[30] While an investigation into the incident later suggested mass poisoning, the evidence overwhelmingly favors mass hysteria. Dr. McLeod notes that confusion over the toxicity of what was in the drums was a major factor in the outbreak of symptoms, which were due to anxiety. Misinformation about the case had sent officials in New Zealand on a roller-coaster ride of fear and confusion. For instance, on February 26, an urgent telegram was sent to Australia to ascertain the contents of the drums. The response: "Good Navigator re damaged drums marked VAL/-54/SYD ex Manzanillo, contents, being herphos, chemical herbicide, no other description available." Unfortunately, the freight manager was not satisfied with the response and assumed that "herphos" was really "merphos." He looked up merphos in a chemical dictionary and it referred to tributyl phosphorotrithioite—a cotton defoliant that was "probably highly toxic."[31] By 4:15 pm on February 26, the same agent responded with further information: good news— the drums contained tributyl phosphorotrithioite—which was only mildly toxic. Soon after, a health department representative mistakenly concluded that the drums contained parathion, a highly toxic chemical.[32] By midday on February 27, Australian officials assured concerned health representatives in New Zealand that the compound had a very low toxicity. An analysis of the compound was soon obtained, and it was found to be relatively harmless.

However, not long after receiving word that there was nothing to worry about, a telex message from Australia brought alarming news: "Good Navigator— Merphos—have now been in contact with head chemist Amalgamated Chemicals, Sydney, who advises as follows: To neutralise, flush with water, douche with soda ash. This will not remove the smell which can be partly neutralised by douching with sodium hydrochlorate. He informs that this chemical is highly toxic and that if inhaled in large quantity could be fatal."

Under the circumstances, one cannot fault New Zealand health officials for erring on the side of caution, though in retrospect, the evidence for mass hysteria is overwhelming. In addition to the conflicting information being received from Australia, it is noteworthy that the compound involved—butyl mercaptan (buta-nethiol)—has a terrible smell and is the major component found in the spray of skunks.[33] In his final report on the outbreak, Dr. McLeod observed that despite the inquiry's findings of poisoning, "the signs and symptoms which were recorded may also be associated with fear, anxiety, exhaustion, and possibly to the use of respirators and protective clothing. Failure to show reduced cholinesterase levels and the non-toxic effects on several people who would otherwise be thought to have been rendered sick by their proximity to the fumes adds further evidence to the idea that the whole episode was more related to mass panic than to toxic phenomena."[34] In fact, there were many people who, unaware of the emergency, remained in the affected area at the height of the fume exposure and did not get sick. In another instance, a truck driver came into contact with the compound and remained symptom free.[35]

Football Swoon, September 12, 1952 (Natchez, Mississippi, USA)

During a Friday-night football game between two rival high schools, 165 cheer-leaders suddenly fainted. The incident happened at the end of the first quarter when the cheerleaders from the visiting team—the Neville High "Tigers" from Monroe, Louisiana—came onto the field to perform. They were under the mistaken belief that it was halftime, and they were embarrassingly asked to return to the sidelines over the loudspeakers.[36] One observer said that the girls, ages fourteen to eighteen, then "fainted like flies."[37] Ambulances and private cars rushed the girls to a nearby hospital where examinations proved unremarkable and they quickly recovered. A physician at the hospital, James Barnes, surmised that once the first two girls fainted, "mass hysteria" took over, prompted by a confluence of factors including the heat, the excitement of the occasion, and the sudden distress of seeing their class-mates collapse.[38] While food poisoning was initially suspected as the girls had eaten hamburgers at a local establishment prior to the game, the possibility was ruled out after their rapid recovery.[39] Neville High won the game, 21–8.

A remarkably similar incident took place during halftime of a tense, fiercely fought high-school football game between two rivals when a marching band suddenly collapsed. The incident happened on a hot, humid Friday night on September 21, 1973, with the score 7–6 in favor of the home team. The performance began with the visiting band executing a seven-and-a-half-minute routine. They then knelt on the field while the opposing band completed their performance, after which the visitors stood at attention and began marching to the grandstand to be seated. Suddenly, a female band member fainted, followed by five more girls over the next ten minutes. Some of the girls were placed on benches to recover, while others were sent to the hospital. Before long, about half of the 123-member visiting band had either collapsed or reported feeling ill. Many of those stricken were clearly overbreathing and reported feeling light-headed and weak, with tingling in their extremities—classic symptoms of hyperventilation. Other symptoms included cramps, abdominal pain, and nausea.[40]

Doctors later concluded that the heat and excitement of the game contributed to the incident, along with some of the band members being overdressed for the occasion. The initial incidents likely generated extreme anxiety among the remaining band members after seeing their colleagues collapse. A second wave of illness broke out as band members boarded busses for the trek home. Over the next three days, ten more band members fell ill—five of whom were among those who had been originally stricken.

Investigators ruled out food poisoning and, to the surprise of many, heat stroke, as a tell-tale indicator—fever—was absent. Dr. Richard Levine of the United States Public Health Service studied the data and noted that while heat may have played a minor role, mass hysteria was the primary culprit. Levine observed that "the discipline of a precision marching drill, the discomfort of wearing heavy clothes in a hot environment, the excitement and disappointment at losing a close game—suggests that the setting was appropriately tense for mass hysteria to occur."[41] Only girls from the wind section were initially affected; coincidentally, they had been dressed in the heaviest clothing. With an air temperature of 73°F, Levine hypothesized that a few girls were likely affected by the heat, but the sudden distress of seeing their bandmates faint was what ultimately triggered mass hysteria.[42]

Insecticide Scare, April 24, 1987 (Tucson, Arizona, USA)

On the morning of Friday April 24, 1987, a man began spraying malathion to control bugs near a high school. Before long, a class of elementary students who had been outside their school, encountered the foul-smelling spray, and retreated to the cafeteria where many reported headaches, dizziness, nausea, difficulty breathing, sweating, watering eyes, and weakness. Medical personnel rushed to the school "on the basis that an unknown and possibly toxic substance was causing illness."[43] All 296 students were taken to area hospitals where their symptoms—which mimicked those of anxiety—rapidly subsided. No evidence of insecticide poisoning was detected.[44]

Authorities checked the spraying equipment and found that based on the residue, the man had diluted the malathion as per the instructions on the label.[45] Investigators concluded that the symptoms were psychogenic and triggered by the bad smell. Malathion is an insecticide with a bad odor, yet it poses little risk to human health. It is widely used in the United States and around the world. It is even approved by the Food and Drug Administration for use to combat head lice in children. During the 1981Mediterranean-fruit-fly infestation in California, which was countered with the widespread spraying of malathion, the director of the California Conservation Corps, Brien Thomas Collins, publicly drank a diluted solution of Malathion to alleviate public fears.[46] One study placed subjects in a sealed room and exposed them to the insecticide sprayed in the air for two hours a day over forty-two consecutive days. No health issues were reported.[47]

Vaccine Panic, October 6, 1992 (Hanza, Iran)

Four days after a routine inoculation for tetanus, a schoolgirl fainted in class and complained of headache, blurred vision, tremor, and "burning" hands. Within a few days, nine classmates—all of whom had received tetanus injections—were afflicted with similar symptoms, prompting fears that they had been injected with a bad batch. Investigators learned that the first victim had long suffered from stress-induced seizures accompanied by symptoms similar to those exhibited in class. She had even been seeing a neurologist at the time of her "attack." Authorities surmised that not knowing of her condition, her classmates grew anxious believing that her symptoms were caused by the injections. The symptoms persisted for five weeks amid rumors of the "bad" batch and only subsided after a dramatic public display by a local physician. In an effort to quell fears and ensure that parents continued to inoculate their children, Dr. M. T. Yasamy invited the community to a meeting, where he had himself injected with vaccine from the same batch that the girls had received. The symptoms soon subsided.[48]

Pokémon Sickness, 1997 (Japan)

Between December 16 and 17, 1997, upward of twelve thousand Japanese children reported feeling unwell after watching an episode of a popular animated cartoon, Pokémon. While a tiny cluster of cases were diagnosed as photosensitive epilepsy, authorities were initially puzzled by the thousands of other students who reported headaches, nausea, vomiting, blurred vision, breathing difficulty, and lethargy. Media coverage of a few early cases appears to have been instrumental in spreading symptoms.[49] Investigators concluded that the outbreak was an episode of mass hysteria triggered by sudden anxiety after the release of dramatic media reports describing a relatively small number of genuine photosensitive epilepsy seizures triggered by the flashing lights.[50]

The cartoon in question first aired on Japanese television in April 1997. Each of the many different Pokémon characters has its own unique personality and powers. Pikachu, for instance, is a popular yellow mouse with the ability to move exceptionally fast and disable opponents with electric shocks. The offending episode aired at 6:30 p.m. on Tuesday, December 16. About twenty minutes into the show, Pikachu is forced to use his electric powers in a battle, a scene that included a sequence of rapid light flashes. The sequence appears to have triggered photosensitive epilepsy.

Twenty-one minutes into the program, at 6:51 p.m., Pikachu's attack began to send flashes across television screens. Japan's Fire Defense division reported that within forty minutes of the flashing sequence airing, 618 children had been taken for hospital evaluation with a variety of complaints. The illnesses were headline news across the country during the evening. Several television stations aired replays of the flash sequence, after which more children reportedly became sick and required medical evaluation.[51] While the light flashes have been blamed for all of the children's symptoms, the same flashes had been previously used many times in animated cartoons, without incident.

Soda Poisoning Scare, June 1999 (Belgium and France)

On June 8, 1999, thirty-three students at a school in Bornem, Belgium, became ill after drinking Coca-Cola. The pupils recovered quickly, and tests, including blood and urine samples, were normal. The attending physicians noted that the students appeared nervous and excited. The following day, four more students from the school were rushed to hospital with similar complaints. Again, nothing out of the ordinary was uncovered except that they seemed anxious.[52] The incidents received widespread media coverage across Europe.

On June 10, alarm grew as eleven more students were affected in Brugge. The next day, seventeen fell ill in Harelbeke, followed by incidents at schools in Lochristi and Kortrijk on June 14, when a total of forty-seven students were reportedly stricken with soda-related illness.[53] At this point, all Coca-Cola products were banned from sale in Belgium. Poisoning reports soon spread to the general population, and, over the ensuing three weeks, 943 calls were recorded by the Belgian Poison Control Centre from people feeling sick after consuming a variety of drinks made by the Coca-Cola Company including Fanta, Sprite, Pepsi, Lipton Ice Tea, Minute Maid, and Nestea. There was no clear pattern, and calls came from scattered locations across the country.[54] Similar symptoms were also reported from citizens in France at this time.[55]

On June 15, Coca-Cola officials announced that they had identified the culprits: a fungicide used to treat transport pallets had tainted the outside of cans. They also blamed "bad carbon dioxide."[56] An independent investigation by a leading Belgian toxicologist, Dominique Lison at the Université catholique de Louvain, concluded that the assessment of the situation by Coca-Cola officials was wrong. Instead, Lison concluded that the illnesses had been triggered by mass hysteria.[57] He continued: "Small amounts of 4-chloro-3-methylphenol were found on the outside of some cans (about 0.4 µg/can). In both cases, it is unlikely that such concentrations caused any toxicity beyond an abnormal odour. No other notable chemicals had been found."[58] A separate investigation by the Belgian Health Ministry reached a similar conclusion.[59] The ban on Belgian Coke products was lifted June 23 and cost Coca-Cola an estimated US$250 million.[60]

The context of the episode is vital to understanding how the events unfolded. The outbreak of illness symptoms coincided with a major food scare in Belgium that became widely known as the "dioxin crisis." The scare began earlier in the year when a tank of recycled fats that were used to make animal feed was contaminated with a variety of toxins including dioxins. The incident led to tainted feed being fed to chickens. There was widespread public suspicion, anger, and distrust of Belgian government officials after the contaminated-feed incident was initially withheld from the public. It was reported in the news only after it had been leaked to the media. The fallout of this delayed public response led to the resignation of the Minister for Agriculture and the Minister for Health.[61] In the month preceding the tainted Coke scare, news outlets reported that the contaminated animal feed in Belgium had contained such toxic agents as dioxins, polychlorinated biphenyls (PCBs), and dibenzofurans. This state of affairs resulted in preexisting anxiety just before the tainted Coke episode, following the highly publicized recall of chicken, eggs, dairy, and meat products. The contaminated food crisis was making headlines in Belgium at the same time that the Coke scare developed.[62]

In commenting on the importance of the context of the scare, Dr. Benoit Nemery and a team of researchers at the Belgian Health Ministry concluded that key factors in the outbreak were Coke's high-profile image, the dioxin crisis, and poor communication by Coke officials.[63] Ironically, part of the failure to communicate effectively with Belgian officials may have been intentional. Nemery suggests that perhaps fearing the disclosure of its secret recipe, Coca-Cola officials "were very casual in providing data from the chemical analyses of their products. The documents that were received were often no more than faxed messages and loose notes, with insufficient details."[64]

It took time for Coke to regain consumer trust in Europe. Writing a year later, Maureen Taylor discussed the fallout from the scare and its impact on the Coca-Cola Company, noting that second-quarter earnings for 1999 had plummeted 21 percent from the previous year. Earnings for the third and fourth quarters were also down from 1998. Taylor writes: "Immediately following the resolution of the crisis, CEO Ivester promised, 'we'll spend whatever is necessary to regain the confidence of the Belgian consumers.' However, Coca-Cola found itself once again in trouble in Belgium. In October of 1999, Alan Cowell of *The New York Times* reported, 'the company confronted another flurry of health scares when four Belgian children reported illness from drinking Coke. Prosecutors cleared the company of responsibility in these incidents but the publicity reminded customers once again about the mass illnesses in June.' No matter what it did, it could do little to regain the trust and support of publics in France, Spain, and Belgium."[65]

British psychiatrist Simon Wessely was confident of the mass-psychogenic-illness diagnosis well before it was officially determined, noting that it had the tell-tale signs of mass hysteria. Unlike the Coca-Cola Company, Wessely cashed in on the crisis. He had placed a wager with two friends that the cause would be determined to be mass hysteria. He received two bottles of champagne.[66]

In a second humorous twist, the initial incident at the school in Bornem, included a fourteen-year-old pupil named Ann DeMann. The Associated Press reported that at the time she felt ill and was taken to the hospital for examination, DeMann was in the lead in a competition with other students to win a portable CD player. The contest was sponsored by Coke.[67]

Itching Outbreak, February 2000 (Free State Province, South Africa)

Between February 14 and 25, 2000, an outbreak of unexplained itching swept through thirteen schools in Free State Province, South Africa. Most of the 1,430 students affected were from the eighth, ninth and tenth grades. The itching developed after the students had entered the school grounds and subsided as they left. A few teachers were also affected. The symptoms spread amid rumors that Satanism was responsible; another rumor held that itching powder had been sprinkled in the toilets. The average length of the outbreaks was six days, although symptoms in any one student never persisted for more than a few hours. Investigators determined that the itching spread by line of sight after seeing other students scratching. Prior to being affected, students typically reported feeling a sensation of hot air, often accompanied by tingling of the limbs, dizziness, headache, and overbreathing. Researchers examined both the schools and the students, but could not identify any trigger. The symptoms soon went away after authorities, in an effort to reassure anxious parents, had the schools fumigated, and new guidelines were implemented which sent any new cases home until the sensations of itching had stopped.[68]

Phantom Bus Terrorist, May 25, 2004 (Vancouver, Canada)

In the aftermath of the September 11, 2001 terror attacks in the United States, North Americans remained on edge for several years, fearful of more attacks, possibly with chemical weapons. It was within this backdrop that at approximately one o'clock on the afternoon of May 25, 2004, an Arab-looking man was stepping off a bus in downtown Vancouver in western Canada. As he passed by, the man made a vague remark to the driver that his day was going to take a turn—

presumably for the worse. Joyce Horton, who was traveling from Richmond to Vancouver to see her daughter, recalled the conversation. "He said how's your day going and the bus driver said good. Then the man said 'it won't be for long.'"[69] Not long after, the driver felt ill and vomited, then asked if any of the passengers felt unwell. When one of them answered in the affirmative, the driver pulled to the roadside and radioed for help. Medics soon arrived and began treating the pair while listening to their accounts of what happened, and felt ill themselves. This triggered a massive government response as emergency personnel rushed to the scene, and police issued a bulletin to be on the lookout for an olive-skinned man in his mid-twenties, of average build, with a thin moustache. He was said to have had a gold chain around his neck and a five o'clock shadow. This description only served to heighten fears that the man may have been of Middle Eastern origin and was carrying out a terrorist act using methyl chloride.[70]

In early June, Vancouver's chief medical officer, Dr. Francis John Blatherwick, became suspicious of the chemical-weapons-attack theory when looking at the data and how the events transpired. He noted that some of the symptoms were inconsistent with methyl chloride exposure, but that they were, however, typical of anxiety. Blatherwick concluded that the trigger was "mass anxiety," and the episode was an outbreak of mass hysteria. This infuriated the police and ambulance unions. During a police press conference held on June 11, a police spokeswoman was highly critical of Blatherwick and suggested that he was ignorant of the facts in the case. As a result of their dispute, police had stopped working with Blatherwick. The spokeswoman told members of the media that "he is not involved in the investigation and he is misinformed. The investigation remains active, as toxicology results are still not complete."[71]

Soon after the incident, University of British Columbia epidemiologist Dr. Richard Mathias reached a similar conclusion to that of Blatherwick, suggesting that the cause of the symptoms were the result of mass psychogenic illness. "An unknown substance which turns out to be harmless, somebody getting sick, nausea, vomiting, all of those kinds of things are associated with this . . . Somebody starts to get sick and then it rapidly spreads to other people," Mathias said.[72]

On June 25, Vancouver police made a dramatic announcement: they had been able to confirm that the incident was indeed a chemical attack. At a press conference, chemical expert Dr. Robert Lockhart announced: "A trace level of Methyl Chloride was found, which in high concentrations is capable of killing someone. While it is impossible to say how much of the gas the victims were exposed to or how it came to be delivered into the air on the bus, it would have taken a fairly high concentration to force the gas into some of the materials on the bus, such as seat fabric and the air filters."[73] One of the investigators, Rodger Shepard, supported the department's interpretation of the methyl chloride traces: "You're talking about two very senior ambulance attendants and they're not going to have psychosomatic symptoms, they've seen everything."[74] Police urged anyone who had been on the bus to go back to their doctors for further tests.[75]

While the announcement of the findings made headlines across the world—it was widely reported that a terrorist had attacked a bus in Canada. In reality, the police had conducted a faulty investigation and let their emotions and their dispute with Dr. Blatherwick influence their findings. For instance, while proclaiming the terrorist link, they could not adequately explain the absence of medical findings in the victims. They also failed to initially acknowledge that methyl chloride was common and builds up in small quantities over time. Even shoddier, no one had bothered to check the filters on other Vancouver public busses to see if there were traces of methyl chloride there as well. As for the amount of methyl chloride found, Lockhart said it was in a quantity of twenty-seven parts per million. When a journalist for the *Richmond Review* asked whether "testing other bus filters might serve as a control with which to gauge these findings," Lockhart's answer was stunning: no one had requested him to do so![76]

It was quickly becoming apparent that the police investigation was far from thorough or scientific. Curiously, the Royal Canadian Mounted Police also tested the bus and found nothing out of the ordinary. It turns out that the minute traces of methyl chloride were nothing unusual, especially for a city near the ocean. The United States Environmental Protection Agency reports that methyl chloride is "formed in the oceans by natural processes" and can be found at low levels around the world.[77] It is also generated by the burning of coal or wood, chlorinated swimming pools and aerosol sprays.

Later that same year, a study of the incident by Dr. Réka Gustafson concluded that the incident was a case of mass hysteria, noting that while the driver and a single passenger felt sick, between twenty and fifty other passengers reported no symptoms. "In addition . . . first responders who boarded the bus prior to the paramedics and . . . did so without personal protective equipment did not get ill. Similarly, the bus mechanic who boarded the bus with the paramedics, also remained asymptomatic."[78] The head of the local paramedics union, Stuart Meyers, was infuriated by the mass-hysteria diagnosis, saying that two experienced paramedics could not be the victims of mass hysteria. "For Dr. Blatherwick to suggest that they are victims of mass hysteria, leads me to believe that he has a narrow and limited understanding of the paramedic profession. These paramedics have suffered enough indignity . . . from having to defecate and vomit in a bucket while quarantined in the back of an ambulance to being stripped naked and scrubbed with a car brush to decontaminate." Mr. Meyers said that Blatherwick's statements "only add to these indignities as he belittles and dismisses their exposure and illness as 'hysteria.'"[79] This was a classic response to many cases of mass psychogenic illness, which typically receive strong opposition within the group that is diagnosed. It is widely asserted among professionals that "mass hysteria" is something that happens to other people but not themselves or their groups.

Anxiety hysteria is a reaction to the sudden, unexpected appearance of a threatening stimulus. The response typically reflects the illness scenario—for example, after the perceived exposure to pesticides, subjects may exhibit watering of the eyes and breathing troubles. A false threat of suspected food poisoning could prompt stomach pain, nausea and vomiting.

In chapter 8, we examine a different type of reaction to a perceived threat: conversion disorder in the form of motor hysteria, as victims convert exposure to long-term emotional distress into physical symptoms. In outbreaks of traditional hysteria, the subjects remain and attempt to deal with the anxiety internally rather than trying to flee. Fear and emotional distress trigger disruptions to the nervous system as messages to the muscles and brain become disordered, resulting in outbreaks of twitching, shaking, and altered states of consciousness.

CHAPTER 8

CLASSICAL MASS HYSTERIA: PSYCHOLOGICAL GREMLINS

British psychiatrist Simon Wessely identifies two types of mass hysteria. In the previous chapter we looked at *mass anxiety hysteria* which is common in developed countries and involves the sudden reaction to an unexpected threat—be it real or imagined. There is no preexisting group stress, and the symptoms—most commonly headache, dizziness, nausea, fainting, and hyperventilating, usually subside within a few hours. Most outbreaks of this type are found in modern Western schools and factories and are prompted by environmental fears over the safety of food, air, and water. The most common triggers are an unfamiliar odor, and rumors of food poisoning or a terrorist attack. The second type of mass hysteria identified by Wessely is the subject of this chapter: *classical mass hysteria*—also known as *motor hysteria*.

Occasionally throughout history, when groups of people have been under great stress for long periods, strange behaviors and symptoms have broken out. Scientists think that pent-up stress disrupts the nerves and neurons that send messages to the muscles and brain. As a result, bodies go haywire with temporary bouts of twitching, spasms, and shaking. Sometimes the messages to the brain are disrupted, resulting in vocal ticks, difficulty speaking, trance-like states, and amnesia. In this chapter we will provide an overview of the history of motor hysteria, which are most commonly reported in schools, factories, and convents, places where groups of people are in an enclosed "captive" environment. While factory workers can quit their jobs, students can walk out of school, and nuns can leave the sisterhood, each action has a high price attached to it, such as being suspended from school, fired from your job, or expelled from a nunnery. Symptoms appear gradually and usually take weeks or months to go away after the anxiety subsides and the nerves begin to settle down and function normally again.[1] Classical mass hysteria is more common in strict schools and factories in Africa and Asia, with spirit possession being the most popular explanation among locals.

EARLY OUTBREAKS: CONVENT HYSTERIA

During the Middle Ages, mass hysteria in European convents was rampant as nuns were seized with bizarre fits, accounts of which seem difficult to believe today. Indeed, there are reports of groups of nuns bleating like sheep, yelping like dogs, meowing like cats, and even biting each other. In some instances, nuns tore off their clothes and began touching or rubbing their genitals, claiming that demons were controlling them. Some gave detailed confessions of copulating with the devil in the form of a dog. The literature on these accounts is so rich and the sources so solid, there is no doubt as to their veracity. But how do we explain the shaking, twitching, strange body movements, lewd gestures, and trance states?

Young girls were often forced by their parents into joining strict religious orders that included vows of poverty, chastity, menial labor, and meager diets. Under these repressive, unnatural conditions, lesbianism became common, as were love affairs with priests, all of which generated tremendous guilt and conflict, culminating in mental gridlock. Also during this time, it was widely believed that humans could be possessed by certain animals, such as wolves, sheep, and dogs. In parts of Europe, cats were particularly despised as they were considered familiars with the devil. It is this context that triggered cases such as the barking and meowing nuns.[2]

FACTORY AND SCHOOL OUTBREAKS

Many cases of classical hysteria occur in factories and schools where the students or workers are under extreme pressure to perform. Between the eighteenth and early twentieth centuries and the industrial revolution, harsh working conditions and weak or nonexistent labor unions led to mass hysteria in factories. Episodes were recorded in England, France, Germany, Italy, and Russia and included convulsions, strange movements, and unusual states of mind. The industrial revolution was notorious for child labor, low wages, and appalling conditions. The first recorded outbreak of motor hysteria in a factory setting occurred in England at a Lancashire cotton mill in February 1787, when twenty-four workers experienced violent convulsions and sensations of suffocation.[3] This episode came just one year after Edmund Cartwright invented the power loom, which revolutionized the textile industry. The absence of similar motor-hysteria reports in Western countries during the second half of the twentieth century may result from union gains and tougher health-and-safety regulations for workers.

During this same period, fits of shaking, trembling, and trance states swept through many authoritarian European schools that shared one common element: they were ridiculously strict and run like military boot camps. In 1893, sixty-two students at a girls' school in Basel, Switzerland, began to shake and convulse. Symptoms subsided after school hours, relapsing only upon reentering school grounds.[4] In Gross-Tinz, Germany, between June and October 1892, hand tremors, trance-like states, and amnesia struck twenty students.[5] At a school in Chemnitz, Germany, in February 1906, arm and hand tremors forced the cancelation of writing drills.[6]

Anxiety generated by sexual tension is evident in many of the few recent Western cases. In 1939, a twitching epidemic broke out among a group of girls at a Louisiana high school in the southeastern United States. At first only one girl was stricken, likely from the stress of having to join dance classes and dealing with a failing relationship. When her classmates saw that the girl's bouts of twitching got her excused from dance class and her boyfriend suddenly grew more affectionate, six more girls suddenly became stricken with bouts of uncontrollable twitching over the ensuing weeks.[7] In 1962, a series of blackout spells affected an African American school in Louisiana that had a significant proportion of pupils who were sexually active. The symptoms began after rumors that authorities were going to administer pregnancy tests, with offenders to be transferred to reform school.[8] During the early 1970s, psychiatrist Silvio Benaim reported on an episode of falling and fainting at a London girls' school. The incident lasted for nine months and was triggered in part by long-term stress caused by the lesbian advances of a teacher at the school.[9]

One of the most bizarre series of incidents involves outbreaks of laughing mania in African schools since the 1960s. Episodes sound more like science fiction than fact, but have been reported in numerous medical journals. Laughing mania has been very selective, usually striking missionary schools in poor, remote locations. A typical African case was investigated in May 1976 by psychiatrists Manohar Dhadphale and S. P. Shaikh. It involved an outbreak of twitching, mental confusion, uncontrollable laughing, and running in 126 students at a secondary school in Zambia. Dhadphale and Shaikh concluded that "recent strict disciplinary measures taken by the new administration" probably contributed to the episode.[10] Physician G. J. Ebrahim notes that African children are dominated by their powerful elders. Conflict arises from exposure to foreign ideas which challenge traditional beliefs, with escape being sought through conversion reactions. Ebrahim believes outbreaks are fueled by "emotional conflict aroused in children who are being brought up at home amidst traditional tribal conservatism, while being exposed in school to thoughts and ideas which challenge accepted beliefs."[11]

OUTBREAKS AMONG NATIVE PEOPLES

Some episodes among indigenous groups have been triggered by such factors as social and geographical isolation and rapid social changes. An example of the former is an episode of mass psychogenic boredom that was investigated by psychiatrists in Canada during 1972. The outbreak of strange behaviors persisted for several months in a small village of Cree and Ojibway peoples. Symptoms were confined to locals between the ages of eleven and eighteen and included headaches, nightmares, irritability, and general fatigue. Often during fits, the affected youth would try to run into the woods and had to be restrained. The outbreaks coincided with their frustration and depression over feeling trapped in such an isolated, impoverished environment with few recreational outlets. The decisions of elders could not be challenged as elders practiced tight control over the actions of the youth, and the youth had little privacy and had to conform to a set of rigid Christian values. Even marriages were prearranged. Investigators observed that outbreaks received a great deal of attention and often turned into social events with neighbors gathering around and snacks and refreshments being served. On several occasions, girls who were affected appeared to intentionally stop breathing in order to create excitement by being the subjects of attempts to resuscitate them. The fits subsided after psychiatrists put an end to the social aspects of the episodes and were able to increase educational and recreational activities.[12]

Another atypical outbreak of mass hysteria in an indigenous backdrop—an epidemic of clay eating—occurred in northern Australia between 1974 and 1978. Investigating anthropologist Harry Eastwell identified nineteen cases among women; all were close to the end of or past childbearing age. Eastwell interpreted the outbreak as hysterical in nature, resulting from rapid social and cultural changes that occurred during the transition from a hunter-gatherer lifestyle to life in Western society. With the appearance of imported foods and the use of Western money, patterns of traditional food gathering, including foraging, hunting, and means of distribution, became obsolete.

The role of females who were past menopause became ill-defined as they were trapped between two worlds. Previously, middle-aged women had the responsibility of childminding for young mothers, but because of the shift to a capitalist society and the resultant high rates of unemployment for young mothers, older mothers lost this valued role, and were left financially poor, dependent, and depressed. Eastwell believes that many of these women, who were no longer valued for their ability to produce babies or be productive members of society, turned to eating clay as it was comforting.[13]

MEMORABLE EXAMPLES

Tarantism, 1200–1600 (Southern Italy)

One of the earliest outbreaks of behaviors to be labeled as mass hysteria was what historian Harold Gloyne refers to as the "mass hysterical reaction" to perceived bites of the tarantula spider in southern Europe during the Middle Ages—most notably in Southern Italy. The first known descriptions of this strange malady were made by local physicians and identified as *tarantism*. Incidents were most common during the hot, dry summer months of July and August and reached a peak in the seventeenth century. Medical historian Henry Sigerist outlines the characteristic features of tarantism: "People, asleep or awake, would suddenly jump up, feeling an acute pain like the sting of a bee. Some saw the spider, others did not, but they knew that it must be the tarantula. They ran out of the house into the street, to the market place dancing in great excitement. Soon they were joined by others who like them had just been bitten, or by people who had been stung in previous years, for the disease was never quite cured. The poison remained in the body and was reactivated every year by the heat of summer."[14] Sigerist also observed that there was believed to be only one cure: dancing to certain types of music.

One of the most effective cures was for victims to dance to certain versions of the tarantella, a well-known Italian folk dance characterized by an upbeat tempo that increases in intensity and features short, repetitive phrases. In an attempt to cure themselves, *taranti* (as victims were referred to) would dance intermittently for several hours, and occasionally days and weeks, until their symptoms disappeared. The following is a typical account of tarantism, published in 1621 and summarized by Martha Baldwin. The case involved a young man named Pietro Simone, a farm worker who had been working on a country estate, who believed he had been bitten by a tarantula. "Suddenly the young harvester felt a strong pain on his leg where he had been stung. In the time in which it took to say three Ave-Marias [Hail Mary prayers] he fell on the ground with chills, and endured strong pains in the chest, priapism [sexual arousal], and convulsions. He breathed heavily, and cried out to bystanders that he was suffocating."[15] As dawn broke, the attending physician called for a musician who played while the young man danced until he was drenched in sweat. Over the next week, he would dance strenuously for between eight and twelve hours daily. As was typical of victims, the young man exhibited odd yearnings and fetishes. Baldwin noted that while not dancing, he slept and ate little, but expressed a strong desire to hear lullabies and asked "to plunge into water, and fondled objects which were red." One week after the alleged spider bite, he "returned to full health, and all traces of his mad behavior vanished."

Common symptoms of tarantism included chest pain, breathing difficulties, headache, fainting, trembling, vomiting, twitching, and delusions. Victims commonly attributed a sore or swelling just prior to the appearance of their symptoms to a tarantula bite, but such claims were difficult to verify. Few people ever saw what bit them, and their skin irritations could have been caused by an array of insects. Furthermore, while the identical species of tarantula was common throughout Southern Europe and is still considered relatively harmless even today, frenzied dancing in reaction to perceived bites was almost exclusively confined to the state of Apulia, along the southeastern coast of what is now Italy. Some early physicians believed that a venomous species of tarantula indigenous to Apulia could produce the bizarre reactions observed in the region, but contemporary investigators have tested the spiders from Apulia and found them to be no different than those of the same species in other parts of Europe.[16] It is also unlikely that a venomous variant of tarantula once existed in Apulia but later died out.

Anthropologist Ioan Lewis reports that *Latrodectus tarantula*—a docile, slow-moving spider found in Apulia—can produce psychoactive symptoms in some victims including nausea, muscle pain, weakness, and shaking.[17] However, another species of spider—*Lycosa tarantula*—was usually blamed for causing tarantism in Apulia as it was bigger than *Latrodectus tarantula* and had a more painful bite.

Tarantism appears to have grown out of ancient Greek rituals in which participants experience a number of similar symptoms while listening to music and dancing. George Mora describes these Corybantic or telete initiation rites, sometimes referred to as ritualized madness. "The candidate was seated in a chair and the ministrants danced around him and raised a great din. The effect of this was to rouse his excitement and stir his emotions, so that he gradually lost consciousness of all but the whirling rhythm of the dance. This was followed by what was called telete proper, in which, we may suppose, the candidate threw himself into the dance with the rest and yielded to the intoxication of the rhythm. In the end, when all was over, the participants emerged from the tumult to a state of calm and tranquility."[18] It is also notable that Apulia was once an extension of ancient Greece, where music was often used to evoke ecstatic healing and mental equilibrium. Tarantism, therefore, may not be a spontaneous, uncontrollable example of both individual and collective hysteria (what contemporary psychiatrists refer to as conversion disorder).

The symptoms associated with tarantism are identical to those of people engaging in both historical and contemporary religious enthusiasms—such as the Shakers and Quakers, whose behaviors were ritualized and institutionalized. While tarantism victims were typically described as uncontrollable and frenzied, like their contemporary counterparts in ecstatic sects, there is a distinct pattern to their behavior. As Jean Russell notes, *taranti* would typically begin dancing at sunrise, would sleep during the midday heat, bathe, then resume dancing until evening when they would eat and sleep until sunrise. This ritual typically persisted over several days and could occasionally endure for weeks.[19] As one medical historian notes, *taranti* "may involve normal, rational people who possess unfamiliar conduct codes, world-views and political agendas that differ significantly from those of Western-trained investigators who often judge these illness behaviours independent of their local context and meanings."[20]

Meowing Nuns, Middle Ages (France)

In 1844, noted German physician Justus Friedrich Hecker wrote: "I have read in a good medical work that a nun, in a very large convent in France, began to meow like a cat; shortly afterwards other nuns also meowed. At last all the nuns meowed together every day at a certain time for several hours together. The whole surrounding Christian neighborhood heard, with equal chagrin and astonishment, this daily cat-concert, which did not cease until all the nuns were informed that a company of soldiers were placed by the police before the entrance of the convent, and that they were provided with rods, and would continue whipping them until they promised not to meow anymore."[21]

While this incident may seem far-fetched, during this time it was widely thought that people could be possessed by certain animals, which some believed were familiars with the devil. Common candidates were wolves, dogs, sheep, and cats, the latter being especially despised in France, where the killing of cats remained a popular pastime until the early sixteenth century.[22] This distain for certain animals in medieval Europe may explain some of these behaviors, with the content of their possession and histrionics being shaped by the prevailing social and cultural beliefs of the times. Many parallel cases have been recorded during this period. For instance, in Xante, Spain, in 1560, a group of nuns "bleated like sheep, tore off their veils, [and] had convulsions in church."[23] In 1491, at Cambrai in France, Sisters at a convent went into fits of hysterics, exhibited feats of strength, and yelped like dogs.[24]

During the later Middle Ages, it was common for people who entered trance and possession states to act like cats. The case of the meowing nuns was far from an isolated example, and thus animals like cats were viewed as posing a threat to society. Due to their reputation of being in cahoots with demonic forces, cats were often rounded up and killed at public functions. Historian Robert Darnton has written extensively on this peculiar aspect of medieval European culture.[25] He observes: "In the Metz region [of France] they burned a dozen cats at a time in a basket on top of a bonfire. The ceremony took place with great pomp until it was abolished in 1765."[26]

Witch Hysteria and Trials, 1691 – 1693
(Salem Village, Massachusetts Bay Colony)

One of the most infamous episodes of mass hysteria occurred at Salem Village (now Danvers, Massachusetts) in the Massachusetts Bay Colony. The village is located just west of Salem Town. Between 1691 and 1693, the community was the scene of a great fear involving claims that witches were casting spells on residents. There is no one cause of the outbreak. The witch scare resulted from a confluence of factors, notably: mass hysteria among young repressed Puritan girls, disputes between members of Salem Town and Salem Village, and a fear of the devil.

On another level, the Salem witch hunts were a moral panic involving a volatile, hostile overreaction to a group of people who were perceived as a threat to Puritan society. As a result, two broad groups were formed—"them" and "us," with the "us" faction exaggerating the threat from dark, outside forces.[27]

While many factors have been attributed to the Salem witch scare, one factor has received scant attention: a fortune-telling fad was sweeping across the Massachusetts Bay Colony at the time. In his book about the life of the colony's governor, Sir William Phips, Cotton Mather writes that books on the art of divining the future were common as the inhabitants were practicing "detestable Conjurations with Sieves, and Keys, and Pease [peas], and Nails, and Horseshoes."[28] A minister from the town of Beverly, John Hale, wrote that he had been "credibly informed" that a young girl in Salem had used an egg, suspended in a glass, "to find her future Husbands Calling" until she was frightened upon seeing a spectre resembling a coffin.[29] The practice of placing an egg white in a glass of water, then interpreting the shapes that would form in terms of future events, was brought from England to the New World.[30] It was akin to using a crystal ball. While such a practice would have no doubt been exciting for a group of repressed girls burdened with laborious chores in the dead of winter, at the time, it was viewed by the clergy as a dangerous pastime that could expose oneself to the dangers of Satan. It was the modern-day equivalent of dabbling with a Ouija board.

In February 1692, not long after some of the Salem girls began meeting secretly to try to divine the future, two from their fold, Betty Paris and Abigail Williams, began exhibiting disordered speech, convulsive movements, and epilepsy-like seizures. Sometimes they would appear to be in a trance, blurt out nonsense words or phrases, or curl up on the floor and contort their bodies. The symptoms were diagnosed as witchcraft and soon spread to other girls. The affected girls were part of a Puritan settlement where they lived cloistered lives that were filled with restrictions; even dancing and singing were prohibited. Still, many were friends with a Barbados slave woman named Tituba who had been telling them scary tales of Caribbean voodoo and magic. Prior to the outbreak, the overexcited girls had experienced difficulty sleeping and nightmares about demons and witches.

When pressed for details of their bewitchers, those accused gave the names of two women and Tituba. All three women were soon arrested. Tituba revealed the names of other conspirators, who in turn gave up the names of even more people. Some of the descriptions of those accused of witchcraft were elaborate. Tituba, for one, even described the devil in detail, noting that it was "a thing all over hairy, all the face hairy, and a long nose."[31]

In June 1692, a court of "Oyer and Terminer" (meaning to hear and determine) was set up by the colony's governor. More than two hundred people were eventually accused of witchcraft and held for trial. Some were tortured into confessing while they waited for their day in court. A few died in jail without ever having their say before the judge. Nineteen residents were executed by hanging (thirteen women, six men), and an eighty-year-old farmer, Giles Corey, was crushed to death with heavy stones after he refused to enter a plea. The stones had been used to force him to talk. Two dogs were even executed.

The episode ended when one of the girls accused the wife of Massachusetts Governor William Phips of being a witch. The governor quickly ordered new trials for the accused. This time "spectral evidence," where the accused witch had appeared in the form of an apparition, was not allowed in court, and all suspects were soon released. On October 29, the governor suspended the court, and the remaining suspects were eventually acquitted. By May 1693, he ordered the release of those remaining in prison.[32]

While psychologist Linnda Caporael has argued that the girls' fits were triggered by ergot contamination of the rye grown by the settlers that was used to make bread. Symptoms include hallucinations, headaches, and confusion.[33] However, the possibility that *Claviceps purpurea* (an ergot fungus) was involved has been dismissed by most researchers on several grounds: hysteria is the more likely explanation. The biggest strike against the ergot hypothesis involved the actions of the afflicted girls who were able to suddenly stop their bizarre behaviors. As toxicologist Alan Woolf notes, this would have been impossible if the girls had eaten ergot. Furthermore, why were the symptoms mainly confined to young girls?[34]

The outbreak of the psychological disturbance and accusations at Salem were not only fueled by a belief in real witches, but an embryonic legal system where those accused were presumed guilty until proven innocent. There were no lawyers to represent the accused; they had to represent themselves. The types of evidence on which the accused witches were charged was flimsy, at best, by modern legal standards. In *Salem Possessed: The Social Origins of Witchcraft*, historians Paul Boyer and Stephen Nissenbaum identify four types of evidence: confession, the appearance of supernatural attributes and deficits, anger followed by mischief, and spectral evidence.

The first type of evidence, outright confession, was not as straightforward as its name implies. On the one hand, if someone confessed to being a witch, they would be freed, but confessing to witchcraft presented its own set of complications. Firstly, if devout Puritans confessed to being a witch when they were not, this was viewed as a lie and could result in their damnation to hell. Given that there were no real witches, the accused, in order to be freed, would have to implicate others as practicing witchcraft, potentially sending more innocent persons to jail or the gallows. Those accused of witchcraft faced a difficult dilemma. As Rickard Werking observes: "An accused person was faced with the bitter choice of calling the accusation lies (which was just what a witch would do according to the judges) or of saving his own life by confessing" and naming their fellow community members as witches.[35]

Another type of evidence was the identification of supernatural attributes and weaknesses. At Salem, six different witnesses testified against George Burroughs, claiming that he possessed superhuman strength and could lift a heavy gun by pushing a single finger into the barrel and hold it at arm's length. This category of evidence also included weaknesses, such as the inability of witches to perform simple feats that others would take for granted, like being unable to recite the Lord's Prayer.[36] However, there were exceptions. When George Burroughs was convicted of witchcraft and wizardry, he was taken to the gallows on August 19, 1692. While on the scaffold, he continued to profess his innocence, then proceeded to recite the Lord's Prayer. "Our father who art in heaven, hallowed be thy name . . ." Much to the astonishment of the crowd, he did so flawlessly. Believing that it was not possible for a witch to perform such a recitation, many in the crowd listened attentively and with new meaning as Burroughs pleaded for his life. Some began to openly doubt his guilt. Ann Putnam cried out that she could see a black man whispering into his ear. Meanwhile, as the crowd hesitated, Cotton Mather reaffirmed Burroughs's guilt, claiming that he was never ordained, and that the devil could also masquerade as an angel. Burroughs was then hanged.[37]

A third type of evidence, anger followed by mischief, involved an expression of anger by the alleged witch, followed shortly after by some misfortune. For instance, when Bridget Bishop entered the courthouse at Salem Town, it was noted that she glanced across the square at a meetinghouse, and at that instant, a heavy timber supporting the roof suddenly crashed onto the floor. Another time, Samuel and Sarah Abbey claimed as confirming evidence of Sarah Good's guilt, that within an hour of her arrest, one of their cows that had appeared to be dying, suddenly recovered.[38] A good example of the ambiguous nature of this category was the incident involving an elderly Salem Town resident named Bray Wilkins.

When John Willard was accused of witchcraft, he visited Wilkins to ask for his prayers, but Wilkins refused. The next time they met and Wilkins glanced at Willard, Wilkins said he soon experienced trouble urinating. In this instance, the bladder difficulties of an elderly man, perhaps exacerbated by anxiety, were viewed as confirming evidence that Willard was indeed a witch.[39]

In the case of spectral evidence, those accused of witchcraft were convicted after accusers claimed that the spirit of the defendant had appeared to them as a spectre. Such visitations were usually at night. It was impossible to refute such claims, which were often made by rivals and may have been a way of settling old scores. In other instances, they could have reflected visions prompted by lucid or waking dreams, reflections in windows that were misidentified as faces of people they knew, or outright fabrications. For example, in May 1692, Ann Putnam testified that two female figures had appeared before her: "The two women turned their faces towards me, and looked as pale as a white wall, and told me that they were Mr. Burroughs's first two wives, and he had murdered them. And one told me that she was his first wife, and he [had] stabbed her under the left arm and put a piece of sealing wax on the wound. And she pulled aside the winding sheet and showed me the place."[40] Boyer and Nissenbaum note that the problem with spectral evidence was that "the spectres were usually visible only to the person or persons for whom the visitation—vision, really—was intended. Others might be present, but they could see nothing."[41] That some people could see the spectre while others nearby could not, was considered to be a sign that the accused was indeed a witch, for how else could such an anomaly be explained? When some of the afflicted girls would scream out, fall to the floor, and claim to have been tormented by the invisible forces controlled by certain people in the courtroom— this too was spectral evidence.[42]

"Possessed" Nuns, 1642–1647 (Normandy, France)

A remarkable outbreak of mass hysteria occurred at the Louviers Convent in Normandy, France, between 1642 and 1647, when a group of nuns fell into hysterical seizures after being forced to worship nude. This unusual practice coupled with harsh and excessive convent rules provided a backdrop for the events that were to follow. One historian observed that the nuns engaged in a variety of self-torments including "passing their nights in prayer, fasting with excessive strictness, torturing their flesh with flagellation, and to crown all these fine works, rolling half-naked in the snow."[43] The saga began in 1616 when the convent opened. Its first chaplain, Father Pierre David was an Adamite and believed that people should worship God naked, just as Adam had presumably done. To demonstrate their poverty and humility, he ordered the nuns to receive communion naked. This created unbearable sexual tension between the convent inhabitants, followed by considerable guilt and conflict after succumbing to their desires of the flesh. In her autobiography, Sister Madeleine Bavent writes of some of what then transpired: "The most holy, virtuous, and faithful nuns were held to be those who stripped themselves completely naked and danced before him in that state, appeared naked in choir, and sauntered naked through the gardens. Nor was that all."[44]

In 1628, Father David passed away and was succeeded by Father Mathurin Picard and his understudy, Father Thomas Boullé. Under their leadership, reports of sexual shenanigans reached new heights until 1642 when Father Picard died. After hearing stories of these sexual escapades, an investigation was conducted the following year, with Father Boullé and another man named Duval being convicted of practicing witchcraft. In 1647, both were burned alive. Church authorities were so upset by what had gone on when Father Picard headed the nunnery, that they had his body dug up and burned as well. Madeleine Bavent died that same year after spending several years in solitary confinement in a dungeon, being fed only bread and water. The possessed nuns were charged with committing immoral acts, became viewed as victims, and were placed in other convents.[45]

Damning testimony that helped to seal the fate of Father Boullé and Duval came from Sister Madeleine Bavent, one of the first nuns to be stricken. Some of the nuns had accused her of consorting with the devil after being instructed in the black arts by Father Picard. At first Bavent denied the charges, but she soon recanted and testified in elaborate detail of her interactions with the two men. Historian Richard Madden writes: "She said, that the infants of several witches had been cut into pieces to make charms, and that Father Picard and she had assisted to put the children to death. . . . She said, that on a Holy Thursday she had eaten a part of a roast child at the Sabbath: the Father Picard was then alive." She claimed that Father Boullé assisted.[46] Madden reports that Bavent claimed to have seen two children at the Sabbath who "were nailed to crosses. . . . They drove nails into the head of this child, so as to make the form of a crown, and until both children were dead assailed them with blasphemous outrages." She also testified that after Father Picard's death, she met his corpse at the Sabbath. "The corpse spoke to her as if it had been living, and recalled to her the promise she had formerly made, never to give herself to any one but the devil . . . A large black beast, which appeared as if from a cloud, and which went three times round the corpse, terrified her greatly in counselling her" to give Father Boullé that same respect that had been afforded to Father Picard.[47]

The Barking Children, 1673 (Hoorn, Holland)

One day at an orphanage in Hoorn, a gang of street children were stricken with fits of shouting and barking. Dutch theologian Balthasar Bekker witnessed the strange happenings. He noted that the children would suddenly collapse, have an unusual look in their eyes, then lose their senses. "They tugged and tore at themselves, striking at the ground with their legs and arms and even with their heads, crying, yelling and barking like dogs so that it was a terrifying thing to see," he wrote.[48] Bekker reported that some of the children's stomachs "pounded so fearfully, that one would have said there was a living creature moving about inside them or even that a barrel was being rolled within their bodies. So strong were these movements that it took three, four, five or even six persons to hold them: one would take the head, two others the hands, one sat on the legs and sometimes another to sit on the belly to prevent them moving." Eventually they lay motionless, their bodies as "stiff as a bar of iron, so that with one person holding the head and another the feet, they could be carried anywhere, without making any movement. Sometimes this happened for several hours on end, and even at night, until 11pm, midnight, one, two or three o'clock."[49]

Bekker described an attack involving a girl named Catherine. He said that she was stricken as the 8:00 a.m. breakfast bell rang and remained in the strange state until 4:00 p.m. "when the bell called the children to their evening collation. [After regaining her senses] she believed she had been in that state only for a moment, because she could hear the bell still ringing, and when she heard grace being said for the evening meal she thought it was for breakfast."[50] The orphans were under great stress and were forced to endure monotonous religious instruction and prayer. Within this repressive atmosphere, the fits grew common. As authorities tried to "save" them from the clutches of Satan, the children were forced to endure lengthier prayer sessions. Unfortunately, the prayer sessions had the opposite effect, and the fits intensified. The fits finally subsided after the orphans were lodged with local families.

Cotton Disease Hysteria, February 1787 (Lancashire, England)

Dr. William St. Clare investigated an outbreak of mass hysteria at a British cotton mill. At the time, such facilities were notorious for long work hours, low salaries, and unsanitary, hazardous working conditions. Within this cauldron of stress, a strange outbreak developed, triggered by a prank. St. Clare wrote: "a girl, on the fifteenth of February, 1787, put a mouse into the bosom of another girl, who had a great dread of mice. The girl was immediately thrown into a fit, and continued in it with the most violent convulsions, for twenty-four hours. On the following day, three more girls were seized in the same manner; and on the 17th, six more. By this time the alarm was so great, that the whole work, in which 200 or 300 were employed, was totally stopped, and an idea prevailed that a particular disease had been introduced by a bag of cotton opened in the house. . . . Dr. St. Clare was sent for from Preston; before he arrived three more were seized, and during that night and the morning of the 19th, eleven more, making in all twenty-four. Of these, twenty-one were young women, two were girls of about ten years of age, and one man, who had been much fatigued with holding the girls. The symptoms were anxiety, strangulation, and very strong convulsions; and these were so violent as to last without any intermission from a quarter of an hour to twenty-four hours, and to require four or five persons to prevent the patients from tearing their hair and dashing their heads against the floor or walls."[51]

The symptoms soon subsided after an unusual method of treating the girls. The local physician brought with him a machine capable of producing mild electric shocks by cranking a generator. He shocked each patient and suggested to them that the symptoms would go away.

Possessed Town, 1857–1877 (Morzine, Italy-France)

An extended outbreak of demonic possession overwhelmed the small, remote town of Morzine, in the region of Haute-Savoie, France, dramatically affecting community life before it finally ended during the 1870s. Hundreds of residents—mostly women and children—were afflicted. The episode occurred at a time when medical knowledge was rapidly expanding. Several medical authorities visited the community, sparking tension between the scientists and local clergy, the latter interpreting the events as the work of the devil.

Many factors may have contributed to the outbreak. For instance, the population was characterized by very low education levels, with only about ten percent able to read and write. Most residents were devout Catholics with a fear of the devil.[52] The year prior to the outbreak, it was reported that there was an upsurge of interest in spiritualism, which may have rendered the population more suggestible.[53] A preponderance of men, who were forced to work outside of the town, left a large number of women behind. As a result, many females were in charge of their households. The normal routine was for the women to meet evenings at each other's homes where they would drink coffee, play games, discuss events of the day, and exchange stories. This state of affairs has been viewed as ideal for propagating rumors and gossip. Also of potential relevance was a dramatic episode of demonic possession that had occurred during the early 1850s, involving a ten-year-old girl from a neighboring community. Her symptoms paralleled those that would appear at Morzine. Church officials took the girl, Sylvie, to Besançon, where she was declared demonically possessed, exorcised, and proclaimed "cured."[54]

The episode in Morzine can be traced to March 14, 1857, when the town was still an Italian territory. A ten-year-old girl, Péronne Tavernier was leaving church. It was an especially exciting day for her as she had been preparing for her first communion. Then, she witnessed an event that likely distressed her: a small girl being rescued after nearly drowning in the nearby river. Several hours later, Péronne fainted at school and was carried home, where she then lay unconscious for many hours before regaining her senses. Weeks later, she was minding goats with her friend, Marie Plagnat, when the pair had attacks and were later found unconscious. From then on, the girls entered trances five to six times daily. As the fits continued, they became more complex, and the girls experienced hallucinations—many about serpents. They also went through the motions of opening and reading letters. Upon regaining awareness, they said that the letters were from the Virgin Mary; occasionally the letter was said to have come from the devil and was very negative in tone. By May, Marie's nine-year-old sister was affected by strange behaviors and began climbing trees. She was "cured" after her father threatened to kill her if she did not stop. Then another sister, Julienne, fifteen, claimed that seven devils had possessed her body. Marie then began to make predictions about the future.[55]

The epidemic spread slowly before picking up pace—first in families, then among neighbors, and later, throughout the whole town. By the end of the year, twenty people were affected; several months later, the number was over one hundred. Symptoms included convulsions, trances, hallucinations, and feats of acrobatics. Victims typically lost their appetite and exhibited a distain for both work and attending church. A belief spread that sorcery was to blame, and residents traded accusations. Some residents called for the execution of these perceived instigators in the public square. One poor person barely eluded a mob of thirty to forty vigilantes armed with forks, axes, and sticks.[56]

A medical official who investigated the outbreak provided the following description of the seizures, which began with a light trembling of the arms. He observed: "The face muscles have light spasms, the eyes flicker and bulge, she utters groans, then, suddenly, her arms bend and stretch, and this spreads to the whole body. Now, her body convulses in all directions . . . until the head nearly touches the feet; the eyes, sometimes open, sometimes closed, roll with an extraordinary rapidity. Then she starts to curse, in an earnest, raised voice. If she is spoken to, without irritating on contradicting her, she replies violently with all kinds of insult. The convulsions grow more violent during the seizure . . . then comes complete anesthesia, at least as regards the skin: you can pinch or prick her, she seems to feel nothing. If the fits are prolonged, the convulsions cease for a while and she will let herself slump against a wall or furniture, or fall as if exhausted: but after a minute or so she will suddenly leap up as though she has acquired a new secretion of nervous energy, and the convulsions begin again with the same intensity."[57] It was noted that when a seizure ends and the victim regains their senses, they exhibit a look of surprise, "as if emerging from a dream, not knowing where she is, and ordinarily starts to laugh, having no memory of what has happened, and returns to normal."

In 1860, the town, which had been a territory of Italy, came under French authority. Many residents believed that both the Church and state were in cahoots against them, and the *sous-préfet*, or government leader of the district, ordered that anyone exhibiting a public seizure would be arrested. This infuriated the townspeople, who then vented their anger against government officials, whom many residents believed, were under the control of Satan.

In January 1864, the Church compromised and sent seven missionaries to the town after requests by the residents. They visited the afflicted in their homes, but the missionaries were strictly forbidden to conduct exorcisms. Instead, they were allowed to offer prayers. In April 1864, when a government leader visited and attempted to meet and talk with those stricken, they went into seizures, rolled on the floor, broke furniture, shouted obscenities, and assaulted him.[58]

The next month, a breakthrough finally came with the visit of Bishop Monseigneur Magnin. At first his appearance triggered more violence, but the outbreak soon died down. As he arrived, those afflicted hurled insults at him. The government report on the visit stated that several girls soon exhibited seizures. Before long, about seventy women fell to the ground and began crying out. Among the insults: "Wolf of a bishop! Tear his eyes out! He hasn't the power to cure a girl! He can't rid a girl of the Devil."[59] As the bishop entered the church, upward of forty women were already having fits. Some of those afflicted had to be moved aside for him to reach the altar. While the women convulsed and flailed about, he offered prayers for them over the next hour. Some of them tried to approach the altar and attack the Bishop but were held back by relatives and a squad of gendarmes (French police). The government report stated: "So passed this terrible evening, which it is impossible to describe precisely. However, it gives some idea of the appalling disorder which reigned everywhere to say that at more or less the same moment, in the entire commune, in the cemetery, on the public square and the streets, and in the interior of the church, women could be seen in prey to atrocious convulsions, rolling on the ground, agitating their legs and their hands, striking the ground and uttering the same words as before and furious cries."

The next day when the Bishop returned to the church, there were wild scenes. An outside observer witnessed the scene firsthand after attending a 7:00 a.m. church service. "I hadn't been in the church five minutes before an unfortunate young girl fell at my feet, in horrible convulsions: four men couldn't hold her; she struck the floor with her feet, hands and head with such rapidity that it was like the beating of a drum. After this another, and then another. Soon the church had become an inferno; on all sides were cries, jostling, cursing and blaspheming enough to make your hair stand on end . . . The entry of the bishop, above all, set everyone shaking: knockings with fists and feet, spitting . . . hair loose in the air together with bonnets, clothing torn, hands bleeding; it was so dreadful that everyone was in tears . . . All the victims, more than a hundred of them, fell rapidly and simultaneously into convulsions, and it was a racket out of this world." The witness noted that the majority of those affected were females between the ages of fifteen and thirty, although a ten-year-old girl was affected, as were a few elderly women and two men. "The bishop, as best he could, bestowed confirmation on some of them. As soon as he approached close to them, they entered into crisis, and with the help of gendarmes and nearby men, he confirmed them all the same in the face of the most horrible curses. . . . They tried to strike him, to bite him, to tear off his official ring; they spat in his face. Only when they were slapped on the face, they let themselves go and fell into a drowsy state which resembled a deep sleep . . . the gendarmes were terrified . . ."[60]

Realizing the inadequacy of their measures to date, government officials soon took a new tactic and ordered a series of public spectacles intended to distract people's minds. Dances were held; music concerts were organized; even lectures were given in the public library. At the same time, religious displays were minimized as even the ringing of a church bell or the sight of a priest walking down the street was known to trigger outbreaks. It was within this secular backdrop that the affliction subsided, and by April 1868, only fifteen cases persisted—cases that were now widely viewed as suffering from an illness, changing the affliction from a collective religious outbreak, to an individual one.

German "Trembling Disease," 1905–1906 (Germany)

A number of schools in east central Germany were affected by a "trembling disease" that seemed to target students with heavy workloads. In October 1905, Meissen, Germany, was the scene of an outbreak that affected students' writing. It started in a thirteen-year-old girl whose hand began to tremble uncontrollably. The malady gradually spread throughout the school, so that by March 20, 237 students were struggling to write. The episode endured for eight months until it ended in mid-May.[61] A report on the outbreaks found that most victims were girls, ages nine to thirteen, with the shaking being confined to their writing hand. "The trembling often extends to the forearm and sometimes it also seizes the left side. The trembling . . . occur[s] with varying frequencies, sometimes also at night, and they last from a few minutes to half an hour. During the intervals the children usually feel entirely well, except for a certain nervous excitement, until the attack again sets in with more or less renewed vigor. This condition can last for weeks or months."[62]

In 1906, the city of Chemnitz was affected when students at the People's Elementary School had difficulty writing. Nearly two dozen girls, ages nine and ten, were affected. The symptoms only affected students when they were being asked to conduct writing drills, and like the pupils in Meissen, it only affected their writing hand. They were even able to attend the rest of their classes without any trouble—even physical education classes. The school physician, Johannes Schoedel, tried to cure the girls by giving them electric shocks, followed by suggestions that the trembling would go away. He believed that the shocks—which were thought to make people more open to suggestions—could stop the ailment. In the aftermath of this treatment, when the girls attended writing classes, their teacher announced: "Since you are not able to write, you must unfortunately have mental arithmetic again."[63] This strategy led to the reduction and eventual cessation of the tremors.[64] There is evidence that newspaper reports on the tremor helped to spread the "tremor disease" to Chemnitz. The first pupil to have been stricken said that they had read about it in a paper.[65]

The outbreaks in Germany were part of a wide incidence of psychogenic writing tremor in many parts of Europe during the late nineteenth and early twentieth centuries. Most of those affected were participating in writing classes where they were forced to undertake repetitive writing drills. One episode was recorded at a school in Gross-Tinz, Germany in 1892, and persisted for three months.[66] The epidemic began on June 28 when the writing hand of a ten-year-old girl started to tremble uncontrollably. The violent shaking eventually spread throughout her body. The very next day, several classmates experienced hand tremors lasting up to an hour. Those afflicted were between the ages of five and twelve. As each new student was stricken, they were removed from their class. The outbreak peaked during mid-July: "On almost every seat were patients having convulsions of the whole body. The girls fell under the seats and had to be carried from the room by the boys."[67] Of thirty-eight girls attending the school, twenty were affected—eight so severely that they temporarily lost consciousness. The bouts of trembling lasted from fifteen minutes to an hour. The principal had little choice but to close the school. When it reopened on August 19, the students were free of their trembling, although school officials were now faced with a new dilemma: widespread complaints of headaches. Those exhibiting these symptoms were sent home, and the school finally got back to normal after the autumn break.[68]

These outbreaks of writing tremors were part of a much wider pattern of maladies that swept through some European schools during this time. These schools had one common thread: very strict instruction where students were pushed to their mental limits with long, tedious exercises. These episodes coincided with the rise of "mental discipline," which became popular in Europe in the nineteenth century and viewed the mind as a muscle whereby to reach their potential, a student must engage in daily mental gymnastics. Many of these exercises involved rote memorization and repetition. The method was later refuted by psychologists such as Edward Thorndike (1874–1949) who soon realized that such efforts were not getting the desired results. For instance, when the test scores of students who had been schooled in math were compared with those with poor math training, there was no difference in their capacity to reason.[69]

While "mental discipline" soon fell out of favor with the advent of World War I, during the previous decades, stress associated with this teaching method was responsible for a variety of bizarre outbreaks among students who were exhibiting what psychologists refer to as "psychomotor agitation." In other words, in intolerable, unescapable settings where people are subjected to stressful conditions over a long period of time, twitching, trembling, and trance states are common as the anxiety disrupts motor neurons that send messages to different parts of the body.[70] Psychiatrists refer to these outbreaks as "motor hysteria." Outbreaks of twitching, shaking, and trance states often persisted for weeks or months in European schools at this time.[71]

The French school system, where a number of outbreaks occurred during this period, was characterized by monotonous performance drills. A 1908 inquiry into the educational practices of European education revealed that French primary schools were "far too much composed of memory work."[72] The French education code discouraged games and other physical activities, as teachers feared the consequences given that they were legally responsible for accidents under their supervision.[73] The inquiry reported that students were under great pressure to perform and faced being kicked out if their grades dipped as there were long waiting lists of students keen on getting accepted. One educator remarked: "With such dismissal constantly hanging over their head, pupils appear to be always at high pressure."[74] The report described secondary schools in France as "a veritable prison-house for all pupils from the youngest equally to the oldest, with a system of continual espionage known as *surveillance* (every minute of the day being duly apportioned, even recreation policed)" and possessing "scarcely a human feature." During a visit to one French school, the observer described the teaching as "monotonous and reiterated preaching" that included considerable memorization.[75] A school inspector in Germany, Joseph Lucas, wrote that in Bavaria "it truly does not matter if one serves his three years in the army or in the schoolhouse."[76] During the latter nineteenth century, the German curriculum was notorious for being unyielding and inflexible.[77] The situation was similar in Swiss schools.[78]

Twitching Epidemic, 1939 (Bellevue, Louisiana, USA)

In 1939, a strange twitching epidemic broke out among a group of girls at a school in Bellevue, Louisiana. Psychiatrists who investigated the case noted that the first person to be stricken was a popular seventeen-year-old student at the high school; she was an awkward dancer and felt very uncomfortable engaging in any dance-related activity. This posed a problem because her boyfriend was an excellent dancer and was showing interest in another girl who was also a very proficient dancer. The psychiatrists concluded that the afflicted girl—Helen—was able to resolve her dilemma subconsciously by developing an involuntary twitch, which excused her from dance classes as she was unwell. When this happened, her boyfriend began to show renewed interest. At one point, the twitching spread to several of Helen's female friends, who subconsciously identified with her, thus gaining attention for themselves. The outbreak began in January during a homecoming dance. Helen attended but only as a spectator. Suddenly, her right leg began twitching uncontrollably while watching her classmates dancing. She was plagued with bouts of leg twitching for several weeks after the event. One day while at school she was playing basketball, her twitching flared up, causing some of her friends to worry that they might "catch" it.[79]

On February 21, a sixteen-year-old girlfriend of Helen was attending a public celebration when her abdomen, chest, and neck started twitching.[80] Even before the episode, she had been under a physician's care for anxiety.[81] Within two days, two more girlfriends began twitching during French class.[82] As the two girls were being treated in the school infirmary, an angry parent burst into the school and made a dramatic scene, fearful that her children might also "catch" the twitching. She demanded that her children be let out of school. The incident heightened anxiety levels among the students, and rumors quickly spread that other parents were going to take their children out of school. The principal closed school early in order to restore calm, but another girlfriend was stricken on the bus.[83]

When school reopened the following Monday, half of the students were absent; attendance did not stabilize for a week. Meanwhile, the twitching slowly subsided. Investigators pinpointed several factors that may have triggered the outbreak. They noted that a few days prior to Helen's twitching, school officials had made dance instruction classes mandatory. The investigators noted: "The jerking of her leg muscles obviously made it impossible for her to dance, so the painful conflict situation was resolved with no discredit to the subject."[84]

They hypothesized that as Helen could not win her boyfriend's waning affection through dancing, subconsciously she used the sick role to gain sympathy and attention. Investigators concluded that "Helen was both by temperament and training entirely incapable of consciously making a bid for the attention of her boyfriend, but unconsciously and involuntarily she may have been achieving precisely this end through [hysteria]."[85] It was believed that Helen's popularity shielded her from being negatively stigmatized and allowed her friends to unconsciously imitate her twitching once they saw the attention she was receiving.[86]

Islamic School Ghost Scare, 1962 (Johor Bahru, Malaysia)

On September 25, 1962, Malaysian psychiatrist Eng-Seng Tan of the Tampoi Mental Hospital in Johor Bahru, was called to an outbreak of mass hysteria at a nearby Islamic school. It was reported that about a dozen female students at the school became disturbed after seeing a spirit from a ghost-infested rambutan (fruit) tree in the schoolyard. The afflicted girls had rapid pulses; otherwise they appeared to be normal. At times, the girls would scream, beat their chests and tear at their hair.[87] Tan described the scene: "The atmosphere of the schoolhouse was tense and electric. There were pupils of the school, some nursing their fainting schoolmates, others milling around quite bewildered. There were the school officials rushing about excitedly trying to pacify the screaming girls, and there was before long a big number of curious spectators crowding in to see what was going on."[88] Eight girls were severely affected, while many others seemed to be caught up in the emotion of the situation. The eight were taken to the Johor Bahru General Hospital and soon released to their parents. In piecing together the circumstances behind the outbreak, Tan learned that it had started during recess when a student named Sariaton, became frightened after claiming to have seen a ghost near the rambutan tree. She screamed and fainted and later said that the entity had threatened to hurt her. Before long, her classmates also reported seeing ghosts near the tree. However, when their descriptions were compared, none of them were the same.

In addition to calling for psychiatric help to aid in the episode, school officials also contacted sought assistance from a *bomoh*—a Malay native healer—an elderly man dressed in yellow garb. Dramatically, he placed a heavy iron nail in his right hand and a lump of clay in his left, then stabbed the clay with the nail. In an effort to exorcise the ghosts, he approached each of the stricken girls, turned over the palms of their hands, and lightly stabbed them with the nail. He eventually approached the rambutan tree and spoke to Dr. Tan: "it was the nest of a mother—and 44 children-ghosts. He said that the girls had trodden on the toes of some of the children ghosts, so that the mother ghost retaliated by haunting the girls. He then stabbed the tree with his big iron nail, by which means he said he had killed a few of the children ghosts and assured us that the incident would not be repeated."[89]

The appearance of the bomoh complicated matters because he was unable to stop the "attacks." Furthermore, his appearance only served to legitimize the reality of the ghosts to the school officials who had called him in. The outbreak persisted over several more days and affected twenty-nine girls in all. Each time the episode would flare up, it began with the same girl—Sariaton—who would scream and then faint, soon followed by her classmates. Besides screaming and fainting, the girls reported a variety of symptoms including heart palpitations, general weakness, insomnia, and visions of a ghost beckoning to them. The psychiatrists were frustrated because only one of the girls was allowed to be treated by them. She recovered after being given a sedative. The remainder of the students sought out the bomoh, though their problems continued. Administrators decided to close the school for several weeks, and Sariaton was told not to return. Dr. Tan reported that prior to the outbreak, there had been tension as a school official had been allegedly favoring some students over others. Tan said that there were claims "of promoting some pupils who had failed their examination, and, in a few cases, who had not even sat for their examination."[90] The symptoms subsided only after the official in question was fired.

The manner in which the case was reported in the press only served to enhance the belief that the school was indeed infested with malicious ghosts. For instance, the influential *Straits Times* proclaimed: "A Vengeful Ghost Tried to Lure a Girl to Its Tree Lair." The paper reported that when the outbreak began and Sariaton had fainted, at about the same time, two other Malay girls, ages sixteen and seventeen, "clutched their throats and screamed that a 'beautiful woman' was threatening to strangle them."[91] According to the paper, "Sariaton said that an old woman with streaming white hair and bloodshot eyes had urged her to come to her lair up the tree." The bomoh who had been called in to help, Inche Haji Mohamed bin Bendera, told school board members that the only way to stop the haunting was to appease the ghosts with a feast. One of the affected girls echoed these sentiments and said that a ghost had demanded a feast of *nasi beryani*—a traditional dish made with rice, meat, spices, and vegetables. She said the ghost also said there would be more trouble if they were not appeased.

One of the girls affected, Zariah binte Jais, described her encounters with one of the ghosts as frightening. "It looked like a very old woman, with long white hair and blood-red eyes in a wrinkled face. Her body was shadowy, but her voice was soft and clear. She kept calling me by name to go and see her sister's wedding. Then I felt as if I was tasting nasi beryani, which she offered me. When I made to leave a dark figure, the same one I saw on Tuesday, threatened to kill me with a parang [machete]."[92] Zariah said that one of the spirits told her that she was unhappy because Sariaton had stepped on one of her ghost friends and failed to apologize. While apparently in a trance-like state, the ghost spoke through Zariah saying that the tree was their home, and she and her friends were planning to have a wedding there. The spirit said she would stop harassing the girls if the nasi beryani feast was held. The bomoh backed up Zariah's claims by saying that there were forty-four female spirits in the tree making preparations for a wedding.[93]

Believing in ghosts and claiming to have encountered them, may have been a culturally acceptable way for the girls to protest the perceived favoritism at the school. Over time, tension from the situation would have built up and led to the mass faintings and altered states of consciousness during which students saw visions related to their concerns. The appearance of ghosts at the school may have been a signal to authorities that something was amiss: in this instance, the allegations of misconduct by the school official who later lost his job. The outbreak of ghosts may have been a subconscious form of negotiation whereby the group of submissive, powerless schoolgirls was able to assert their authority by bringing unresolved issues to the fore. As a result, the corrupt official was fired and the girls' demands were indirectly met.

Outbreaks of mass hysteria in Malaysia experienced a sudden upsurge in about 1960, coinciding with the rise of the Islamic *dakwah* movement, which spread its conservative values across the country. As a result, a strict Muslim code of behavior was instituted in the Malay education system. This helps to explain why those affected by outbreaks are predominantly Malay females, as ethnic Indian and Chinese schools in Malaysia did not have rigid rules and regulations. One of the authors (RB) writes that it is no coincidence that outbreaks of collective spirit possession became common in Islamic Malay boarding schools where girls are often subjected to strict rules and little privacy, and "where students must account for their whereabouts at all times. Interaction with boys is forbidden, as is dating. Even visits by family and friends take place in rooms that resemble fishbowls—under the watchful eye of adult monitors. The formula for mass hysteria here is simple: all work and no play fosters abnormal states of mind that reflect local beliefs in the existence of an array of supernatural creatures."[94] However, these outbreaks ultimately serve a function of creating change when their needs are being blatantly ignored. In such situations, as a result of the pent-up stress and frustration, "students may collapse on the floor and enter trances, leading to a widespread belief that they have been the victims of demonic attacks. A few girls act as a mouthpiece for the class, publicly voicing complaints and frustrations with the way the school is being operated. The spirits are thought to be speaking through the girls, who negotiate better conditions with administrators, such as more recreation time and less homework. In reality, their subconscious is expressing what they cannot voice aloud. The girls avoid punishment for speaking out because the spirits are seen as wresting temporary control of their minds and bodies."[95]

Pregnancy Panic, early 1960s (Welsh, Louisiana, USA)

In 1960, a girl fell pregnant at an African American school in the town of Welsh in rural Louisiana. Authorities acted swiftly, and before long, the two students involved were sent away to reform school.[96] During this time in American history, a high-school girl becoming pregnant was a major offense and was looked upon negatively for both the girl and her family. A pregnant teenager was a scandal for both the families involved and the community.

It was within this hotbed of anxiety that a strange malady broke out at the school as twenty-one girls and one boy complained of dizziness, headaches, overwhelming drowsiness, tremor, epileptic-like fits, and catatonic posturing. The fits would persist for up to an hour. A study found that most of those with the affliction had been sexually active. It would later be discovered that sexual rendezvous had been occurring in the photography darkroom at lunchtime. Investigators believe that at least thirty different boys had partaken in the secret rendezvous. The outbreak coincided with rumors that pregnancy tests were to be given to all of the girls, and anyone testing positive would be sent to a correctional school. Sedatives were ineffective, and visits by outside authorities only made the symptoms worse. Only with the gradual reduction of anxiety did the outbreak subside seven months later.[97] It was later uncovered that sexual activity among students had been rampant, and the reform-school rumors caused great anxiety.

The first girl was stricken in a dramatic fashion when she began to hyperventilate at a nearby church choir concert on February 14 and was carried out unconscious. The next day, a schoolmate who had witnessed the incident "blacked out" at school. Soon more and more students were stricken. By early April, an alarming twenty girls and one boy were experiencing spells.

The Louisiana Health Department ruled out an environmental cause and eventually concluded that the culprit was stress-induced mass hysteria. Their investigation was extremely thorough, and they even conducted painful lumbar spine punctures on some of those affected so as to rule out the possibility of exotic causes. They also tested gum and candy found at the school after hearing rumors that a student had spiked them with drugs. The affected girls were given sedatives, but they failed to work because the underlying cause of the anxiety remained: the constant fear of being tested for pregnancy.[98]

As for the lone boy affected, he may have been fearful of having fathered a child or of being turned in for having been sexually active. Hence, when he suffered a fit, his fellow students jokingly speculated as to whether he would be the father of a boy or a girl.[99] By August, a more supportive principal took over, the students no longer feared being tested for pregnancy, and their fits subsided.

Possessed Factory Workers, 1973 (Singapore)

In 1973, mass hysteria swept across factories on the tiny island city-state of Singapore in Southeast Asia. W. H. Phoon of Singapore's Ministry of Labour documented several episodes.[100]

One incident occurred at a television assembly plant during January 1973. A female worker began to scream, then fainted. As her supervisor and several colleagues carried her to the medical clinic on a different floor, she screamed out and struggled against them. Before long, other female workers exhibited similar symptoms, and plant officials closed the factory later that night, reopening it the following Tuesday. Of the plant's 899 employees, each of the eighty-four workers stricken with "spells" were female Malays. During the two days the plant was shut down, management hired a bomoh, or witchdoctor, to exorcise the evil spirits. The day the factory reopened, more women had spells.[101]

Two nearby factories were soon affected—and again most victims were female

Malays. Investigators identified three types of cases. First were "hysterical sei-zures," which were typified by screaming, fierce struggling, and violence. Many exhibited extraordinary strength, often requiring several men to restrain them. Tranquilizers were ineffective. Those affected would ignore attempts to reassure them or not respond to any questions posed to them or would scream even more after inquiries were made. Between screams and shouts, some would break into nervous laughter, followed by more screaming. Some said they could see "a dark figure" that was about to strangle them.[102] The second category of cases included people who went into trance states. "While being violent, or before becoming violent, a worker would suddenly speak as though she was someone else, and claim that a spirit was speaking through her."[103] Such states persisted for no more than several minutes. The third group was of people who exhibited "frightened spells" and were fearful that something bad was going to happen. Their fear was often accompanied by feeling a cold chill, numbness, or dizziness.

The recipe for the Singaporean factory hysteria is similar to that of the convent and school hysterias. Most Malay females are enculturated to be seen and not heard and to avoid challenging male authorities.[104] With no way to vent frustra-tions, hysteria results. In Singapore, a former Malaysian state, spirit possession is an accepted part of everyday life and generates great concern and sympathy from relatives and coworkers.[105] This helps to explain why episodes are predominately confined to Malay females and occur amid a backdrop of employee dissatisfaction and management conflict. Faced with limited or nonexistent channels of protest and no union to address grievances, the workers are able to fight back indirectly. Trapped in an intolerable situation and facing financial stress and peer pressure to remain on the job, the anger and frustration felt by workers leads to a small number of people twitching, shaking, convulsing, and experiencing trance states. Many workers believe that the factory is possessed by evil spirits, which exacer-bates the situation and further raises anxiety levels. Such beliefs are reinforced by popular Malay folk beliefs. Each new outbreak of spirit possession is interpreted within the Malay worldview that holds to the reality of animistic spirits (toyols), roaming ghosts (hantus), and Jinn creatures as mentioned in the Koran.[106]

In Malaysian and Singaporean factory settings, management may call on the services of a bomoh, or native healer, to appease the spirits. It is not uncommon for the possessed workers to tell the bomoh about their unhappiness with conditions at the factory—conditions that are blamed for attracting the spirits. In this way, the bomoh sometimes serves as a mediator between the dissatisfied workers and management, which often leads to better conditions, thus reducing stress levels and a subsiding of the outbreak. However, episodes may persist if the underlying conditions for the dissatisfaction remain, in which case the cycle is repeated. In this regard, anthropologist Aihwa Ong believes that outbreaks of mass hysteria in Malaysian factories are a form of covert political resistance. She writes that these episodes of spirit possession "are acts of rebellion, symbolizing what cannot be spoken directly, calling for a renegotiation of obligations between the management and workers. However, technocrats have turned a deaf ear to such protests . . . choosing to view possession episodes narrowly as sickness caused by physiological and psychological maladjustment."[107]

Poisoning Scare, 1983 (Israeli Occupied West Bank, Middle East)

Between March and April 1983, disturbing news reports from the Middle East claimed that over one thousand Palestinian schoolgirls had been poisoned—most likely by agents of Israel. Even major Israeli newspapers published the claims of the attack, which was said to have taken place in the Israeli-occupied West Bank. The victims complained of headaches, dizziness, fainting, abdominal pain, blurred vision, blindness, and weakness of their limbs. Investigations by health researchers would later determine that the outbreak was psychological in nature and had been triggered by an odor from a school latrine, amidst a backdrop of long-standing Palestinian mistrust of Israel. The symptoms appeared over a stretch of fifteen days and coincided with rumors of poison-gas attacks. The episode was mostly confined to schools in several adjacent villages in this bitterly disputed region. The case became known as the Arjenyattah epidemic as it affected the communities of Arrabah, Djenin, and Yattah.[108] The West Bank region of Jordan has been occupied by Israeli forces since 1967, a source of long-standing political tension with the presence of the Israelis generating intense hatred. While many Palestinians believe that one day the land will be returned, one observer noted, "some tend to believe that the Israelis would do anything to perpetuate the status quo."[109] Within this climate of hatred and distrust, suspicion naturally fell on Israeli agents or civilian extremists for perpetrating such a heinous act—poisoning young girls.

The outbreak spread in three waves, with the first wave of illness occurring on March 21, 1983, after a mysterious rotten egg smell was detected near the Arrabah Girls' School. During class, a seventeen-year-old student reported suffering from dizziness, difficulty breathing, a headache, and blurred vision. Before long, fifteen classmates were also stricken. The rotten-egg smell seemed to emanate from a schoolyard bathroom.[110] The next day, five adults and sixty-one students were evaluated by medical personnel. Medical authorities investigating the outbreak noted a definite relationship between the proximity of those affected and the bathroom where the bad smell was reported. The highest attack rates were in those rooms nearest to the bathroom where the foul smell was reported to have come from.[111]

On March 22, *Yedi'ot Ahronot*, an Israeli newspaper, reported on the incident, with the journalist suggesting that toxic gas was involved, observing that the girls "were suddenly afflicted by an attack of blindness, headache and stomach pain." In reality, the symptoms were exaggerated by the reporter, who, instead of listing "blurred vision," wrote "blindness."[112]

A second clustering of similar symptoms occurred near Djenin on March 26 and affected 246 girls at six schools. Some staff were also sickened. The following evening, sixty-four Djenin residents exhibited similar complaints after a passing car emitted a cloud of gas.[113] That same day, press reports, including many papers in Israel, were describing the wave of illnesses as attempted genocide. For example, *Ma'Ariv*, said that the Djenin gas cloud was a clear instance of mass poisoning. Their headline proclaimed: "The Mysterious Poisoning Goes On: 56 High School Girls in Djenin Poisoned." The report read: "The mysterious poisoning of 50 students that took place last week in Arraba [village] affected 56 additional students yesterday in Djenin. Currently no definite evidence exists as to the source of the poison. Yesterday morning, 29 schoolgirls were admitted to the hospital from Djenin High School with difficulty breathing, cyanosis, and dizziness."[114] According to the paper, the "gassing" was an accepted fact, only the source was in question. On March 28, *Ha'Aretz* claimed that tests had determined that the Djenin students had been sickened by a nerve agent.[115]

The Israeli government dispatched prominent psychiatrist Albert Hafez and epidemiologist Baruch Modan to investigate the incidents. Hafez found that press reports clearly fueled the episode, which was an outbreak of mass hysteria. Meanwhile, a third cluster of cases occurred on April 3 at a Yattah girls' school and spread to several nearby schools.[116] Modan traced the origin of the outbreak to a latrine near the Arrabah school and concluded that an episode of mass psychogenic illness had been triggered by the bad smell coming from the bathroom. Later that same day, another wave was touched off during recess, as rumors spread when friends of the first group of girls to become sickened discussed the possibility that they, too, had been poisoned.

Modan and his team also found that the media played an influential role, especially during the second wave that raced through several Jenin schools and adjacent villages. As for the sixty-four Djenin residents who were reportedly sickened by poison gas from a speeding car, it was later determined that the "toxic gas" was actually black smoke from a faulty exhaust system. The final illness wave was attributed to the continuous spreading of rumors and media reports that the girls were being targeted in a series of poison-gas attacks.[117]

As some suspicious Arabs refused to accept the findings, the United States sent physicians Philip Landrigan and Bess Miller to conduct an independent inquiry that included samples of soil, water, and air: all tested negative for toxic agents. It was concluded that fear and mass suggestion took over after students detected the smell of hydrogen sulfide gas escaping from the latrine of the first school affected, in Arrabah.[118] Landrigan and Miller's findings were in agreement with those of Modan and Hafez.

Social Network Hysteria, 2011–2012 (LeRoy, New York, USA)

In 2011, over a dozen girls and one boy at LeRoy Central School in Western New York, were stricken with a mysterious ailment that included facial tics, twitching muscles, and garbled verbal outbursts similar to Tourette's syndrome. The outbreak was frightening to people in the community and made headlines across the United States as media outlets speculated as to the existence of a mystery illness. The symptoms were so severe that some of the students were unable to complete a sentence without muddling their words. After a series of exhaustive tests that were all negative, health officials concluded that the students were suffering from mass hysteria, a diagnosis that resulted in community outcry as many believed that some other trigger was responsible.

The outbreak in LeRoy does not fit the typical spread of symptoms in cases, as the students were spread across the school, not from a single class. Further, mass hysteria is traditionally spread by direct sight and sound—that is, seeing and hearing other people affected. This case was different. Investigators noted the important role played by social media, including Facebook, Twitter, and YouTube, to communicate about the outbreak, as well as e-mail, blogs, and text messages. Dr. David Lichter observed: "It's remarkable to see how one individual posts something, and then the next person who posts something—not only are the movements bizarre and not consistent with known movement disorders, but it's the same kind of movements. This mimicry goes on with Facebook."[119] Neurologists treating fourteen of the victims also reported that "exacerbation and prolongation of symptomatology was observed with increased media attention and psychosocial stressors."[120]

Critics of the mass hysteria diagnosis have claimed that the victims, which included a nurse from the town, had little in common. James Dupont, a parent of one of the girls, asserted: "For us to try to buy that our girls all seem to have a traumatic experience within a couple of months . . . and all seem to have handled it the same way with the same symptoms, that don't even know each other, it's just unbelievable."[122] However, neurologist Laszlo Mechtler, who treated many of the girls, observed that they were not exactly strangers: "Some of them were friends, some played on the same soccer team and all are in the same high school."[123]

The public reaction to the outbreak was remarkable in the annals of mass-hysteria literature. For instance, when the popular *Huffington Post* published an article about the outbreak in January 2012, no less than one thousand blog postings were recorded on their site in a single week. Concerned people proposed dozens of possible triggers, everything from Lyme disease caused by ticks to pesticide poisoning. No theory seemed too outrageous. One person suggested the likelihood of copper poisoning on the assumption that the affected girls had been abusing alcohol. It was thought that they may have been placing copper pennies in their mouths to cover up the smell of alcohol! The idea was quickly shot down when someone noted that since 1982, American "copper pennies" have contained just two and a half percent copper; the rest is zinc. Other theories ranged from the victims having abused drugs such as Ecstasy or Ritalin to magnesium deficiency and exposure to electromagnetic fields. The most common belief locally was the existence of a toxic dumpsite near the school, although tests by the New York State Department of Health and the federal Environmental Protection Agency were negative.[123] However, if toxic chemicals *had* been involved, why would they almost exclusively affect only young girls and not others at the school such as teachers?

Another popular theory held that PANDAS disorder was the culprit. A form of chronic streptococcus, or strep throat infection, PANDAS stands for Pediatric Autoimmune Disorders Associated with Strep. This possibility was championed by neurologist Rosario Trifiletti who tested many of the girls, and on February

7, he announced the results: at least eight of the victims had tested positive for a "PANDAS-like illness." Fox News medical reporter Dr. Marc Siegel confidently supported the hypothesis. But the researcher who discovered PANDAS syndrome, Dr. Susan Swedo, immediately challenged the likelihood, noting that high levels of strep antibodies (which some of the girls had) does not necessarily mean that the patients had PANDAS. She said that the presence of such antibodies were extremely common in school-age students.[124]

Since 2000, researchers have noted a series of similar mass hysteria outbreaks—each of which appear to have social media as a key component of their spread.[125] One group of researchers observes that while in the past, outbreaks of mass psychogenic illness in school settings have been typically confined to a classroom, a grade level, or a close group of acquaintances, social media may be changing this pattern. They write: "This may explain why in LeRoy, symptoms are not confined to a class or group but are scattered throughout the school. We may be witnessing a milestone in the history of MPI (mass psychogenic illness) where the primary agent of spread will be the Internet and social media networks."[126] Another unusual aspect to these new cases is the absence of a clear stressor. It may be that interpersonal conflict, which has always been common in the adolescent world, is a major factor, but social media is now able to amplify these anxieties in ways that did not exist in the past.

Outbreaks of conversion disorder prompted by repression have a long history. Perhaps the most famous instance occurred during the Salem witch hunts of 1691–1693. Episodes of motor hysteria remain common in parts of rural Africa and Asia where they often take the form of shaking, twitching, and possession states, the presence of which reinforces traditional beliefs in the existence of demons and evil spirits. While episodes have been rarely reported in Western countries, since the dawn of the twenty-first century, there has been a spike in the number of cases that may be a result of social media and new communication technologies.

In chapter 9, we review episodes of immediate community threats that may affect regions or entire countries. Unlike anxiety hysteria, the threat arises from preexisting tensions and often persists for weeks or months and occasionally years. During outbreaks, residents often redefine a variety of ambiguous stimuli as being related to the threat, giving rise to sightings of mad gassers, flying saucers, or in the case of eighteenth- and nineteenth-century New England—imaginary vampires.

CHAPTER 9

IMMEDIATE COMMUNITY THREATS: DEFENDING THE HOMELAND

Immediate community threats involve exaggerated feelings of danger within communities at-large, where members of the affected population are concerned over what is believed to be a personal threat. Episodes usually persist from a few weeks to several months and often recur periodically. Participants may express fear and concern, but rarely attempt to take flight. The underlying process of fantasy creation and spread is the fallibility of human perception, and the tendency for people sharing similar beliefs in group settings is to accept the opinion of the majority.

The mass media typically play a pivotal role in creating, maintaining, and eventually extinguishing episodes. At the beginning of outbreaks, they often exaggerate the perceived threat and report on it in an uncritical or sensational manner. These initial accounts may cause people to scrutinize their environment in an effort to confirm or deny the existence of the reported threat, giving rise to more sightings, and in turn, more media reports. During the American kissing-bug scare of 1899, people were warned to be on the lookout for the dreaded insect. While that year was no different than previous ones for the prevalence of the bug, people were looking out for kissing bugs and reported a spate of "attacks." These had been from a variety of insects that had been mistaken for the kissing bug. No one ever saw the bug doing the dirty deed as they were said to attack while people were asleep. Once the media begins to turn critical and produce skeptical articles that often ridicule believers, the wave usually experiences a precipitous decline.

Occasionally the feared agent is a mysterious attacker believed to be terrorizing a community, such as the phantom slasher of Taipei, Taiwan. During a

191

two-week period in 1956, nearly two dozen people claimed to have been slashed by a man welding a razor-blade-type object. Taiwanese police later determined the episode to have been imaginary. In the wake of rumors, lacerations caused by everything from incidental paper cuts or bumping into an umbrella on a crowded bus were redefined as slashings.[1]

Sometimes the imaginary threat is from an agent that is believed to cause illness, such as the series of phantom attacks in Mattoon, Illinois, during two weeks in 1944, that was believed to involve a "mad gasser."[2] On other occasions, the perceived agent of threat is more global and diffuse, such as the belief that poison gas from the tail of Halley's Comet posed a threat to all life on earth during its closest point of rendezvous in May 1910. The threat is often exaggerated by authority figures, such as the small number of scientists who expressed their opinion that the comet posed a danger.

Examining the social and cultural content of episodes is useful in understanding outbreaks. For instance, during the "ghost rocket" scare of 1946, authorities in Sweden were inundated with sightings of rockets that were believed to have been test-fired by Russia as a means to intimidate the country in the political uncertainty that followed the close of World War II. While rumors and sensational press coverage helped to fuel the episode, the poor state of relations between the two countries was also important as they have a longstanding history of border disputes and invasion fears. It was within this context that people began to redefine known astronomical and meteorological events as ghost-rocket related.[3]

MEMORABLE IMMEDIATE COMMUNITY THREATS

The London Monster, 1788–1790 (England)

Between March 1788 and June 1790, nearly sixty women were reportedly assaulted (usually stabbed or slashed) by a supposed maniac who became known as the "London Monster."[4] An artificial flower-maker named Rhynwick Williams was eventually arrested and put on trial for the attacks. He was sentenced to six years in jail and disappeared into obscurity after his release. Due to the vagaries of English law, Williams was not charged with assault on the body of one of his victims (Ann Porter) but instead with "an intent to tear, spoil, cut, and deface her garments and clothes."[5] A subsequent analysis of the case has led some investigators to believe that there was no "monster" at all and that the scare was actually a form of social panic.

There are numerous cases of stabbers, slashers, dress cutters, hair snippers, oil throwers, foot stompers, shoe stealers, etc., right into the present day. These violent fetishist attacks are invariably committed by men on women. The attackers typically get sexual gratification from the attacks and are impotent if they attempt normal intercourse.[6] However, the London Monster case was not as clear cut as other fetish attacks. Rhynwick Williams certainly appeared to have had the habit of verbally harassing women on the street, but there is no firm evidence that he did anything more. There is also evidence that he had normal sexual intercourse (albeit with prostitutes). Lastly, Williams also had a fairly solid alibi from coworkers who testified he was with them at the time of one of the attacks. As with some other cases of mass attacks—both real (Jack the Ripper) and imagined (the Halifax Slasher)—the precise number of victims is in dispute. This is due to a wide variety of attacks that, at a time of public panic and hysteria, are lumped together as the work of one person.

The London Monster either slashed or stabbed his victims with a knife held by hand, a knife hidden in a cane, a spike attached to his knee, an iron claw, or an artificial flower with a spike that he would persuade victims to smell. It was this last, unusual weapon that drew attention to Williams because of his occupation.[7] Another factor that casts doubt upon a single attacker is the multiple descriptions of the London Monster. He was variously described as a pale, thin man or a tall, large man and wore a wide variety of different civilian clothes or a uniform.[8] These discrepancies led to theories about one man wearing multiple disguises or blundering pickpockets accidentally injuring people.[9]

Many aspects of the London Monster scare were repeated in the 1938 Halifax Slasher scare: multiple attack methods, varied descriptions, copycat attacks, and innocent pedestrians in the vicinity of an attack being mistakenly thought to be the slasher and set upon by mobs. Little had changed in 150 years! There are two possible interpretations of the London Monster attacks: most of the attacks were by one man (with either the correct attacker or an innocent man being blamed and jailed) or all of the attacks were a combination of deliberate hoaxes, imagined assaults, and "normal" street crimes of the time committed by multiple people.

New England Vampire Scare, eighteenth and nineteenth centuries (USA)

During the eighteenth and nineteenth centuries, a fear of vampires swept through New England, resulting in dozens of bodies being dug up and either dismembered or burned—sometimes both. The scare was triggered by a confluence of factors, particularly the belief in vampires, brought from Old World Europe where accounts of undead corpses were common.[10] The prevalence of consumption (tuberculosis) was another key to the scare. TB made a victim's skin pale and gave the appearance that the blood had been sucked from their body. Michael D'Agostino notes that a regional belief evolved that the spirit of a recently deceased family member would rise from the grave to attack other family members. It was within this environment of fear and uncertainty that folklore took over where medicine had failed. When graves were exhumed on suspicion that the deceased was a vampire, they looked for telltale signs including the apparent growth of hair and fingernails, blood near the mouth, and little outward decay.[11] Once a body was dug up, the most common procedure was to remove key organs, such as the heart, liver, and lungs, and burn them. The ashes were then mixed with water or medicine and fed to the afflicted, as a possible cure.[12]

Folklorist Michael Bell has documented numerous vampire exhumations in small towns across New England during this period.[13] A typical case took place in 1793 in Manchester, Vermont. Several years earlier, in 1789, Isaac Burton married Rachel Harris, who was young and vibrant: a picture of health. Within a year, she had died of TB. Soon after, Mr. Burton took a second wife—Hulda Powell—who, within a short time, also fell ill with the disease. Little was known about the origin and nature of TB, and her dramatic decline in health was attributed by friends and relatives to Burton's first wife returning from the grave as a vampire to torment Hulda. Judge John Pettibone, writing in the *History of Manchester, Vermont*, describes the incident: "She became ill soon after they were married and when she was in the last stages of consumption, a strange infatuation took possession of the minds of the connections and friends of the family. They were induced to believe that if the vitals of the first wife could be consumed by being burned in a charcoal fire it would effect a cure of the sick second wife. Such was the strange delusion that they disinterred the first wife who had been buried about three years. They took out the liver, heart, and lungs, what remained of them, and burned them to ashes on the blacksmith's forge of Jacob Mead. Timothy Mead officiated at the altar in the sacrifice to the Demon Vampire who it was believed was still sucking the blood of the then living wife of Captain Burton. It was the month of February and good sleighing. Such was the excitement that from five hundred to one thousand people were present. This account is furnished . . . by an eyewitness to the transaction."[14]

Another incident occurred in Woodstock, Vermont, in 1817. On February 14, a local man named Frederick Ransom died of TB. Soon after, his father, fearing that his son might attack his family from the grave, exhumed the body, cut out his heart, and set fire to his remains. Journalist Gareth Henderson writes that due to the high mortality rates at the time, when medical treatments failed, residents often turned to supernatural explanations such as vampires. "This feared specter of the night helped explain why tuberculosis spread so rapidly among families—it had to be the result of a predeceased loved one coming back as a blood-sucking vampire."[15]

Writing in the *Journal of American Folklore* in 1889, Jeremiah Curtin describes another Vermont account of a vampire exhumation in about 1830, at Woodstock Green. When a brother of the deceased became ill shortly after the funeral, he states that "the family decided at once to disinter the body . . . and examine his heart," which was found to have been well-preserved.[16] This was viewed as a sure sign of vampirism. The organ was removed, placed in an iron pot and reduced to ashes under a fire.

One of the earliest known accounts of a vampire exhumation in New England occurred in 1784 at Willington, Connecticut. Local resident Moses Holmes was an eyewitness. His account appears in John Warner Barber's book, *Connecticut Historical Collection*, published in 1836. Holmes said that a "foreigner," whom he described as a "quack doctor," claimed that consumption could be cured by digging up the remains of deceased family members and examining them for vines and sprouts growing from their vital organs. He said that both the vitals and vegetation should be harvested and burned in order to cure other stricken family members. Under the doctor's guidance, he had the remains of Isaac Johnson's two children, who had died of tuberculosis, dug up. However, nothing unusual was found. There is no mention of the bodies being burned. Holmes refers to the doctor as an "impostor" and warns his fellow residents to beware of him.[17]

Another representative case occurred in 1799 in Exeter, Rhode Island, and highlights the tragic and fragile nature of life in colonial America. Six members of the Tillinghast family died of consumption. Beginning with the second child to die, each of the five other children complained that the first child to succumb—

Sarah—would torment them by sitting on different parts of their body in order to cause "great pain and misery." In an effort to save the rest of the family, the desperate father exhumed the bodies, cut out their hearts, and incinerated them. The body of Sarah was the most preserved, which was taken as evidence that she was a vampire. Michael Bell writes: "The eyes were open and fixed. The hair and nails had grown, and the heart and arteries were filled with fresh red blood. It was clear at once to these astonished people that the cause of their trouble lay before them. All the conditions of the vampire were present in the corpse of Sarah, the first that had died, and against whom all the others had so bitterly complained."[18] Her heart was cut out and burned on a rock.

Nearly a century later, in 1892, Exeter was the site of another vampire exhumation involving the body of nineteen-year-old Mercy Brown, who may have been the last person in New England to have her body dug up on suspicion of stalking the living from her grave. Brown died of TB on January 17, 1892. Two months later, her body was exhumed as she was suspected of sucking the life from her sick brother Edwin.[19] Bell recounts the story, observing that the body was in a reasonably preserved state. "The heart and liver were removed, and in cutting open the heart, clotted and decomposed blood was found, which was what might be expected at that stage of decomposition. The liver showed no blood, though it was in a well-preserved state. These two organs were removed, and a fire being kindled in the cemetery, they were reduced to ashes, and the attendants seemed satisfied."[20] In order to ensure that the cure would take effect, the afflicted person was to eat the heart and liver. With the death of Mercy Brown, the great New England vampire scare subsided as people began to gain a better understanding of tuberculosis and its origins.

The Kissing Bug Scare, 1899 (USA)

The term *kissing bug* is used to describe several species of insects that suck blood from mammals by piercing the skin of sleeping victims, typically on the face and especially the lips. After biting, kissing bugs defecate on their victims. This practice can transmit potentially fatal Chagas disease as a parasite that lives in the feces can severely damage the heart, nervous system, brain, colon, and esophagus. Kissing bugs are much feared in parts of Central and South America where an estimated fifty thousand deaths occur annually.[21] While the bug's notorious reputation outside the United States may have contributed to the scare of 1899, kissing bugs on the mainland United States rarely bite people and do not defecate while feeding, making the risk of transmitting Chagas disease rare.[22]

During the summer of 1899, a *Washington Post* police reporter James F. McElhone triggered a nationwide scare when, while making his usual journalistic inquiries, he became aware of a sudden surge of patients who were being treated for strange bug bites at the Washington City Emergency Hospital. The bites caused redness and swelling, typically on the lips.[23] Oddly, no one ever caught the offending culprit in the act, and it was assumed to have attacked while the patient was asleep. On June 20, McElhone's article on the spate of bug-bite victims appeared in the *Post* in sensational fashion, describing victims as "badly poisoned" and warning that the bugs threatened to become something of "a plague."[24] The story was quickly published in papers across the country.[25] Soon any insect bite, swelling, or pain of any kind on or near the face was attributed to the nefarious kissing bug. McElhone wrote: "Lookout for the new bug. It is an insidious insect that bites without causing pain and escapes unnoticed. But afterward the place where it has bitten swells to ten times its normal size. The Emergency Hospital has had several victims of this insect as patients lately and the number is increasing."[26] McElhone cited an "attack" from the previous night on a newspaper agent named William Smith who presented to the Emergency Department "with his upper lip swollen to many times its natural size. The symptoms are in every case the same, and there is indication of poisoning from an insect's bite."

As the story appeared in papers across the country, accounts of kissing-bug attacks began to pour in. A typical encounter was reported in Alameda, California. The *San Francisco Call* stated that John McCulley had been found unconscious after he claimed to have been attacked by what he presumed was a kissing bug on Saturday night while waiting for a train. According to the paper, McCulley insisted "that the thing was black and unlike any insect he had ever seen before."[27] In Mt. Pleasant, Utah, when a boy named Sophus Jensen was bitten on the lip while at school by an unidentified insect that caused his face to swell, a front-page story in the *Salt Lake City Herald* proclaimed: "Mt. Pleasant Boy Attacked by the Mysterious Insect."[28] Following three "attacks" in La Salle, Ohio, it was reported that "every residence in the town is closed airtight every night" for fear of being bitten. On a lighter note, a group of young girls in La Salle had reportedly formed a "kissing bug club" and were keeping the suspects in glass jars, "with the object of acquiring one specimen for each member."[29]

Fears were heightened when a Chicago coroner signed a death certificate that the demise of Mary Steger had been precipitated by the bite of a kissing bug. Dr. George Illingworth who attended the autopsy, stated: "Mrs. Steger was stung six days before her death . . . She distinctly remembered having been stung, but did not succeed in capturing the bug. The sting was on the upper lip, and the mark was plainly perceptible, even before the face swelled."[30] However, there were suspicious circumstances that called into question the kissing-bug hypothesis. While the death certificate officially read that the cause of death was "the sting of a kissing bug," and that is what grabbed press headlines—the document also stated that a contributing cause was tonsillitis. While massive swelling had been noted and presumed associated with the bite, this was problematic because when the coroner examined the body, he also observed that it had already been treated with embalming fluid, and therefore, "he could not definitely determine the cause of death." This did not stop the newspaper—the *San Francisco Call*—from printing the headline: "Cause of Death a Kissing Bug." Another death attributed to the bug occurred when a two-year-old girl in Trenton, New Jersey, died myste-riously on the night of July 9. This diagnosis was based on a physician finding an ambiguous "red spot" on the toddler's leg shortly before her death.[31]

A Chicago preacher, "Professor" A. M. Leonard, has the distinction of taking the most dire and extreme position on the "outbreak." He claimed the presence of the insect to be the locust foretold in the book of Revelation portending the end of the world. He believed the insects were deliberately targeting nonbelievers. He cited the following passages: "And there came out of the smoke locusts upon the earth; and unto them was given power, as the scorpions of the earth have power . . . And it was commanded them that they should not hurt the grass of the earth, neither any green thing, neither any tree, but only those men which have not the seal of God upon their foreheads."[32]

The scare began to subside with a number of scientists speaking out in the press and calling for calm. During late July, attempting to downplay fears over the bugs in an article in *Scientific American*, Dr. Eugene Murray-Aaron observed that the insect was no more common in 1899 than in years past and that its bite was not poisonous.[33] One influential article was written by Leland Howard, chief of entomology for the US Department of Agriculture, in *Popular Science Monthly*. He described the scare as a *"newspaper* epidemic, for every insect bite where the biter was not at once recognized was attributed to the popular and somewhat mysterious creature."[34]

At the height of the scare, the Philadelphia Academy of Natural Sciences was inundated with specimens of alleged attackers. Entomologists who analyzed their remains identified houseflies, bees, beetles, and even a butterfly as the culprit. In all, they identified twenty-one different types of insects.[35] During the summer of 1899, the annual meeting of the American Association for the Advancement of Science in Columbus, Ohio, was dubbed "the Convention of Kissing Bug Experts" due to the number of entomology papers that were presented on the subject.[36] The state of New Jersey's official entomologist, Professor John B. Smith, also tried to quell public fears about kissing bugs by issuing a challenge. "I have been bitten by them many a time," he said, "and if anyone will bring me a live kissing bug I will let it sting to its heart's content. We are simply going through a craze like the one we had when spider bites were popular. Everybody who was bitten by any kind of an insect was bitten by a spider. The same is true now."[37] He observed that kissing bugs feed on caterpillars and other insects, and "sometimes convey poisons, but the insect is no more numerous or dangerous now than it ever was."

Newspapers clearly fanned the flames of fear.[38] One report from a woman in Chicago sounded more like a vampire attack than a relatively mundane insect bite.[39] There were even accounts of homeless people in Washington, DC, wrapping themselves in bandages and soliciting donations on the street. They claimed to have been out of work and in need of funds in order to survive while they recovered from their wounds.[40] Dr. Howard described the episode as a form of mass hysteria and considered it likely that many of the bites were from mosquitoes. Some press coverage appeared to recognize the scare for what it was—and made light of the episode. In Illinois, the *Rockford Register-Gazette* stated that several local girls had "been on the streets every night in the hope of meeting a kissing bug."[41] One newspaper editorial perhaps aptly summed up the great kissing-bug scare. John McNaught of the *San Francisco Call* wrote: "The prevailing sputter and flurry over the kissing bug is a striking illustration of the old proverb, 'We always see what we look for.'"[42] Alluding to the power of the press and the propensity for human imagination to run wild, he observed that "all at once, the creature appears simultaneously all over the United States; and every community has its thrilling tale to tell of the terrors of the creature's kiss."

Some newspaper editors clearly did not take the threat posed by the bug too seriously. When an August "attack" was claimed by Miss Annette Grogan of Hillsboro, Ohio, the local *News-Herald* made light of the incident, claiming that just prior to the encounter with the insect, she had remarked to her companions "that she was sweet sixteen and had never been kissed."[43] In Kenosha, Wisconsin, the *Milwaukee Journal* reported that Katherine Kluetz claimed to have been bitten by a kissing bug in her sleep, and, having swatted the insect, it was found in the morning dead next to her bed. After seeking treatment for her swollen lip at the office of Dr. Paul Malmstrom, he pronounced it to have been a kissing bug and placed it on display in a bottle of alcohol. However, a reporter who visited the office noted that it bore a remarkable resemblance to an undernourished June bug, which was common at the time. The incident was said to have triggered an upsurge in sales of door and window screens in the city.[44] By early September, some residents were attempting to ward off kissing-bug attacks in their sleep by placing drops of rhodium oil on their bed quilts.[45]

"Jersey Devil," January 1909 (New Jersey, USA)

Between January 16 and 23, 1909, the Pine Barrens region of New Jersey was overwhelmed with reports of a mysterious creature and its footprints. Many said that the creature stood three to four feet tall with a head resembling a horse and bat-like wings. Others said it was only as big as a dog. During the brief scare, most residents stayed inside behind locked doors; factories and schools closed, and search parties scoured the countryside for the creature. One of the first reported sightings was made by James Sackville, a Woodbury, New Jersey, police officer, who said he spotted a winged beast at 2:00 a.m. on January 17, hopping like a bird and giving off a screech before it flew into the darkness. According to press reports, over one hundred people in more than two dozen communities saw the devil.[46]

A typical description was that of E. W. Minster, a postmaster living in Bristol, Pennsylvania, who reported a strange encounter on the weekend of January 16 and 17: "I awoke about two o'clock in the morning . . . and finding myself unable to sleep, I arose and wet my head with cold water as a cure for insomnia. As I got up I heard an eerie, almost supernatural sound from the direction of the river . . . I looked out upon the Delaware and saw flying diagonally across what appeared to be a large crane but which was emitting a glow like a firefly. Its head resembled that of a ram, with curled horns, and its long thin neck was thrust forward in flight. It had long thin wings and short legs, the front legs shorter than the hind."[47] He described the sound it made as a cross between a whistle and a squawk.

On January 19, Mr. and Mrs. Nelson Evans saw the "monster" at close range for ten minutes at about 2:30 a.m. It was "about three feet and a half high, with a head like a collie dog and a face like a horse. It had a long neck, wings about two feet long, and its back legs were like those of a crane, and it had horse's hooves. It walked on its back legs and held up two short front legs with paws on them."[48] It flew away after they yelled at it.

Sporadic sightings have been recorded since the 1909 episodes. In 1924, Emil Schneider, a milk driver, allegedly followed a creature like an overgrown calf or giant dog through the woods for hours. "Once it turned and bared fangs eight inches long at me," he claimed.[49] In 1960, mysterious screams and tracks in the region were dismissed by police as being caused by Halloween pranksters.[50] In 1993, a park ranger allegedly saw a creature that was "approximately 6-feet-tall, with horns on its head and matted black fur."[51]

The outbreak of January 1909 and subsequent occasional sightings did not appear out of thin air, but have evolved out of a long tradition. Since the 1730s, the desolate Pine Barrens forest region of central and southern New Jersey and adjacent eastern Pennsylvania has been the site of stories of the "Jersey Devil." Historian Brian Regal observes that according to Jersey Devil lore, when a local women gave birth to a thirteenth baby, she reportedly cursed it, resulting in the infant being born with a hideous horselike head and wings resembling a bat. He writes: "It yelped menacingly and flew up and out of the chimney, disappearing into the dark to spend the centuries accosting anyone unfortunate enough to encounter it."[52] Prior to 1909, the legend was not only spread by word-of-mouth, but through the area, regional, and occasionally, the national press.

The Jersey Devil flap of 1909 is a classic example of an immediate community threat, steeped in a longstanding regional urban legend, which primed residents just prior to the wave. Locals grew up hearing tales of the devil. Former New Jersey Governor Walter Edge once remarked that as a boy growing up in Atlantic County, "we were threatened with the Jersey Devil, morning, noon, and night," as it became a popular way to scare children; a local version of the bogeyman.[53]

As is typical in community-threat outbreaks, the beginning of the wave was marked by a high-profile sighting that received widespread press coverage: the report by Officer Sackville. Soon, anything odd or unusual was quickly defined as devil-related. The misidentification of vague tracks and figures, hoaxes, rumors, and local press coverage combined to fuel the wave. The 1909 sighting flap soon collapsed as no body or other indisputable physical evidence of the creature was found, and before long, normal life resumed. Folklorists James McCloy and Roy Miller suggest the possibility that many people could have mistaken a Sandhill crane for the devil, which coincidentally gyrates as it flies and emits a bloodcurdling screech—common features in many reports. They write: "The Sandhill crane averages about 12 pounds and is 4 feet long, with an 80-inch wingspan. When in danger, the bird becomes very fierce. These birds have an eerie cry, and participate in a rather striking group mating dance of jumping and hoping."[54] The birds are also aggressive and are known for stealing corn and potatoes from gardens and farm fields. The Jersey Devil continues to live on in popular culture and has been featured in novels, several low-budget movies, and even an episode of *The X-Files* television series.

Halley's Comet Fear, 1910 (Worldwide)

Halley's Comet passes close to the earth every seventy-five years. In 1910, French astronomer Camille Flammarion stated his opinion that if it were to pass close enough, cyanogen (a.k.a. cyanide) gas in the comet's tail could potentially kill all life on Earth.[55] Professor Edwin Booth at the University of California agreed, saying that if estimates of the gas in the comet's tail were correct, "we may have a chance to feel the sensations of the bugs and insects which are killed by the use of this deadly gas as an exterminator."[56] Although other astronomers and commentators disagreed that there was any danger (many noted that the amount of gas in the comet's tail was too diffuse to cause any harm), some members of the public became frightened. The scare was fueled by the discovery of deadly cyanogen gas in the comet's tail in 1881 and speculative newspaper articles quoting rogue scientists on the threat.

The appearance of the comet had caused little concern until February 6, 1910, when the *Washington Post* published an alarmist story, exaggerating the threat. While citing other astronomers who were skeptical of the doom and gloom claims, it also highlighted Flammarion's fears that the atmosphere could become tainted with poison gas. It stated in part: "On the other hand there is a large quantity of cyanogen gas in the atmosphere surrounding Halley's Comet. A mixture of this gas with air would lead to certain poisoning."[57] If that was not alarmist enough, the reporter mentioned French astronomer M. Armand Gautier's concerns of a possible explosion, noting that, "in the presence of fire or a small electric spark, a mixture of cyanogen gas and air will explode."[58]

An even more chilling account appeared in the *New York Times* the next day. The writer observed that cyanogen was so lethal that if "a grain of its potassium salt touched to the tongue [it was] sufficient to cause instant death."[59] The article was misleading in that it conveyed an image of growing alarm in the astronomical community. It read: "The fact that cyanogen is present in the comet . . . is causing much discussion as to the probable effect on the earth should it pass through the comet's tail. Prof. Flammarion is of the opinion that the cyanogen gas would impregnate the atmosphere and possibly snuff out all life on the planet." Flammarion soon changed his mind as to the threat, but this received less press coverage. Recognizing the potential for panic, the *Times* published an editorial downplaying the threat. To underscore the harmless nature of the upcoming encounter, it confidently claimed that Earth could pass through a dozen comet tails without any harm to life.[60] The editorial did little to allay fears.

As Earth passed through the comet's tail on Wednesday evening, May 18, New York time, there were scattered reports of panic. In Lexington, Kentucky, it was reported that "excited people are tonight holding all-night services, praying and singing to prepare [to] meet their doom."[61] There were similar reactions in North Carolina[62] and Georgia.[63] Near Denver, Colorado, miners went into the mines in hopes of limiting their exposure to cyanogen.[64] Meanwhile, in Chicago, the head keeper at the Lincoln Park Zoo, Cy DeVry, was expressing concern over the health of the animals, especially a baby kangaroo. The Associated Press reported: "The animal keeper fears that next Wednesday night when the tail of the comet sweeps Lincoln Park some of the gasses may be breathed by the baby kangaroo and result in sudden death. To guard against any danger, the young kangaroo and its mother will be locked in the head animal keeper's house, behind tightly closed doors and windows during the night."[65] DeVry explained that he was taking the action because he had heard stories of dead baby kangaroos in Australia, coinciding with the last appearance of the comet seventy-five years earlier.

Overseas, the reaction was more dramatic. Hundreds marched in a candlelight parade through the streets of San Juan, Puerto Rico, singing religious songs.[66] In Rome, the pope pleaded with citizens to stop hoarding oxygen cylinders after pharmacies had sold out.[67] In France, residents were reported to have hoarded the cylinders and placed them in their cellars, which were sealed off in hopes of keeping out the cyanogen gas.[68] In parts of South Africa, the comet fostered "an extraordinary amount of nervousness," as one man placed a newspaper ad reading: "Gentleman having secured several cylinders of oxygen and having bricked up a capacious room wishes to meet others who would share the expense for Wednesday night. Numbers strictly limited."[69]

Several suicide attempts were linked to anxiety over the comet's arrival.[70]

Among them was that of forty-year-old Stephen Conner of New York, who cut his own throat. Seventeen stitches were needed to save him. "I tried to die because the world is coming to an end," he said.[71] There were people prepared to profit from the gullible. A voodoo man in Haiti sold many boxes of anticomet pills at $1 a box. Exactly how they were supposed to protect against poisonous gas in the comet's tail or an actual collision of the comet with the earth was not stated.[72] One of the biggest scams related to the scare occurred in Texas. The *Los Angeles Times* reported that two Ohio men were arrested in Texas after selling hundreds of mouth inhalers and "comet pills" to fearful residents in four southern counties. The men had distributed the pills to agents who were selling them on their behalf and managed to collect several thousand dollars. The pills were believed to be composed of quinine and sugar. The pills cost between $5 and $10, with some people buying up to fifty. The inhalers ranged in price from $2 to $24 and were to be worn while asleep.[73]

Halifax Slasher, November–December 1938 (England)

Nearly 150 years after the London Monster panic, there was a very similar scare in the large town of Halifax, Yorkshire. A mad slasher was at large and no pedestrian—especially female—was safe at night.

The first attack was on November 21, 1938. Shortly after 10:00 p.m., Mary Sutcliffe was walking home from her late shift at the Mackintosh's toffee factory. A man stepped directly in her path with an arm raised. She threw up an arm to block his attack and felt a sudden pain in her wrist. Sutcliffe ran away and later needed four stitches to close the cut on her wrist.[74] The attacks continued for the next ten nights until a surprising denouncement. Almost all the victims were women, and the Halifax Slasher's weapon of choice was apparently a razor blade.

Public alarm increased rapidly as the attacks continued. Cinema attendance plummeted, and evening trade in shops was greatly reduced. Fish-and-chip shops were hit particularly hard. A fish wholesaler in Hull claimed "the takings of one fish fryer have dropped 7s. 6d. per night."[75] Men and women alike armed themselves if they had to go out at night. Protective devices included truncheons, hammers, lead pipes, and Indian clubs (normally used for exercise, these look like modern-day juggling clubs).[76] Shop owners sold large numbers of walking sticks and knuckle dusters![77]

Up to twenty thousand men joined vigilante groups that patrolled the streets. Halifax's total population was about 100,000 at the time.[78] Inevitably, the vigilantes made mistakes. On November 25, a crowd of about a hundred men roughed up Clifford Edwards after he was mistaken for the slasher.[79] Two days later, fifteen-year-old Fred Baldwin was falsely identified as the slasher by half a dozen men as they left a pub. Dozens of others came from their homes and joined in the attack on Baldwin. A general melee ensued. Baldwin was only saved from serious injury with the arrival of several car loads of police.[80]

Just as with the earlier London Monster scare, there were numerous problems with blaming the attacks on a single assailant. The attacks were also scattered over several towns and even as far as two hundred miles away in London.[81] There were several different methods of attack (from the front in passing, from the rear, and from in hiding). There were even three different brands of razor blades found at the attack sites.[82] These factors led to a police release that stated "There is probably more than one person concerned—probably about three."[83]

The scare quickly subsided as police began to realize the psychological nature of the events, as slasher "victims," began to buckle under questioning by detectives, one after another, admitting to having faked the attacks.[84] For instance, Hilda Lodge told police that she had been slashed on November 25 but later admitted that she had scratched her face and arms with a broken bottle, apparently to gain attention. Another "victim," nineteen-year-old Beatrice Sorrell, confessed that she had argued with her boyfriend and, in a bid to gain his waning affection, bought a razor blade and slashed her sweater. Another woman with boyfriend issues was Lily Woodhead. After having an argument, her boyfriend reportedly refused to walk her to the bus and said: "I should not be surprised if there was a slasher in the road tonight," giving the distinct impression that he didn't care about her safety. Woodhead claimed that the slasher appeared, knocked her to the ground, and cut her. She later confessed to carrying a razor, apparently in self-defense in case she was attacked by the slasher.[85] During early December, a spate of confessions were recorded. In Manchester, Marjorie Murphy told police that the "slashing" injuries she received while going to the laundry were an accident, while in Doncaster, a young girl admitted to having fabricated her slasher attack after reading about the accounts in the paper.[86]

The whole affair was over. But at what cost? Tens of thousands of people had been gripped in an unnecessary state of fear for the better part of two weeks. Local businesses had suffered heavy financial losses. In addition, "304 police officers were engaged in making inquiries; 200 special constables were sworn in;

400 motor-cars were used; and 130 A.R.P. auxiliary firemen and wardens were engaged."[87] There were consequences for the fake victims—but only for some. Several were fined either five pounds or ten pounds, and some also received four-week jail terms.

Mad Gasser, September 1944 (Mattoon, Illinois, USA)

A series of wartime "attacks" on the home front by a "mad gasser" were reported over a two-week stretch in early September 1944 in the small city of Mattoon, Illinois (pop. 17,000). Authorities would later determine that the episode was entirely imaginary. The saga began at about 11:00 p.m. on September 1, when Aline Kearney was at home and smelled a sweet, nauseating odor that paralyzed her legs. She yelled to her sister, Martha Reedy, who was staying with her. A neighbor was called and contacted police. Kearney's three-year-old daughter also became sick from the smell (although her son and other daughter were unaffected). At the time, the women felt particularly vulnerable as Aline's husband was out driving a taxi, while Martha's spouse was away fighting in World War II. This undoubtedly added to the tension. Police soon arrived but found no evidence of a gasser. After learning of the incident, Mr. Kearney rushed home, and, upon arriving at about 12:30 a.m., he spotted a shadowy figure near their bedroom window. The entire family slept elsewhere overnight. The symptoms were vague, such as headache and dizziness, and the "victims" never even sought medical attention. Mr. Kearney's fleeting glimpse of a figure was equally nebulous, yet the local paper reported on the "attack" as a fact, proclaiming in large headlines: "'Anesthetic Prowler' on Loose." The subheadline read: "Mrs. Kearney and Daughter First Victims."[88] Soon, a deluge of similar "gassings" were reported across the city.

On September 5, Mrs. Carl Cordes found a small folded cloth on her porch, sniffed it, and began to feel unwell. Analysis of the fabric at a police laboratory yielded no trace of gas. Police speculated that it had evaporated.[89] On September 8, it was reported that Mr. and Mrs. Orban Raef had been attacked at their home on the night *before* the Kearney "gassing." He and his wife were asleep at 3:00 a.m. when, Mr. Raef claimed, fumes came through their bedroom window. Both experienced "the same feeling of paralysis" and felt ill.[90] Others sleeping in the house were unaffected. Mrs. Olive Brown told police that she had been "gassed" months earlier but did not report it.

None of these or the many other reported "attacks" could have been very serious at the time that they supposedly happened, as not a single "victim" thought to contact police or seek medical attention.[91] However, both the press and the behavior of local authorities gave the impression that the gasser was real. Mattoon mayor E. Richardson suggested the possibility that mustard gas was used as it could explain the numbness reported by victims. Experts from the US Army stationed at the Chicago-based Chemical Warfare Service hypothesized that chloropicrin was the agent used.[92] Richard Piper of the Illinois Bureau of Criminal Identification and Investigation proclaimed: "The existence of the anesthetic, or whatever it is, is genuine."[93]

Perhaps the most dramatic and vivid claim involved two sisters—Frances and Maxine Smith—who reported a series of attacks in their home. Frances was a respected grade-school principal. During the first nighttime attack, they reported being frightened by "noises outside their bedroom windows" and assumed it was the gasser.[94] The next night, they claimed three more attacks. On September 9, the *Gazette* presented the encounters as a fact: "The first infiltration of gas caught them in their beds. Gasping and choking, they awoke and soon felt partial paralysis grip their legs and arms. Later, while awake, the other attacks came and they saw a thin, blue smoke-like vapor spreading throughout the room . . . Just before the gas with its 'flower-like' odor came pouring into the room they heard a strange 'buzzing' sound outside the house and expressed the belief that the sound probably was made by the 'madman's spraying apparatus' in operations."[95]

Mattoon's modest police force of two officers and eight patrolmen was soon overwhelmed with gassing reports.[96] On September 8, about seventy people poured onto Dewitt Avenue after hearing that the gasser was seen nearby. Many in the group soon became convinced that they had been "gassed."[97] The *Chicago Herald-American* described the incident with an alarmist, page-one account: "Groggy as Londoners under protracted aerial blitzing, this town's bewildered citizens reeled today under repeated attacks of a mad anesthetist who has sprayed deadly nerve gas into 13 homes and has knocked out 27 known victims."[98]

The psychological nature of the "attacks" soon became evident. By September 9 and 10, hundreds of residents had gathered near City Hall to await the latest reports. As patrol cars responded to each call suspected of being the gasser, a procession of vehicles filled with curious occupants followed closely behind, prompting Police Commissioner Wright to order their arrest.[99] Vigilante gangs roamed the streets, both on foot and in vehicles, brandishing everything from baseball bats to shotguns. The commissioner was forced to issue a plea to residents to cease such activities, fearful that innocent people would be killed.[100] In one instance, a woman, home alone, accidentally blew a hole in the kitchen wall when her husband's shotgun inadvertently discharged.[101] In another case, Mrs. Eaton Paradise frantically phoned police, saying: "I've just been gassed." After speeding to the house, they quickly located the offender—a bottle of spilled nail-polish remover.[102] This and many other obvious false alarms prompted Police Chief Cole to announce on the 12th that it was *all* "mass hysteria" triggered by chemicals from local factories that drifted across the city by shifting winds.[103]

The content of the outbreak is crucial and coincided with the poison-gas scare, as popular and scientific periodicals at this time discussed the threat of poison gas attacks on the United States.[104] As the war turned in favor of the Allies, concern rose that German commanders might resort to gas warfare.[105] The Allies were so concerned about such a scenario, that during the D-day invasion of Normandy in June 1944, they had a plan to hit selected targets with chemical weapons if the Germans had used poison gas first.

On Wednesday, September 13, newspapers were publishing stories ridiculing the "gasser," using such descriptions as the "phantom anesthetist" and "Mattoon Will-o'-the-Wisp." By the 14th, the reports ceased as the *Gazette* began its account of a prowler claim the previous night as follows: "One call! No paralyzing gas! No madman! No prowler!"[106] On the 15th, the *Gazette* reported on an apparent gasser incident in Cedar Rapids, Iowa. Police there reported receiving a telephone call from a frantic woman claiming to have been gassed by a man outside her window brandishing a spray gun. Police said "they found no madman and no gas, but did find a billy goat tied in the yard and an odor that seemed to come from the animal."[107] The "mad gasser" scare was over.

The Rock 'n' Roll Peril, 1956–1961 (Worldwide)

During the 1950s, the rise of rock 'n' roll music was widely viewed as portending the decline of Western youth and civilization. Numerous local communities in many countries feared its arrival. Martin Bleyer, a psychiatrist, stated that after a rock 'n' roll session, a young woman said to him, "I am gone, man. I am really dreamy. Nothing matters to me. I am walking on air."[108] He was concerned that a drug addict had said almost the exact same words to him only a week earlier. "It appeals to adolescent insecurity and drives teenagers to do outlandish things.

It's cannibalistic—tribalistic," complained Dr. Francis Braceland, another psychiatrist.[109] "The music inflames teenagers and is obscenely suggestive. Some of these records are so vulgar they are sold under the counter," claimed Barret Byrne, a district attorney.[110]

The perceived instigator of the emerging evil was Elvis "The Pelvis" Presley, who received particularly harsh criticism. "He wiggles itches and scratches, spins and gyrates as if he were doing a loathsome take-off on a victim of St. Vitus' dance. And all the while his face is distorted in suggestive smirks and leers," said horrified New York critic Ben Gross.[111] "The gyrations . . . were such an assault to the senses as to repel even the most tolerant observer . . . one begins to understand the present-day attitude of our youth."[112]

Individual communities worldwide felt the effect of rock 'n' roll most often when it visited in the form of local cinema screenings of the movie *Rock Around the Clock* in 1956. "It started with hand-clapping and banging of seats, but soon they were out in the gangway dancing," reported cinema manager Mr. E. Herbert of Essex, England. [113] It ended with the cinema seats all torn and smashed. After a London screening of the movie, teenagers threw bottles and fireworks. Shop windows were smashed. Two policemen were injured.[114] In Helsinki, Finland, teenagers struggled against police to try and get in to a sold out premiere of the film. Two were arrested.[115] Rock 'n' roll concerts also caused problems. Ten teenagers were arrested when they fought police outside one in Australia.[116]

After a rock 'n' roll session in Boston, ten people (including two young girls) were robbed or attacked. Albert Raggiani, a nineteen-year-old sailor, was stabbed. Famous disc jockey Alan Freed was charged with "inciting the unlawful destruction of property."[117] Freed responded that police used him as a scapegoat. About eighty teenagers rioted at a Bo Diddley, Fats Domino, and Chubby Checker concert in Ohio. Many windows were broken. Nineteen-year-old Dale Miller was dragged from his car then beaten and stabbed in the shoulder.[118] At a Vince Taylor concert in Paris, France, about 3,500 teenagers smashed two thousand chairs plus numerous windows. Fourteen police were injured. The riot kicked off before Taylor even got on stage! A second concert was canceled.[119]

Was it really valid to blame rock 'n' roll for all the violence and destruction? On at least some occasions there were other causes. Teenage gate crashers— seventy boys and twelve girls—forced their way into a private party at a Chicago home. Windows and furniture were broken. The sixteen-year-old host's face was gashed with a broken bottle. The party, held when the host's parents were out and unaware, was for members of the "Dukes" gang. The crashers were members of two rival gangs—"The Hung" and "Mumchecks."[120] The type of music being played had nothing to do with the fracas. When two plainclothes policemen tried to gain access to an ex-servicemen's club to investigate the noise, the result was one officer shot in the hand, one civilian shot in an arm and another civilian shot in his stomach.[121] It is doubtful that the type of music being played—or the volume—played any part in what happened.

Newspapers typically reported on stories related to rock 'n' roll in the most sensational terms. After a midnight screening of *Rock Around the Clock* in a Singapore cinema, six British soldiers jive danced for thirty minutes while others stood in a circle and sung and clapped. Then police stepped in and told them to leave—which they did, peacefully. Yet this nonevent received international press coverage as an "incident."[122] "There's nothing wrong with rock 'n' roll music. The trouble is started by a handful of determined mischief makers who use rock 'n' roll as an excuse for their behavior. They'd tear the cinema down with Mickey Mouse on the screen," said one London psychologist.[123]

Young people have pushed back against their parents and other authority figures for hundreds of years. The latest popular form of entertainment of each generation has always been blamed as the cause of their rebellious behavior: penny-dreadful plays and novels, cinema films, comic books, music, videos, video games, computer games, the Internet, etc. In December 1961, concern shifted from the evils of rock 'n' roll to the threat posed by a new dance craze called the twist, which by any standard of contemporary Western society, would be considered quite tame![124]

"Jawsmania," 1975 and 2001 (USA)

In the summer of 1975, a medium-budget film directed by a fresh, young director hit cinema screens. The movie was *Jaws*. The director was Steven Spielberg. Previously, Spielberg had only directed television shows, one made-for-TV movie (*Duel* in 1971), and one low-budget feature film (*The Sugarland Express* in 1974). Surprisingly, *Jaws* was a huge hit. During the normally lackluster summer months, *Jaws* had record box-office takings. It cost $8 million to make and an additional $1.8 million was spent on advertising. During the first thirteen days following its release, the film sold a then astonishing $25.7 million worth of tickets at 450 cinemas in the United States and Canada.[125]

Jaws had an unsettling effect on many people who saw it. They either became too scared to swim in the ocean or their usual behavior changed when they entered the water. Reporter Tom Cardy vividly recalled his memories of that summer (when he was fifteen) for a retrospective holiday piece: "A couple of steps into the water at Caroline Bay and the *Jaws* theme—the deep, creepy, cell-based *Jaws* theme—went through my head. Was that a flick of white surf to my right a few waves away? Or was it the tip of the fin of nature's most efficient killing machine? A few steps further out. What was that that just grazed my foot? A bit of seaweed? A bit of driftwood? . . . What if that was a shark doing a shark version of testing me? A bit like poking your fork the first time into an unfamiliar piece of meat straight off the barbie [bar-b-que]. I'm outta here!"[126]

Jaws caused people to become hypervigilent and imagine they saw sharks when there were none—or certainly no more than usual. Despite a large increase in shark sightings in the Rhode Island area, marine biologist John G. Casey said there was no sign that "the number of sharks is any higher than in past years . . . Instead of a few lifeguards looking out towards the ocean, there will be thousands of eyes looking out there after swimmers see *Jaws*."[127] "Any fish in the water now becomes a shark. The majority of people are staying closer to the shore this summer. My lifeguards report there are no distance swimmers at all this year," said Jim Holland, a Dade County lifeguard.[128]

At the Menemsha Coast Guard station in Martha's Vineyard, Massachusetts (where *Jaws* was filmed), there had been twenty reports of sharks partway through the summer when there were only six all season the previous year.[129] In some areas, beach-visitor numbers had dropped. Ted Seawell, Treasure Island tourist-business director, said room bookings were down about 15 percent. "We thought it might just be the economy in general but then we checked with the resorts in the mountains and they're having a great season—100 percent capacity," he added.[130]

There was an intense interest in everything *Jaws*-related, from board games to hair-cut styles. Over the next few decades, millions of sharks were unnecessarily killed out of fear or to supply the demand for shark products. In New Bedford, Massachusetts, marine specialty shop owner Joseph Piva estimated he had sold several hundred pairs of shark jaws and forty thousand individual shark teeth in four months.[131] Shark was added to the cafeteria offerings at the University of Iowa. In two days, 150 pounds were sold. New Orleans public schools bought twenty thousand pounds of shark meat for school lunches. Preston Battistella, a New Orleans fish monger doubled his shark-meat sales from 150,000 pounds to

300,000 pounds in a year.[132] Humans were not really in danger from sharks. There was a far greater chance of being killed driving to the beach than by a shark when swimming in the ocean. Every year in the United States alone, more people are killed by bees and wasps than are killed by sharks worldwide.

Years later, Peter Benchley, author of the novel that *Jaws* was based on, felt guilty about the skewed public perception of sharks caused by the novel and the film. "More than twenty years ago, I set out to write a story about a town menaced by a marine predator. Intrigued by a newspaper item about a fisherman who had caught a 4,550-pound Great White Shark off the coast of Long Island, I wondered what would happen if such a creature were to visit a resort community . . . and wouldn't go away. I've often been asked why *Jaws* became the weird cultural phenomenon it did, and to this day I have no satisfactory answer."[133] Benchley believes that in writing best-selling books, luck and timing are key factors. He says that he may have tapped into "a profound, subconscious, atavistic fear . . . not only of sharks but of the sea itself, of deep water and of the unknown."

Today, Benchley has a much more sympathetic view of sharks. "I could not, for instance, portray the shark as a villain, especially not as a mindless omnivore that attacks boats and humans with reckless abandon. We know now, as we didn't then, that the majority of shark attacks on human beings are accidents (often cases of mistaken identity), that a person has a much greater chance of being killed by lightning, bee stings, or feral pigs than by sharks, and that even the most formidable great white shark does not attack boats: rather, responding to complex and confusing electromagnetic signals in the water, it tests a boat, exploring it with its mouth to determine if it is edible."[134] Rather than viewing sharks as the oppressors, Benchley now views them as the oppressed. He said that "the shark in an updated Jaws could not be the villain; it would have to be written as the victim . . . Every year, more than a hundred million sharks are slaughtered by man. It has been estimated that for every human life taken by a shark, 4.5 million sharks are killed by humans."

The exaggerated fear of sharks flared up again twenty-six years later when, during the summer of 2001, the US media created the widespread belief that the public menace posed by sharks was far greater than it actually was. Newspapers, radio stations, television stations, and the Internet fueled the scare and were quick to pass on the latest shark sightings and attacks. The extent of the scare was underscored by some television stations that oversaw twenty-four hour shark-cams near supposed hotspots so that viewers could watch at their computer.

The 2001 outbreak can be traced to a spectacular incident that received saturation media coverage when a boy named Jessie Arbogast had his arm torn from his body by a shark while swimming off the coast of Pensacola, Florida. In a remarkable display of courage, the boy's uncle grabbed the shark's tail and wrestled it to shore, while a park ranger pulled out a gun and shot the creature. Jessie survived the ordeal, and his arm was reattached by surgeons. The story captivated the American media, with some outlets giving daily updates on the boy's recovery and running stories about how to avoid being attacked yourself.[135]

In the wake of the sudden media interest in sharks, any shark-related incident received prominent news attention. *Time* magazine would later typify this media hype with a cover story titled: "The Summer of the Shark." Coincidence also played a role, such as the release of two popular books on shark attacks: Richard Fernicola's *Twelve Days of Terror* and *Close to Shore* by Michael Capuzzo. Both chronicled a series of incidents off the New Jersey coast in 1916. In reality, the statistical probability of any one person being attacked or killed by a shark is remarkably small. For instance, between 1990 and 2009, 15,011 Americans died in bicycle accidents, while a mere fourteen died from shark attacks.[136] Tanya Basu of National Geographic has calculated the odds of being killed by a shark; she places them at one in 3.7 million.[137] Perhaps the science publication *New Scientist* best summed up the danger in an article titled: "Relax: You're Not That Tempting."[138] Ironically, the sudden media frenzy for everything shark ended as sharply and suddenly as any news story in the history of journalism. It went from front-page news to virtually no reports overnight. Shark summer ended abruptly on September 11, when the attention of most Americans was focused on another threat that was far more grounded in reality: terrorism.

El Chupacabra Scare, 1995 and ongoing (Puerto Rico and the Americas)

Beginning in 1995, a spate of rumors and mysterious sightings involving a strange, blood-thirsty creature referred to as the chupacabra—Spanish for "goat sucker"—cropped up across the US territory of Puerto Rico. The creature received its name for its reported affinity for killing and draining the blood of goats. Sightings soon spread throughout portions of South, Central, and North America and were typically confined to members of the Hispanic community. In his 2011 book, *Tracking the Chupacabra*, which traces the history of the enigmatic beast, Ben Radford writes that there is no agreed upon uniform description. "It is a shapeshifter, changing its appearance and characteristics according to the time and place it is seen, and according to the beliefs and expectations of those who see it."[139] While descriptions vary widely, Radford states that the creature typically stands on two legs and is four to five feet tall. "It has short but powerful legs that allow it to leap fantastic distances, long claws, and terrifying black or glowing red eyes. Some claim it has spikes down its back; others report seeing stubby, bat-like wings. Some say the stench of sulfur taints the air around chupacabras, or that it emits a terrifying hiss when threatened."[140]

Radford found that one of Puerto Rico's most popular newspapers, the sensational tabloid *El Vocero,* had been influential in spreading the scare across the island by producing numerous stories on the menace. He writes: "This strong bias toward sensationalism affected the information that most Puerto Ricans got about the monster. Because the respectable, credible newspapers largely ignored the chupacabra stories, *El Vocero* happily filled the news void with its own dramatic brand of tabloid reporting. As a result, few Puerto Ricans who followed the mystery were exposed to the more level-headed, skeptical, and scientific analyses: panicked housewives and gun-toting farers would always crowd out the calm skeptics and scientists on newspaper pages."[141]

As more and more sightings accumulated, a discernible pattern appeared—a pattern that was first identified in Puerto Rico during the mid-1990s and continues to be repeated. Radford states that "animals thought to have been 'mysteriously' killed by the chupacabra (or, far more rarely, a sighting of the creature), occurred, and were reported to the press. Those news reports, most of them alarmist and sensationalized, told hundreds of thousands (and eventually millions) of people about the chupacabra. The news reports in turn spawned more reports and sightings, and the process began anew, stronger than before. The chupacabra's meteoric rise in popularity was closely tied to the amount of publicity it received."[142]

After gaining widespread media attention in Puerto Rico in 1995, by the next year encounters with the creature quickly spread throughout much of the Americas. For instance, in May 1996, a thirty-one-year-old construction worker in Santa Ana, California, said that he had dozed off to sleep while lying on his sofa when he was attacked and bitten by the creature. Roberto Garcia told a reporter for the *Santa Ana Orange County Register*: "Suddenly, I felt something strong tugging my arm through the window and I woke up . . . I yanked my arm back and I saw this large, shadowy figure moving away very fast. I thought this was strange because I live on the third floor and there is nothing next to the window except the alley below."[143] Garcia's encounter could be potentially explained as a hypnagogic dream, which can produce vivid images and occur as one is falling asleep. The rumors among the Hispanic community and media accounts of sightings may have colored the content of the images.[144] The vast majority of incidents attributed to the mysterious chupacabra were findings of dead animals that were assumed to have been killed by the creature without anyone actually seeing it. An analysis of the ten most notable chupacabra reports for which a body was recovered revealed that four were later identified as dogs, one turned out to be a coyote, another was a suspected coyote, and another was determined to have been a raccoon.[145]

The chupacabra scare has also been fueled by a number of fictional books on the topic that have helped to solidify its existence within the popular imagination. These include: *Curse of the ChupaCabra*,[146] *El Chupacabra: The Beast*,[147] *Night of the Chupacabra*,[148] and *Taken by the Chupacabra*.[149] Sightings of chupacabras continue to be reported—typically in clusters, in a waxing-waning fashion—fueled by media reports of sightings, the publication and broadcast of which motivate people to scrutinize their surroundings for evidence of these fantastic creatures of the night. As a result, people become prone to misidentifying a variety of mundane stimuli and shadowy figures as chupacabra-related.

Radford has located the original sighting—what he calls "case zero"—in the scare from Puerto Rico during 1995. When this case was reported in the media, a deluge of further sightings followed. He flew to Puerto Rico and interviewed the woman who made the first sighting claim, Madelyne Tolentino of Canóvanas. What Radford uncovered is revealing. Tolentino claims to have spotted the creature during the second week of August (exact date unknown). She said it walked on two legs, had black or dark gray eyes, "three, long, skinny fingers," long, thin legs "with three separate toes," and where the nose would be, "it had two little holes."[150] Radford observes that the woman's story is incredulous because of the fine detail including the eye color and the three-toed feet. Such detail is remarkable as she saw it from a distance through a window! Radford remarks that for such an important case, chupacabra researchers in Puerto Rico never conducted an investigation into the validity of the report. Yet, despite all of the red flags and Tolentino's description having been fabricated or embellished, the case "is regularly presented as one of the best, most important pieces of evidence for the chupacabra."

Monkey Man Fear, 2001 (New Delhi, India)

In May 2001, New Delhi was the scene of a scare over the alleged existence of a half-human, half-monkey creature dubbed by locals as "the monkey man." In addition to the many sightings, several people claimed to have been attacked by the creature, which purportedly had long claws, the ability to leap great distances, and superhuman strength. East Delhi appeared to be the epicenter of the reports. Most encounters occurred at night to people who were trying to stay cool in the summer heat by sleeping on the tops of their homes, as a result of ongoing electricity blackouts.[151]

Two people reportedly died as a result of the scare, while others suffered minor cuts and bruises. One man was awakened by cries in the night, and, assuming that the creature was coming for him, he jumped off a one-story building. In another incident, a pregnant woman awoke and thought she was being attacked by the creature. In her haste to get away, she fell down a staircase.[152] One witness described their encounter in broken English: "I open the curtain and I saw a hand. Then I heard a noise, a noise like a monkey makes, and I started running towards the stairs and he chased me. Then I tripped over something in the hall and fell down the stairs. He didn't follow, but I could see he had a dark face and an iron hand."[153]

By the middle of May, the scare peaked and gangs of vigilantes roamed the streets, on the lookout for the creature. An account of the episode in *Time Asia* depicted a tense scene: "Wandering bands of vigilantes guard neighborhoods with wooden cudgels, daggers, field-hockey sticks, ceremonial swords and pikes made from butchers' cleavers. In the early hours, police fire flares over cultivated ground to see if the Monkey Man is hiding in the darkness. The area's 500-strong police force has been tripled. Some legislators are demanding the central government send in elite commandos to deal with what they call 'the crisis.'"[154]

While most witnesses described seeing a half-human, half-monkey creature, descriptions varied widely. According to some accounts, it had steel claws and an invisibility button on a belt encircling its waist. While most observers said it stood between three and six feet tall, a few said it was the size of a cat. Monkeys are common on the outskirts of New Delhi, where the sightings were concentrated, and the heat wave and corresponding power cuts forced many residents to sleep on their rooftops, where they may have felt vulnerable to attacks. This may have generated anxiety, rumors, and misperceptions of mundane occurrences such as seeing monkeys or shadowy figures. Curiously, the outbreak coincided with the airing of an Indian television series on "Hanuman," a popular Hindu monkey deity with superhuman strength and the ability to leap incredible distances.[155] Dr. D. K. Srivastava of the University College of Medical Sciences in Dilshad Garden, Delhi, conducted a study of victims who were treated in the hospital. He found that 94 percent of cases were poorly educated, and most attacks happened between midnight and 6:00 a.m., during power outages.[156] Srivastava concluded that most people were injured while fleeing.

The Ebola Scare, 2014 (USA)

In 1976, researchers discovered the Ebola virus in what is now the Democratic Republic of Congo. Since then, and prior to 2014, the World Health Organization (WHO) reports that there have been thirty-two known outbreaks resulting in 2,361 infections and 1,438 deaths.[157] While Ebola has a high mortality rate for those who contract it, it is a very difficult virus to catch—even for those treating patients in close proximity, if proper precautions are taken.

Despite the relatively low threat to the US population, a media-driven scare erupted in the United States and across the world in 2014, after an initial outbreak in March. While there was a fear of a global Ebola pandemic, the WHO reported that 99 percent of cases were confined to just a few countries that had experienced widespread, intense transmission: Guinea, Liberia, and Sierra Leone. Another cluster of countries, such as in Mali, Nigeria, Senegal, Spain, and the Unites States, had either one or a small number of cases. As of November 7, 2014, the United States had reported four cases and one death, yet the public and media reactions were disproportionate to the threat.[158]

Ebola is spread through direct contact with an infected, symptomatic person's body fluids including blood, sweat, saliva, mucus, feces, urine, and vomit. According to the Center for Disease Control, there is no evidence that the virus "is spread by coughing and sneezing. Ebola virus is transmitted through direct contact with the blood or body fluids of a person who is sick with Ebola; the virus is not transmitted through the air."[159]

A major reason for the spread of Ebola involves cultural patterns in Africa: patterns that do not generally exist in countries like the United States. While physicians and hospitals are specifically designed to diagnose and treat the sick in West Africa, friends and relatives play a much more influential role than in the West. In many parts of West Africa, the relatives of hospitalized patients are responsible for their other basic needs including providing them with food and fluids and washing them. With Ebola, touching and hugging patients without the proper protective equipment places family members at great risk of contracting the disease.[160]

The Ebola scare is rooted in a long history of similar disease epidemics where certain groups are targeted. For instance, when the Black Death erupted in Europe during the fourteenth century, Jews became scapegoats. During a nineteenth-century cholera outbreak in New York City, former mayor Philip Hone placed blame on the habits of "filthy, intemperate" immigrants from Germany and Ireland.[161] Psychologist Kurt Gray observes that people typically look to assign blame for epidemics, which explains why during the Middle Ages, when a locust swarm caused serious crop damage in France, authorities put the insects on trial. Gray notes that a virus does not "have a mind that would allow it to choose to do harm, so when it comes to Ebola, we blame the outsider instead."[162] In fact, in medieval Europe, there are records of all types of animals and insects being placed on trial for assorted crimes.[163]

Immediate community threats have the power to severely disrupt everyday life as residents live in fear of the perceived threatening agent. They often give rise to the presence of vigilante gangs that can potentially cause more harm than the threat itself. In most episodes, the mass media plays an influential role in triggering the false alarm with the publication or airing of initial sensational reports that exaggerate the danger. Conversely, the decline of outbreaks coincides with the appearance of skeptical press coverage. Eventually, the absence of confirming evidence, in conjunction with negative media coverage, results in a rapid end to the scare.

In chapter 10, however, we examine a more specific type of community threat: moral panics, which are incubated during periods of social upheaval and crisis. During such times, people subconsciously search for scapegoats in the form of deviants, who are blamed for causing the hard times. Moral panics have a notorious history that includes the incarceration, torture, expulsion, and even death of many innocent people, from the medieval-European witch burnings and the Salem witch trials, to the American communist Red Scare after World War II and more recently, the demonization of Muslims as terrorists after the September 11, 2001 attacks on the United States.

CHAPTER 10
MORAL PANICS:
IMAGINING OUR WORST FEARS

From time to time, communities are gripped by general fears about a person, group, or condition in society that is deemed to be a grave threat and must be addressed. These perceived threats to societal values and interests appear in the media in the form of reports that stereotype the offending moral deviants as evildoers. Sociologist Jeffrey Victor notes that in periods of turmoil, societies unconsciously create new deviants who serve as scapegoats.[1] Social scientists have dubbed these outbreaks *moral panics*—a term popularized by Stanley Cohen in his 1972 landmark study of two British youth groups, the Mods and the Rockers, and their distorted portrayal in the media. Cohen refers to the perceived evildoers as "folk devils" and observes that such episodes, also called *social panics* or *symbolic scares*, spark community outrage, with local and national leaders, such as politicians, bishops, editors "and other right-thinking people," manning the "moral barricades."[2] He also notes that while these panics often fade from memory, they may have lasting impacts such as new laws or changes in social policies.

Moral panics commonly persist in a waxing-waning fashion for years and last about a decade before fading away. There is usually a "grain of truth" to the fears, but the threat is exaggerated. For instance, during the American communism scare of the 1950s, a few Reds had infiltrated the country and were attempting to ferment revolution. Yet, given their small numbers and minor influence, the notion that these communists could successfully foster even a minimal shift in public opinion and threaten the government was totally unrealistic, and their actual impact was negligible. During this period, many Americans were blacklisted and unfairly stigmatized. Once outbreaks have passed, Victor notes that a close examination of the facts and figures surrounding the panic "reveals that the perceived threat was either greatly exaggerated or nonexistent."[3]

Moral panics often affect entire countries or regions and may be impossible to eradicate as every society constantly faces threats from some type of evil—be it real or imagined. Moral panics function by unifying communities against a common threat and serving to channel aggression. A common motif of many social panics in Western countries over the past century has been the sudden perceived influx of psychoactive drug use.[4] Another has been the portrayal of Muslims in general as terrorists in the wake of the September 11 attacks on the United States and the attempts by a relatively small number of Islamic radicals to set up an Islamic state in parts of Syria and Iraq in 2014. In 2010—nearly a decade after the 9/11 attacks, the reaction to the proposed construction of a mosque at Ground Zero was a classic instance of a social panic reflecting global Islamophobia. While many social commentators agreed with attempts to stop the project on the grounds that it was a scared site, the reality was far different.

In *Intimate Enemies: Moral Panics in Contemporary Great Britain*, criminologist Philip Jenkins documents a variety of social panics in the United Kingdom involving the exaggerated threat from a variety of deviants, from serial killers to pedophiles and child murderers.[5] Other documented moral panics include exaggerated claims over the threat and prevalence of AIDS, welfare cheats, child abuse, pornography, Halloween candy tampering, school homicides, and the Salem witch hunts of 1692.[6] Michael Welch has even examined the waxing and waning of the ongoing American moral panic over flag burning and desecration as a form of political protest.[7]

Historically, the most common theme in these outbreaks is the perceived erosion of traditional values, and the most common scapegoats are ethnic minorities, heretics, deviants and the poor. Jews, foreigners, and recent migrants have been favorite targets. One of the most far-reaching and long-lasting moral panics in human history was the widespread persecution of "witches" in continental Europe from 1400 to 1650. These witch hunts coincided with the disintegration of the Roman Catholic Church and the feudal hierarchy.[8] Under siege from new denominations that were outside the control of the Church in Rome, and threatened by the rising influence of science, new deviants were created in an attempt to reassert the authority of the Church. It cannot be overemphasized that this is not a conscious process: most people do not realize they are doing it. Another particularly destructive moral panic involved the portrayal of Jews by the Nazis as threatening the very existence of the Third Reich and the German way of life.

Sociologists Erich Goode and Nachman Ben-Yehuda identify five indicators of moral panics.[9] The first element is *concern*; the perceived threat must be of sufficient gravity as to worry members of the community, and this concern should be measurable in some way, such as with opinion polls or the appearance of new social movements. The second element is *hostility* toward the person or group that is viewed as being behind the threat. This may take the form of public protests or posters warning members of the community as to the existence and activities of the nefarious deviants. Third, there must be a *consensus* within the population that the threat posed by the "folk devils" is real and serious. A fourth indicator is *disproportionality*, in which the perceived threat is not in proportion to the reality. According to Goode and Ben-Yehuda, during moral panics, generating and disseminating statistics about the danger of the threat is vital. Figures typically take the form of deaths, crimes, injuries, and monetary amounts, which are usually wildly inflated by moral crusaders. Lastly, moral panics must exhibit *volatility* by their nature. They may erupt suddenly, then subside for a time, only to suddenly gain prominence again.

Key players in moral panics who are responsible for creating and perpetrating the exaggerated threat include the media, the public, law enforcement agencies, politicians and lawmakers, and action groups.[10] The first group of social actors that play a vital role in both triggering and perpetuating moral panics is the mass media, which does so by publishing and broadcasting stories that exaggerate the perceived threat posed to society. For instance, in the lead-up to America's entrance into World War I, the *Washington Post* published thirty articles on the threat from homeland spies and saboteurs, including the sensational headline: "100,000 Spies in Country." The *New York Tribune* proclaimed: "Spies are everywhere! They occupy hundreds of observation posts . . . they are in all the drug and chemical laboratories."[11]

Another factor that was essential in generating widespread public worry over the threat from German Americans involved existing public fears. There was public concern because the threat from spies and saboteurs in America was real—but the actual extent of the threat was minor. Politicians and legislators attempted to organize public campaigns against the threat. Even the president of the United States asserted that there were spies in every community, overstating the threat and fueling fears among the public that the danger was far greater than it was. During the panic over the loyalty of German Americans during the First World War, legislators passed a spate of laws that would seem ridiculous by today's standards. For instance, historian Ronald Schaffer writes that during the summer of 1918, nearly half of all US states had either banned or restricted the use of German as a language. He remarks: "The South Dakota council of defense ordered the state's elementary and secondary schools to stop teaching it and prohibited people from using it in telephone conversations." The Governor of Iowa issued a proclamation that banned the speaking of any language but English in public places including on trains and in phone conversations.[12] Law enforcement carried out the new laws.

The final major players in moral panics are action groups, which attempt to counter the new threat. Sociologist Howard Becker refers to these people as "moral entrepreneurs" who are upset that authorities are not doing enough, necessitating an organized response to remedy the situation in acting for the public good.[13] For instance, in East Alton, Illinois, a local German American merchant was forced to kiss the US flag and threatened with hanging by a group of young vigilantes. New groups were formed that engaged in harassing German Americans, with such names as "Knights of Liberty" and "Sedition Slammers." During March 1918, one observer in the Midwest wrote: "All over this part of the country men are being tarred and feathered and some are being lynched . . . These cases do not get into the newspapers nor is an effort ever made to punish the individuals concerned. In fact, as a rule, it has the complete backing of public opinion."[14]

MEMORABLE MORAL PANICS

Catholic Scare, 1830–1860 (USA)

Beginning in about 1830, fear and suspicion of Catholics swept across the United States and culminated in violence. During this period, Catholics were widely portrayed as cultists who posed a danger to the American way of life, both morally and economically. The scare coincided with an influx of new immigrants, especially German and Irish Catholics.[15] Rumors spread that these new immigrants were intent on undermining or overthrowing the government, as their authority came from the pope, not the American president.

Anti-Catholic publications became common and included over two dozen newspapers, thirteen magazines, and hundreds of books.[16] Novels fueled rumors and mistrust, often describing nuns living in virtual captivity within convents, serving as sex slaves for perverted priests.[17] These depictions generated anger that such evildoers could be allowed to ply their trade and coexist with law-abiding

Americans. In 1834, a convent in Charlestown, Massachusetts, was set alight by an angry mob after hearing rumors that the building had been the scene of abuse. In 1844, anti-Catholic riots left thirteen people dead in Philadelphia as the homes of many Catholics were burned along with two churches. In 1854, riots claimed the lives of ten people in St. Louis, while at least twenty died the following year in Louisville, Kentucky.[18] The anti-Catholic hysteria abated when more pending matters rose to the fore, most notably the outbreak of the Civil War.

White Slavery Scare, 1880 to 1917 (United States and Europe), 1969 (France)

During the late nineteenth and early twentieth century, there was widespread outrage in Europe and North America over reports that young white women and girls were being abducted by criminal gangs and forced into a life of prostitution. The scare peaked in the years leading up to the Great War. Some accounts held that the women were kept high on drugs. The scare coincided with the growing influence of women's rights groups and their crusade against prostitution. Those in opposition to greater independence for females used the scare to highlight the traditional role of women as mothers and housekeepers. Historian Donna Guy concludes that the appearance of "white slavery" horror stories functioned as cautionary tales about the dangers posed to women who strove to be too independent.[19]

Immigrants, especially Jews, were blamed for the defiling and exploitation of young white women. In both the United States and Europe, the primary motif centered on the virtuous "country girl" who's innocence was shattered after being lured to the city, which was rife with danger and corruption.[20] The scare abated with new restrictions on immigration surrounding the outbreak of World War I.

A similar scare surfaced in France during May 1969, amid claims that desirable women were being drugged in the changing rooms of Jewish-operated clothing stores and smuggled to North Africa to be sold as prostitutes. Authorities were said to have turned a blind eye to the trade after receiving Jewish bribes. Historian Edgar Morin viewed the stories as cautionary tales about the dangers of dressing provocatively and shopping at avant-garde clothing stores as they could lead to moral decay and prostitution.[21]

Anti-German Scare, 1914-1918 (USA and Canada)

During World War I, the widespread fear of all things German swept across North America as the threat of German infiltration by the "fifth column" (subversive agents) was wildly exaggerated. German spies were said to be lurking in every town and holding government posts. In Canada, the Anti-German League was formed to rid the dominion of all German influences. One historian noted that in Canada "there was hardly a major fire, explosion, or industrial accident which was not attributed to enemy sabotage," and further investigation "invariably led elsewhere."[22] Between 1914 and 1918, 8,579 German and Austro-Hungarian Canadian men were placed in internment camps.[23] So deep was the fear, that the names of some communities with Germanic names were renamed. Berlin, Canada, for instance, was renamed Kitchener, and the German-language curricula was removed from schools and universities. Historian Paul Magocsi reports that by 1917, nearly all German ethnic associations had been dissolved, and the German-language press was "totally suppressed" near the end of the war.[24]

The scare was equally as intense in the United States, where President Woodrow Wilson warned Congress that disloyal Americans with an allegiance to the kaiser "filled our unsuspecting communities with spies and conspirators."[25] In the Unites States, streets, schools, businesses, and cities with Germanic names were renamed. There was even a public campaign to change the name of sauerkraut to "Liberty Cabbage." Many communities prohibited the playing of German music or theater performances.[26] Predictably, a flurry of silent films appeared about German spies infiltrating the country. In the 1915 film *Her Country First*, Vivian Martin, whose father was a munitions maker, became convinced that their butler was a spy. She eventually learns that their entire staff is made up of spies—except the butler, who turns out to be an undercover Secret Service agent![27] Historian Fraser Sherman writes that "mobs assaulted German-Americans who showed signs of disloyalty—which included speaking German in public, or not giving enough to bond drives. The victims were tarred and feathered, beaten or forced to kiss the American flag. The worst incident was the 1918 lynching of German immigrant Richard Prager."[28] Prager was hanged by a mob after being accused of spying and reportedly making disloyal comments about the president. He vehemently denied the charges.

Communist Red Scare, 1946–1955 (USA)

Soon after the United States dropped the atomic bomb on Japan to force their surrender, a number of people were arrested and charged with spying for the Soviets. These fears culminated in the sensational case of Ethel and Julius Rosenberg, who were found guilty of passing secrets of the atom bomb to the Soviets and were executed in 1953. Communists were demonized.

The widespread public fear of Russian spies and sleeper agents having infiltrated the country was epitomized in a statement issued by the US Attorney General in 1947. J. Howard McGrath warned: "American Reds are everywhere—in factories, offices, butcher stores, on street corners, in private businesses—and each carries in himself the germ of death for society."[29] During this period, newspapers and magazines published alarmist articles reaffirming the Red threat, while Hollywood produced such films as *I Married a Communist* (1949), *I Was a Communist for the FBI* (1951), *Red Snow*, and *The Thief* (1952). Many science-fiction movies also had a distinct anticommunist theme, such as *The Flying Saucer* (1950), in which Soviet agents try to steal a secret device invented by an American scientist.

Amid rumors of communist sympathizers in Hollywood, in 1947, the House Un-American Activities Committee held a series of hearings to determine the extent of the problem. As a result, many actors, producers, and writers lost their jobs and were placed on "do not hire" blacklists after being suspected of supporting communists. Wisconsin Senator Joseph McCarthy spearheaded the campaign to identify communist sympathizers. He caused great alarm in 1950, when he spoke on the threat. "In my opinion the State Department, which is one of the most important government departments, is thoroughly infested with Communists. I have in my hand fifty-seven cases of individuals who would appear to be either card-carrying members or certainly loyal to the Communist Party, but who nevertheless are still helping to shape our foreign policy."[30] McCarthy's popularity grew, culminating in a series of televised hearings in 1954, but his campaign quickly lost momentum after he failed to support his claims and appeared to bully those testifying.

Halloween Sadism and Poisoned Candy, 1958–1984 (USA)

For decades, the mass media has presented accounts of evildoers tampering with candy and apples and dispensing them to trick-or-treaters at Halloween. Stories of tainted sweets and apples embedded with razor blades abound. Sociologist Joel Best and Gerald Horiuchi reviewed news reports of such cases and failed to find even one substantiated report of a child being seriously injured or dying as a result of eating contaminated treats collected while trick-or-treating. They concluded that the panic over tainted Halloween treats was a media-created scare that began during the early 1970s. Contrary to widespread media claims, "there were no reports where an anonymous sadist caused death or a life-threatening injury; there is no justification for the claim that Halloween sadism stands as a major threat to US children."[31]

While there have been reports of tainted treats causing death, these cases have turned out to have been unfounded. Far from having been caused by Halloween sadists, the deaths were perpetrated by relatives. For instance, in 1970, five-year-old Kevin Totson died after reportedly ingesting heroin from Halloween candy in Detroit, Michigan. While this case caused great media fanfare, authorities later concluded that the boy had found the heroin at the home of a family member. The death was unrelated to Halloween, but this information received far less media coverage than the original report. Another supposed Halloween poisoning occurred in Pasadena, Texas, in 1974. Eight-year-old Timothy O'Bryan died after eating treats laced with cyanide. An investigation revealed that the boy had been murdered by his father who had given him the candy in order to collect on an insurance policy.

Best and Horiuchi note that survey data during the early 1970s revealed increasing levels of general mistrust, including the fear of strangers in urban settings. "The social conflicts of the 1960s and early 1970s may have encouraged doubts about the trustworthiness of other people. Such doubts provided another form of strain during the period when the belief in Halloween sadism spread."[32] These social anxieties are what they believe fueled the trick-or-treat-sadist myth. "These sources of strain — threats to children, fear of crime, and mistrust of others—provided a context within which the concern about Halloween sadism could flourish. The Halloween sadist emerged as a symbolic expression of this strain: the sadist, like other dangers, attacks children—society's most vulnerable members; the sadist, like the stereotypical criminal, is an anonymous, unprovoked assailant; and the sadist, like other strangers, must be met by doubt, rather than trust. Placed in the context of the late 1960s and early 1970s, the spread of Halloween sadism is easily understood."

A 1972 study by the newspaper and magazine industry to determine the extent of Halloween sadism found that almost all claims were hoaxes. A separate study in 1982 examined 270 claims of tampering. According to the Food and Drug Administration, which analyzed the treats, in 95 percent of cases, no evidence of tampering was found, leading an FDA investigator to conclude that it was an episode of "mass hysteria."[33] Ben Radford observes that in instances "where children weren't perpetrating deliberate hoaxes for mischief or attention, a knick on an apple or innocent tear of a candy wrapper, was redefined as the work of the sadist!"[34] The epidemic of tampering can be viewed as part of the moral panic over the safety of children. Halloween sadism tales are an urban legend embedded within a moral panic which reflects fears that Americans no longer feel safe.[35]

Video Nasties Scare, early 1980s (England, Australia, and New Zealand)

With the widespread appearance of video players in Western homes during the 1980s, video shops popped up like mushrooms, and, for the first time, people with average incomes could buy or rent a range of videos. It was within this backdrop that a flurry of media reports appeared, warning of the harmful effects of horror videos on young, impressionable minds. Dubbed "video nasties," the scare was stoked by the British media and peaked between 1983 and 1984. Conservative social commentators and religious groups railed against this new form of moral decay corrupting innocent youth, and extreme claims were the order of the day. British sociologist Clifford Hill led the crusade against the new evil. An ordained minister worried about a perceived decline in moral values, Hill claimed that a "significant number of children of all ages reported that they had suffered nightmares which they attributed to watching video nasties."[36] One survey reported that 40 percent of six-year-olds had seen at least one of the suspect videos.[37] Dubious of these results, independent researchers gave a similar survey to eleven-year-olds but added several bogus titles. A whopping 68 percent of those questioned claimed they had watched the fictional titles.[38]

The panic over "video nasties" soon gained momentum in New Zealand.[39] During 1985, the battle raged. The New Zealand Minister of Women's Affairs, Ann Hercus, called for all videos to be censored and some even banned. "I do not believe they should be available to anyone. While I understand the argument that says you cannot interfere in the privacy of what happens in a person's home, I believe there is another set of values that is as important—a community interest that says in a modern democratic society we should not portray women in filthy, degrading circumstances."[40] The August 1985 issue of *Grapevine*, a popular Christian family magazine, carried the alarmist headline: "Video Nasties: Loose in Your Living Room?" It claimed that the same video rental shops that stocked *The Sound of Music* and Mickey Mouse, offered videos that were "sick and even down-right savage. . . . On any given evening, adults who normally WOULDN'T—and kids who certainly SHOULDN'T—are treating their eyeballs and their memory-banks to movies that in many cases have never been permitted on a cinema screen (at least in their uncut version).[41]

The absurdity of the "video nasties" scare was highlighted by the tussle over *The Driller Killer*. While banned in England, the film carried an R18 rating in New Zealand. The low-budget flick told the story of "Reno," who, by night, left his New York City apartment and hunted prostitutes, drunks, and indigents using a cordless power drill. While alarmists warned against viewing the film, two journalists decided to see what all the fuss was about and rented it. Far from horrifying, Colin Hogg found it boring: noting that Reno "was part of a very, very boring exploitation pic. A film so inept, so badly acted, so utterly boring, that it's no wonder when I rang my local video shop and asked to book it, they said they'd withdrawn it."[42] Journalist Marianne Nørgaard was similarly underwhelmed, writing that Reno "manages to bore his victims into the pavement while he's boring us to death on the couch." She said that "the film is so cliché-ridden and badly produced, it's impossible to view it as anything other than pathetically ridiculous twaddle. It's even too absurd to rate as a cult movie."[43]

In the end, the "video nasties" did not lead to the decline of Western youth and soon passed. This was just one in a long series of panics about wayward youth. British sociologist Geoffrey Pearson observes that during the 1960s and 70s, the concern was about television shows and superhero comics. In the 1950s, it was rock 'n' roll music, jukebox hangouts, and comic books about horror and true crime. During the 1930s, there was widespread concern over copycat crimes caused by watching cinema movies.[44]

McMartin Preschool "Satanic Cult," 1983–1990 (California, USA)

One of the most remarkable cases of moral panic in modern times began in 1983 at the Virginia McMartin Preschool after seven teachers were accused of abusing children, and in some cases, of taking children by helicopter to an isolated farm where fantastic things occurred. The case has many parallels with the infamous

Salem witch trials of 1692 and is a sober reminder of how innocent people can be falsely accused.

At its face value, the story sounds unbelievable. The teachers were arrested and placed on trial after no less than 360 children had testified that adults at the facility had molested them. This raises the obvious question: How could so many people claim that something happened to them when it did not? Especially when it is now clear that it did *not* happen and the accused were all innocent.[45] The legal case endured for seven years before those accused were acquitted of all charges. In the end, what appeared to have been the strongest evidence for the guilt of the "McMartin Seven" turned out to have been their greatest strength: the videotaped testimonies of the preschoolers describing what had supposedly happened.

As news of the charges were initially made public, the mass media—far from being a neutral source for news—suggested that those accused were guilty, even before their trial was completed. Many television reports were blatantly biased for the prosecution.[46] The same was true of press reports. *People* magazine typified the coverage and made reference to the school as "California's Nightmare Nursery." *Time* magazine reported the story under the headline: "Brutalized."[47] The trial coincided with a number of similar scares involving false accusations of the mistreatment of children in preschools in many Western countries. The tide of justice did not turn in these cases until the early 1990s, with the publication of several studies showing that the testimony of children is highly suggestible and easily manipulated by adult interviewers.

The allegations occurred within a backdrop of fear about declining sexual morality. During the early 1980s, there was an explosion of media coverage in the Los Angeles area on an array of sexual ills including rape, juvenile prostitution, child abuse, and sexually explicit advertisements. It was within this context of anxiety and suspicion about a decline in sexual morals that, by late summer 1983, there was growing concern among parents as to the safety of local preschools. The center of the scare, the McMartin Preschool, was owned by Peggy McMartin Buckey and her mother, Virginia McMartin. The school had an outstanding reputation, as did Virginia, who had once been named Local Citizen of the Year.[48]

The scare can be traced to the mother of one of the children at the school—Judy Johnson, who told local police that she suspected that school aid Ray Buckey, son of Peggy Buckey, had molested her son. Her evidence was circumstantial and flimsy. She said that one day, upon returning from school, she noticed that her son had a red, itchy bottom. She also repeated rumors of the possibility that the practice of Satanism may have been going on at the school. Mrs. Johnson was later found to have been mentally ill. However, as a result of her worries, police put the school under surveillance.[49]

On September 8, the Manhattan Beach Police Chief, Harry Kuhlmeyer Jr., mailed letters to two hundred parents, informing them that Ray was being investigated on suspicion of child molestation. He wrote: "This Department is conducting a criminal investigation involving child molestation. Ray Buckey, an employee of Virginia McMartin's Pre-School, was arrested September 7, 1983 by this Department."[50] The letter asked parents to discuss the matter with their children in order to determine if they may have also been a victim of abuse or had witnessed a crime. "Our investigation indicates that possible criminal acts include: oral sex, fondling of genitals, buttock or chest area, and sodomy, possibly committed under the pretense of 'taking the child's temperature.'" The letter also claimed that Ray may have taken nude photos of the children and asked if anyone had observed Ray "leave a classroom alone with a child during any nap period, or if they had ever observed Ray Buckey tie up a child."

Kuhlmeyer's letter, and the manner in which the children would later be interviewed by investigators, resulted in a swarm of claims by the children. While the letter had stated that Buckey had been arrested, this was deceptive because he was soon released due to insufficient evidence. Typically, when police interview witnesses, they separate them and take down their stories to see if they match. However, the letter by Chief Kuhlmeyer had immediately tainted the investigation into the allegations as it revealed the specific claims not only to the parents— who in turn repeated them to their children—but to the entire community. This letter meant that the investigation was flawed from the beginning. However, once the case went to trial, the evidence against the defendants was so weak that District Attorney Glenn Stevens was so disturbed by the lack of concrete evidence that he quit and actually joined the defense team, commenting that the evidence used to lay the original charges, was "very weak, if not false."[51]

In a stunning reversal of fortune, once the prosecution began to produce the videotaped interviews with the children, the case turned in favor of the defense as it became clear that the interviews were flawed. The interviewers tended to dominate the young children and ask them leading questions—that is, questions suggesting an answer. Under intense questioning by poorly trained interviewers, a number of claims about real events became jumbled. A classic example involved details surrounding "the naked movie star game." Authorities had asked children about a game they had supposedly played while naked at the school. After asking leading questions, it appeared that some of the children had engaged in this bizarre, sexual game. While this is a very specific allegation that sounds too bizarre to have been made up, it later became apparent that the "game" was actually a rhyme used to tease children. During the trial, one of the children said: "There was no naked movie star game. If someone made fun of you, you'd say, 'What you see is what you are. You're a naked movie star.'"[52]

Psychologist Daniel Wright uses this example to highlight the dangers of poor interviewing techniques. He and his colleagues observed that the acts of praising the interviewee or putting them down had a powerful effect on their responses. "This can be a powerful suggestive technique, particularly when the interviewer is an authority figure and the interviewee a child. Consider the McMartin preschool case, in which positive statements included 'Oh, you're so smart. I knew you'd remember,' while negative statements included 'Well, what good are you? You must be dumb.' This was coupled with providing information about what other children allegedly said."[53]

In one example, when a preschooler was asked about the game and the child said that they did not remember the game, the interviewer responded: "Everybody remembered that game. Let's see if we can figure it out."[54] In looking back on the case, Wright and his team noted that such questioning "established a situation in which the cost of disagreeing with the alleged statements of the other children was large. Under such situations, normative influences come into play, and a person may comply with others for instrumental reasons: to gain acceptance and affiliation, and to avoid censure or disapproval."[55] This was especially true in the McMartin case, as the interviewers were dealing with preschoolers who were easily manipulated.

Poor interviewing techniques marked by leading questions posed to the children eventually led to a wave of false allegations that resulted in a group of innocent people having to live under a cloud of suspicion for the rest of their lives. For instance, even after the accused were acquitted on all counts, they were still viewed with suspicion. When jurors were asked if they believed that some of the molestations had taken place, eight thought that was the case, but the evidence was too weak to convict![56] However, once experts had a chance to scrutinize the evidence, a research team who observed some of the interviews wrote: "There was not one spontaneous 'disclosure' on any of these tapes . . . On all of the videotapes shown, the children repeatedly denied witnessing any act of sexual abuse of children. The interviewer ignored these exonerating statements and continued to coax and pressure the child for accusations."[57]

While the accused were eventually set free, they had to live with the allegations for the rest of their lives. At the time of their acquittal, Peggy had served two years in jail, and Ray had lost five years behind bars. They had spent most of their money on lawyers' fees.[58]

The "Knockout Game," 1992 and ongoing (USA)

The first known reference to the "knockout game" appeared in a 1992 newspaper article by the Associated Press. Journalist Tony Rogers wrote that the objective of the game was "to knock someone unconscious with one punch. Until this week, it was apparently something youths on the street only whispered about. But prosecutors Monday charged that three Cambridge teen-agers were playing the brutal game when they robbed and killed a Massachusetts Institute of Technology student Friday."[59] Seventeen-year-old Joseph Donovan was with two teenage friends when he allegedly punched and then stabbed twenty-one-year-old Yngve Raustein, from Norway, who was out with a friend. Howard Spivak, director of the New England Medical Center, said: "This doesn't surprise me. We're creating an environment in which kids do this."[60] Police were unsure that this was really a new craze among teenagers. "Nobody's heard of this. This could be something one or two kids have started as something they did among themselves," said Frank Pasquarello, a detective in Cambridge, Massachusetts.[61] Curiously, four days earlier, the first newspaper account of this murder had no mention of the "knockout game" and stated that the sole motive was robbery.[62]

There were a relatively small number of isolated cases of the "knockout game" reported between 1992 and 2012, and there was a sharp increase in reported "knockout game" assaults and deaths in 2013 and 2014. During this time, awareness of the "knockout game" was increased by more newspaper coverage, online blogging, and posting of YouTube videos about it. While "knockout game" attacks do exist and are not an urban legend, the number of attacks and the threat that they pose to society has been greatly exaggerated, and as such, they constitute a moral panic.

In the course of investigating incidents of the game in 2013, *New York Times* reporter Cara Buckley contacted police in several American cites who said that the game was more mythical than real. They suggested that such attacks were simply random assaults that have always been recorded by police. Even after supposedly occurring for over two decades, Buckley wrote in 2013 that New York City police officials were still "struggling to determine whether they should advise the public to take precautions against the Knockout Game — or whether in fact it existed."[63] If, after twenty years, police are unable to conclusively confirm the existence of a particular crime, it probably doesn't exist—or at the very least, is far less significant than previously thought.

A flare up in concern over the prevalence of the "knockout game" took place in 2012 with saturated media coverage of an attack in Pittsburgh, Pennsylvania, where the incident was captured by surveillance cameras. The video showed fifty-year-old high-school teacher James Addlespurger being struck by a young man who was walking in a group. However, despite the media attention, the attacker told Pittsburgh police that the incident had no connection with any organized game. Eric Holmes of the Pittsburgh Police Department said that based on talking to the suspect, it "was just a random act of violence," noting that the man said he had been having a bad day.[64] Addlespurger also believes it was a random assault and not part of any organized game. "I feel like I'm exploited. People need a label. If they're selling toothpaste or CDs, or news stories, they need a label. . . . To me it's an assault, plain and simple," he said.[65]

The "knockout game" was reported to have occurred in Jersey City, New Jersey, with videos circulating in which youths describe perpetrating such acts. But when Buckley talked to Bob McHugh, a Jersey City police spokesman, McHugh said that there had not been a single local incident reported to police. It was a similar response in Hoboken, New Jersey, when the "knockout game" was blamed for the death of a man after three youths approached him and he was punched. Hoboken Police Chief Anthony Falco said he had no reason to believe it was anything other than an isolated incident—a view echoed by Hudson County Assistant Prosecutor Gene Rubino: "We keep getting asked that question . . . there is no noticeable trend."[66]

Remarkably, just two days after the *New York Times* article questioning the existence of the "knockout game" appeared, CNN also interviewed New York City police officials and made it sound like the game was alive and well. Reporter Morgan Winsor filed a story with the alarming headline: "Police Keep Close Eye on Reports of Disturbing 'Knockout' Game." Winsor asserted: "A sick so-called game known as 'knockout'—where teens appear to randomly sucker-punch strangers with the goal of knocking them unconscious with a single blow—is catching the attention of law enforcement throughout the nation. . . . The assaults can be fatal. In New Jersey, Ralph Santiago, 46, a homeless man, was walking alone in Hoboken on the night of September 10 when he was suddenly struck from behind, said Hoboken Detective Anthony Caruso. . . . The blow knocked out Santiago, who had a pre-existing brain injury. He suffered a seizure. The victim's body struck a nearby fence, with part of the wrought iron fence piercing his body and killing him, Caruso said." Winsor claimed that "Authorities have reported similar incidents in New York, Illinois, Missouri and Washington."[67]

A research fellow for the Center on Juvenile and Criminal Justice, Mike Males, says that the mass media tend to cherry-pick isolated incidents of violence in order to create sensational headlines that demonize youth. Males said it was the equivalent of randomly highlighting scattered incidents of violence against people with Jewish surnames and proclaiming it to be a "troubling new trend."[68] Ironically, he said, the media had "picked a few real and anecdotal assaults by black youths across the nation, some years apart, and applied the label. Then, in standard self-reverence, reporters and sources worried that media publicity—that is, their own made-up panic—might stimulate more knockout attacks by 'idiotic, impulsive . . . insensitive, uncaring' teenagers." [69] Males cites a statistic from the US Department of Justice that over the past two decades, violent crime by strangers was down 77 percent.

In Australia, for instance, it was reported in 2013 that since 2000, there were ninety reported deaths from single-punch assaults, but these attacks were not made by people playing the "knockout game." They were alcohol-fueled arguments—mostly in or just outside bars and pubs—when one person king-hit another. A "king-hit" is American slang for a sudden knockout blow. "There was a brief altercation with someone they just met five minutes ago. One person throws a punch. A person goes down, hits their head and never again regains consciousness," said Dr. Jennifer Pilgrim, a researcher at Monash University's Department of Forensic Medicine.[70] Nearly half of the fatal single-punch assaults happened between midnight and six in the morning. "There is no reason for it. Usually the person is not expecting it," said Gordian Fulde, director of St. Vincent's Hospital's emergency department, of the four or five king-hit assault victims he treats every Friday or Saturday night at the hospital.[71]

Less than one hundred alleged instances of the "knockout game" were reported in the United States in 2013. According to FBI statistics, that same year there were "an estimated 724,149 aggravated assaults in the nation."[72] So, worst case scenario, less than one in every 7,200 assaults could be attributed to the "knockout game." Also, when an examination is made of recent reported cases of the "knockout game" from 2013 and 2014, it is clear that some are ordinary assaults—or even accidents rather than assaults—and have nothing to do with the "knockout game." This fact reduces the already minute percentage of assaults that are actually "knockout game" related.

In March 2014 it was reported that a sixty-five-year-old Orthodox Jew—a tourist from England—was a victim of the "knockout game" in Borough Park, Brooklyn. The victim was grabbed by the head, and his face was smashed into the pavement. He suffered a chipped tooth and a split lip.[73] "It is shocking and disturbing to hear about yet another apparent anti-Semitic assault in our community, especially after so many similar incidents over the past months. Simply put, there is no place for this type of heinous behavior in our city, as nobody should be afraid to walk the streets of their community at any time of day or night," stated City Councilman David Greenfield.[74] "He was attacked from behind by two individuals, brutally attacked. . . . They did not take anything from him, and he was in such bad condition that he had to be hospitalized," said Greenfield, who believed it was a "knockout game" attack.[75] However, the alleged victim then told police that he had actually just fallen over.[76]

Some people claim the "knockout game" is gang related (implying gangs of African American teenagers). As with claims about the increasing spread and growing number of "knockout game" attacks, this claim should be treated with great suspicion. Brian Chapman cautions that while there has been much hoopla about gang initiations and the "knockout game," the association remains dubious. "In the last few years gang initiates have been accused of asking for directions from passersby and killing them if they respond; throwing bricks through car windshields; rear-ending cars and killing the occupants; leaving a doll or car-seat on the roadside and doing in anyone who stops; driving without headlights on and shooting any drivers who helpfully flash their own lights; killing tourists on a certain day; killing state employees; raping or killing college students; killing white people on crosswalks; murdering women on Halloween or at shopping malls; hiding under cars and slashing women's ankles; and so on. The knockout game would fit nicely in this list, no doubt about it. That in itself should make us hesitant to claim it's a type of gang initiation, at least until good evidence comes along."[77]

"Kill the Cat Killers" Moral Panic, 2000 (Slovenia)

In March 2000, a moral panic erupted that involved claims of widespread cat killings and torture. The episode was triggered by sensational media coverage in the wake of the arrest of three high-school teenagers who were accused of having killed and tortured over forty cats during the previous fifteen months. The dramatic response helped to fuel an exaggerated belief that killing cats was a major issue in Slovenian society. The extreme nature of the reaction culminated in experts suggesting that those accused would likely become serial killers, and a leader of the Slovene Animal Protection Organization called for the teens to be executed.

Gregor Bulc analyzed media reports on the concern over cat abuse and noted that it was out of proportion to the reality. "The cases of serial pet killing are exceedingly rare or even nonexistent in Slovenia: there have been no reports on such behavior in the past decade. Although five cases of deliberate animal torturing appeared in the year 1999, they were all characterized as one time only incidents. The Tržič cat-killing case was an idiosyncratic event and not a part of any recognizable trend. Yet somehow the case has crystallized an amorphous national sense of unease into rage over delinquent boys."[78] Bulc said there was irony in the reaction as the issue had received intense media coverage due to "the infrequency of these occurrences rather than their frequency."[79] Bulc found that the media had created a new issue where none had previously existed in Slovenian society. For instance, media outlets proclaimed that "lately, more and more similar cases are appearing," and one of the main television stations reported: "Not a day goes by that we do not hear about torturers."[80] In going overboard in their response, Bulc states that the media flooded the airwaves and newspapers with "images of dead cats and cute kittens" that even included pictures of an infamous Slovene serial killer and photographs of the three teens on "Wanted" posters.[81] "It can be argued that the response to the cat killings was, in large part, created by the media. The media ignited the moral panic, confirming, distorting, and structuring the whole case; they kept the public attention focused on the problem and contributed to a definition of cat-killing youth as highly dangerous for Slovene society. This heightened the public awareness of the problem."[82]

Claims about the case of the three teens were often incorrect as reported in the media. Also, representatives of animal-protection organizations were cited as experts on the issue when they were clearly not. "Apparently, this interest group found it necessary to exaggerate their claims so as to distinguish themselves from other groups seeking recognition for their goals. Therefore, they presented their concern through statements about a high degree of animal torturing in Slovenia (which calls for tougher penalties) and claims about a definite, scientifically proven fact that young animal torturers become serial killers when they grow up."[83] For instance, the director of one animal-protection group made the dubious claim on television "that in one Slovene tavern, cats can be found on the menu: 'they bring the cats, they roast them in the traditional oven and then they have a public feast and they eat those cats.'"

Politicians also engaged in the moral panic, including the mayor of Tržič and a member of Parliament, who was scathing in his attack on the boys and called for harsher penalties. The mayor described them as "satanic" and called for their names and addresses to be published—quite illegally![84] Bulc writes: "The condemnation of evildoers and the promotion of tougher legislation by politicians is, then, a consequence of their acknowledgment of a large public concern and a relatively big public consensus that something must be done about it so it does not happen again. This generates a temptation to reach for simple, often punitive, solutions to complex problems."[85]

The Great Hoodie Scare, 2005–2006 (England)

During the mid-2000s, Great Britain experienced the "Great Hoodie Scare," as the British media and politicians began to warn against those wearing hooded sweatshirts and expressed the need to ban the wearing of them. Hoodies began to gain a bad reputation during the 1990s when they were commonly worn by skateboarders and disaffected youth. By 2005, the term "hoodie culture" emerged and some shopping centers began to ban hoodies and other youth-related items, such as baseball caps, allegedly on the grounds that they obscured the wearer's face. British criminologists Ian Marsh and Gaynor Melville document how the hoodie became a temporary symbol of evil, for youth who were seemingly "up to no good," and note the irony of how shoppers in many malls were barred from wearing an item that was on sale in the very building they could not wear them in![86] At the time, Prime Minister Tony Blair welcomed the shopping-center bans as a way of controlling threatening and antisocial behavior. The scare was triggered when the Bluewater shopping mall in Kent announced their ban, sparking an intense debate in the media and among politicians. *Guardian* journalist Patrick

Barkham wrote: "Street rats, says Ainsley, 17. 'That's what they're called.' 'They sit on the streets and drink,' explains Lauren, 16 . . . The teenagers from Bexleyheath describe the disrespectful youths of today as they glide along the Bluewater shopping centre in Kent. Street rats wear hooded tops and baseball caps."[87]

To its credit, the *Guardian* eventually recognized the hoodie scare for what it was and published an article on the affair by British sociologist Jack Fawbert, who wrote in 2008 that once the panic was underway, journalists began trying to outdo themselves with the most sensational hoodie story. As a consequence of the media hyperbole, Fawbert wrote that "one youngster was prevented from sitting a GCSE exam for wearing one, a two-year-old was banned from a shop for wearing one and a pensioner was prevented from wearing his trilby hat in a public house." Fawbert found that authorities grew more and more extreme in addressing the issue. One of the more outlandish claims was made by the former Metropolitan police commissioner, Sir John Stevens, who advocated for longer prison terms for so-called thugs donning hoods. Ironically, the public condemnation by adults and authorities only made hoodies more attractive, and they soon became "hot" fashion items as reflected in soaring sales of hooded tops. Fawbert observed that the peak of the panic was relatively short-lived due to the difficulty in sustaining "a fever-pitch level of antagonism for any length of time."[88]

Moral panics have had a prominent place in world history. They prey on prevalent stereotypes and fears, especially involving unpopular groups such as Jews, gypsies, communists, homosexuals, and Muslims. For instance allowing gays to adopt children or marry has been viewed by some religious conservatives as portending a moral decline in Western civilization and going against god's will as outlined in the Bible. Whether it is a fear of tainted Halloween candy or concern over Satanists infiltrating our day-care centers, moral panics are based on preexisting prejudices and legitimated in the media with exaggerated facts and figures that highlight the threat. While the threat exists—people can and have tainted candy, and children have been molested in nurseries—the degree of exaggeration in relation to the actual threat posed, is extreme.

In chapter 11, we survey what is perhaps the most dramatic and explosive form of collective behavior: riots. While they occasionally result from moral panics, they never arise from a social vacuum. They are always incubated in a backdrop of prejudice and unrest.

CHAPTER 11

RIOTS:
THE BREAKDOWN
OF SOCIAL ORDER

A riot is a relatively spontaneous gathering of people who break traditional standards of behavior by engaging in destructive acts to people or property. Most riots are a form of collective grievance in response to a perceived social injustice and are essentially an exercise in collective problem solving that is triggered by anger, frustration, and societal strains. The goal is to force change by challenging authorities and attacking the existing social order. A minority of outbreaks that do not fit this pattern include collective excitements and celebrations that turn destructive, such as after a sporting event. Most outbreaks of public disorders last from a few hours to several days or weeks. On rare occasions, they endure for months. While rioters come from all walks of life, and there is no clear indication that they are disproportionately composed of people with criminal records, in his analysis of the Los Angeles Race Riots of 1965, Anthony Oberschall found that of the nearly four thousand people arrested, most were of low social and economic status.[1]

Sometimes riots are important initiators of social change. On June 28, 1969, rioting broke out in New York City after a police raid on a popular gay nightclub. Dubbed the Stonewall riots after the club's name, the event has been credited with marking the start of the gay rights movement and helped to focus attention on the treatment of homosexuals.[2] The Rodney King riots of 1992 in South Central Los Angeles were triggered by video footage of police using excessive force to subdue Mr. King and led to improvements in the way police handle such incidents and placed greater focus on the economic disparity experienced by the community. It is important to recognize that riots are rarely triggered by one event, although a single incident can often be pinpointed as being "the straw that broke the camel's back." During the King riots, a special California commission concluded that several key factors had been incubating the unrest among the local population for years, including segregation, poverty, unemployment, police mistrust, and a lack of educational opportunities.[3]

Riots can be coordinated and uncoordinated. The latter involve acts of random destruction and looting as an expression of dissatisfaction, with no target group in mind. In contrast, coordinated riots are purposeful, and anger is vented with a specific target in mind—sometimes a person, such as a government leader, or a group, such as an ethnic minority. Occasionally, a commodity is the target of the rioters. An example of a coordinated riot was the storming of the Bastille in France on July 14, 1789, when a mob destroyed the huge fort, a symbol of government power that housed prisoners. Lynchings are another example. Between 1865 and 1955, it is estimated that upward of five thousand African Americans were lynched for such infractions as looking at a white woman in the eyes, showing disrespect, asserting their right to vote, and riding with white passengers on a train.[4] On rare occasions, hostile crowds that appeared potentially riotous have quickly changed into festive gatherings, highlighting the difficulty in predicting the appearance of riots. In 1977, a one-day national strike in France turned into what one news outlet reported to have been "closer to that of a national holiday than a national crisis."[5]

American psychiatrist John Spiegel identifies four stages that all riots pass through.[6] First is the *precipitating incident*: an act, event, or situation that is interpreted as proof of social injustice. Sociologist Reid Luhman remarks that "riots form around some kind of precipitating event, or spark, that sets things off. As with checking a gas tank with a lighted match, the cause of the conflagration is more the gas than the match, but both are necessary."[7] In their study of seventy-six race riots, Stanley Lieberman and Arnold Silverman found a variety of precipitating factors: interracial fights, shootings, murder, desecration of the American flag, violations of civil liberties, and the attack, rape, murder, or robbery of white females by black males.[8]

Precipitating events may be imagined and are often exaggerated. During the Gordon riots in London during 1780, unrest broke out after Parliament passed a law extending the rights of Catholics; a move which reinforced preexisting sentiments among Protestants that the government viewed them as second-class citizens.[9] Precipitating incidents never occur in isolation; there are always preexisting hostilities in the community affected. Sociologist Neil Smelser writes that "hostile outbursts" are frequently preceded by stereotypic attitudes about the

despised group that is the focus of their anger.[10] He notes that "anti-Semitic attitudes traditionally have emphasized the Jew as an unfair competitor; anti-Negro
attitudes in this country [the US] center on economic competition and sexual
perils; anti-Catholic attitudes have clustered around the problems of public education and the interference of the Church in political affairs."

Rumors may also reinforce existing stereotypes. The Detroit race riots of June
1943 were accompanied by separate rumors demonizing both blacks and whites.
One version of events held that white sailors had tossed a black baby off a bridge,
while another version held that a white baby had been thrown off the same bridge
by a group of blacks. Other accounts claim that a white female "had been attacked
on the bridge by colored men; white sailors had insulted colored girls; white girls
had been accosted by Negroes while swimming" and so on.[11]

Phase two is the *confrontation*, where potential rioters are incited to right the
perceived injustice. Outraged participants may have gathered publicly and vocal-
ized the perceived injustices and made demands. During the 1971 Attica prison
riot in Western New York, prisoners formed a committee to represent the group
and attempted to address their grievances. They also composed a list of reforms.[12]

Often, the confrontation develops after police arrive at the scene, immediately after the precipitating incident, and become the subject of taunts. As they
try to disperse or arrest crowd members, violence grows rapidly. At this juncture,
if the police show force that is disproportionate to the situation and act aggres-
sively toward the crowd, it often can inflame the unrest and incite even greater,
widespread violence. On the other hand, if police show up with a scant force and
appear not in control, it can encourage more unrest.[13]

The third stage of a riot is the *Roman holiday*, where authorities lose control
and violence breaks out. The term refers to holidays in ancient Rome that were
given so that members of the public could attend combat spectacles between
gladiators. Its common contemporary usage is, according to the *Merriam-Webster
Dictionary*, "a destructive or tumultuous disturbance."[14] Crowd members may
toss projectiles at law enforcement officers, burn down buildings, fire weapons,
or attempt to bull-rush authorities. Often a symbol of their anger is targeted. For
instance, if the riot begins over the perceived unjust killing of a black teenager
by a white police officer, the mob may vent their anger on police headquarters or
a government building.

During the final stage—the *siege*—the violence, looting, and destruction
of property have ceased as reinforcements have arrived to regain control. Here

marshal law is often declared, protest leaders may be arrested for inciting the riot, and the battle lines are clearly drawn. In rare instances, snipers may prevent fire-fighters from doing their job, and firebombings may continue.

Some sociologists discuss *communal riots* which are typified by violent confrontations between groups that are divided along ethnic or religious beliefs. So-called race riots would fall under this heading. However, as many scientists now view race as a mythical concept as we are all part of the same race—the human race—we prefer to use the term *ethnic riot* in place of race riot. These conflicts often involve turf wars in which competing groups vie for the control of a patch of land such as a street, a park, or beach. For this reason they are sometimes called *contested area riots*. In prison riots, outbursts may involve part of the recreation area.

During the Los Angeles zoot-suit riots of June 1943, a series of fights erupted between a group of American sailors and young, male Mexican American gang members dressed in "zoot suits" (loose-fitting jackets with padded shoulders and high-waisted pants). The disputed turf was downtown Los Angeles. The riots were driven by white stereotypes of Hispanics. It should come as no surprise that the police, press, and public all backed the servicemen who were supporting the war effort. The rioting endured for several days until the City Council proclaimed the wearing of zoot suits to be a misdemeanor, and the military issued orders declaring the city off limits to service personnel.[15] The Nazi pogrom (a deliberate, organized riot) against Jews in November 1938 known as "The Night of Broken Glass" also qualifies as a communal riot.

Commodity riots involve civil disorder where the target of attack is the property of a particular group and usually take the form of looting buildings that store goods and equipment. While violence often occurs, it usually involves police and National Guard officers in the course of trying to stop looting or destruction of property. Commodity riots became frequent in the United States during the 1960s as segregated African Americans engaged in looting and destroying property in order to protest perceived inequalities. Targets of the rage included white-operated businesses and government buildings. During these riots, Douglas Massey notes that whites "were not singled out for assault . . . The participants did not express a racial hatred of whites but an anger with the conditions of racial oppression and economic deprivation that had been allowed to fester in the ghetto."[16]

Protest riots are common and involve reactions to government policy. They usually involve civilians refusing to obey official directives, often by physically or verbally attacking government agents. The 2014 democracy protests in Hong Kong are an illustration of this type of riot. The police or military may be called in to restore order and stop the unrest from spreading. However, such actions often backfire by inciting protesters. Sticks, stones, bottles, and fruit may be hurled at police.

During the infamous Boston Massacre of March 5, 1770, a mob of colonists were protesting the collection of taxes near a customs house—a symbol of their anger. They began taunting the British redcoats who guarded the building. When the colonists started tossing snowballs and oyster shells at them and daring them to shoot, the frightened soldiers shot dead five colonists. This event increased resentment of King George and furthered the attempts by colonists to break away from the British government and form a new nation.

Arguably the worst riot in US history involved the protest of drafting soldiers to fight in the Civil War. On March 3, 1863, Congress passed the Conscription Act requiring all able-bodied men between twenty and forty-five to join the military if called upon. The draft triggered anger and resentment that the poor were being unfairly treated as a man could avoid the draft by paying $300 to the US government to pay a "hired soldier" to go in the man's place. New York City was the epicenter of the riots as many there could not afford to pay to avoid going to war, especially Irish Americans, who reacted by rampaging through the city in July. The targets of the Irish community's wrath were the wealthy, who had paid to avoid military service, and blacks, who were blamed for causing the war. During the unrest that ensued, many government buildings were set alight, including conscription offices. At least seventy people died in the violence.[17]

Some researchers discuss *celebration riots*, which involve mass joys and exuberance, usually after sporting events when one team wins a championship. Excited fans may overturn vehicles, start fires, toss bottles, and break windows.[18] Sometimes referred to as "sore-loser riots," *defeat riots* are also common as participants exhibit anger after their team's loss. The nature of human perception may help to drive these events. For instance, studies of sports events have found that people rooting for one side tend only to see infractions committed by the opposing side. After a defeat, supporters tend to blame the loss on outside factors—poor refereeing, bad luck, and dirty play by the other team—and express their dissatisfaction through protest.[19] Some riots involve exuberant crowds unrelated to sports, such as in March 1986, when thousands of university students descended on Palm Springs, California, to enjoy spring break. Many students became so excited and high-spirited that they began tearing clothing off women and throwing rocks at cars. One hundred students were arrested.[20]

MEMORABLE RIOTS

New York City Draft Riots, 1863 (USA)

While riots are relatively rare in modern America, between 1712 and 1873 there were nearly fifty large riots in New York alone.[21] They occurred for a variety of reasons: religious differences, food shortages, even corpse stealing by medical students. One of the worst riots of all was caused by an unpopular war draft. By 1863 the Civil War between the northern and southern United States had entered a second year. The Union army needed more troops than had volunteered to fight against the Confederates. So in March 1863, a national draft was initiated. The names of all men ages twenty and forty-five were put into a draw. Those selected had to serve in the Union army for three years. However, by paying $300, a man could buy his way out of serving if his name had been pulled. As a laborer was paid about $20 a week at the time, the poor were angered by the new legislation and called it "a rich man's war; a poor man's fight."[22] On July 13, 1863, a huge mob marched to the building where the draft names were drawn. The small number of heavily outnumbered police guarding the building wisely chose to retreat. The draft officers fled out the rear of the building as the protesters trashed the inside and set it alight.[23]

The telegraph wire system was a great communications tool that the authorities used to keep track of the rioters and deploy police and troops where they were most needed. Despite some telegraph poles being chopped down and wires cut by rioters, at least five thousand messages were sent during the four-day spectacle.[24] Even though they were often heavily outnumbered, police and troops fought back. Sergeant Daniel Carpenter of the New York City Police Department commanded two hundred men who managed to hold back a violent mob estimated at five thousand.[25] When deadly stones and bricks rained down on Carpenter's men from rioters standing on rooftops, he ordered Captain Mount of the Eleventh Precinct to take fifty men and clear them. The fighting was vicious—some rioters "dropped from second and third story windows, and met with a worse fate than those who stayed behind. One huge fellow received such a tremendous blow, that he was knocked off his feet and over the edge of the roof, and fell headlong down a height of four stories to the pavement beneath. Crushed to death by the force of the fall, he lay a mangled heap at the feet of his companions."[26]

The worst violence was against African Americans, who were perceived by many as the cause of the riots as the stimulus for the draft was the enslavement of blacks. As a result, the four-story Fifth Avenue Colored Orphan Asylum was burned to the ground. Only the courageous actions of the staff saved two hundred infants and children.[27] African American victims included a baby thrown from the upper window of a house on East Twenty-Eighth Street, a young cripple who was beaten then hung in front of his parents, and a man hung from a lamp post with a fire lit beneath his still-writhing body.[28] After four days of violence and looting, order was eventually restored. The final death toll, while initially placed at over one thousand, has been revised downward by contemporary researchers. There is a consensus that the final figures were between 105 and 119.[29]

Battle of Manners Street, 1943 (Wellington, New Zealand)

On Saturday night, April 3, 1943, hundreds of American servicemen (popularly referred to as GIs—General Infantrymen) who were stationed in New Zealand fought a running battle with local soldiers and civilians in the small city of Wellington. It started during the early evening in the Allied Services club on Manners Street. Allegedly, one or two racist Americans from southern states had harassed local Maori troops: the brown-skinned indigenous people of New Zealand. The Kiwis retaliated, and the fight rapidly escalated as more troops and civilians joined in. It spread through the inner city including Cuba Street and Courtenay Place. Most male New Zealanders already resented their American visitors—a popular saying was that they were "overpaid, oversexed, and over here." Historian Jock Phillips observes: "The Americans were a bit more sophisticated and had more money to spend."[30] It was a similar situation in Australia, where many GIs had also been posted. Historian John Costello noted that the GIs "had the money, taxicabs, cigarettes—and the girls. A spot survey at a busy Brisbane intersection at six o'clock on a September evening revealed ninety three American servicemen were in the company of 126 girls; fifty-two Australian servicemen in the company of 27 girls . . ."[31] He includes a report from the *Chicago Sun* which stated: "Australian troops resent the fact that the Americans are better dressed, more affluent, and by reason of their manners, appearance etc., seem to have taken an unfair share of Australian womanhood."

The Battle of Manners Street was fought on and off for two hours. One witness, New Zealander Sol Heperi, remarked: "No one was really hurt. There were black eyes which take a week to cure and bloody noses that stop in 10 minutes. More things happen in rugby," he recalled, playing down the skirmish.[32] John Owen, a thirteen-year-old newspaper-delivery boy, remembered the event well: "I was on the tram and when we got to Manners St I could see there was an enormous crowd gathered. There would be a group of two or three men fist-fighting, and then crowds of hundreds of people cheering them on. The shore patrol, they were kind of the American police, were . . . on either side of the tram with big truncheons and they were just knocking the American soldiers out. The thing I remember most clearly was them placing the soldiers they had hit on the back of these flat-bed trucks they had. They looked like they were knocked clean out."[33] Heperi remembers a tram driver who stopped in Manners street:. "He got out, left his passengers and joined the fight. I don't know who he was or what kind of an axe he had to grind."[34]

Due to war-time censorship that was in place, the Battle of Manners Street was never reported in newspapers or on radio when it happened. Word-of-mouth transfer of information about it inevitably led to exaggeration including talk that two Americans had actually been killed. For the same reason, there are several conflicting versions of exactly how the fighting started. There were other smaller-scale incidents between Americans and locals in both Wellington and Auckland, New Zealand, and Brisbane, Australia. However, the Battle of Manners Street is remembered most today, largely due to the aura of secrecy that concealed it for many decades.

Zoot-Suit Riots, 1943 (Los Angeles, California, USA)

The zoot suit was an item of clothing that sparked full-scale riots and was banned for being unpatriotic. Zoot-suit style started in Harlem, New York, during the 1930s, and many individual tailors have claimed to have created the style.[35] The zoot suit was a wide, long jacket paired with pants that were baggy to the knee then tapered to a tight cuff at the ankle. The look was often added to with a wide-brimmed hat and a chain dangling from the waist to below the knee. In Los Angeles in the 1940s, the style was mainly worn by Mexican immigrants and lower-class African Americans. The need for wartime factory workers had boosted their incomes. With spare money in hand, they spent it on zoot suits, alcohol, and entertainment. The influx of large numbers of both races into the city and their new-found affluence were sources of anger for some whites. From 1942 onward, the zoot-suit style fell afoul of regulations designed to reduce the wastage of clothing materials during World War II. As such, zoot suits were widely viewed as unpatriotic. The highlight of propaganda against zoot suits was a Walt Disney short cartoon called *Spirit of '43*, in which Donald Duck is tempted to waste his money in a bar by a zoot-suited duck with a swastika bow tie.[36]

The Los Angeles zoot-suit riots were fueled by both actual and rumored attacks on servicemen by zoot-suiters. Whatever the truth about violent harassment by zoot-suiters, the riots themselves were violence on a much larger scale, perpetrated against zoot-suit wearers by larger numbers of roaming servicemen. On June 8, 1943, at least fifty zoot-suiters were stripped of their finery. Cars and taxis were used to go from one theater and dance hall to another searching for zoot-suiters. Two hundred servicemen entered one theater, pulled twenty zoot-suiters from the audience, and "left them lying on the footpath in the nude. Ambulances took three to hospital."[37] A large group of almost four hundred sailors roamed the Long Beach area "to search for Mexican and Negro youths sporting the reat pleats."[38]

After several nights of rioting, ninety-two civilians and eighteen servicemen were hospitalized with serious injuries. An estimated 100–150 more were treated by private doctors. Ninety-four civilians and twenty servicemen were arrested. An additional four hundred zoot-suiters were held in custody until tensions eased.[39] California Governor Earl Warren would later proclaim: "Without regard to the basic cause of these riots they promote disunity, develop race hatred, and create an unwholesome relationship between our men in arms and the citizenry. They create doubts of our solidarity in our own minds and bring joy to the hearts of our enemies."[40]

Also of great concern was the damage caused to America's relationship with Mexico as Mexican labor was needed for wartime factories due to the large number of men serving overseas. Rafael de la Colina, the Minister-Counselor of the Mexican embassy in Washington, described the riots as "mob violence" directed against the Mexican community in Los Angeles.[41]

Drag Racers' Riot, 1956 (Daytona Beach, Florida, USA)

At about 8:30 p.m. on February 25, 1956, teenagers watching illegal street drag racing mistakenly thought someone from their group had been arrested. They broke the windows of one police car and slashed the tires on two others. That night nearly one hundred teens were arrested out of the angry mob of three thousand to four thousand people. Fifteen people were injured—one policeman and five firemen among them.[42] Just as the mob looked like it would disperse, firemen had arrived and reeled out hoses. This incited the crowd to attack. The hoses were slashed and the firemen were pelted with rocks, bricks, and fireworks. Shop windows were also smashed, and passing cars were attacked.[43] A National Guard platoon of thirty armed men moved in at 1:00 a.m. and, with aid from one hundred city and state police, closed all bars and restaurants and cleared a three-square-mile area of pedestrians. With that, the riot was over. Only a single warning shot had been fired.[44] Remarkably, no one had been killed.

Student Sports Riots, 1964 (Gainesville, Florida, USA)

At 11:00 p.m. on the night of December 5, 1964, over 2,500 students had gathered on the University of Florida campus to celebrate twin football and basketball victories. Their basketball team beat Stetson University 90–57, and the football team beat Louisiana State 20–6. The crowd swelled to as many as eight thousand.[45] Press reports attributed the cause of the riots to groups of female students who waved their underwear out of their dormitory windows at the crowd of young men and yelled "come and get it!" Such claims seem simplistic and naive. The violence quickly escalated; before it was over, sixteen people were arrested for disorderly conduct and four were injured (two students and two policemen).[46] A bonfire was lit on Highway 441 and blocked traffic. Students ran down streets and set fire to cars and trees. A mobile coaching tower was also set alight. Wooden bleachers were ripped apart to provide fuel for more bonfires.[47] A subsequent investigation led to one student being expelled, nine suspended, and thirteen placed on probation. Nine of the students were also fined $50 each.[48]

Stonewall Inn Riots, 1969 (New York, USA)

"There was never any time that I felt more scared than I felt that night," said Deputy Inspector Seymour Pine, a World War II veteran and author of the official US Army hand-to-hand combat manual.[49] Pine had been trapped inside the Stonewall Inn after a violent crowd of homosexuals and transsexuals battled police. In 1969, most gays were forced to hide their sexuality. Even in New York City there were only a few gay restaurants and bars at the time. Raids and harassment by police meant risking arrest and public exposure. Gay men were often fired from their jobs if they were outed.

The Stonewall Inn on Christopher Street in the bohemian Greenwich Village area was a Mafia-run bar that flouted numerous city health-and-safety laws. Despite protection payouts to city officials and police, raids were still common. The bar was a cash cow for the owners—it was run as cheaply as possible, sold overpriced, watered-down drinks, and packed in far more patrons than were allowed for the size of the property.

Historian David Carter has produced a detailed analysis of the riots. On the night of Tuesday, June 24, the Stonewall Inn was raided by police. Bar staff were arrested and alcohol was seized. As usual, the bar soon reopened. At 1:20 a.m. on Saturday, June 28, eight members of the police department raided the inn again, assisted by four undercover police officers who had been inside gathering intelligence. As patrons and staff were either held inside the bar (if they had identification) or taken to a waiting paddy wagon and police cars, anger against the police grew in the form of a large crowd of onlookers. This was highly unusual—in past raids released patrons had soon made themselves scarce. Inside the bar, police encountered resistance from transvestites who refused to be examined in the toilets (this had to be done to confirm they were men—a man dressing as a woman in public was illegal).

When a mannish lesbian was dragged from the bar, she fiercely resisted being put in a police car and was beaten with billy clubs by several cops. The crowd erupted in violence.[50] A rain of projectiles was hurled at the police including coins, cans, and bottles. Police retreated and barricaded themselves inside the Stonewall Inn, and the barrage increased. Cobblestones, bricks, and trash cans were thrown at the building. An uprooted parking meter was used as an improvised battering ram on the main door. Burning rubbish and Molotov cocktails were thrown through the broken windows. The cops inside used a single fire extinguisher and a fire hose against the flames. Their radio calls for assistance were countermanded by someone on the frequency saying to disregard them. The bar's phone line was cut. The situation was desperate. Eventually a small policewoman squeezed through an air duct to the roof to call for help from a nearby fire station. Only when reinforcements arrived —including two buses full of the Police Tactical Force—did they feel it was safe to leave the bar.

"When they tried to clear the streets is when people resented it, 'cause it came down to 'Whose streets are these? They are our streets. And you cops are not from this area. It's gay people's streets,'" recalled gay activist John O'Brien.[51] The bar was on one side of a narrow triangle of streets with a park opposite it. This made it easy for the crowd to repeatedly circle around behind the police lines. Each time one end of the street was cleared of rioters, the other would then be filled up. Eventually the crowd tired of this and dispersed near dawn.

The next day, news of the confrontation spread rapidly through the local community. That night a crowd of thousands gathered in Christopher Street. Gay and transgender participants blocked traffic as locals and tourists looked on. One hundred local police were supplemented by 150 riot police. Tension rose as did the temperature. It was the hottest June 28 in New York history.[52] Journalist David Carter writes that a solid wall of riot police prepared to clear the street. "The queens—they were extremely effeminate young men—formed this kicking line all across Christopher Street, and started to do a Rockettes kick. . . . And the police started moving ahead, moving towards them. And the queens did not move, they just continued to kick and to sing as the police just moved closer and closer . . . with their clubs and their helmets and their riot gear and the whole thing . . . They were waiting until the very last minute, and it wasn't until the police were eight feet away from them that the crowd finally broke and ran," recalls Robert Bryan.[53]

The protesters used side streets to circle behind the police as each section of the street was cleared, although authorities did manage to seal off one block immediately around the inn. After several hours of street fighting, police eventually managed to disperse the crowd. On Sunday, Monday, and Tuesday nights there were only minor altercations between police and protesters, but the gay community was infuriated when the latest issue of the *Village Voice* came out on Wednesday. Two negative articles appeared that included derogatory terms to describe the protesters including "limp wrist," "fag follies," "dancing faggots," and "dyke."[54] From 10:00 p.m. on, hundreds of people fought both regular and riot police. Many protesters were badly injured. Dick Leitsch saw that "young people, many of them queens, were lying on the sidewalk, bleeding from the head, face, mouth, and even the eyes. Others were nursing bruised and often bleeding arms, legs, backs, and necks."[55]

A variety of factors contributed to make perfect-storm conditions for the Stonewall riots: the gay community reaching breaking point over harassment and raids, the unusual layout of streets that favored guerilla tactics by the rioters, and the extreme heat. After Stonewall, the face of gay-rights protests changed. Prior to the riots, a gay protest comprised a handful of polite men wearing suits and ties and carrying neatly stenciled placards. After, a typical protest consisted of hundreds of rowdy, casually dressed young people. In the years since the Stonewall riots, the LGBT (lesbian, gay, bisexual, and transgender) community has continued to gain equality with heterosexuals, and in June 2015, the United States Supreme Court ruled that same sex couples could legally marry in all fifty states. Despite these gains, there are still battles being fought, particularly in the area of transgender rights.

Blackout Riot, 1977 (New York City, New York, USA)

On July 13, 1977, a wave of arson and looting started during a twenty-five-hour electricity "blackout" caused by lightning strikes in New York City. Before it was over, more than 3,800 people were arrested, over one thousand fires had been set, and property damage was estimated at one billion dollars. "The looters were looting other looters, and the fists and the knives were coming out," remembers Carl St. Martin, a Queens neurologist.[56] Thousands of looters stole everything they could get their hands on: television sets, clothing, furniture, jewelry, liquor, and drugs. "It's like a fever struck them. They were out there with trucks, vans, trailers, everything that could roll," said Frank Ross, an African American policeman.[57] *Time* reporter Paul Witteman noted, "The evidence of looting was numbing. As firemen fought blazes from cherrypickers, the looters went about their business virtually unmolested. Periodically when a rumor swept through the pack that the police were coming the looters would break and run. But the police, outnumbered and fatigued, often did not try to chase them. When I left the area, [Broadway in the Bushwick part of Brooklyn] it was burning, the flames taking what little the looters left behind."[58]

"Prices have gone too high. Now we're going to have no prices. When we get done, there ain't gonna be no more Broadway," said one looter with a television set in one hand and a wine bottle in the other. "You take your chance when you get a chance. We're poor, and this is our way of getting rich," said another.[59] Two main reasons were proposed for why the 1977 blackout was so violent compared to an even-more-widespread (but peaceful) blackout that had occurred on November 9, 1965 across the northeastern US and Ontario, Canada, including New York City. The 1965 blackout happened on a cool November evening, whereas the 1977 experience occurred in sweltering summer heat. Economic conditions in 1977 were also worse than they were a decade earlier: unemployment among young African Americans in the ghettos was almost 40 percent: double what it was in

1965.[60] Whatever the full causes, the 1977 night of terror will long be remembered by those who lived through it.

"Rodney King" Riots, 1992 (Los Angeles, California, USA)

Rodney King was no angel. On March 3, 1991, he led police on a high-speed chase. King had previous convictions and was on parole so he only stopped when forced to. King was savagely beaten with police batons as he attempted to crawl away. Police later claimed that he was high on the drug PCP and resisted arrest. Fortunately for King, the entire incident was caught on video tape.[61] Despite the damning video evidence of police brutality, the four officers charged with beating King were acquitted on April 29, 1992. Widespread anger about the verdict in the African American community triggered five days of rioting. Fifty-three people were killed, 2,383 were injured, and over twelve thousand were arrested for their part in the chaos. The tally of riot-related criminal acts was placed at sixteen thousand, with property damage estimated at nearly a billion dollars. More than ten thousand California National Guard members were deployed, aided by at least 3,500 US Marines, in a show of force that was needed to eventually restore order. The riots did not subside until May 4.[62]

During the riots, there were extraordinary attacks against drivers including white truck driver Reginald Denny who was dragged from his cab, viciously beaten, then hit on the head with a cement slab and left for dead. Local African American resident Bobby Green Jr. risked his own life to save him. Denny forgave his attackers even though he required years of rehabilitation and never fully recovered from his injuries.[63] One of the attackers, twenty-year-old Damien Williams, was sentenced to ten years in prison for his part in the assault.[64] At the same intersection, only minutes after Denny was dragged from his truck, self-employed construction worker Fidel Lopez was dragged from his vehicle and kicked. As he lay on the ground, a car stereo was smashed onto his head. Then Lopez "was doused with gasoline, his ear was nearly severed and he was stripped and spray-painted black as he lay semi-conscious. He might well have died if not for the arrival of the Rev. Bennie Newton, who appeared on the hellish scene like an angel, raised a Bible and warned the rioters: 'Kill him, and you have to kill me too.'"[65] Shocked by the violence, Rodney King pleaded for calm: "We can all get along. We've just got to stop. . . . Let's try to work it out."[66] Unfortunately, as the more recent events in Ferguson, Missouri, and Baltimore, Maryland, have shown, history is still repeating itself.

British Riots, 2011 (England)

Between August 6 and 10, 2011, upward of fifteen thousand people rioted and looted in English cities, with the bulk of events taking place in Manchester, Liverpool, Nottingham, Birmingham, and several boroughs of London. While sporadic incidents were reported after this time, the major unrest had been quelled. By the time the riots were over, property damage was estimated at £300 million, lost tourism revenue at £250 million, and lost business revenue at £80 million. In all, a panel investigating the riots estimated that the total damage bill was half a billion pounds.[67] These events were also referred to as the Blackberry riots for the widespread use of mobile devices and the influential role of social media in organizing the unrest. British criminologist Daniel Briggs remarks that while politicians and journalists tended to focus the blame on "feral youth," gangs, criminals, the lower classes, and dysfunctional families, such claims were unfounded.[68]

The unrest can be traced to the death of Tottenham resident Mark Duggan, who was shot by police on August 4. Local residents organized a peaceful protest in front of the Tottenham Police Station on the night of August 7 to express displeasure with the circumstances surrounding the shooting and to demand answers. The protest turned violent, and the rioting that began that night in Tottenham soon spread across the country. The unrest was marked by widespread looting of consumer goods, fires, and assaults. One of the poorest suburbs of London, Tottenham had over one hundred different ethnic minorities and an unemployment rate of nearly 9 percent—twice the national average.

An inquiry into the riots, which focused on London and its suburbs, identified several underlying causes. These included a breakdown in community-police relations fueled in part by the lack of representation of minority ethnic groups on the police force and a feeling by these minorities of being unfairly targeted by police carrying out their stop-and-search law. The discretional practice of this law clearly generated resentment and hostility among blacks. For instance, between 2009 and 2010, 28 percent of people stopped and searched by London police were black, yet they represented just 11 percent of the population. Other factors cited were poverty, unemployment, a lack of confidence in the government, and a sense of powerlessness and alienation from the rest of British society.[69] The Metropolitan Police Service reported 4,019 arrests connected to the disorder. They recorded 880 acts of criminal damage attributed to the unrest, 467 robberies, and 166 arsons.[70]

Some of the events were clearly open to interpretation: while Metropolitan police stated that two people died in the riots, Daniel Briggs places the number at five.[71]

Ferguson, Missouri, Riots, 2014 and ongoing (USA)

On August 9, 2014, a young black man named Michael Brown was fatally shot by Darren Wilson, a white police officer in the small town of Ferguson, Missouri. Brown and a friend had been walking down the middle of the street when Wilson ordered them to move off the road. Accounts about what happened next differ. According to some, Wilson was attacked by Brown and shot him in self-defense. Others say Wilson shot an unarmed Brown multiple times when there was no provocation.

There was already tension in the town due largely to a feeling that the mainly white police force unfairly targeted African Americans for harassment. This feeling is borne out by the statistics. Ferguson's population is 63 percent African American, but, on average, ten times as many blacks than whites are stopped, searched, or arrested.[72] An initially peaceful vigil on August 10 turned into a night of rioting and looting. Over two dozen businesses in Ferguson and nearby Dellwood were damaged or looted. Zisser Tire & Auto owner John Zisser said that looters stole display wheels and tires as well as a customer's car. "I don't understand. We've never had black-white issues here in the store," he said.[73]

Protests and outbreaks of violence continued for over a week. Police tactics, including unjustified attempts to stop journalists from filming, were criticized as contributing to the violence. On a CNN live news feed on August 9, at 11:46 p.m., a policeman on a bullhorn ordered: "If you are credentialed media you need to move to your designated area now." On another occasion two reporters were harassed by police in a local McDonald's.[74] Police also arbitrarily introduced a five-second rule, saying that protesters had to be moving at all times.[75] The greatest criticism was about the militarized clothing, vehicles, and weaponry used by the police that made them look more like soldiers. Police wearing riot gear, backed up by urban assault vehicles, used smoke bombs, tear gas, and plastic bullets to force everyone out of the area.[76] "Everyone in our immediate vicinity is being overcome with tear gas," said a CNN reporter at 11:33 p.m. on August 19, during a live news feed. President Obama ordered a review of the use of surplus military equipment and additional funds given to police agencies after the September 11 attacks. Body armor, military weapons, and armored vehicles were now available to many police departments.[77]

It cannot be denied that a portion of the protesters looted businesses and attacked police. However, many of those appear to have been opportunists and not those trying to make a legitimate, peaceful (and legal) protest. A *Time* magazine journalist observed that "Ferguson became a magnet for troublemakers from every point on the compass, from as near as next-door St. Louis and as far as California and New York. They seeded themselves in the ranks of peaceful protesters and in the throngs of visiting reporters, and no one could predict just when one of them would brandish a gun or fling a bottle."[78] This is clearly shown in the arrest statistics from August 12 to 21. Of the 179 people who were arrested, only ten were actually from Ferguson, and more than forty were from states other than Missouri. Almost all of the arrests were for refusal to disperse, and only a few were for burglary and other offenses.[79] Discontent and sporadic rioting continued into 2015.

Riots are arguably the most dramatic and visible form of collective behavior and usually involve violent outbursts by those on the margins of society who are unhappy with the existing social order and want immediate change. There are many types of riots, and it is possible to identify the different stages or phases that they pass through: from the precipitating incident to the confrontation, the Roman holiday, and lastly the siege where authorities regain control. On rare occasions, riots occur during mass celebrations and collective excitements. Riots are a culmination of many factors, with the trigger or precipitating incident being "the straw that broke the camel's back." Riots can last a single day, but more often they endure for weeks or months, and occasionally in a waxing-waning fashion over years. Historically, the most common riots are those that break out along political and ethnic lines.

In chapter 12, we look at an entirely different type of social delusion on which little has been written: small-group scares, whereby a close-knit unit in a tense, restricted setting with limited escape routes, literally scare themselves. Episodes are triggered when a belief emerges in the existence of a threatening agent, be it a mythical monster, space aliens, or enemy troops. The driving mechanism behind these episodes is the imperfect nature of human perception, as individuals in small groups—often suffering from fatigue and living under intense stress in dark environments—become prone to defining a variety of mundane stimuli as reflecting the perceived threat.

CHAPTER 12

SMALL-GROUP PANICS: PEOPLE WHO SCARED THEMSELVES

T his category has received scant attention from sociologists and social psychologists. Episodes involve relatively small groups of people in close physical proximity, in an isolated environment, who panic when they perceive an immediate threat to their well-being. The threat is amplified because escape routes are either difficult or temporarily cut off. The panic usually occurs at night. Often, those involved feel trapped inside a house or car. The fear may be intensified by physical or mental fatigue. Within this backdrop, people begin to redefine a variety of mundane objects and events, as providing evidence of the threat. Darkness further intensifies the perceived threat. For instance, if three people were at a well-attended party in a house on a busy street during the day and a picture frame suddenly fell from a wall and smashed onto the floor, the trio are not likely to become overly concerned for their safety. However, if they were the only occupants in an isolated house at midnight, and they had just heard strange noises outside after watching a scary movie, they might flee, thinking the house was haunted.

Episodes of phantom sieges, attacks, and pursuits have been recorded throughout history. The ambiguous stimulus often reflects popular cultural beliefs. For example, campers hearing rustling leaves might shine a flashlight in the direction of some trees and redefine the outline of the tree as a towering Bigfoot. Once the incident is over, the only concrete evidence of the perceived threat is eyewitness testimony from people within the group. In each case, a false consensus is soon reached that the group was the subject of an attack. The stimulus—be it ambiguous noises, strange lights, or rustling bushes—is quickly redefined within popular cultural labels and interpreted as an extraterrestrial spacecraft, Bigfoot, raiding Indians, and the like.

Underpinning episodes is the inaccuracy of eyewitness testimony and memory reconstruction.[1] During situations of extreme stress, such as believing that one's family or friends face possible death or serious injury, this effect is especially pronounced. As most people are not experts in human perception, they are susceptible to misidentifying a variety of phenomena. A person's education level or training offers little protection from making such mistakes. For instance, it is often said that the police are "trained observers," yet this does not render them immune from identifying the wrong suspect or mistaking a light in the sky for an extraterrestrial spaceship. Even former US President Jimmy Carter mistook Venus for a UFO.[2] Human perception is highly selective and based more on inference than reality; as a result, it is not unusual for different people observing the same event to give very different interpretations. This occurs because "inference can perform the work of perception by filling in missing information in instances where perception is either inefficient or inadequate."[3] Hence, a person's background, experiences, and expectations have a major influence on the interpretations of what they see. This is especially pronounced when people are viewing ambiguous stimuli within a group setting, as they compare their perceptions to those around them. As psychologist Leon Festinger once noted, a person's perspective "is 'correct,' 'valid,' and 'proper' to the extent that it is anchored in a group of people with similar beliefs, opinions and attitudes."[4]

A classic illustration of the circumstances that are conducive to small-group panics is related by Upstate New York historian Fred Stiles who has written about an incident that happened to his neighbor, Hail Hall.[5] Hall had been using a metal detector to search for lost coins and other valuables. At the time, there had been several sightings of a large, hairy, two-legged Bigfoot-like creature in the area. While digging out a find, he glanced up and spotted "a giant form about 10 feet tall with a great bushy head." Hall raced off on foot, believing that he had seen the famous creature. Moments later, he realized that his expensive machine was lying in the woods and got up the pluck to return for it. Arriving at the scene of the encounter, Hall glanced at the spot where the creature had been and saw the animal, a huge porcupine, shaking its head about ten feet up in a tree. "I guess he believes as I do, if the people who see Bigfoot had time to look more closely, they would find something which could be explained."[6] While this was an individual incident, it is certainly applicable to small group settings.

In some phantom sieges, those involved report shooting the assailant at close range, yet upon closer examination, no blood is ever found. While it is difficult to imagine how the victims could have recalled such a vivid experience, several factors may be at play here. First, it is important not to underestimate just how imperfect humans are at perceiving their environment. For example, one sunny afternoon during the nineteenth century, sailors on board a French frigate saw a life raft adrift in the ocean. Those on the ship, including officers, "clearly saw a raft covered with men towed by boats."[7] A rescue operation was quickly launched and a boat was soon rushing toward the men who were "clearly seen stretching out their hands and clearly heard." The sailors were stunned when they reached the spot, and found that the "raft" was comprised of "but a few branches of trees covered with leaves" that had been swept out to sea from the nearby land mass.

A second major factor involves how people reconstruct past events from memory. It is important to realize that people do not recall memories like a video recorder—instead memories are interpreted. A person's mind set at the time is very influential in their memories. For instance, during the infamous 1938 "War of the Worlds" hoax radio broadcast directed by Orson Welles, some people believed that the earth was under attack by Martians. A devoutly religious woman was interviewed by a team of researchers led by Princeton University psychologist Hadley Cantril. The woman said that as she was listening to the program, she became convinced that it was real when she heard the part that described "the sheet of flame that swept over the entire country" because it "was just the way I pictured the end."[8] In reality, the broadcast was devoid of any mention of a sheet of flame.

It is also easy to mix up memories. For instance, in 1975, an Australian expert on eyewitness testimony appeared on a television program. Shortly after the show ended, he was arrested on charges of rape after a woman identified him as her rapist. Curiously, the woman was raped at the same time of his appearance on television. When police questioned the woman in greater detail, she admitted to watching the program. She had confused Donald Thompson's face with the face of her attacker! Harvard psychologist Daniel Schacter observes that memory does not function like a videotape but is "a reconstruction using bits of sound, sights, words, and even tastes stored in different parts of the brain. Gaps in such reproductions, filled by imagination, cause error and distortions in eyewitness recollections and other aspects of everyday memory."[9]

There is a third possible factor that may contribute to participants seeing and even shooting at what they perceived to have been people or creatures at close range: hypnagogic and hypnopompic hallucinations. These are images that occur on the awake/sleep interface and are well known to psychologists. Hypnagogic imagery occurs as people are falling asleep, while hypnopompic visions happen when people are waking up. It may be significant that the several episodes of small-group scares that we document where people shot at entities at close range all took place in darkness, and most occurred during the early morning after those involved had been in an aroused, fatigued state throughout the night. Under such conditions, the mind can produce a temporary hallucination that reflects the attack scenario. Psychologist Tony Jinks writes that when someone is drowsy, they experience "a decrease in self-awareness and attentiveness to the external environment. Time perception becomes poor (an expression of the *missing time* phenomenon), and control over mental thoughts is lost. This altered state might explain the subsequent appearance of strange visual imagery."[10] What's more, Jinks notes that imagery on the awake/sleep interface is also induced in sensory-deprivation environments such as darkness—an integral feature of most small-group scares.[11]

Another common feature of episodes is the presence of sleep deprivation, which is known to trigger vivid hallucinations. Jinks cites the example of British nurse Ruth Booker, who, during a period of extended sleep deprivation, was working in the casualty ward of a hospital at 5:00 a.m. when she was helping to pump the stomach of a female patient who had overdosed on drugs in a suicide attempt. "Half way through the procedure, she noticed that the woman's head had come off in her hands. She felt not a little bit surprised, distressed, or alarmed about this appalling development. Instead, with great effort she tried recalling whether she'd ever seen or read about this type of thing happening before, and came to the conclusion that she hadn't. Soon . . . she became aware that what she was in fact holding was the woman's wig in her hands, not the patient's head at all."[12]

A fourth possibility is that the primary observer, whose observations excite other group members, possesses a fantasy-prone personality (FPP). During the 1970s and early 80s, psychologists discovered that a small percentage of normal, healthy people are prone to extraordinarily vivid and involved fantasies. Even more remarkable: most of these people lead secret lives, and, in many instances, not even their siblings or closest friends were aware of their rich fantasy worlds. Persons living within their self-absorbed "Walter Mitty" worlds have trouble differentiating between imagination and reality. Based on early research by Ernest 'Jack' Hilgard in the 1970s,[13] and later studies by hypnosis researchers Cheryl Wilson and Theodore Barber,[14] it is believed that up to four percent of the population may qualify as FPPs, ranging from mild to intense. The breakthrough came when Wilson and Barber were administering a number of tests and interviews to both excellent and poor hypnotic subjects. They found that 92 percent of fantasy-prone subjects estimated that they spent at least half of their working day engaged in rich fantasizing. Not one subject in their control group reported doing the same. They discovered that FPPs often "see," "hear," "smell," and "feel" what is being described in conversations or on television. Sixty-five percent had difficulties differentiating between their fantasy world and reality. As Wilson and Barber observe: "They see sights equally well with their eyes opened or closed. Also, imagined aromas are sensed, imagined sounds are heard, and imagined tactile sensations are felt as convincingly as those produced by actual stimuli. . . . almost all of the fantasy-prone subjects have vivid sexual fantasies that they experience 'as real as real' with all the sights, sounds, smells, emotions, feelings, and physical sensations."[15] The fantasies were so realistic that three out of four fantasizers reported orgasms that were generated solely by imagining the experience.

Fifty-eight percent of the fantasy-prone subjects (compared to 8 percent in the control group) reported spending much of their childhood interacting with fantasized people or animals ("imaginary companions") and reported having "clearly seen, heard and felt them in the same way that they perceived living people and animals."[16] Imaginary playmates are common in childhood and viewed as a sign of creativity and mental health, yet in fantasy-prone individuals there is a deeper, richer involvement.[17] Of those playing with dolls or toy animals, 80 percent believed them to be alive, with unique personalities. "Many of the 25 subjects in the comparison group also pretended their dolls or stuffed animals were alive; however, with three exceptions, they did so only when they were playing with them. Although they made-believe that the dolls and toy animals had personalities and said and did specific things, the make-believe play was always confined to a specific period and the toys did not seem to have an independent life."[18] As adults, the extensiveness and vividness of imaginary companions does not decrease substantially in FPPs. Based on their findings, Wilson and Barber believe that many figures from the past who claimed to have supernatural experiences may have been fantasy-prone.

MEMORABLE SMALL-GROUP SCARES

Phantom Frenchmen and Indians, 1692 (Cape Ann, Massachusetts Bay Colony)

Near the height of the witch trails in Salem Village, in an atmosphere of great suspicion and fear, a curious incident was recorded at Cape Ann in the Massachusetts Bay Colony and caused great alarm. The Reverend Cotton Mather, who played an integral part in fostering the Salem witch scare of 1691–1693, documented an episode in the form of a detailed report from a local minister, John Emerson, who had gathered accounts from those involved.[19] Over several nights in the middle of summer, Ebenezer Babson and his family were at their home in Gloucester when they heard noises outside, and it was thought that people were up to some clandestine activity. Then, one night while returning home at a late hour, Babson reported seeing two men exit a door from his home and run into a nearby cornfield. Babson rushed into the house to check on the welfare of his wife and children, who insisted that they had not seen or heard anything out of the ordinary. Unconvinced, Babson grabbed a gun and went looking for the intruders. Shortly thereafter, "he saw the two men start up from behind a log, and run into a little swamp, saying to each other, 'The man of the house is come now, else we might have taken the house.'"[20] Shaken by the incident, Babson took his family to the nearby garrison. Just as they arrived, they heard noises that sounded like men moving around outside. Babson ran out with his gun and saw two men running down a hill and into a swamp. On a subsequent night, Babson was heading toward a meadow when he spotted what appeared to be two Frenchmen, one with a gun on his back, running toward him. He raced back to the safety of the garrison where several people heard noises outside—as if men were walking about. Within a night or two, people in the garrison heard sounds like someone throwing stones at the side of the barn. Not long after, Babson and John Brown saw the figures of three men in the distance, running from the corn path and into the bushes.[21]

On July 14, 1692, half a dozen men were spotted in the distance, marching toward the garrison. Most of the men inside left in pursuit of the party, which resulted in a strange chase with the shadowy figures of the night. According to the report to Mather, Babson overtook two of the men after they ran out of some bushes. He said he tried to shoot them but his gun misfired. Meanwhile, they ran back into the bushes and escaped. Babson called out to his fellow garrison members across the swamp, "Here they are! Here they are!" What happened next is bizarre. Babson spotted three men walking "softly out of the swamp" side by side, the one in the middle wearing "a white waistcoat. So being within two or three rod of them, he shot, and as soon as his gun was off, they all fell down." Babson ran toward the fallen prey, "cried out unto his companions, whom he heard on the other side of the swamp, and said, 'he had kill'd three! He had kill'd three!' But coming almost unto them, they all rose up, and one of them shot at him, and hearing the bullet whist by him, he ran behind a tree, and loaded his gun, and seeing them lye behind a log, he crept toward them again, telling his companions, 'they were here!'" One of the men was eventually surrounded, and as he approached, Babson said that he fired at him, and watched as he fell to the ground. But, as he reached the spot where the man fell, the man had seemingly vanished. The men searched the corn in a vain effort to find the phantom attacker. In the minister's report to Mather, he wrote that "as they were searching, they heard a great discoursing in the swamp, but could not understand what they said; for they spoke in an *unknown tongue*. Afterwards, looking out from the garrison, they saw several men skulking among the corn and bushes, but could not get a shot at them."[22] The next morning at daybreak, a man was spotted coming out of the swamp and was shot at with a long gun, but he quickly vanished out of sight.[23]

Help was summoned and arrived on July 18 in the form of sixty soldiers. Historian John Babson writes that none of the "mysterious invaders" were ever captured and notes that the "strange beings . . . were too ethereal to leave a foot-print upon the soft and miry places over which they were pursued."[24] With the arrival of reinforcements, the sightings quickly died down. Another major encounter with these phantoms had occurred on July 15 when Ezekiel Day and several others were scouting the woods. They reported seeing an Indian dressed in blue in the distance and say they shot at the figure. On the same day, another scouting party watching the woods in the area "saw another of these 'strange men,' having on a blue shirt and white breeches . . . but could not overtake him."[25]

The last major incident was recorded on about July 25. Ebenezer Babson went into some woods to locate his cattle and spotted three men standing on some rocks. "So he crept along the bushes till he came within forty yards of them . . . presented his gun at them, and snapt, but his gun miss'd fire, and so it did above a dozen times, till they all three came up towards him, walking a slow pace, one of them having a gun upon his back. Nor did they take any more notice of him, than just to give him a *look*; though he snapt his gun at them all the while they walked toward him, and by him: neither did they quicken their pace at all, but went into a parcel of bushes, and he saw them no more."[26] After this incident, Babson believed that he was dealing with specters and not intruders, so little notice of them was taken again.

At the time of the phantom guerillas, one historian observes that Gloucester was engulfed in an invasion fear, which was likely instigated by the Reverend John Emerson himself. In 1690, Emerson had been instrumental in getting forty-seven members of the village militia to join the army. Afterward, he expressed fear that local residents would be vulnerable to attack. It was within this context that Ebenezer Babson reported his phantom attackers.[27] Historian Peter Muise also suggests that Babson's mysterious visitors were likely a product of the anxieties of the time. He notes that after fleeing to the garrison, the sightings were mostly fleeting "glimpses of strange men running back and forth outside, but more often they just heard them. One night, unseen hands threw stones against the side of the building. The strange men never attacked the garrison, which seemed a little odd. If they were really French invaders, wouldn't they have fired at the Gloucester residents or set fire to the garrison?"[28] Given the supernatural events that were believed to be afoot in the region, Babson's phantom encounters were interpreted by Emerson as stemming from "the Devil and his Agents."[29] Cotton Mather concurred, suggesting that Satan may have "'set ambushments' against the good people of Gloucester, with demons in the shape of armed Indians and Frenchmen."[30] Shortly after this episode, in September 1692, Ebenezer Babson himself became directly involved in the witch hunts, accusing two local women of being witches.[31]

Frog Pond Indian Scare, 1758 (Windham, Connecticut, USA)

Occasional raiding parties from the north during the French and Indian War (1754–1763), resulted in frayed nerves. It was within this context that one night during July 1758, after midnight, the inhabitants of Windham, Connecticut, were awakened by strange noises. Men grabbed their muskets and prepared to defend themselves, believing that the town was under threat of imminent attack by French and Indian raiders. Throughout the night, the men waited anxiously for an attack as the strange noises grew louder. In the distance, they could clearly hear the screeches and war whoops of Indians preparing for an attack. In his 1836 book, *Connecticut Historical Collections*, John Barber recounts the story from a local broadsheet (an oversized newspaper of the time). It stated: "At intervals, many supposed they could distinguish the calling out of the particular names, as of Cols. Dyer and Elderkin two eminent lawyers, and this increased the general terror."[32] Soon, amidst the clamor, people rushed "from every house, the tumult in the air still increasing—old and young, male and female, poured forth into the streets." Convinced they were hearing the yells of Indians massing for an attack, they ascended the hill on the eastern side of the village. The next morning a scouting party discovered the source of the commotion in the night: in the midst of a summer drought, bullfrogs had been fighting over a small patch of water in puddles of what was left of a pond. Barber reports that many of the frogs were found dead in the wake of the battle with each other.[33]

The extraordinary nature of the sounds during the incident may owe to atmospheric conditions (warm and foggy) and the geography—Frog Pond being located only one mile from the Village of Windham, separated only by a sloping hill. For whatever reason, related to either the weather or internal biology, the bullfrogs were particularly loud on that fateful morning. The community, however, embraced the incident and now has a frog as their official town seal. The event has even been the subject of an opera, postcards, ballads, and poems.[34]

Space Goblins, 1955 (Kelly, Kentucky, USA)

On the evening of August 21, 1955, an extraordinary series of events were reported to have occurred at a rural farmhouse in Kelly, Kentucky, after the occupants claimed they were under siege by creatures from outer space. The claims were made by the Sutton family who were living eight miles north of the small hamlet of Hopkinsville. At least seven adults and three children were at the house at the time, along with their landlord, William Taylor. At about seven o'clock, Taylor was visiting with his tenants when he decided to fetch water from a well. Upon his return, he told of having seen a glowing saucer-shaped object that appeared to land in a nearby gully. Skeptical family members thought that while Taylor was being truthful, he was likely overreacting to seeing a "shooting star."

When a pet dog began to bark at about 7:30, Taylor and Lucky Sutton decided to have a look around. As they reached the back door, they noticed a faint light in a field. The illumination appeared to be moving toward the house. As the men left the house, Taylor, who was in front, said that a massive hand reached down from the roof and grabbed his hair. He pulled away, and the pair quickly withdrew into the house where they raised the alarm, grabbed their guns, and began firing at what appeared to be diminutive creatures standing three-and-a half-feet tall. The creatures had oversized heads with large elephant-like ears on either side. Sutton grabbed his shotgun, while Taylor brandished a .22-caliber pistol. For the next three and a half hours, the family claims that they were terrorized by the creatures, which jumped on the roof and peered through windows. During this period, countless rounds of gunfire were directed at the entities. At one point, the two men were so frightened that at times they shot *through* a screen window.

Emotionally distraught and both physically and mentally fatigued from the ordeal, by eleven o'clock, family members realized that their only means of escape was to make a dash for one of two cars. They did not have a telephone. Everyone scrambled to the car, and they sped off to summon help. They returned with the police, who carefully searched the grounds but found nothing out of the ordinary—with the exception of bullet holes in the house and shell casings littering the area. They remained on the scene until about 2:15 a.m. Soon after, one of the occupants was staring at a window when she swore she saw a creature peering back, and she alerted the rest of the household. Sporadic gunfire rang out for the next three hours, as the creatures were spotted around the house. Near sunrise, the family again summoned police, who searched the area for a second time but could find no evidence of extraterrestrials.[35]

A local newspaper reporter for the *Kentucky New Era*, Joe Dorris, visited the house with police. The next day, Dorris wrote that "more than a dozen state, county, and city officers from Christian and Hopkins counties went to the scene between 11 p.m. and midnight and remained until after 2 a.m. without seeing anything either to prove or disprove the story about the ship and its occupants." The paper's headline was reserved and read: "Story of Space-Ship . . . Kelly Farmhouse Scene of Alleged Raid by Strange Crew Last Night; Reports Say Bullets Failed to Affect Visitors." Police reported that the men had expended four boxes of bullets in their frantic attempt to fend off the creatures.

On the surface, it sounds difficult to believe that so many people could have been deceived into thinking that they had been under siege by space aliens. Upon closer inspection, several of the occupants saw nothing. For instance, eighteen-year-old June Taylor reported that she was "too frightened to look,"[36] while Lonnie Langford, then age twelve, had been hidden under a bed with his brother by their terrified mother.[37]

Former detective Joe Nickell has concluded that what the occupants of the house saw was one or more Great Horned Owls. They are also known as "hoot owls." Nickell observes that they stand around two feet tall, and have "very large, staring, yellow eyes; long ear tufts; a large head, set (without apparent neck) on its shoulders; a light-grey underside; long wings that, seen on edge, could be mistaken for arms; spindly legs; claws with talons; and so on."[38] He also notes that the behavior of such owls is consistent with what was reported. "An owl could be on a roof or in a tree and be perceived to 'float' to the ground." He further notes that they are known to be aggressive when defending their nest and typically become active at dusk. But if owls were to blame, why were there no bodies of the creatures found nearby? It may be that the owls caused the initial scare, and later fatigue and imagination took over as the occupants began firing at shadows and any rustling in the bushes.[39]

It is also noteworthy that at the time of Taylor's "flying saucer" sighting, there had been other reports of meteors nearby. The mid-1950s was a period characterized by a surge of interest in UFOs, with numerous flying-saucer films and books having been released. This environment may have led Taylor to redefine a relatively common fireball as an alien spaceship. As to why the aliens would have been interpreted as hostile, films from this period featured distinctly unfriendly extraterrestrials. For example, 1953 saw the release of such movies as *Invaders from Mars*, *It Came from Outer Space*, and *Phantom from Space*. The year before the encounter, Hollywood released *Killers from Space*, *Devil Girls from Mars*, and *Target Earth*. The year 1954 also featured the book, *Flying Saucers on the Attack* by Harold T. Wilkins.[40] As an interesting aside, the US Air Force officially investigated UFO reports from 1952 to 1969 and informally looked into the incident as Case 10073. According to Air Force Captain Edward J. Ruppelt, information gathered on the case was placed in the "C.P." file. "C.P." stood for crackpot.[41]

UFO Chase and Abduction, 1961 (Indian Head, New Hampshire, USA)

It is arguably the most publicized case in UFO history, and it has been the subject of a major motion picture and countless books. Known simply as "the Betty and Barney Hill case," the saga involved a married couple from Portsmouth, New Hampshire, who claimed to have been captured by UFO beings while driving on a remote stretch of the Daniel Webster Highway. At about midnight on September 20, 1961, Betty became aware of a bright object in the sky. Over the next thirty miles, she and her husband grew more and more excited by the light, with Barney pulling the car to the roadside on several occasions so they could get out and get a better look with binoculars. While initially believing that they were looking at either a star or satellite, the Hills soon reached a more exotic hypothesis. During one stop, Barney claimed to see what appeared to have been a fuselage without wings.[42] Betty eventually determined that the light was an extraterrestrial spaceship that was pursuing them. There also seemed to be a series of lights along the apparent fuselage, blinking in an alternating pattern. When Betty took the binoculars, the object passed in front of the moon in silhouette. It appeared to be flashing thin beams of different colored lights that were rotating around the object, which appeared to have been cigar-shaped. Just a moment before, it had changed its speed from slow to fast, then slowed down again as it crossed the face of the moon. The lights were flashing persistently, red, amber, green, and blue.

Eventually, Barney thought he could discern what appeared to be windows and "at least half a dozen living things" inside that were "staring directly at him."[43] He panicked, ran back to the car, and sped off, believing that the aliens were trying to capture them. When the Hills arrived home at 2:00 a.m., they realized that their trip had taken two and a half hours too long, and they were unable to account for the missing time. They later experienced nightmares about the incident. After suffering from nervous tension and high blood pressure, Barney visited Boston neurologist and psychiatrist Dr. Benjamin Simon, and as part of his treatment, underwent regressive hypnosis. While hypnotized, Barney told how he and Betty had been taken aboard a spacecraft by slender beings with large heads and slits for nostrils. He described being forced to undergo medical probes. Dr. Simon later regressed Betty, who recounted a similar story. She said that the creatures had pushed a needle-like instrument into her naval and was told that it was a pregnancy test. Barney said that a cup-like device was placed over his groin area. Later he developed warts there.[44]

Robert Sheaffer has shown that based on the astronomical alignment of the night in question, the Hills likely mistook the planet Jupiter for the mysterious light. Mrs. Hill reported two objects near the moon. One was a star below the moon; the other was a brilliant starlike object above it, which she said was the alien spaceship. Sheaffer writes that on the night in question, Saturn was the bright star below the moon, "with Jupiter a more illuminated star-like object above it. Thus, Mrs. Hill's description of the initial sighting of the supposed UFO strongly suggests that she mistook the planet Jupiter for a UFO."[45]

The psychiatrist who conducted the hypnosis sessions with the Hills, Dr. Benjamin Simon, also did not believe the abduction occurred. Astronomer Walter

Webb later interviewed Dr. Simon, who concluded that the initial UFO experience had triggered Betty's dreams about having been abducted. Webb summarizes Simon's position: "At first Barney was skeptical and believed they were just dreams. But gradually Barney's suggestibility took hold and he, like his wife, finally accepted the dreams as manifestation of a real experience, that is, that they both were abducted and then made to forget the experience by a form of hypnotic amnesia. It is readily apparent that Betty's account of the kidnapping and medical examination aboard the UFO is quite elaborate and detailed while Barney's account of his own experience is very brief and sketchy—an indication to Dr. Simon that the whole second encounter originated in Betty's mind and then was duplicated, at least in part, in Barney's mind by the process of suggestion. The doctor told me if one believes in anything strong enough, whether it really happened or not, it can be repeated under hypnosis."[46]

As for the "missing time" element of their story, time estimates are notoriously unreliable under stress.[47] Returning from a vacation in Canada, their trek home was lengthy and on desolate roads in the early morning hours. Their situation was exacerbated by fatigue. It was not your typical leisurely trip. As psychologist Don Donderi points out, "Barney took a wrong turn in Montreal, couldn't understand the directions he was offered in French, so instead of staying in Montreal for another night as planned, they drove back to the United States . . . They arrived home, exhausted, as the sun rose, about two hours later than the trip should have taken."[48]

Phantom Gunboat Attack, 1964 (Gulf of Tonkin, North Vietnam)

In 2005, the United States National Security Agency released a number of previously classified documents pertaining to a reported attack on US warships off North Vietnam in the Gulf of Tonkin. The "attack," was viewed as the reason for America to dramatically escalate its involvement in the Vietnam War, which would result in the deaths of over fifty-eight thousand Americans. However, after a perusal of the official records on the incident, and based on interviews with those involved, a consensus has emerged that the attack never happened, and American naval forces had been firing at radar phantoms. The incident is a classic example of what has been described as "the fog of war."

The context of the Gulf of Tonkin incident is essential in understanding the scare. Tensions between the United States and North Vietnam were high. On

August 2, 1964, the USS *Maddox* was on intelligence patrol in the Gulf when it encountered three North Vietnamese torpedo boats. The close proximity of the *Maddox* to the North Vietnamese coast was seen as provocative and threatening, and the ship was met with aggressive maneuvers. The *Maddox*, supported by several fighter jets, fired on and damaged the enemy vessels, killing four soldiers and wounding several others. The United States suffered no casualties.[49] As a result of the incident, tensions were strained and US forces in the Gulf were on high alert for other attacks. While this initial encounter could have been viewed as a misunderstanding, a second attack would be interpreted as a clear sign of North Vietnamese aggression.

On the night of August 4, members of the Chinese military who were positioned along the nearby coast heard the echo of gunfire and saw exploding shells lighting up the night sky. They quickly contacted their Vietnamese comrades to ask if they were involved in a firefight with the Americans. "No" came the reply. Curiously, at about the same time, the Vietnamese were contacting the Chinese to inquire if *they* were currently engaged in battle with the Americans.[50] Two destroyers, the USS *Maddox* and the USS *Turner Joy*, were patrolling off the coast when enemy vessels were detected on both radar and sonar. While no one actually spotted the enemy, there were several sightings of torpedo wakes as the sailors scrutinized the waters around their vessels. The ships took evasive action and began firing back. It is now clear that they were firing at phantoms on a stormy night when visibility was low and tensions were high. When air support was called in from the USS *Ticonderoga*, one of the pilots who was dispatched was James Stockdale. He said that for the next ninety minutes, he flew low over the exact area where the enemy vessels supposedly were. He reported that there was "not a ship, not the outline of a ship, not a wake. Not the light of a single tracer bullet. Nothing."[51] Even when *Maddox* Captain John Herrick called off the attack, he had serious doubts and cabled his superiors with the following urgent message: "Entire action leaves many doubts. Suggest complete evaluation before any further action."[52]

In *Tonkin Gulf and the Escalation of the Vietnam War*, historian Edwin Moïse observes that the stormy weather which coincided with the incident is known to pose challenges for radar operators who must interpret images on their screens. He believes that the phantom images spotted on radar were not of Vietnamese war vessels but American aircraft. While it may sound far-fetched to think that the two could be confused, the nature of radar in 1964 was such that such misidentifications were not uncommon, usually under certain weather conditions—conditions that were recorded on the evening of the "attack." Moïse writes: "Normally one would think it impossible for airplanes to be confused with surface vessels on radar, since the slowest airplane moves so much faster than the fastest surface vessel. Commander George Edmondson . . . confirms that such confusion can occur in weather of the sort he remembers encountering on the night of August 4. He served as Navigator of the aircraft carrier *Kitty Hawk*, operating in this area not long after the Tonkin Gulf incidents, and states that there were 'numerous times' when weather anomalies caused the carrier's radar to mistake the carrier's own aircraft for surface vessels. . . . [on the evening of August 4] the radar operators on the destroyers tended to report surface vessels in just the locations where he and his wingman were flying low and slow over the water."[53] Edmondson concluded that in all likelihood "the radar on the destroyers was mistaking aircraft for surface vessels."

The weather and geography of the Gulf also created unique challenges for radar operators as these factors were known to generate a radar anomaly called "Tonkin Spooks," or "Tonkin Gulf Ghosts." While the exact cause of these phantom radar returns in the region is unknown, they appear to be more frequent during periods of high humidity—a feature of the evening of August 4. Because the images appear to move so fast, it is also believed that flocks of birds may also be involved. Early on in the United States' involvement in the Gulf, radar operators were unfamiliar with the unique features of the region. Over time, the area became notorious for the high number of spurious radar images that were reported there.[54] Yet another contributing factor of the scare was a nervous, inexperienced sonar operator on the *Maddox*, who appears to have mistaken his ship's rudder for the sounds of torpedoes.[55]

The officer in charge of the main gun director on the *Maddox* that night was Patrick Park. A veteran sonar specialist, Park was interviewed in 1971, once the war had become unpopular, by the investigative television program *60 Minutes*. When asked about the incident that triggered the entry of the United States into the Vietnam War, Park said: "I'm certain there was not anything to shoot at right from the beginning. The captain asked me immediately after the attack to go down and evaluate all the recordings that had been made of noise that sonar was reporting . . . to determine if we had heard anything that might have been, even a question mark that it might have been a torpedo or anything else in the water, not related to the two ships or noise of any one of them."[56] Park added that his evaluation of the various recordings from that night turned up "absolutely nothing."

Phantom Apemen, 1924 (Ape Canyon, Washington, USA)

During the summer of 1924, a group of mining prospectors reported being attacked by several hulking apelike creatures with long, black hair, in a remote, mountainous region of Washington State. In the days leading up to the encounter, the men had heard strange sounds in the woods. Prospector Fred Beck later recalled: "We had been hearing noises in the evening for about a week. We heard a shrill, peculiar whistling each evening. We would hear it coming from one ridge, and then hear an answering whistling from another ridge. We also heard a sound which I could best describe as a booming, thumping sound—just like something was hitting its self on its chest."[57] The five men in the mining party were clearly on an emotional knife-edge as they were aware of local folk stories of Bigfoot-like animals in the area, and on a previous occasion, one of them claimed to have spotted suspicious footprints attributed to the creature on a river sandbar.

On the day of the "attack," Beck and his friend Hank (a pseudonym to protect his identity) walked to a spring about one hundred yards from their cabin to collect water. Beck said: "We walked to the spring, and then, Hank yelled and raised his rifle, and at that instant, I saw it. It was a hairy creature, and he was about a hundred yards away, on the other side of a little canyon, standing by a pine tree. It dodged behind the tree, and poked its head out from the side of the tree. And at the same time, Hank shot. I could see the bark fly out from the tree from each of his three shots. Someone may say that that was quite a distance to see the bark fly, but I saw it. The creature I judged to have been about seven feet tall with blackish-brown hair. It disappeared from our view for a short time, but then we saw it, running fast and upright, about two hundred yards down the little canyon. I shot three times before it disappeared from view."[58]

After recounting his exciting story to the three other miners in the party that night, their remote cabin reportedly came under siege by the apemen. News of the sensational attack attracted the attention of a journalist from the *Portland Oregonian*, who visited the site and interviewed the witnesses. The paper published an account of the claims several days later on July 16, under the headline: "Fight with Big Apes Reported by Miners. Fabled Beasts Are Said to Have Bombarded Cabin."[59]

"The strangest story to come from the Cascade mountains was brought to Kelso today by Marion Smith, his son Roy Smith, Fred Beck, Roy Lefever and John Peterson, who encountered the fabled 'mountain devils' or mountain gorillas of Mount St. Helens this week, shooting one of them and being attacked throughout the night by rock bombardments of the beasts.

The men had been prospecting a claim on the Muddy, a branch of the Lewis River . . . They declared that they saw four of the huge animals, which were about 7 feet tall, weighed about 400 pounds and walked erect."

In the week prior to the encounter, the men had heard strange high-pitched shrills. They also described hearing thumping and booming sounds echoing through the canyon that was reminiscent of something pounding its chest.

After the pair returned to the cabin and related their encounter, the miners wanted to go home, but given that darkness had set in, it was deemed prudent to wait until daybreak. In the middle of the night, the men were awakened by rocks showering down on the cabin. Beck recounted the frightening events, noting that the men opened fire when they thought they heard the creatures climbing onto the roof. "We shot round after round through the roof. We had to brace the hewed-logged door with a long pole taken from the bunk bed. The creatures were pushing against it and the whole door vibrated from the impact. We responded by firing many more rounds through the door. They pushed against the walls of the cabin as if trying to push the cabin over, but this was pretty much an impossibility, as previously stated the cabin was a sturdy made building."[60] Beck said that he and Hank fired most of the shots, while the rest of the men huddled at "the far end of the cabin, guns in their hands. One had a pistol, which still is in my family's possession, the others clutched their rifles. They seemed stunned and incredulous. . . . The attack continued the remainder of the night, with only short intervals between." As the sun began to rise, the men fled the cabin. As they did, Beck reported seeing one of the creatures about eighty yards distance, standing at the edge of Ape Canyon. "I shot three times, and it toppled over the cliff, down into the gorge, some four hundred feet below."[61]

Based on a perusal of Beck's 1967 book, *I Fought the Apemen of Mt. St. Helens*, his "encounter" the morning after the "siege" may have occurred only in his imagination, as he was prone to visions and hallucinations throughout his life. Beck told of frequently encountering and sometimes communicating with "spirit beings." On one occasion, Beck told of encountering a spirit being in the form of "a large Indian dressed in buckskin."[62] Another time he encountered "a beautiful young lady" at a campsite, who appeared to be from the spirit world. He said: "She would be talking on a subject, then pause and say, 'Isn't that right, Dad?' This she said several times. There was no tent, cooking utensils, no food, and certainly no visible father. The most amazing thing was I did not at the time think her different than any other person. When she spoke to her invisible Dad, I felt just like her Dad was there. . . . I do not know anyone who had seen her but myself."[63] Beck's fantasy-prone personality coupled with apeman folklore in the region and the mysterious noises the mining party heard just prior to their "attack" may have combined to create an apeman state of mind, anticipating an encounter. This situation would have likely made the men anxious and left them feeling trapped, with a potential threat lurking just outside their windowless, wooden cabin, far from civilization.

Several forest rangers and journalists visited the area shortly after the episode, and could find no trace of the apemen. They also searched the ravine where Beck said he shot one of the creatures. The investigators had reportedly reached the conclusion that the events were "either a hoax or the result of imagination."[64] Canadian journalist John Green interviewed Beck, concluding: "There isn't a shadow of a suggestion as to why they would make up such a story and keep telling it all their lives."[65]

In 1982, eighty-six-year-old Rant Mullens gave a newspaper interview in which he confessed to triggering the Ape Canyon scare. While returning from a fishing trip, he said that he and his uncle decided to play a joke on the miners by rolling rocks onto their cabin.[66] It is plausible that the preexisting folklore about the apemen, the redefinition of ambiguous sounds in the night, coupled with fear and isolation, played a major role in the affair. It may be that the "attack" on the cabin was actually Mullens and his uncle playing a prank by rolling and raining down rocks, giving the bewildered miners the fright of their lives.

It may be significant that the cabin siege occurred shortly after Beck and his friend "Hank" claimed to have spotted and shot at one of the apemen. The claim of this dramatic encounter clearly heightened the anxieties of his fellow miners, and that night they would have been on alert—an alert that was no doubt exacerbated by the mysterious "thudding" and "thumping" sounds that had spooked the party the night prior to the "attack" and the realization that they would have to wait until daylight to make it out of the canyon.

Perron Family Haunting, 1971–1980 (Rhode Island, USA)

Soon after Carolyn and Roger Perron moved into a remote farmhouse in Harrisville, Rhode Island, in January 1971, strange happenings began to occur. Before long, Mrs. Perron had concluded that the house was haunted by an array of mostly mischievous spirits. Roger was skeptical of these paranormal claims, but Carolyn exerted a significant influence over her daughters and subconsciously convinced them that the house was filled with spirits. The tale of the haunting has been the subject of several books, and, in 2013, it was used as the foundation of a "based on a true story" movie, *The Conjuring*. This is an unusual example of a small-group panic because it endured in a waxing-waning fashion until 1980, when the family finally left the house. There is no indication that the infestation of spirits was a collective hoax. However, closer examination of the mysterious occurrences suggests that the family had literally scared themselves, with occasional pranking by Cindy – one of the Perron's young daughters.

A number of circumstances combined to create a belief that their house was haunted. Roger was a traveling salesman, and his absence much of the time, coupled with the remote location of the farmstead, only served to amplify the vulnerability of Carolyn and her daughters. Another factor was Carolyn's preexisting belief in the paranormal and her penchant for exaggeration, transforming mundane happenings into supernatural ones. For instance, as they were moving into the house, Mrs. Perron noticed that an antique clock had stopped. While it is not uncommon for a clock to stop, she transformed it into a mysterious event by remarking that "its pendulum [was] stilled by some unknown force."[67]

Before long, Carolyn was convinced that she was being watched—feelings that greatly influenced her daughters. The strange happenings began slowly and graduated to more significant events over time. Early on, someone thought they heard an intruder, but nothing was found. While another daughter, April, was asleep, she awoke with a startle and concluded that someone or something had shaken her. Eventually, the family—with the exception of Roger—was routinely interacting with "spirits." Occasionally when answering the phone, there was only static. Instead of accepting that they had a bad line, such happenings were interpreted as supernatural. Daughter Andrea suggests that otherworldly forces were attempting to communicate: "More frequently there would be an unnerving noise, a crackling rather convoluted sound, as if someone was calling from far beyond the realm of possibility; from long ago and far away."[68]

The arrival of two self-proclaimed ghost hunters, Ed and Lorraine Warren, in October 1973, only fueled the social panic. Lorraine suggested that knocking sounds and rattling in the house were not from the wind, but were "demonic in nature."[69] When she learned that the girls played with a Ouija board, Lorraine alarmed them by proclaiming: "Under *no* circumstances should a Ouija Board be allowed in this house."[70] She called it a "very dangerous game" and said that was "inviting disaster." Carolyn had also concluded that the appearance of flies swarming in window sills during winter were supernatural in origin, based on advice from Lorraine. "Those flies were all sent here on a mission, to observe the new occupants . . . to size us up." Carolyn also observed: "No one has thousands of flies in the dead of winter. No one. Certainly not in Rhode Island! . . . they'd attack us and buzz our heads . . . They'd stare at us! They did not even look like normal flies."[71] However, according to a local pest-control company, winter fly swarms in windows sills are a common occurrence in Rhode Island.[72]

Once, Lorraine was walking near the Perron's bedroom when she closed her eyes and began shaking. "No one should sleep in this bedroom," she asserted.[73] Shortly after, Lorraine stepped inside the laundry room and a visible look of disturbance came over her face: "Something awful happened in there. Violent. The poor thing. So young. A girl. Blood. Definitely a female."

It is also evident that several family members were exhibiting different psychological conditions that were redefined as supernatural. If they had visited a psychologist early on, instead of consulting with paranormal investigators for the answers to the strange happenings, the "haunting" may have ceased. On one occasion, while Carolyn was in bed, she watched in horror as the room erupted in flames. Despite her terror, she could only look on, as her body was paralyzed. She recalled seeing "sparks jumping from a fireball, the core of which burned so brightly she could barely gaze into it. Off-shoots sprung from its center, appearing like wild sparklers out-of-control, pinging then popping in every direction."[74] Suddenly, "in a mere fraction of a second, it was gone." After regaining her movement, Carolyn was baffled to realize that there was no evidence of fire.[75]

What happened to Carolyn that night, and also on other occasions, is a classic example of a *waking dream*, which occurs as one is dozing off or awakening from sleep. Such dreams are typically described as having exceptionally bright and vivid colors and are often accompanied by paralysis.[76] During a separate waking dream, Carolyn awoke to the sense of a presence. She opened her eyes and saw a grotesque-looking woman hovering above her. Once again, she was paralyzed and saw brilliant scenes, as recounted by Andrea during an interview: "The image of it leapt through her eyes into her mind, impaling her memory with a spectral wonder so vivid and compelling, it had to be processed in tiny patterns and fragments. . . . slicing into her consciousness . . . bombarding the senses . . ."[77] Mrs.

Perron assumed that she had been attacked by an evil spirit. In fact, her experience closely parallels reports of waking dreams accompanied by temporary paralysis from around the world and throughout history, as collected by psychologist
David Hufford.[78] Other family members were also prone to waking dreams. For
instance, one morning at 3:00 a.m., Cindy reported encountering a "dark presence" in the room, hovering above her sister Andrea. It was a "black, vaporous
apparition" and resembled a storm cloud.[79] As it began to move toward her, she
realized that she was paralyzed.

The youngest child, April, was five when the Perrons moved into the house.
She soon talked of having an imaginary companion named Oliver, with whom
she frequently played. Mrs. Perron assumed that "Oliver" was from the spirit
world, yet imaginary friends are a common childhood occurrence. One study of
children between ages five and twelve, found that 46 percent had such companions although the phenomena quickly declines in adulthood.[80] Such experiences
are viewed as mentally healthy and normal, providing entertainment and stemming from boredom.[81] Once Carolyn and her daughters had become convinced
that their house was haunted, their common, everyday occurrences were viewed
in a different light.

One of the girls—Cindy—appears to have been responsible for several of
the supposed poltergeist incidents. Andrea wrote that Cindy "attracted supernatural activity unlike any of her siblings" and had "passive/aggressive tendencies."[82]
As with most poltergeist outbreaks, strange happenings tended to center on one
person; in this case, Cindy. She claimed that on several occasions the refrigerator
door would suddenly begin to open and shut, flapping wildly back and forth, as
food "would fly out all over the place." Andrea wrote that "for some reason, Cindy
was the one most frequently subjected to the cruel and unusual behavior, a particular stunt occurring in her presence on a fairly regular basis. It seemed to be a
deliberate act, initiated with some forethought and malice."[83] Curiously, Cindy's
strange encounters with the so-called haunted fridge "almost always occurred just
prior to Roger's return home."[84] This may have been a ploy to gain the attention
of an absentee father who was frequently away on sales trips, in an attempt to get
him to stay at home more often.

Once Mrs. Perron had convinced her daughters that their house was filled
with an array of spirits—both good and evil—the girls became prone to redefining a variety of mundane events as paranormal. A good example of this tendency
occurred in 2012, decades after the haunting, when family members gathered on

the set of the film *The Conjuring*. Andrea was giving a promotional interview on the movie when she noted that "a bizarre wind" suddenly knocked over much of the set and cameras. She immediately concluded that it was Bathsheba's curse—in reference to one of the spirits that supposedly haunted the house.[85]

Phantom Siege, 1978 (Lowell, Michigan, USA)

In November 1978, police were called on to investigate a strange "siege" that reportedly took place at a house in a sparsely populated area of southwestern Michigan. Investigators would eventually conclude that the episode was the result of paranoia, fatigue, and overactive imaginations. One of those who investigated the incident was respected, Harvard-educated sociologist Dr. Ronald Westrum. Westrum interviewed the two frightened occupants of the house and was able to examine the scene.[86]

One of the men involved, identified by the pseudonym of "Masters," was a twenty-four-year-old suspected drug dealer. His companion, "Cordell," was twenty-nine. The strange affair began in the early morning of November 7, when the pair grew suspicious over a series of relatively mundane events. For instance, during the afternoon part of a grape-bubble-gum wrapper was found on the roof. What appeared to be the other half of the wrapper was picked up near a wood pile. In their paranoid state, the two young men viewed this as a significant event, and they were soon convinced that the house was under surveillance. That same afternoon, Masters and Cordell were "on the lookout" for intruders. Their fears were soon confirmed as they caught fleeting glimpses of what appeared to be people sneaking around the outside of the house. As dusk neared, they thought they saw someone lurking near the house wearing camouflage gear. Cordell ran after the figure, but it melted into the night. He then shouted that if those hiding did not stop, "somebody was going to get shot."

A short time later, voices were heard at the back door. Cordell fired off a warning shot to scare the perceived intruders away, and events quickly spiraled out of control. Fearful of imminent danger, Masters contacted his friend Hamby who dropped off an assortment of weapons to deal with the crisis. By 1:30 a.m., the three men were keeping a careful watch on the house, when Cordell and Masters suddenly spotted shadowy figures outside and fired off ten shots. Hamby didn't see or hear anything, prompting the others to consider the possibility that they were imagining things. During the next several hours, the three men kept vigil over the house, intermittently reporting shadowy figures and vague noises.

At about 5:00 a.m., the three sleep-deprived men, in a state of physical and emotional exhaustion, thought they were under attack and responded accordingly by firing indiscriminately. Cordell thought he saw someone hanging from the roof by a bedroom window and shot at them. He was certain that he had hit his mark, but there was no body or blood. Westrum writes: "Hamby fired a .44 magnum through a refrigerator—I saw the hole myself—at a person in the kitchen, whom he heard slam against the sink, fall on the floor, and make gurgling noises, as if critically wounded . . . All three were extremely scared; Masters to the point where he was re-loading spent cartridges into the revolver."[87] By 5:50 a.m., they had phoned the sheriff's department. "Because one of them was on parole, and had a real interest in not being associated with firearms or drugs, it demonstrates the degree of their desperation."

Hamby was so excited and emotionally distraught, that when he saw a police car, he discharged a shot to get their attention. Unfortunately, it struck the vehicle's windshield and resulted in his being charged with attempted murder! Lucky for him, the charge was eventually reduced to misuse of a firearm. Police combed through the house searching for clues but could find no evidence of intruders. The only clear physical evidence of a confrontation was the damage left behind by the three men, including a house ridden with bullet holes and empty shell casings.

The social context of the "siege" may be significant. Cordell had only lived at the house for three weeks; Masters about one week. In the month leading up to the incident, Masters had been exhibiting paranoia, and Cordell noted that the more time he spent with him the more fearful he (Cordell) became. As Masters was a suspected drug dealer, he may have been afraid of being arrested or provoking violence from competing dealers.[88] Dr. Westrum conducted four hours of interviews with the men and said that they were surprised when police were unable to find any bodies or blood on the premises. He writes: "On reflection, *none* of the three remembers being shot at by the mystery assailants. The three were then taken away, under the cameras of the media, and booked on charges of assault with intent to commit murder. In later weeks the charge was changed to misuse of a firearm."[89] Westrum observes that a remarkable aspect of the case is the vivid recollection that the men had of the events. He notes that "the three remembered having shot and *hit* the people they were shooting at—even taking into account their state of mind, it is hard to discount their testimony about this entirely."[90]

In reviewing the case, Dr. Westrum writes that the most likely explanation for the "siege" was that the three occupants suffered hallucinations "due to the effect of fear and drugs. They never actually saw their assailants. They saw silhouettes and heard noises, although very distinct ones. The entire sequence took place at night and in a context of fear, suspicion and insecurity."[91] If there had been real assailants engaged in drug-related activity, those involved "must have been extremely hardy or very foolish because the three men shot to kill with weapons which would have been fatal (I counted five large .444 holes in the back wall of the house)."

Bigfoot Confrontation, summer 1981 (Rome, Ohio, USA)

On July 1, 1981, a curious article appeared in the *Valley News* of Orwell, Ohio, under the headline: "Strange Beast Roams in Rome." The article stated that a local family had been terrorized by a large black animal that stood between seven and nine feet tall. Family members had reportedly fired shots at the creature, which made growling noises and was blamed for taking several ducks and chickens. Local Bigfoot investigator Dennis Pilichis interviewed the witnesses and was so moved by the series of encounters, that he self-published a booklet, *Night Siege*, that detailed their experience.[92] Researcher Ron Schaffner has also chronicled the episode.[93]

As soon as Pilichis arrived at the scene, he searched for evidence of a possible hoax, but quickly ruled it out. In his final report on the episode, he wrote that the physical evidence at the scene substantiated their story. "There were two ladders up against the family house, up on the roof were coffee cups, flashlights and coats. The yard was covered with spent shotgun shells. The family was in a great state of agitation and stress. The family appeared to be honest, troubled, and confused by what they were going through."[94]

In the early morning hours of June 25, a man and his sons heard their ducks making a ruckus, and, looking at their front yard, they reportedly saw an eight-foot-tall "thing" standing on four legs and sporting large, glowing red eyes as big as baseballs. The father, Robert, shot at the creature. At about 2:00 a.m. the following morning, after hearing his dog barking, Robert went outside with a flashlight and spotted a gorilla-like creature with bright red eyes, snorting and growling. Running back into the house, Robert roused his sons and grabbed his shotgun. They jumped into his truck and chased the figure until it disappeared into a nearby wooded area. When Robert told a neighbor what had happened, the neighbor said that his kids had seen a strange bear-like creature and were afraid to camp in their own backyard. The creature reportedly had one-and-a-half-inch fangs protruding from its mouth and long arms that hung below its waist.[95]

Three days later, in the early morning, mysterious forms were spotted by a wood line near the house. Several family members entered the field and spotted figures with glowing red eyes. The figures appeared to be waving flashlights. Robert began firing his 12-gauge shotgun, emptying two boxes of shells. He thought he struck one of the creatures as he saw two eyes drop to the ground. Then, many sets of glowing eyes appeared, and everyone raced back to the security of their house. Throughout the night they said they could see the creatures from their window, roaming about. The next day, Bigfoot researcher Dennis Pilichis arrived and found three-toed tracks that were attributed to the creatures. They measured seven inches by eight inches.[96]

On June 29, the family had grown panicky and at 5:00 a.m. they phoned the Ashtabula County Sheriff's Department. Deputies drove their cruiser around the field where the creatures had been spotted, but saw nothing out of the ordinary. While the police were there, family members claimed to have spotted mysterious figures in the distance, but when the deputies spotlight was shone in that direction, they saw nothing. The following report is taken from the police log, under the heading, "Suspicious Activity."

Robert S. reported that on Wed and Thurs evening of late last week he and his family were awakened by loud growling and activity in the front and back-yard. When we went to check the disturbance they reportedly saw a large black colored animal standing about 7 to 9 feet tall. Each time they shined a light on the animal or attempted to shoot it, it would run off into the woods. Last evening the animal returned and was in the north field behind the house. Robert S. and his sons chased the animal toward a clearing in the north tree line where they said they saw three pairs of large eyes. They fired several shots at the animal and were waiting for daylight to check for any signs. I checked the area along with Mr. S. and saw no signs of blood or tissue. We did discover a few large prints in the ground but they were distorted. Mr. S. said he had called our offices and game Warden Kelly last week and was told nothing could be done unless a clear print could be obtained. Mr. S. mentioned that he had lost four ducks and a chicken since the activity had started and advised of other incidents where horses belonging to Amish loggers, and other farm animals had been attacked.[97]

On the night of the 29th at 11:00 p.m., the police were again called to the farm after the family heard mysterious noises. The investigating deputy wrote in his log:

I arrived at the above location and met with the Robert S. family. They explained that they have been hearing strange noises around their property for the last week or so. Mr. S. said that they have seen a huge animal also, at nighttime. He said that it looked like it stood about 9 feet tall. The animal makes a real loud growl. HE SAID IT LOOKED LIKE IT COULD BE A BEAR. It has always been dark when they see it. So he hasn't got a real good look at it. They have found large paw marks in the ground around his property. Deputy D. came to the scene with a shotgun, and Sgt. F. arrived also. We checked the area with our spotlights but didn't see anything. Resumed patrol.[98]

Family members spent the rest of the night sitting on the roof, guarding the house. Schaffner reports that they had been doing so since the activity began.

The sightings would continue sporadically after the arrival of several Bigfoot researchers who appear to have legitimated the reality of the creatures to the family and themselves. By August 13, events were resembling a scene from a grade-B science-fiction movie. Schaffner writes that a Maryland Bigfoot investigator, Willard McIntyre, contacted Pilichis by phone to discuss what could be done if the creatures returned. McIntyre arrived a few days later. The men went over a variety of exotic methods to kill the creatures, including luring them out with tape recordings of rabbits and ducks. "McIntyre would use the live rabbits and use cyanide capsules on them. In this manner, the capsules would be broken if the rabbits were eaten alive. Other defenses were brought out, such as flares, cylinders of pressurized hydrofluoric acid, loaded guns of various powers and a '40.00 crucifix' in case the phenomena were demonic."[99] Considering the many weapons that were eventually in use, and the nervousness exhibited by those there, it is remarkable that no one was accidentally shot.

On August 21, a dead chicken was found on the farm—a sure sign that the creatures had returned. Robert also reported that a fuse box had been smashed in the cellar. During the evening, McIntyre and another researcher put the rabbits out as bait. One end of a parachute chord was tied to the rabbits' back feet, and the other end was attached to a metal milk crate. About an hour later, glowing red eyes were spotted in a field and along a tree line, heading straight for the rabbits. Strange "phantom flashlight beams" were also spotted. While Robert accompanied his family to the barn to illuminate the yard, McIntyre was on the roof of the house with a rifle. McIntyre saw a small figure near the tree line and called out: "Are you human or animal?"[100] Not receiving a response, he opened fire; the creature screamed and ran into the woods. When McIntyre returned the next day to kill the rabbits, one was missing and the parachute cord had been snapped. The investigators concluded that the creatures had broken the cord while holding the crate with their feet.

The events soon died down. Over the course of several weeks, the family, encouraged by several Bigfoot researchers, appeared to have reinforced each other's beliefs in the existence of a small group of Bigfoot creatures outside their farm. The appearance of missing, killed, and wounded animals, strange noises, shadowy apelike figures with glowing red eyes, and mysterious lights seem to have given rise to the belief that the farm was under siege. The family took to sitting on the roof of their home at night with guns, guarding their buildings and land from the perceived threat. When that didn't work, they did what most people would have done in their situation: they rang law enforcement. When authorities could find nothing unusual and no tangible evidence of the creatures' existence, the family turned to Bigfoot investigators for help—investigators who shared their belief in the creatures.

As family members and the Bigfoot researchers stayed awake on many nights until daybreak, the darkness, anxiety, and fatigue may have compromised their judgment. Their paranoia and tendency to jump to far-fetched conclusions were no more evident than on the night of July 1. Pilichis wrote that on that night, family members suggested that the sightings of glowing red eyes in the distance may have been a deliberate attempt to divert their attention away from the sightings of shadowy figures. At one point, "while taking turns shooting at these forms" after spotting them near the tree line, family members saw what appeared to be a horse standing in a field. Because it resembled their horse, which was secure in a barn, they attached great significance to the sighting. They immediately opened fire on the figure from their vantage point on the rooftop of the house, believing the figure was some type of supernatural entity. When they went to look for the body, they found nothing.[101]

A few nights later, when several forms were spotted near the tree line, Pilichis later acknowledged that he had difficulty seeing what the others had seen. When members of the group opened fire on one of the figures and were sure they hit it, they found nothing. Pilichis wrote: "A glowing form stepped out of the woodline on the other side of the field. The three family members fired upon it, hitting it, with it looking like the form fell down into the high grass. We all ran toward this area . . . with the grass smashed down, and another path leading away, as if something had dragged it's self [sic] away into the woods. No human or animal had been in this area to create the ground effects we observed."[102]

On several occasions the Bigfoot researchers and family members also shot at UFOs. There was even a suggestion that one of the family members may have been abducted by a UFO. In the end, after extensive investigation by the researchers, no concrete evidence of the existence of the creatures was found.

Nullarbor UFO Chase, 1988 (Mundrabilla, Australia)

On January 22, 1988, the Associated Press reported that four Australians claimed their car had been chased by a UFO and lifted off the ground. South Australian police sergeant Jim Furnell was quoted as saying that while initially skeptical, upon investigating, they were taking the report "very seriously."[103] He told South Australian TV that after talking with the victims: "They were certainly scared; they were visibly shaken. . . . I have no reason to doubt that something happened."[104]

The story began on January 19, 1988, when Faye Knowles, age forty-three, set off on a cross country trek from Perth, Western Australia, to the east coast. She was accompanied by her three sons: eighteen-year-old Wayne, twenty-one-year-old Sean, and twenty-four-year-old Patrick. They traveled virtually nonstop for the next thirteen hours by alternating drivers. As dawn was approaching, their blue Telstar sedan was near the tiny, remote outpost of Mundrabilla in the remote Western Australian desert. It was Sean's turn at the wheel. Sean noticed a mysterious light in front of him that he initially assumed to have been from a truck, though he eventually decided that it resembled a "spaceship." The light soon disappeared. A short time later, a mysterious light appeared behind the car, frightening Sean, who believed the object was chasing them. He responded by pressing the accelerator; the car raced down the desolate highway at great speed. Suddenly the light appeared in front again.[105]

Family members later told authorities that at one point while trying to escape the object, a beam enveloped their car and lifted it off the ground, before dropping it. As the vehicle impacted, a tire burst, disabling the car. The shaken occupants nervously replaced the flat tire and continued on to nearby Mundrabilla. During the encounter and "chase," several events were reported by the family, although the exact sequence is not known.[106] Mrs. Knowles rolled down her window and placed her hand on the roof—that is when she felt a "spongy substance." During the encounter a "greyish-black mist" was reported to fill the vehicle. Family members also observed that their voices appeared to slow down and change in pitch during the chase. They also reported hearing a humming sound. At one point, they thought that the craft had landed on the roof and lifted the vehicle into the air. However, they neither saw anything protruding down the sides from the roof, nor had any one looked out the windows at the time and seen the vehicle airborne. A mysterious, black ash-like deposit was found coating the outside of the car; it was also found inside the vehicle. On the roof of the car were indentations. During the incident, they said that the car shook violently, a foul odor filled the inside of the car, and their two dogs reportedly went "crazy."[107]

Two truck drivers who met the family after the incident reported that they were visibly distraught. Upon arriving in South Australia, police conducted interviews as the incident was now the subject of global headlines. NASA space scientist Richard Haines was sent a sample of the mysterious ash and concluded that it was mundane road dirt, typically found on vehicles and consistent with a car that had just crossed the sand-laden Nullarbor Plains, which border the Great Southern Ocean.[108]

Monty Luke from the Australian Mineral Development Authority also conducted a series of tests on the car. His report stated: "The investigation revealed that the damage to the tyre was consistent with running on a deflated tyre for an extended period. It is considered that this would account for the odour, smoke and vibrations sensed during the incident. . . . The material taken from around the front wheels was typical of residual dust from wearing brake pads and discs. No significant dust was observed on the vehicle as presented for inspection."[109] The report also noted that the shallow dents on the car roof—supposedly created when a force or magnet grabbed onto the car—were consistent with an object that was pressed down on the vehicle, not lifting it.[110] Sean said that he was driving at nearly 200 kmph as he sped away. Given the lack of corroborating physical evidence and the frightened state of the occupants, it appears that family members, fatigued from a long trip, under the cover of darkness while traveling on an unfamiliar, desolate road, mistook an anomalous light for an extraterrestrial space craft that they believed was pursuing them. It is also notable that, based on interviews, the entire family appeared to have been in an extremely emotional state, "shouting and crying" while Mrs. Knowles said they thought they were going to die.[111]

The former head of the Bureau of Meteorology for the region, Allan Brunt, believes that weather played an integral role in the "encounter." He said that at the time of the episode there had been a temperature inversion in the area, where warmer air becomes trapped below colder air. Such events are notorious for refracting light and distorting the sizes, shapes, and colors of objects. Brunt concludes that the Knowles family saw the distorted image of the headlights of a truck in the distance, which appeared to them as "frightening and bizarre." As for the other aspects of the encounter that could not be explained by weather conditions, he attributes "their own imagination whilst in a state of fright."[112] This assessment was supported by Ceduna police officer Sergeant Fred Longley, who said that when the family entered the police station, they appeared to be emotionally distraught. "They were in a terrible state—even though it was five hours after the incident. Something happened out there. Their car, even after being driven all that way, still had black ash—or dust—over it. Even on the inside. Where did that come from? There's no soil like that out there, only sand."

The gullibility and social ineptitude of the Knowles family may have contributed to their perceived encounter. Faye Knowles later complained that they had been taken advantage of by people who had promised they would gain financially from their experience. She said an advertising executive told them that their car "could be used in television commercials, a documentary and taken around shopping centres where people would pay to see it . . . But we didn't get a cent; we don't even know if the car was promoted at all, and now we have lost it."[113] They said the vehicle was auctioned off for $7,050 in June 1988 after they failed to make the repayments. Patrick Knowles said that the family was trying to put the experience behind them. "We are trying to forget the sharks who promised us money from our experience — they only wanted to use us."

There is no evidence to suggest the case is a hoax. Two separate truck drivers confirmed the family's UFO story. Fifty-seven-year-old Graham Henley from Victoria, and John Dejong were both truckers from Norseman in Western Australia that had been in the vicinity at the time of the "encounter." Henley reported seeing the family filling up a petrol can during a stop at Caiguna at 1:30 a.m. At 4:00 a.m. he had passed Madura when he spotted a bright egg-like object in his rearview mirror. Arriving in Mundrabilla at about 4:30 a.m., he said the Knowles car pulled in soon after, and the occupants appeared frightened. Henley observed that the family members were excited and claimed that a "flying saucer" had picked up and dropped their car. He said that one of the males in the car had bare feet and they were bloody. Dejong and a companion who shared his driving duties, caught up with Henley and the Knowles family as they were discussing the incident. The truckers pulled in and listened to the family's story.[114]

Small-group scares are a fascinating form of social delusion, which is a virgin area for research. For instance, on a number of occasions, people have come to believe that they have shot and killed or injured imaginary intruders at almost point-blank range, only to have forensic investigators find no trace of the trespasser's presence. These shooting incidents may reflect the mind playing tricks on the participants, who were in a fatigued, frightened state that is known to trigger fleeting hallucinations on the sleep-awake interface. These episodes certainly deserve more study.

CHAPTER 13
POSTSCRIPT: LESSONS TO HEED

Those who cannot remember the past are condemned to repeat it.
—George Santayana, *The Life of Reason*

Information is not power. It does not necessarily make us any smarter or better able to cope with social delusions. English philosopher Francis Bacon knew this centuries ago when he wrote in 1597 that "knowledge itself is power."[1] In this chapter, we will outline the lessons that can be gleaned from our foray into the history of popular delusions. We must emphasize from the onset that many people may recognize the appearance of a particular delusion, but that is no guarantee that they will avoid being caught up in the fear or excitement. An apt example is the typical stock market crash. The old adage of buy low and sell high is considered by most economists to be sage advice. Yet, during a bull market, shareholders are often reluctant to sell for fear of missing out on even greater profits. Conversely, when the market has taken a sudden plunge, there is usually widespread reluctance to buy, fearing that prices may spiral even further downward. When a major move in share prices occurs, many people fail to act. This state of affairs has given rise to another adage: that markets are driven up by greed and fall on fear. If the advice in this section is to be useful, it is important to heed the lessons and remember that we are all susceptible to popular delusions.

We have learned that rumors are unverified stories of perceived importance that cannot be immediately substantiated. As they emerge, they tend to become shorter (leveling), more specific (sharpening), and reflective of prevailing stereotypes (assimilation). Rumors are ever-present, but flourish when there is scant information and conflicting claims. They are incubated in situations of anxiety and ambiguity. A key determinant of whether a rumor will flourish or fade is its degree of plausibility: the more credible the rumor, the more likely it is to be believed. It is impossible to control the content or outcome of a rumor.

Most rumors arise spontaneously in a cauldron of uncertainty and fear that typify times of financial crisis, political turmoil, and war. The construction and circulation of rumors provides a degree of certainty which reduces tensions. Humans can deal with just about anything, but they cannot cope with uncertainty. The bottom line is that, in times of crisis, expect the appearance of wild claims and unverified tales, but exercise caution as to their truth or falsity until they have been confirmed. If rumors should arise, address them promptly, refute each claim point by point, and offer evidence. Never issue statements like "no comment," as in the public eye, this is the equivalent to admitting guilt, whether you are guilty or not.

As for gossip, talking about someone who is not present—especially in negative ways—appears to be part of the human condition. We have all gossiped at some point. While it can be considered cruel and divisive, recent studies suggest that the benefits of gossiping may outweigh the negatives as it provides several key functions. Gossip binds people together as they share personal information about third parties. It fosters alliances and provides clear standards of behavior. Gossip can also enhance the prestige and social status of those taking part and allows one person to keep tabs on a large number of people without meeting them. However, we should be mindful that there is a potential dark side to gossip; it can alienate and victimize others and create group dissent. At its worst, it is a form of group bullying; at its best, it gives us clear behavioral boundaries. For better or worse, to be human is to gossip.

In reviewing fads, those who become familiar with their phases (the dormant period, the breakout phase, the peak, and the rapid decline) will be better able to track the life stage of any given outbreak. Fads are far from innocent distractions and preoccupations: while the focus may be on the trivial, familiarity with these phases can reap large monetary rewards if you know the difference between a fad and a trend. One is fleeting, the other is enduring. Trends fit with changing lifestyles; fads do not. Trends typically offer health and monetary benefits to those who adopt them; fads do not. People are unlikely to become wealthy or gain health benefits from swallowing goldfish or nurturing a pet rock, yet a trend featuring a new health food that is convenient to cook and affordably priced is likely to endure. Businesses that sell items that they have identified as fads need to ascertain the life-stage that each item is passing through and guard against being left with thousands of units that no one wants to buy.

Crazes are like being in a bad relationship: friends may urge you to break it off and list the negative qualities of the object of your affections, but more often than not, their advice goes unheeded until it is too late. Whether it is a get-rich-quick scheme or a religious figure promising salvation through collective suicide, crazes have a far greater potential for harm. There is perhaps no better advice in dealing with crazes than the old chestnut, "If it sounds too good to be true, it probably is." Use logic: How is it possible that this person claims to have a "hotline" to God or the ability to create vast wealth when others do not? If a religious leader or a financial advisor ever complains that you are asking too many questions, it is a good indicator that it is time to get out.

Powerful psychological processes, such as the autokinetic effect, are often instrumental in triggering social delusions. Stare at an object in the night sky or a terrestrial object in a darkened environment, and it can appear to move and be interpreted as a supernatural occurrence. We are also prone to interpreting information patterns that reflect our expectations: we tend to see what we expect to see. Hence, depending on our preexisting beliefs, one is susceptible to misidentifying a wake at Loch Ness as a prehistoric creature, an aerial light in the night as a flying saucer, or rustling in the woods as a chupacabra. The mind fills in the missing information.

Similar processes are at work in small-group scares. Regardless of one's education level, we are all prone to misidentifying people and objects in the environment. Our memories do not work like a video recorder. Not only is our perception of the world imperfect, what we do recall changes over time. Episodes involving phantom attackers underscore how vulnerable we are to self-deception, especially when facing what is perceived to be an imminent threat, under conditions of prolonged fear, mental fatigue, and sleep deprivation—the combination of which can not only blur judgement, but can also trigger fleeting images and hallucinations that reflect the attack scenario. Preventing small-group scares is problematic as they are usually only recognized as such after the fact, once one has been able to assess the circumstances and facts. Fortunately, these are relatively rare occurrences.

In the case of moral panics, when communities feel threatened by so-called evildoers ("folk devils") who have breached the moral standards of society, it is vital to keep the threat in perspective and obtain accurate information. Scrutinize facts and figures presented by the media, law enforcement agencies, lawmakers, and action groups, and compare them with those of independent, neutral experts. Look for the key, measurable indicators of moral panics such as widespread hostility toward the demonized agent. One sure red flag is any attempt to villainize an entire group or ethnic minority. Identify exaggerated claims and statistics, especially those involving the number of deaths or crimes, or the amount of damage. Remember, it is easy to create a drop in crime statistics if authorities have narrowed the definition of a particular act. Also ask yourself: Do reports of the threat fluctuate wildly over time? Does the threat play into existing public fears?

Incidents of mass hysteria are notoriously difficult to identify in their early stages. Contagious conversion disorder is most common in close-knit groups occupying enclosed settings such as schools and factories. The best advice is to exercise caution and assume the worst: that it is a real contamination or poisoning event. However, once you have been cleared by a doctor and tests of the air, water, food, and soil have been completed and excluded as possible causes, mass hysteria must be considered the most likely cause.

Next, you need to identify the type of conversion disorder you are dealing with: anxiety hysteria or motor hysteria. The former is common in Western countries. There is a rapid onset triggered by the sudden perception of a threatening agent such as a strange odor or a rumor of tainted food. Symptoms are transient and benign and commonly include overbreathing, headache, dizziness, nausea, and weakness. The second possibility—motor hysteria—occurs in an atmosphere of preexisting group anxiety and builds over weeks or months, resulting in disruptions to the nervous system and subsequent bouts of twitching, shaking, and trance-like states. These episodes often take weeks or months to subside.

The best way to deal with an outbreak once it has been identified is to stay calm, offer reassurance, and above all, avoid using emotionally charged words like "hysteria." Instead use "stress reaction" or "psychogenic illness." Emergency responders should separate victims from nonpatients and avoid speculating on the cause. Once a diagnosis of mass psychogenic illness has been made, authorities should avoid making comments like "it's all in their heads" as the symptoms are real. If a school or business is involved, you should limit the number of media contacts. It is best to have only one or two people commenting. Sending victims home and keeping them separated from nonvictims until their symptoms have resolved has been an effective strategy over the years. However, outbreaks of either type are likely to continue unless authorities can convince the victims and their relatives that the perceived threat either never existed or has since been resolved.

Stampedes and flight panics continue to take lives every year. To combat the possibility of being caught up in an event, it would be wise to avoid large groups in confined spaces. If you are going to place yourself in an at-risk situation, ensure that there are an adequate number of functioning exits and situate yourself in close proximity of one. If a panic breaks out and you are not near an exit, remain calm and avoid being swept up in the crowd. In many panics, people did not die from fire or smoke inhalation; they were crushed to death in the frantic attempt to leave the premises. The best advice of all is to avoid placing yourself in a compromising situation.

Our last category is riots, which can break out spontaneously at any time, and hence, there is no set strategy for avoiding them. However, if hostilities break out and you find yourself in the middle of a potentially violent situation, the best advice is to maintain a low profile and leave the affected area as quickly and quietly as possible until emotions have settled down. If there have been simmering tensions and you suspect that hostilities may break out, avoid the business districts, especially at night, where looting is likely.

The history of social delusions showcases the remarkably broad spectrum of human behavior and beliefs and can range from the trivial and humorous such as fads, to claims about the threat from deviants like Jews and other ethnic minorities who become scapegoats during moral panics. Social delusions can take many forms, and while impossible to predict, each has characteristic features that can enable us to recognize them. If we have learned one paramount lesson, it is that these outbreaks will continue to both plague and delight generations to come. Ultimately, social delusions are a barometer of the state of society at any given time; they are reflections of humanity itself as they mirror our prevailing hopes and fears.

NOTES

INTRODUCTION

1. Charles Mackay, *Memoirs of Extraordinary Popular Delusions and the Madness of Crowds*, vol. 2 (London: Office of the National Illustrated Library, 1852).

CHAPTER 1: RUMOR AND GOSSIP

1. Arlette Farge and Jacques Revel, *Logiques de la Foule* (Paris: Hachette, 1988).

2. Tamotsu Shibutani, *Improvised News: A Sociological Study of Rumor* (Indianapolis: Bobbs-Merrill, 1966).

3. Nicholas DiFonzo, "Rumor," in *The Corsini Encyclopedia of Psychology*, ed. Irving Weiner and W. Edward Craighead, vol. 4 (New York: John Wiley, 2010), pp. 1480–81. See p. 1481.

4. Richard T. LaPiere, *Collective Behavior* (New York: McGraw-Hill, 1938), p. 199.

5. Jean-Noel Kapferer, "How Rumors Are Born," *Society* 29, no. 5 (July–August 1992): 53–60.

6. Gary Allan Fine, "Rumor Matters: An Introductory Essay," in *Rumor Mills: The Social Impact of Rumor and Legend* (Piscataway, NJ: Transaction, 2009), pp. 3–6.

7. Ibid., p. 5.

8. Gordon Allport and Leo Postman, *The Psychology of Rumor* (New York: H. Holt, 1947).

9. Ibid., p. 150.

10. Ibid.; Allan Kimmel, *Rumors and Rumor Control: A Manager's Guide to Understanding and Combatting Rumors* (Mahwah, NJ: Lawrence Erlbaum, 1991), pp. 91–92.

11. Shibutani, *Improvised News*, pp. 133–34.

12. David L. Miller, *Introduction to Collective Behavior and Collective Action*, 2nd ed. (Prospect Heights, IL: Waveland, 2000), p. 95.

13. P. Bordia and Ralph Rosnow, "Rumor Rest Stops on the Information Highway: Transmission Patterns in a Computer-Mediated Rumor Chain," *Human Communication Research* 25 (1998): 163–79.

14. Ralph L. Rosnow and Gary Allen Fine, *Rumor and Gossip* (New York: Elsevier, 1976), p. 20.

15. David Samper, "Cannibalizing Kids: Rumor and Resistance in Latin America," *Journal of Folklore Research* 39, no. 1 (2002): 1–32. See p. 5.

16. Jean-Noel Kapferer, *Rumors: Uses, Interpretations, and Images* (New Brunswick, CT: Transaction Publishers, 1990), p. 24.

17. Charles Mackay, *Memoirs of Extraordinary Popular Delusions and the Madness of Crowds*, vol. 2 (London: Office of the National Illustrated Library, 1852), p. 259.

18. B. A. Robinson, "An Overview of the Persecution of Jews for the Past 2,000 Years," ReligiousTolerance.org, February 7, 2010 http://www.religioustolerance.org/jud _pers.htm (accessed September 30, 2014).

19. Pamela Stewart and Andrew Strathern, *Witchcraft, Sorcery, Rumors, and Gossip* (Cambridge: Cambridge University Press, 2004), p. 198.

20. Richard A. Drake, "Construction Sacrifice and Kidnapping: Rumor Panics in Borneo," *Oceania* 59 (1989): 269–78; G. Forth, "Construction Sacrifice and Head-Hunting Rumours in Central Flores (Eastern Indonesia): A Comparative Note," *Oceania* 61 (1991): 257–66.

21. Miller, *Introduction to Collective Behavior*, p. 86.

22. Ibid., p. 87.

23. DiFonzo, "Rumor," p. 1481.

24. Christopher Matthews, "How Does One Fake Tweet Cause a Stock Market Crash?" Time.com, April 24, 2013, http://business.time.com/2013/04/24/how-does-one-fake-tweet-cause-a-stock-market-crash/ (accessed January 11, 2014).

25. Joseph Epstein, *Gossip: The Untrivial Pursuit* (Boston: Houghton Mifflin Harcourt, 2011), p. 3.

26. Anatoly Liberman, *Word Origins and How We Know Them* (New York: Oxford University Press, 2009), p. 78; Gary Alan Fine and Ralph Rosnow, "Gossip, Gossipers, and Gossiping," *Personality and Social Psychology Bulletin* 4, no. 1 (1978): 161–68. See p. 161.

27. Epstein, *Gossip*, p. 5.

28. Nicholas DiFonzo and Prashant Bordia, "Rumor, Gossip and Urban Legends," *Diogenes* 213 (2007): 19–35. See p. 19.

29. Epstein, *Gossip*, p. xi.

30. Grant Michelson, Ad Iterson, and Kathryn Waddington, "Gossip in Organizations: Contexts, Consequences, and Controversies," *Group & Organization Management* 35, no. 4 (2010): 371–90. See p. 378.

31. Alexander Cowan, "Gossip and Street Culture in Early Modern Venice," pp. 119–40, in *Cultural History of Early Modern European Streets*, ed. R. Laitinen and Thomas Cohen (Leiden, Netherlands: Koninklijke Brill NV, 2009), p. 121.

32. Nicholas DiFonzo and Prashant Bordia, *Rumor Psychology: Social and Organizational Approaches* (Washington, DC: American Psychological Association, 2007), p. 13; William Kornblum, *Sociology in a Changing World*, 9th ed. (Belmont, CA: Wadsworth, 2011), p. 213.

33. DiFonzo and Bordia, "Rumor, Gossip and Urban Legends," p. 26.

34. Ibid.

35. Ibid., pp. 26–27.

36. Ibid., p. 27.

37. Eric K. Foster, "Research on Gossip: Taxonomy, Methods, and Future Directions," *Review of General Psychology* 8, no. 2 (2004): 78–99.

38. Tim Hallett, Brent Harger, and Donna Eder, "Gossip at Work: Unsanctioned Evaluative Talk in Formal School Meetings," *Journal of Contemporary Ethnography* 38, no. 5 (2009): 584–618. See p. 587.

39. David Hernandez, *The Greatest Story Ever Forged: Curse of the Christ Myth* (Pittsburgh, PA: Red Lead, 2009), p. 119.

40. Mattis Kantor, *The Jewish Timeline Encyclopedia* (Lanham, MD: Rowman & Littlefield, 2004), p. 168.

41. Howard N. Lupovitch, *Jews and Judaism in World History* (New York: Routledge, 2010), p. 92.

42. Mackay, *Memoirs of Extraordinary Popular Delusions and the Madness of Crowds*, p. 264.

43. Alessandro Manzoni, *I Promessi Sposi* (The Betrothed), in *Harvard Classics*, vol. 21, ed. Charles W. Eliot (New York: P. F. Collier & Son, 1909), p. 534.

44. Ibid., p. 535.

45. Ibid.

46. Ibid., p. 541.

47. Ibid., p. 542.

48. Georges Lefebvre, *La Grande Peur de 1789* (Paris: Armand Colin, 1988), p. 146.

49. Journal de Troyes, cited in ibid., p. 167.

50. Ibid., p. 84.

51. Ibid., p. 189.

52. M. Kitchen, "The German Invasion of Canada in the First World War," *International History Review* 7, no. 2 (1985): 245–60.

53. G. S. Mount, *Canada's Enemies: Spies and Spying in the Peaceable Kingdom* (Toronto: Dundurn, 1993), p. 40.

54. Ibid.

55. Terry Ann Knopf, *Rumors, Race and Riots* (New Brunswick, NJ: Transaction, 2009), p. 24.

56. Ibid., p. 26.

57. Sutan Sjahrir, *Out of Exile*, trans. Charles Wolf (New York: Greenwood, 1949), p. 164.

58. Ibid.

59. Ibid.

60. Drake, "Construction Sacrifice and Kidnapping," p. 275.

61. Anna Lowenhaupt Tsing, *In the Realm of the Diamond Queen: Marginality in an Out-of-the-Way Place* (Princeton, NJ: Princeton University Press, 1993), p. 86.

62. Forth, "Construction Sacrifice," pp. 257–66; R. H. Barnes, "Construction Sacrifice, Kidnapping and Head-Hunting Rumours on Flores and Elsewhere in Indonesia," *Oceania* 64 (1993): 146–58.

63. Barbara Suczek, "The Curious Case of the 'Death' of Paul McCartney," *Journal of Contemporary Ethnography* 1, no. 1 (1972): 61–76. See pp. 63–64.

64. Hal Morgan and Kerry Tucker, *Rumor!* (New York: Penguin, 1984), p. 82.

65. Ronald P. Grelsamer, *Into the Sky with Diamonds* (Bloomington, IN: Author-House, 2010), p. 353.

66. Kapferer, *Rumors*, p. 22; Rosnow and Fine, *Rumor and Gossip*, p. 14.

67. Suczek, "Curious Case," p. 62.

68. Rosnow and Fine, *Rumor and Gossip*, p. 22.

69. "Kids New Macabre Game: Is Paul McCartney Dead?" *Variety*, October 22, 1969, 67.

70. Rosnow and Fine, *Rumor and Gossip*, pp. 14–20; Kapferer, *Rumors*, pp. 22–23.

71. Suczek, "Curious Case," p. 62.

72. Kapferer, *Rumors*, p. 23.

73. John Neary, "The Magical McCartney Mystery," *Life* 67, no. 19 (1969): 103–106. See p. 105.

74. Ibid., p. 105.

75. Suczek, "Curious Case," p. 66.

76. Ibid., pp. 66–67.

77. Neary, "Magical McCartney Mystery," p. 104.

78. R. Gary Patterson, *The Walrus Was Paul: The Great Beatle Death Clues* (New York: Fireside, 1998), p. 57.

79. Douglas Jehl, "Of College Girls Betrayed and Vile Chewing Gum," *New York Times*, July 10, 1996; and discussion in *Fortean Times*, no. 91, October 1996, p. 14.

80. Barton Gellman, "Pop! Went the Tale of the Bubble Gum Spiked with Sex Hormones," *Washington Post Foreign Service*, July 28, 1997, p. A14.

81. Ibid.

82. Nicholas Herriman, "The Great Rumor Mill: Gossip, Mass Media, and the Ninja Fear," *Journal of Asian Studies* 60, no. 3 (2010): 723–48. See p. 726.

83. Ibid., p. 727.

84. Bianca Beersma and Gerben Van Kleef, "How the Grapevine Keeps You in Line: Gossip Increases Contributions to the Group," *Social Psychological and Personality Science* 2, no. 6 (2011): 642–49. See p. 644.

85. Ibid., p. 646.

86. Ibid.

87. Clifton B. Parker, "Stanford Research: Hidden Benefits of Gossip, Ostracism," *Stanford Report*, January 27, 2014, http://news.stanford.edu/news/2014/january/upside-of -gossip-012714.html (accessed January 8, 2014).

88. Ibid.

89. Ibid.

90. Matthew Feinberg, Robb Willer, and Michael Schultz, "Gossip and Ostracism Promote Cooperation in Groups," *Psychological Science* 25, no. 3 (2014): 656–64. See p. 663.

CHAPTER 2: FADS

1. *The Concise Oxford Dictionary*, 10th ed., ed. Judy Pearsall (Oxford: Oxford University Press, 1999), pp. 509 and 526.

2. Ian Robertson, *Sociology*, 3rd ed. (New York: Worth, 1987), p. 549.

3. Ralph Turner and Lewis Killian, *Collective Behavior*, 2nd ed. (Englewood Cliffs, NJ: Prentice-Hall, 1972), pp. 129–30.

4. "Fads: Did We Really Do Those Silly Things," *Life* 9 (1986): 65–69.

5. Martin Gardner, *Fads and Fallacies in the Name of Science* (Mineola, NY: Dover, 1957), pp. 16–19.

6. "Riots, Girls, Fads: Spring's Ode on Campuses," *Life* 46, no. 13 (March 1959): 15–19. See p. 18.

7. Emory Stephen Bogardus, *Fundamentals of Social Psychology* (New York: Arno, 1973).

8. Richard T. LaPiere, *Collective Behavior* (New York: McGraw-Hill, 1938), p. 160.

9. See: David L. Miller, *Introduction to Collective Behavior* (Belmont, CA: Wadsworth, 1985); David L. Miller, *Introduction to Collective Behavior and Collective Action*, 2nd ed. (Prospect Heights, IL: Waveland, 2000); Rolf Meyersohn and Elihiu Katz, "Notes on a Natural History of Fads," *American Journal of Sociology* 62 (1957): 594–601; L. S. Penrose, *On the Objective Study of Crowd Behavior* (London: H. K. Lewis, 1952).

10. LaPiere, *Collective Behavior*, p. 203.

11. Judith Lanigan, *The Hoola Hoop: A Study of the Subject* (printed by author, 2007), pp. 60–64.

12. Alan C. Elliott, *A Little Book of Big Dreams* (Nashville, TN: Rutledge Hills), p. 112.

13. Frederick Lewis Allen, *Only Yesterday: An Informal History of the 1920's* (New York: John Wiley and Sons, 1997), p. 267.

14. Valerie J. Nelson, "Milton Levine Dies at 97; Co-Creator of Popular Ant Farm Toys," *Los Angeles Times*, January 26, 2011.

15. Miller, *Introduction to Collective Behavior and Collective Action*, p. 185.

16. Turner and Killian, *Collective Behavior*, p. 146.

17. Emily Spivack, "Paint-On Hosiery during the War Years," Smithsonian.com, September 10, 2012, http://www.smithsonianmag.com/arts-culture/paint-on-hosiery -during-the-war-years-29864389/?no-ist (accessed September 28, 2014).

18. Jack Hart, "Fad Words," *Editor & Publisher* 129, no. 19 (May 11, 1996): 5.

19. William Noble, *Noble's Book of Writing Blunders and How to Avoid Them* (Cincinnati, OH: Writer's Digest Books, 2006), p. 111.

20. Mary Lou Widmer, *New Orleans in the Forties* (Gretna, LA: Pelican Publishing, 2007), p. 162.

21. Joel Best, *Flavor of the Month: Why Smart People Fall for Fads* (Berkeley: University of California Press, 2006), p. 12.

22. Ibid., pp. 12–13.

23. Margaret Andersen and Howard Taylor, *Sociology: Understanding a Diverse Society* (Belmont, CA: Thompson Wadsworth, 2008), pp. 598–99.

24. Ibid., p. 599.

25. Martin G. Letscher, "How to Tell Fads from Trends," *American Demographics* 16, no. 12 (December 1994).

26. Frank W. Hoffmann and William G. Bailey, *Sports and Recreation Fads* (New York: Harrington Park, 1991), p. 33.

27. Ibid.

28. M. Babache, *The Diabolo from A to Z* (Geneva, Switzerland: Jongierie Diffusion S. A., 1995), p. 6.

29. Philip Orbanes, *The Game Makers: The Story of Parker Brothers, From Tiddledy Winks to Trivial Pursuit* (Boston: Harvard Business Review, 2003), p. 47.

30. "Playing Diabolo on Common," *Boston Evening Transcript*, December 3, 1907, p. 20.

31. Orbanes, *Game Makers*, p. 47.

32. Ibid.

33. Charles Panati, *Panati's Parade of Fads, Fallacies, and Manias* (New York: Harper-Collins, 1991), p. 151; Andrew Marum and Frank Parise, *Follies and Foibles: A View of 20th Century Fads* (New York: Facts on File, 1984), p. 57.

34. Marum and Parise, *Follies and Foibles*, p. 57.

35. Sylvester Monroe, "Welcome to Putters Paradise: Miniature Golf, a '20s Fad, Comes back in Style," *Time* 131, no. 11, September 11, 1989, p. 73.

36. "Mini Golf: A Hole in One," *Business Week* (August 27, 2001): 16.

37. "People," *Life* 6, no. 12 (March 20, 1939): 69.

38. Richard A. Burgheim, "Goldfish Swallowing: College Fad Started Here, Spread over World," *Harvard Crimson*, May 6, 1952, http://www.thecrimson.com/article .aspx?ref=483444 (accessed May 18, 2013).

39. "Goldfish Eaters," *Life* 6, no. 16 (April 17, 1939): 84.

40. Ibid.

41. Burgheim, "Goldfish Swallowing."

42. The general overview of the goldfish swallowing fad was gleaned from the following sources: Panati, *Panati's Parade of Fads*, pp. 156–57; Hoffmann and Bailey, *Sports and Recreation Fads*, pp. 33–34; Peter L. Skolnik, *Fads: America's Crazes, Fevers & Fancies From the 1890s to the 1970s* (New York: Thomas Y. Crowell, 1978), pp. 73–75.

43. Panati, *Panati's Parade of Fads*, p. 156; Marum and Parise, *Follies and Foibles*, p. 68.

44. Mark Long, *Bad Fads* (Toronto: ECW, 2002), p. 27.

45. Burgheim, "Goldfish Swallowing."

46. Paul Sann, *Fads, Follies and Delusions of the American People* (New York: Crown, 1967), p. 145.

47. Worth Reporting, *Australian Women's Weekly*, December 31, 1958, p. 42.

48. "Indonesia Frowns on Hula Hoop Due to 'Degenerative Tendencies,'" *Milwaukee (WI) Journal*, May 7, 1959, p. 3.

49. Hoffmann and Bailey, *Sports and Recreation Fads*, pp. 185–87; Skolnik, *Fads*, pp. 112–15; Panati, *Panati's Parade of Fads*, pp. 264–65.

50. Robert R. Evans and Jerry L. Miller, "Barely an End in Sight," in *Readings in Collective Behavior*, ed. Robert R. Evans (Chicago: Rand McNally, 1975), pp. 401–15; William A. Anderson, "The Social Organization and Social Control of a Fad," *Urban Life* 6 (1977): 221–40; Marum and Parise, *Follies and Foibles*; Miller, *Introduction to Collective Behavior*; Ben Aguirre, E. Quarantelli, and J. Mendoza, "The Collective Behavior of Fads: The Characteristics, Effects, and Career of Streaking," *American Sociological Review* 53 (1988): 569–84.

51. Jack Levin, *Sociological Snapshots 5: Seeing Social Structure and Change in Everyday Life* (Thousand Oaks, CA: Pine Forge, 2008), p. 181.

52. Anderson, "Social Organization," p. 236.

53. Ibid., p. 237.

54. Ibid.

55. Ibid.

56. Ibid., p. 238.

57. Ibid., pp. 234–35.

58. Ibid., pp. 238–39.

59. Hoffmann and Bailey, *Sports and Recreation Fads*, p. 352.

60. Albert Goldman, "The Life and Death of Bruce Lee: His Final Victim," *Penthouse* (February 1983): 185–86.

61. "Enter the Dragon," IMDb, http://www.imdb.com/title/tt0070034/business ?ref_=tt_ql_dt_4 (accessed September 29, 2014).

62. Metrowebukmetro, "Biddu," Metro, October 27, 2009, http://metro.co .uk/2009/10/27/biddu-636450/ (accessed September 29, 2014).

63. Associated Press, "Kung-Fu Step Is Latest Dance Craze," *Gettysburg (PA) Times*, January 7, 1975, p. 2.

64. "Kung-Fu Craze Spreads," *Sarasota (FL) Herald-Tribune*, January 10, 1975, p. 12A.

65. Jachinson W. Chan, "Bruce Lee's Fictional Models of Masculinity," *Men and Masculinities* 2, no. 4 (2000): 371–87.

66. David L. Miller, *Introduction to Collective Behavior and Collective Action*, 3rd ed. (Long Grove, IL: Waveland, 2013), p. 198.

67. Kara Keeling and Josh Kun, *Sound Clash: Listening to American Studies* (Baltimore, MD: Johns Hopkins University Press, 2012), p. 91.

68. From author Robert Bartholomew's personal experience as an avid CB user at this time in rural upstate New York.

69. Harold Kerbo, Karrie Marshall, and Philip Holley, "Reestablishing 'Gemein-schaft'? An Examination of the CB Radio Fad," *Journal of Contemporary Ethnography* 7, no. 3 (1978): 337–58. See pp. 343–44.

70. Miller, *Collective Behavior and Collective Action*, 3rd ed., p. 199; Kerbo, Marshall, and Holley, "Reestablishing 'Gemeinschaft?'" p. 338.

71. Joel Whitburn, *The Billboard Book of Top 40 Country Hits: 1944–2006*, 2nd ed. (Menomonee Falls, WI: Record Research, 2006), p. 220.

72. Miller, *Collective Behavior and Collective Action*, 3rd ed., p. 199.

73. Ibid., pp. 199–200.

74. Kerbo, Marshall, and Holley, "Reestablishing 'Gemeinschaft'?" p. 347.

75. Ibid.

76. Kelly Sagert, *The 1970s: American Popular Culture through History* (Westport, CT: Greenwood Publishing, 2007), p. 128.

77. "Pet Rock Total Sales Soar Past One Million," *Gazette* (Montreal, Canada), December 26, 1975, p. 27.

78. Carol Olten, "Pet Craze Is Nowhere near Rock Bottom," *Beaver County (PA) Times*, April 14, 1976, p. 4A.

79. "Pet Rock Fad Falls," *Daytona Beach (FL) Morning Journal*, December 21, 1976, p. 5A.

CHAPTER 3: CRAZES

1. *The Concise Oxford Dictionary*, 10th ed., ed. Judy Pearsall (Oxford: Oxford University Press, 1999), p. 334; Erich Goode, *Sociology*, 2nd ed. (New York: Harcourt Brace Jovanovich, 1992), p. 516.

2. Justin Hayes, *The Unexpected Evolution of Language* (Avon, MA: Adams Media, 2012), pp. 71–72.

3. *The Century Dictionary and Cyclopedia*, ed. William Dwight Whitney (New York: Century, 1902).

4. Vladimir Mikhailovich Bekhterev, *Suggestion and Its Role in Social Life*, 3rd ed., trans. Tzvetanka Dobreva-Martinova (New Brunswick, NJ: Transaction Publishers, 1998 [1908]), pp. 96–97.

5. Richard T. LaPiere, *Collective Behavior* (New York: McGraw-Hill, 1938), p. 512.

6. Larry D. Neal, ed., "How the South Sea Bubble Was Blown Up and Burst: A New Look at Old Data," pp. 33–56, in *Crashes and Panics: The Lessons from History*, ed. Eugene N. White (Homewood, IL: Business One Irwin, 1990).

7. LaPiere, *Collective Behavior*, p. 512.

8. Robert E. Park and Ernest W. Burgess, *Introduction to the Science of Sociology* (Chicago: University of Chicago Press, 1969), pp. 895–98.

9. E. A. Ross, *Social Psychology* (New York: Macmillan, 1916), pp. 65–76.

10. Neil J. Smelser, *Theory of Collective Behavior* (New York: Free Press, 1965).

11. Charles Mackay, *Memoirs of Extraordinary Popular Delusions and the Madness of Crowds*, vol. 1, 2nd ed. (London: Office of the National Illustrated Library, 1852), p. 90.

12. Ibid., p. 95.

13. Ibid., p. 92.

14. Peter M. Garber, "Tulipmania," *Journal of Political Economy* 97 (1989): 535–60; Peter M. Garber, "Who Put the Mania in the Tulip Mania?" pp. 3–32, in White, *Crashes and Panics*.

15. Peter M. Garber, *Famous First Bubbles: The Fundamentals of Early Manias* (Cambridge, MA: MIT Press, 2000).

16. Ibid., p. 83.

17. Bekhterev, *Suggestion*, p. 74.

18. Norman Cohn, *The Pursuit of the Millennium* (Fair Lawn, NJ: Essential Books, 1957), p. 127.

19. Charles Mackay, *Memoirs of Extraordinary Popular Delusions and the Madness of Crowds*, vol. 2 (London: Office of the National Illustrated Library, 1852), p. 203.

20. Ibid., p. 205.

21. Ibid., pp. 205–206.

22. Ibid., p. 215.

23. Ibid., p. 216.

24. Ronald A. Knox, *Enthusiasm: A Chapter in the History of Religion* (London: Oxford University Press, 1950), pp. 560–61.

25. George Rosen, "Psychopathology in the Social Process: Dance Frenzies, Demonic Possession, Revival Movements and Similar So-Called Psychic Epidemics, an Interpretation," *Bulletin of the History of Medicine* 36 (1962): 13–44. See p. 35.

26. Hilary Evans, *Visions, Apparitions, Alien Visitors: A Comparative Study of the Entity Enigma* (London: Book Club Associates, 1984), p. 223.

27. Ibid., p. 224.

28. Andrew Lang, "From India to Mars," *Evening News* (Sydney, Australia), August 25, 1900, p. 3.

29. Ibid.

30. Theo Paijmans, "From Paddington to the Planet Mars," Blasts from the Past no. 51, *Fortean Times*, no. 315, June 2014, pp. 28–29.

31. Joseph Dunninger, "Seers and Suckers—No. 4 Martian Cults Exploited," *San Antonio (TX) Light*, July 9, 1944.

32. Ibid.

33. John Clucas Cannell, *The Secrets of Houdini* (Mineola, NY: Dover, 1973 [1931]), p. 63.

34. Ibid., pp. 64–65.

35. Ibid., pp. 87–88.

36. Ruth Brandon, *The Spiritualists* (London: Weidenfeld & Nicolson, 1983), p. 281.

37. Cannell, *Secrets of Houdini*, p. 98.

38. Brandon, *Spiritualists*, p. 277.

39. Ibid., p. 281.

40. Paul Sann, *Fads, Follies and Delusions of the American People* (New York: Crown, 1967), p. 140.

41. Robert K. Utley, *The Last Days of the Sioux Nation* (New Haven, CT: Yale University Press, 1963).

42. Serena Nanda and Richard Warms, *Culture Counts: A Concise Introduction to Cultural Anthropology* (Belmont, CA: Wadsworth, 2009), p. 279; Emily A. Schultz and Robert H. Lavenda, *Anthropology: A Perspective on Human Culture* (Mountain View, CA: Mayfield Publishing, 1995), p. 545; James Davidson, Pedro Castillo, and Michael Stoff, *The American Nation* (Upper Saddle River, NJ: Prentice-Hall, 2000), pp. 519–20; Paul Boyer, ed., *The Oxford Companion to United States History* (New York: Oxford University Press, 2000), p. 851.

43. David L. Miller, *Introduction to Collective Behavior and Collective Action*, 2nd ed. (Prospect Heights, IL: Waveland, 2000), p. 423.

44. See also: Schultz and Lavenda, *Anthropology*, p. 545; Davidson, Castillo, and Stoff, *American Nation*, pp. 519–20.

45. Joseph Bulgatz, *Ponzi Schemes, Invaders from Mars & More Extraordinary Popular Delusions and the Madness of Crowds* (New York: Harmony Books, 1992), p. 51.

46. Frederick Lewis Allen, *Only Yesterday: An Informal History of the 1920s* (New York: John Wiley and Sons, 1997 [1932]), p. 209.

47. Ibid.

48. Angus Gunn, *Encyclopedia of Disasters: Environmental Catastrophes and Human Tragedies* (Westport, CT: Greenwood, 2008), pp. 307–309.

49. John Kenneth Galbraith, *The Great Crash, 1929* (Boston: Houghton Mifflin, 1961), pp. 8–9.

50. For an excellent overview of this movement, see Friedrich Steinbauer, *Melanesian Cargo Cults*, trans. Max Wohlwill (London: George Prior Publishers, 1979), pp. 88–90.

51. J. Graham Miller, "Naked Cult in Central West Santo," *Journal of the Polynesian Society* 57, no. 4 (1948): 330–41.

52. Steinbauer, *Melanesian Cargo Cults*, pp. 88–90.

53. Gottfried Oosterwal, "Cargo Cults as Missionary Challenge," *International Review of Mission* 56, no. 224 (1967): 469–77. See p. 469.

54. Dyron Daughrity, *The Changing World of Christianity: The Global History of a Borderless Religion* (New York: Lang Publishing, 2010), p. 236.

55. John Hamilton, "Where Philip Is God," *Sydney Morning Herald*, December 1, 1983, p. 9. While accounts differ as to how the prince came to be worshipped as a god, I use the information given by journalist John Hamilton because he traveled to the island and interviewed the key leaders of the movement. This is more reliable than accounts given by armchair researchers using questionable sources.

56. Ibid.

57. Ibid.

58. Matthew Baylis, "The Tribe That Worships Prince Philip," *Daily Express* (London), October 26, 2013, http://www.express.co.uk/news/royal/439264/The-Tribe-that-worships-Prince-Philip (accessed January 14, 2015).

59. Michelle Locke, "Heaven's Gate Members on Sci-Fi Trip to Paradise," *Southeast Missourian* (Cape Girardeau, MO), March 31, 1997, pp. 1–2. See p. 2.

60. "Suicides May Be Harbinger of Bizarre Behavior as Millennium Approaches," *Tuscaloosa (AL) News*, March 29, 1997, p. 1D.

61. Bill Hoffmann and Cathy Burke, *Heaven's Gate: Cult Suicide in San Diego* (New York: HarperCollins, 1997).

62. Locke, "Heaven's Gate," p. 2.

63. Frederick E. Pope, "The Psychic Infection of Heaven's Gate," *Humanist* 57, no. 4 (1997): 41–42. See p. 41.

64. Martin Gardner, "Heaven's Gate: The UFO Cult of Bo and Peep," *Skeptical Inquirer* 21, no. 4 (1997): 15–17. See p. 17.

65. Ibid.

66. James Rosenfield, "The Cultural Logic of Heaven's Gate," *American Demographics* 19, no. 12 (1997): 50.

67. Benjamin E. Zeller, "Extraterrestrial Biblical Hermeneutics and the Making of Heaven's Gate," *Nova Religio* 14, no. 2 (2010): 34–60. See p. 38.

68. Ibid., p. 41.

69. Ronald Steel, "Ordinary People: Heaven's Gate Suicides," *New Republic* 216, no. 16 (April 21, 1997): 25.

70. Mark Muesse, "Religious Studies and 'Heaven's Gate': Making the Strange Familiar and the Familiar Strange," *Chronicle of Higher Education* 43, no. 33 (April 25, 1997): B6–B7. See p. B7.

71. Ibid., p. B7.

72. Ibid.

CHAPTER 4: MANIAS

1. Young cited in K. L. Roberts, comp., *Hoyt's New Cyclopedia of Practical Quotations* (Funk & Wagnalls: New York, 1940), p. 67.

2. Carl Jung, *Flying Saucers: A Modern Myth of Things Seen in the Sky* (New York: Harcourt, Brace & World, 1959).

3. Thomas Edward Bullard, "UFO Abduction Reports: The Supernatural Kidnap Narrative Returns in Technological Guise," *Journal of American Folklore* 102, no. 404 (1989): 147–70. See p. 168.

4. Robert E. Bartholomew, "The Symbolic Significance of Modern Myths," *Skeptical Inquirer* 15 (1991): 430–31.

5. Colm Tóibín, *Moving Statues in Ireland: Seeing Is Believing* (County Laois, Ireland: Pilgrim, 1985).

6. Tim Ryan and Jurek Kirakowski, *Ballinspittle: Moving Statues and Faith* (Cork, Ireland: Mercier, 1985), p. 53.

7. J. Sabini, *Social Psychology* (New York: W. W. Norton, 1992), pp. 24–25.

8. M. Sherif, *The Psychology of Social Norms* (New York: Harper & Row, 1936).

9. R. Beeson, "The Improbable Primate and the Modern Myth," pp. 166–95, in *The Scientist Looks at the Sasquatch II*, ed. G. Krantz and R. Sprague (Moscow: University Press of Idaho, 1979), p. 180.

10. Robert E. Bartholomew, "Technology and Mass Delusion: Remembering Edison's 'Electric Star' Hysteria," *Technology: Journal of the Franklin Institute* 335A, no. 1 (1998): 65–67.

11. Robert E. Bartholomew and Steven Whalen, "The Great New England Airship

Hoax of 1909," *New England Quarterly* 75, no. 3 (2002): 466–76; Robert E. Bartholomew, "Two Mass Delusions in New England: 'Light Bulb' Mania of 1897, and the Great Airship Hoax of 1909–1910," *New England Journal of Skepticism* 1, no. 2 (1998): 10–13.

12. Based on information recounted by astronomer Gerard Tsonakwa, a member of the Abenaki tribe of Southern Québec, as chronicled by the Fairbanks Museum and Planetarium (St. Johnsbury, VT), in *Pathways to History Curriculum Guide II*, "Misingwe ta Gitaskogak: The Masked Hunter and the Great Serpent (Mars and Scorpio) Abenaki Nation," reprinted from a special section of the *Arizona Daily Star* titled "Return to Mars," April 6, 2001. There were many other Abenaki names for Lake Champlain, including *bitawbágw* (double lake) and *sitoâmbogook* (double bay). See Gordon M. Day, *In Search of New England's Native Past: Selected Essays by Gordon Day*, ed. Michael K. Foster and William Cowan (Amherst: University of Massachusetts Press, 1998), pp. 240–41.

13. William A. Haviland and Marjory W. Power, *The Original Vermonters: Native Inhabitants Past and Present* (Hanover, NH: University Press of New England, 1994), p. 194; Thomas D. S. Bassett, *The God of the Hills: Piety and Society in Nineteenth Century Vermont* (Montpelier: Vermont Historical Society, 2000), p. 5; Philip M. Parker, *Webster's Abenaki-English Dictionary Thesaurus Dictionary* (Las Vegas, NV: ICON Group International, 2008), p. 5.

14. Adrienne Mayor, *Fossil Legends of the First Americans* (Princeton, NJ: Princeton University Press, 2005), p. 13.

15. "Lake Champlain," *Public Advertiser* (NY), May 18, 1808, p. 2. See also: "Lake Champlain," *Republican Star* (MD), May 31, 1808, p. 2.

16. Robert E. Bartholomew, *The Untold Story of Champ: A Social History of America's Loch Ness Monster* (Albany: State University of New York Press, 2012).

17. Majorie Porter, "Essex County Notes," *Plattsburgh Press-Republican*, February 4, 1966.

18. *Whitehall (NY) Times*, July 9, 1873.

19. "Lake Champlain Sea Serpent 'Seen' Again near Rouses Point Bridge Last Thursday," *North Countryman*, September 9, 1937.

20. Ibid.

21. Bartholomew, *Untold Story of Champ*, p. 166.

22. Marjorie L. Porter, "The Champlain Monster," *Vermont Life* 24, no. 4 (1970): 47–50. Most historians list his birth as 1567, although a few contend that it is open to debate. See, for instance, Susan Castillo and Ivy Schweitzer, *The Literatures of Colonial America: An Anthology* (Malden, MA: Blackwell, 2001), p. 99.

23. Ibid.

24. Samuel de Champlain, *Voyages of Samuel de Champlain*, vol. 2, *1604–1610*, trans. Charles Pomeroy Otis, with historical illustrations and a memoir by Charles F. Slafter (New York: Ben Franklin, 1966), at http://www.canadachannel.ca/ champlain/index.php/ Samuel_de_Champlain%2C_Voyages%2C_Vol._II_1608–1612 (accessed September 12, 2010).

25. Connie Pope publicly pointed this out in "Rotary News: Unusual Topic Chosen by Guest Speaker," *Chateaugay (NY) Record*, June 17, 1971. This was followed by John Ross in his article "Sidelight on History," *North Countryman* (NY), August 23, 1978, p. 16. This was also noted by Michel Meurger and Claude Gagnon, *Monstres des Lacs du Québec: Mythes et Troublantes Réalités* (Montreal: Stanké, 1982). In 1988, the book was updated and translated into English as *Lake Monster Traditions: A Cross Cultural Analysis* (London: Fortean Times Publishing).

26. Christopher Morgan and Edmund B. O'Callaghan, *The Documentary History of the State of New York*, vol. 3 (Albany, NY: Weed, Parsons, 1850), pp. 5, 6, citing a translation of Champlain's original log.

27. "The MonsterQuest Look at the Lake Champlain Monster," MonsterQuest Review, July 9, 2009, http://monsterquestreview.blogspot.com/2009/07/monsterquest -look-at-lake-champlain.html (accessed December 25, 2010).

28. Dick Teresi, "Monster of the Tub," *Discover* 19, no. 4 (April 1998): 87–92.

29. Bartholomew, *Untold Story of Champ*, pp. 196–97.

30. "Great Astronomical Discoveries Lately Made by Sir John Herschel, L.L.D, F.R.S, &c. at the Cape of Good Hope," *New York Sun*, August 25, 1835, p. 2.

31. "Great Astronomical Discoveries Lately Made by Sir John Herschel," *New York Sun*, August 26, 1835.

32. "Great Astronomical Discoveries Lately Made by Sir John Herschel," *New York Sun*, August 27, 1835.

33. "Great Astronomical Discoveries Lately Made by Sir John Herschel," *New York Sun*, August 28, 1835.

34. "Great Astronomical Discoveries Lately Made by Sir John Herschel," *New York Sun*, August 31, 1835.

35. Asa Greene, *A Glance at New York* (New York: A. Greene, 1837), p. 246.

36. Ibid., p. 245.

37. Joseph Bulgatz, *Ponzi Schemes, Invaders from Mars & More Extraordinary Popular Delusions and the Madness of Crowds* (New York: Harmony Books, 1992), p. 147.

38. Hy Turner, *When Giants Ruled: The Story of Park Row, New York's Great Newspaper Street* (New York: Fordham University Press, 1999), p. 8.

39. Lynda Walsh, *Sins against Science: The Scientific Media Hoaxes of Poe, Twain, and Others* (Albany: State University of New York Press, 2006), p. 246.

40. Ibid., p. 245.

41. Turner, *When Giants Ruled*, p. 9.

42. Bulgatz, *Ponzi Schemes*, p. 150.

43. Brian Thornton, "The Moon Hoax: Debates about Ethics in 1835 New York Newspapers," *Journal of Mass Media Ethics* 15, no. 2 (2000): 89–100.

44. Walsh, *Sins against Science*, p. 245.

45. "There Is No String to It. Venus, the Evening Star," *Daily Tribune* (Iron Mountain, MI), March 30, 1897, p. 3.

46. "See That Balloon? Everybody Is Staring at Venus and Venus Is Fooling Everybody," *Bangor (ME) Daily Commercial*, April 2, 1897, p. 7.

47. Ibid.

48. "A Light in the East," *Times and Democrat* (Orangeburg, SC), April 7, 1897, p. 4, citing the *Augusta (ME) Chronicle*.

49. Ivan Frederick Clarke, "American Anticipations: The First of the Futurists," *Futures* 18, no. 4 (1986): 584–96.

50. Matthew Josephson, *Edison: A Biography* (London: Eyre & Spottiswoode, 1961), p. 170.

51. Margaret Staggs, "The Miracle of Sabana Grande," *San Juan Review* 1, no. 4 (1964): 16–18. See p. 16.

52. Tamotsu Shibutani, *Improvised News: A Sociological Study of Rumor* (Indianapolis, IN: Bobbs-Merrill, 1966), p. 115.

53. Ibid.

54. Staggs, "Miracle of Sabana Grande," p. 17.

55. Ibid., p. 18.

56. Melvin M. Tumin and Arnold S. Feldman, "The Miracle at Sabana Grande," *Public Opinion Quarterly* 19 (1955): 124–39.

57. Staggs, "Miracle of Sabana Grande," p. 17.

58. Bob Greene, "They Come to Worship at the Tortilla Shrine," *Free Lance-Star* (Fredericksburg, VA), July 17, 1978, p. 2.

59. Ibid.

60. "Shrine of the Miracle Tortilla," RoadsideAmerica.com, http://www.roadsideamerica.com/story/10166 (accessed January 17, 2015).

61. "Believers See Christ's Image on Soybean Tank," *Mohave Daily Miner* (Kingman, AZ), August 21, 1986, p. 7.

62. Ibid.

63. Leonard Zusne and Warren Jones, *Anomalistic Psychology: A Study of Magical Thinking*, 2nd ed. (New York: Psychology, 2014), p. 77.

64. Ibid.

65. Vinita Srivastava, "Milking a Miracle," *Village Voice* (NY), October 17, 1995, pp. 12, 16.

66. K. S. Jayaraman, "India's 'Milk Miracle' Is Hard to Swallow," *Nature* 377, no. 6547 (September 28, 1995): 280.

67. Joe Nickell, "Milk-Drinking Idols," *Skeptical Inquirer* 20, no. 2 (1996): 7.

68. Ibid.

69. "Milk-Drinking Idols Draw Millions in India," *Syracuse (NY) Post-Standard*, September 22, 1995, p. 1D.

70. Srivastava, "Milking a Miracle," p. 12; Anonymous, "Milk Miracle Makes Masses Mental," *Skeptic* 3, no. 4 (1995): 13.

71. Anil Bhanot, "How I Witnessed a Miracle," *New Statesman*, January 22, 2007, http://www.newstatesman.com/blogs/the-faith-column/2007/01/lord-shiva-hinduism-milk (accessed January 9, 2014).

CHAPTER 5: URBAN LEGENDS

1. Thomas Craughwell, *Urban Legends: 666 Absolutely True Stories That Happened to a Friend . . . of a Friend . . . of a Friend* (New York: Black Dog & Leventhal, 2005), p. 15.

2. See: Jan Harold Brunvand, *Encyclopedia of Urban Legends* (Santa Barbara, CA: ABC-CLIO, 2012), pp. 173–77.

3. Jan Harold Brunvand, *The Vanishing Hitchhiker: American Urban Legends and Their Meanings* (New York: W. W. Norton, 1981).

4. Ibid., p. 21.

5. Nicholas DiFonzo and Prashant Bordia, "Rumor, Gossip and Urban Legends," *Diogenes* 213 (2007): 19–35. See p. 32.

6. Erich Goode, *Collective Behavior* (New York: Harcourt Brace Jovanovich, 1992), pp. 324–30.

7. Brunvand, *Vanishing Hitchhiker*, pp. 160–71; Gary Allen Fine, "Mercantile Legends and the World Economy: Dangerous Imports from the Third World," *Western Folklore* 48 (1989): 169–77.

8. Jeffrey S. Victor, *Satanic Panic: The Creation of a Contemporary Legend* (Chicago: Open Court, 1993); Jeffrey S. Victor, "The Dynamics of Rumor-Panics about Satanic Cults," pp. 221–36, in *The Satanism Scare*, ed. James Richardson, Joel Best, and David Bromley (New York: Aldine de Gruyter, 1991); R. Hicks, "Police Pursuit of Satanic Crime Part II: The Satanic Conspiracy and Urban Legends," *Skeptical Inquirer* 14 (1990): 378–89.

9. Jeffrey S. Victor, "The Search for Scapegoat Deviants," *Humanist* (September–October, 1992): 10–13. See p. 13.

10. Michael Georges and Michael Owen Jones, *Folkloristics: An Introduction* (Bloomington: Indiana University Press, 1995), p. 167.

11. Todd D. Donavan, John C. Mowen, and Goutam Chakraborty, "Urban Legends: Diffusion Processes and the Exchange of Resources," *Journal of Consumer Marketing* 18, no. 6 (2001): 521–31. See p. 523.

12. Ibid.

13. Donna Wyckoff, "Why a Legend? Contemporary Legends as Community Ritual," *Contemporary Legend* 3 (1993): 1–36. See p. 6.

14. Pamela Donovan, "How Idle Is Idle Talk? One Hundred Years of Rumor Research," *Diogenes* 54, no. 1 (2007): 159–82. See p. 162.

15. Brunvand, *Vanishing Hitchhiker*; Jan Harold Brunvand, *The Choking Doberman and Other 'New' Urban Legends* (New York: W. W. Norton, 1984); Jan Harold Brunvand, *Curses! Broiled Again! The Hottest Urban Legends Going* (New York: W. W. Norton, 1989).

16. Donovan, "How Idle Is Idle Talk?" p. 168.

17. Jan Harold Brunvand, *The Mexican Pet* (Ontario: Penguin, 1986), pp. 49–50.

18. Jan Harold Brunvand, *The Baby Train and Other Lusty Urban Legends* (New York: W. W. Norton, 1993), p. 251.

19. Michael Goss, *The Evidence for Phantom Hitch-Hikers* (Wellingborough, UK: Aquarian, 1984), p. 90.

20. Elizabeth Tucker, *Haunted Southern Tier* (Charleston, SC: Haunted America, 2011), p. 95.

21. Ibid., pp. 95–97.

22. W. McNeil and William Clements, *Arkansas Folklore Sourcebook* (Fayetteville: University of Arkansas Press, 1992), p. 9.

23. Gail De Vos, *Tales, Rumors, and Gossip: Exploring Contemporary Folk Literature in Grades 7–12* (Westport, CT: Greenwood, 1996), p. 351.

24. Ibid.

25. Alan Dundes, *Bloody Mary in the Mirror: Essays in Psychoanalytic Folkloristics* (Jackson: University of Mississippi Press, 2002), p. 89.

26. "Alligator Found in Uptown Sewer," *New York Times*, February 10, 1935, p. 29F.

27. "Mayer's Saurian," *Dallas Morning News*, October 12, 1886, p. 8; "A Curious Sewer Resident," *Philadelphia Inquirer*, November 8, 1886, p. 3.

28. "Lacerta Carnegiensis in Water Pipe Two Years," *Stevens Point (WI) Daily Journal*, October 2, 1913, p. 7.

29. *Mansfield (OH) News*, May 7, 1919, p. 15.

30. Anna Quindlen, "Debunking the Myth of Subterranean Saurians," *New York Times*, May 19, 1982, p. 3B.

31. Mark Barber, *Urban Legends: An Investigation into the Truth behind the Myth* (Kent Town, South Australia: Wakefield, 2007), p. 113.

32. Jean-Noel Kapferer, *Rumors: Uses, Interpretations, and Images* (New Brunswick, NJ: Transaction, 1990), p. 159.

33. Gary Turbak, "The Truth about Urban Legends," *Rotarian* 173, no. 3 (September, 1988): 22–25. See p. 24.

34. Steve Roud, *London Lore: The Legends and Traditions of the World's Most Vibrant City* (London: Arrow Books, 2008), p. 220.

35. Ben Ikenson, *Patents: Ingenious Inventions: How They Work and How They Came to Be* (New York: Black Dog & Leventhal, 2004), p. 214.

36. Craughwell, *Urban Legends*, pp. 252–53.

37. R. C. Alexander, J. A. Surrell, and S. D. Cohle, "Microwave Oven Burns to Children: An Unusual Manifestation of Child Abuse," *Pediatrics* 79, no. 2 (1987): 255–60.

38. "Ohio Woman Indicted . . . Accused of Putting Baby in Microwave," *Ludington Daily News*, December 8, 2006, p. 5B.

39. "Woman Who Killed Baby in Microwave Sentenced to 5 Years," *Daily News* (Bowling Green, KY), December 14, 2000, p. 14A.

40. Jack Nachbar and Kevin Lause, *Popular Culture: An Introductory Text* (Madison: University of Wisconsin Press, 1992), p. 63.

41. Jan Harold Brunvand, "New Legends for Old," pp. 56–67, in *Popular Culture: An Introductory Text*, ed. Jack Nachbar and Kevin Lause (Madison: University of Wisconsin Press, 1992), p. 60.

42. Ibid.

43. Simon J. Bonner, *Campus Traditions: Folklore from the Old-Time College to the Modern Mega University* (Jackson: University Press of Mississippi, 2012), p. 353.

44. Linda Dégh, *Legend and Belief: Dialectics of a Folklore Genre* (Bloomington: Indiana University Press, 2001), p. 106.

45. Brunvand, *Vanishing Hitchhiker*, p. 82.

46. Gary Alan Fine, *Manufacturing Tales: Sex and Money in Contemporary Legends* (Knoxville: University of Tennessee Press, 1992), p. 132.

47. Ibid., p. 129.

48. "McDonald's Customer Gets Chicken Head," ABCNews.com, November 30, 2000, http://abcnews.go.com/US/story?id=94840&page=1 (accessed January 4, 2014).

49. Jan Harold Brunvand, "Kidnappers in the Restroom," *Deseret News* (Salt Lake City, UT), July 15, 1987, p. 4-WV.

50. Lauren Ritchie, "Here's a Fantasy Disney Hates, Fib about Park Kidnapping Grows Like Pinocchio's Nose," *Orlando (FL) Sentinel*, August 4, 1989.

51. Ibid.

52. Ibid.

53. Joseph Bosco, "The Hong Kong Ocean Park Kidnapping Rumor," *Ethnology* 50, no. 2 (2011): 135–51. See p. 135.

54. Ibid., p. 149.

55. Pamela Donovan, "Crime Legends in a New Medium: Fact, Fiction and Loss of Authority," *Theoretical Criminology* 6, no. 2 (2002): 189–215. See p. 203.

56. Ibid.

57. Ole Rekdal, "Academic Urban Legends," *Social Studies of Science* 44, no. 4 (2014): 638–54. See p. 640.

58. Ibid., p. 647.

59. Ibid., p. 651.

60. Jan Harold Brunvand, "'Lights Out!' A Faxlore Phenomenon," *Skeptical Inquirer* 19, no. 2 (March–April, 1995): 32–37. See p. 33.

61. Ibid., p. 35.

CHAPTER 6: STAMPEDES AND PANICS

1. Dirk Helbing, Illés Farkas, and Tamás Vicsek, "Simulating Dynamical Features of Escape Panic," *Nature* 407, no. 6803 (2000): 487–90.

2. Diana Kendall, *Sociology in Our Time* (Stamford, CT: Cengage, 2014), p. 617.

3. G. A. Frank and C. O. Dorso, "Room Evacuation in the Presence of an Obstacle," *Physica A* 390, no. 11 (2001): 2135–45.

4. Lee Clarke, "Panic: Myth or Reality," *Contexts* 1, no. 3 (2002): 21–26. See p. 22.

5. William A. Sherden, *Best Laid Plans: The Tyranny of Unintended Consequences and How to Avoid Them* (Santa Barbara, CA: ABC-CLIO, 2011), p. 32.

6. Robert E. Bartholomew, "A Brief History of 'Mass Hysteria' in Australia," *Skeptic* (Australia), (1992): 23–26.

7. Charles Mackay, *Memoirs of Extraordinary Popular Delusions*, vol. 1 (London: Richard Bentley, 1841), p. 172.

8. Ibid.

9. James L. Baggett, "'Keep Still': Booker T. Washington and the Shiloh Church Tragedy," *Alabama Heritage* 95 (Winter 2010): 20–25.

10. "Hundred Fifteen Killed," *Boston Evening Transcript*, September 20, 1902, p. 3.

11. Baggett, "'Keep Still,'" p. 22.

12. "Hundred Fifteen Killed."

13. Baggett, "'Keep Still,'" p. 24.

14. Ibid., p. 23.

15. Ibid., p. 24.

16. Ibid.

17. Ibid.

18. Jeffrey Tubbs and Brian Meacham, *Egress Design Solutions* (Hoboken, NJ: John Wiley, 2007), pp. 54–57.

19. Duane P. Schultz, *Panic Behavior: Discussion and Readings* (New York: Random House, 1964), p. 9.

20. Angus Gunn, *Encyclopedia of Disasters: Environmental Catastrophes and Human Tragedies* (Westport, CT: Greenwood, 2008), pp. 202–203.

21. "Mars Raiders Caused Quito Panic; Mob Burns Radio Plant, Kills 15," *New York Times*, February 14, 1949, pp. 1, 7. Quote appears on p. 1.

22. Ibid.

23. Ibid.

24. Ibid.

25. "Mob Kills 15," *Modesto (CA) Bee*, February 14, 1949, p. 1.

26. "Wolf, Wolf," *Newsweek* 33, no. 8 (February 21, 1949), p. 44.

27. "Mob Kills 15," p. 1.

28. "'Invasion from Mars,'" *Times of London*, February 14, 1949, p. 4; Anonymous, "When You Say That, Smile," *Commonweal XLIX*, no. 20:483–84.

29. "Radio: Boomerang in Ecuador: A Mob Takes Revenge," *Independent Record* (Sedalia, MO), February 20, 1949; "Mob Kills 15," p. 1.

30. Kenneth D. MacHarg, "War of the Worlds—Ecuadorian Style," *Monitoring Times*, September 25, 2000, http://www.missionaryjournalist.net/images/Ecuador-_War _of_the_Worlds.pdf (accessed January 15, 2015).

31. "Jittery World," *Portland (ME) Press Herald*, February 15, 1949.

32. Associated Press, "Two Officials Indicted," *Times of London*, February 15, 1949, p. 4.

33. "Mars Raiders Caused Quito Panic."

34. Enrique Tovar, "The Martians Cause Panic," *La Nación* (Costa Rica), March 3, 1996.

35. "20 Dead in Quito Riot," *New York Times*, February 15, 1949, p. 5; Anonymous, "Quito Holds 3 for 'Mars' Script," *New York Times*, February 16, 1949, p. 15.

36. "Soccer Riot Quotient High," *Lawrence (KS) Journal-World*, August 28, 1975, p. 20.

37. John Nauright and Charles Parrish, *Sports around the World: History, Culture, and Practice* (Santa Barbara, CA: ABC-CLIO, 2012), p. 97.

38. "Stadium Panic Death Toll at 328," *Amsterdam (NY) Evening Recorder and Daily Democrat*, May 26, 1964, p. 1.

39. Robert Bianchi, *Guests of God: Pilgrimage and Politics in the Islamic World* (Oxford: Oxford University Press, 2004), p. 11.

40. Donelson Forsyth, *Group Dynamics*, 5th ed. (Belmont, CA: Wadsworth, 2009), p. 510.

41. Julius Ballanco, "The Night Club Disasters," *PM Engineer* 9, no. 4 (2003): 20; Robert McGill, "Stage Fright," *Fire Chief* 47, no. 4 (2003): 26–29; Lisa Nadile, "E2," *National Fire Protection Association Journal* 102, no 2 (2008): 68–73, see p. 69.

42. Nadile, "E2," p. 69.

43. Ibid. While later claiming that this decision was revered, eyewitnesses say that at least one door was locked when the panic broke out.

44. Robert Siegel, "Georgia 'Invasion' Report Stirs Panic," *All Things Considered*, American National Public Radio (March 15, 2010).

45. Ivan Watson, "Fake Russian Invasion Broadcast Sparks Georgian Panic," *CNN News*, March 14, 2010, http://www.cnn.com/2010/WORLD/europe/03/14/georgia .invasion.scare/index.html (accessed April 6, 2010).

46. Ibid.

47. "False Report of Russian Invasion Spurs Panic," *Reuters News Agency*, March 14, 2010.

48. Shaun Walker, "Fellow Georgians, Russia Has Declared War, the President Is Dead . . . Er, Only Joking," *Independent* (UK), March 15, 2010.

49. Sarah Marcus, "Panic and Fury over Fake Television Report on Russian Invasion of Georgia," *Telegraph* (UK), March 15, 2010.

50. Siegel, "Georgia 'Invasion' Report Stirs Panic."

51. Luke Harding, "Russian Invasion Scare Sweeps Georgia after TV Hoax," *Guardian* (London), March 14, 2010.

52. Robert Bridge, "Georgia Suffering Backlash over Media-Staged Russian Attack," Russian Television, March 16, 2010, http://rt.com/politics/georgia-backlash-media -russian/ (accessed online January 15, 2015).

CHAPTER 7: ANXIETY HYSTERIA

1. K. T. Goh, "Epidemiological Enquiries into a School Outbreak of an Unusual Illness," *International Journal of Epidemiology* 16, no. 2 (1987): 265–70.

2. Y. K. Tam et al., "Psychological Epidemic in Hong Kong, Part 2: Psychological and Physiological Characteristics of Children Who Were Affected," *Acta Psychiatrica Scandinavica* 65 (1982): 437–49; S. W. Wong et al., "Psychological Epidemic in Hong Kong," *Acta Psychiatrica Scandinavica* 65 (1982): 421–36.

3. H. C. T. Smith and E. J. Eastham, "Outbreak of Abdominal Pain," *Lancet* 2 (1973): 956–58; *Daily Mirror* (London), July 10, 1972.

4. Y. Amin, E. Hamdi, and V. Eapen, "Mass Hysteria in an Arab Culture," *International Journal of Social Psychology* 43, no. 4 (1997): 303–306.

5. Randy Rockney and Thomas Lemke, "Response," letter, *Journal of Developmental and Behavioral Pediatrics* 15, no. 1 (1994): 64–65; Randy Rockney and T. Lemke, "Casualties from a Junior High School during the Persian Gulf War: Toxic Poisoning or Mass Hysteria?" *Journal of Developmental and Behavioral Pediatrics* 13 (1992): 339–42.

6. "On a Spot of Bother," *Sydney Morning Herald*, October 10, 1944, p. 1.

7. "Hypnotist Lectures Pupils, Gets Unexpected Reaction," *Wisconsin Rapids Daily Tribune*, January 17, 1953, p. 8.

8. CBC News Canada, "Hypnotized Students in Mass Trance Needed Emergency Help," June 15, 2012, http://news.ca.msn.com/top-stories/hypnotized-students-in-mass -trance-needed-emergency-help (accessed October 12, 2012).

9. "Exhaust Fumes and Hysteria KO Some 500 Students at Festival," *Stevens Point (WI) Daily Journal*, November 24, 1959, p. 2.

10. R. W. McLeod, "Merphos Poisoning or Mass Panic?" *Australian and New Zealand Journal of Psychiatry* 9:225–29. See p. 225.

11. "Hundreds Evacuated—Insecticide Fumes Spread in Parnell," *Auckland Star* (New Zealand), February 27, 1973, p. 1.

12. "4000 Flee Toxic Fumes—200 Ill after Chemical Drums Leak," *New Zealand Herald*, February 28, 1973, p. 1.

13. Ibid.

14. "First Sign Was Strange Smell," *New Zealand Herald*, February 28, 1973, p. 1.

15. "What an Anniversary Gift!" *Auckland Star*, February 28, 1973, p. 1.

16. McLeod, "Merphos Poisoning," p. 225.

17. "Ambulances for Pets," *New Zealand Herald*, February 28, 1973, p. 1.

18. "SPCA Provides Pet Haven," *Auckland Star* (New Zealand), February 28, 1973, p. 3.

19. "Empty Silence Follows Gas Leak into Parnell," *New Zealand Herald*, March 1, 1973, p. 2.

20. "Wind Sends Fumes into Wider Area—More in Hospital," *Auckland Star* (New Zealand), February 28, 1973, p. 1.

21. Ibid.

22. McLeod, "Merphos Poisoning," p. 227.

23. "Vessel Still Smells but Crew Blasé," *New Zealand Herald*, March 1, 1973, p. 1.

24. "Launched by the Nazis—Behind the News," *New Zealand Herald*, March 1, 1973, p. 1.

25. Ibid.

26. "Be It Ever So Humble," *New Zealand Herald*, March 2, 1973, p. 1.

27. "Contaminated Soil for Meola Rd Tip," *Auckland Star* (New Zealand), March 2, 1973, p. 1.

28. "Last of Parnell People Go Back," *Auckland Star* (New Zealand), March 3, 1973, p. 1.

29. "After-Effects of Fumes and Drugs Are Not Expected," *Auckland Star* (New Zealand), March 3, 1973, p. 3.

30. "All Clear Signal Given in Parnell," *New Zealand Herald*, March 5, 1973, p. 1.

31. McLeod, "Merphos Poisoning," p. 225.

32. Ibid., pp. 225–26.

33. Ibid., p. 226.

34. Ibid., p. 227.

35. Ibid., pp. 227–28.

36. "165 Girls Faint at Football Game; Mass Hysteria Grips 'Pep Squad,'" *New York Times*, September 14, 1952, p. 1.

37. "'Tigerettes' Faint Like Flies; Gridiron Looks Like Race Track," *Waukesha (WI) Daily Freeman*, September 13, 1952, p. 1.

38. "Mass Hysteria Sends 165 Girls to Hospital," *Daily Redlands (CA) Facts*, September 13, 1953, p. 1.

39. "160 H.S. Must Take Football Less Seriously," *Mt. Pleasant (IA) News*, September

13, 1952, p. 1; "Mass Hysteria Sends 165 Girls to Hospital," *Daily Redlands Facts* (Redlands, CA), September 13, 1952, p. 1.

40. R. Levine, "Epidemic Faintness and Syncope in a School Marching Band," *Journal of the American Medical Association* 238, no. 22 (1977): 2373–76. See pp. 2373–74.

41. Ibid., p. 2376.

42. Ibid.

43. P. Baker and D. Selvey, "Malathion-Induced Epidemic Hysteria in an Elementary School," *Veterinary and Human Toxicology* 34:156–60. See p. 157. It is difficult to fault the actions of the secretary, who chose to err on the side of caution.

44. Ibid., p. 160.

45. Ibid., p. 159.

46. Jordan Bonfante, "Medfly Madness," *Time*, January 8, 1990.

47. Baker and Selvey, "Malathion-Induced Epidemic," p. 159.

48. M. T. Yasamy, A. Bahramnezhad, and H. Ziaaddini, "Postvaccination Mass Psychogenic Illness in an Iranian Rural School," *East Mediterranean Health Journal* 5, no. 4 (1999): 710–15.

49. "'Pocket Monsters' Shocks TV Viewers into Convulsions," *Japan Times*, December 17, 1997; "Govt Launches Probe of 'Monster' Cartoon," *Yomiuri Shimbun*, December 18, 1997; "Psychiatrists Seek Animation Probe," *Yomiuri Shimbun*, December 19, 1997; Y. Yamashita et al., "Pocket Monsters Attacks Japanese Children via Media," *Annals of Neurology* 44, no. 3 (1998): 428; T. Hayashi et al., "Pocket Monsters, a Popular Television Cartoon, Attacks Japanese Children," *Annals of Neurology* 44, no. 3 (1998): 427; S. Tobimatsu et al., "Chromatic Sensitive Epilepsy: A Variant of Photosensitive Epilepsy," *Annals of Neurology* 45, no. 6 (1999): 790.

50. Benjamin Radford and Robert E. Bartholomew, "Pokémon Contagion: Photosensitive Epilepsy or Mass Psychogenic Illness?" *Southern Medical Journal* 94, no. 2 (February 2001): 197–204.

51. J. Snyder, "Cartoon Sickens Children," *American Broadcasting Corporation News*, December 17, 1997; J. Snyder, "'Monster' TV Cartoon Illness Mystifies Japan," Reuters, December 17, 1997; "Govt Launches Probe of 'Monster' Cartoon," *Yomiuri Shimbun*, December 18, 1997.

52. B. Nemery et al., "The Coca-Cola Incident in Belgium, June 1999," *Food and Chemical Toxicology* 40 (2000): 1657–67, see pp. 1657–58; Anne Gallay and Stefaan Demarest, *Case Control Study among Schoolchildren on the Incident Related to Complaints following the Consumption of Coca-Cola Company Products, Belgium, 1999*, Scientific Institute of Public Health, Epidemiology Unit (November 1999), http://www.iph.fgov.be/epidemio/epien/cocacola.htm (accessed April 10, 2002).

53. Nemery et al., "Coca-Cola Incident," p. 1658.

54. Ibid., pp. 1659–60.

55. Ibid., p. 1662.

56. B. Nemery et al., "Dioxins, Coca-Cola, and Mass Sociogenic Illness in Belgium," *Lancet* 354, no. 9172 (July 3, 1999): 77.

57. Ibid.

58. Ibid.

59. "Het Coca-Cola Incident Juni 1999 in België, Evaluatie van de Gebeurtenissen, Discussie, Besluit en Aanbevelingen," Ad Hoc Werkgroep van de Hoge Gezondheidsraad, Ministerie van Volksgezondheid, Brussels, March 2000, http://www.health.fgov.be/CSHHGR/Nederlands/Advies/Coca-colaNl.Htm (accessed April 10, 2013).

60. "Coke Adds Life, but Cannot Always Explain It," editorial, *Lancet* 354, no. 9174 (July 17, 1999): 173; Scott Leith, "3 Years after Recall, Coke Sales in Belgium at Their Best," *Atlanta Journal-Constitution*, August 26, 2002.

61. A. Bernard and S. Fierens, "The Belgian PCB/Dioxin Incident: A Critical Review of Health Risks Evaluations," *International Journal of Toxicology* 21, no. 5 (2002): 333–40.

62. P. J. Schepens et al., "Surprising Findings following a Belgian Food Contamination with Polychlorobiphenyls and Dioxins," *Environmental Health Perspectives* 109, no. 2 (2001): 101–103; N. van Larebeke et al., "The Belgian PCB and Dioxin Incident of January–June 1999: Exposure Data and Potential Impact on Health," *Environmental Health Perspectives* 109, no. 3 (2001): 265–73; K. Bester et al., "Preparation and Certification of a Reference Material on PCBs in Pig Fat and Its Application in Quality Control in Monitoring Laboratories during the Belgian 'PCB-Crisis,'" *Chemosphere* 44, no. 4 (2001): 529–37.

63. Nemery et al., "Dioxins," p. 77.

64. Nemery et al., "Coca-Cola Incident in Belgium," p. 1665.

65. Maureen Taylor, "Cultural Variance as a Challenge to Global Public Relations: A Case Study of the Coca-Cola Scare in Europe," *Public Relations Review* 26, no. 3 (2000): 277–93. See p. 289.

66. "Coke Adds Life, but Cannot Always Explain it."

67. Cassert Raf, "Belgian Students Back at School as Coke Sickness Still Unexplained," Associated Press, June 29, 1999.

68. S. T. Rataemane, L. U. Z. Rataemane, and J. Mohlahle, "Mass Hysteria among Learners at Mangaung Schools in Bloemfontein, South Africa," *International Journal of Psychosocial Rehabilitation* 6 (2000): 61–67.

69. "Passenger Said She Heard Man Make Cryptic Remark before B.C. Driver Fell Ill," CNews, May 26, 2004, http://cnews.canoe.ca/CNEWS/Canada/2004/ 05/25/472732-cp .html (accessed March 28, 2012).

70. "Highlights from Morning Media Briefing," Vancouver Police Department, May 26, 2004, http://www.City.Vancouver.Bc.Ca/Police/Media/Summaries/2004may26.html (accessed March 27, 2012); "Highlights from Morning Media Briefing," Vancouver Police

Department, May 28, 2004. "Update—Contaminated Bus Incident," Vancouver Police Department.

71. "Highlights from Morning Media Briefing," Vancouver Police Department, June 11, 2004, http://www.City.Vancouver.BC.CA/Police/Media/Summaries/2004may26. htm (accessed March 27, 2012).

72. Tiffany Crawford, "Mystery Illness—or Anxiety—on Vancouver Bus," Canadian Press Bureau, May 30, 2004, http://www.canada.com/search/story.html?id=57ecc518 -8b7c-4a8b-97b0-deb5b4c5074d (accessed March 27, 2005).

73. "Highlights from the Morning Press Conference, Update—Toxic Bus," Vancouver Police Department, June 25, 2004.

74. Tiffany Crawford, "Chemical Probable Cause of Bus Mystery," C-News Canada, June 25, 2004, http://cnews.canoe.ca/CNEWS/Canada/2004/06/25/pf-514533.html (accessed March 27, 2005).

75. "Dangerous Chemical Detected on 'Toxic Bus,'" CBC News, Canadian Broadcasting Corporation, June 25, 2004, http://vancouver.cbc.ca/regional/servlet/PrintStory ?filename=bc_bus20040625&region=Vancouver (accessed March 28, 2005).

76. Martin van den Hemel, "Toxic Bus Mystery Continues: Health Officer Not Convinced by Finding of Dangerous Chemical," *Richmond Review* (Richmond, BC, Canada), July 3–4, 2004.

77. Ibid.

78. Reka Gustafson, *Summary of Findings of Epidemiologic Investigation of Bus Incident* (Vancouver, BC, Canada: printed by author, 2004).

79. Stuart Myers, "Paramedics Did Not Suffer Mass Hysteria," letter, *Richmond Times* (Richmond, BC, Canada), July 8, 2004.

CHAPTER 8: CLASSICAL MASS HYSTERIA

1. Robert E. Bartholomew and Simon Wessely, "Protean Nature of Mass Sociogenic Illness: From Possessed Nuns to Chemical and Biological Terrorism Fears," *British Journal of Psychiatry* 180 (2002): 300–306.

2. Robert Darnton, *The Great Cat Massacre and Other Episodes in French Cultural History* (New York: Basic Books, 1984); Richard Robert Madden, *Phantasmata or Illusions and Fanaticisms of Protean Forms Productive of Great Evils* (London: T. C. Newby, 1857).

3. W. St. Clare, *Gentleman's Magazine* 57 (1787): 268.

4. Fritz Aemmer, "Eine Schulepidemie von Tremor Hystericus [A School Epidemic of Hysterical Tremor]," (Inaugural dissertation, Basel, 1893).

5. L. Hirt, "Eine Epidemie von Hysterischen Krampfen in einer Schleisischen Dorfschule" [An Epidemic of Hysterical Cramp in a Village School in Schleisischen], *Zeitschrift fur Schulgesundheitspflege* 6 (1893): 225–29. (Summary of an article by L. Hirt in *Berliner Klinische Wochenschrift*.)

6. Johannes Schoedel, "Uber Induzierte Krankheiten" [On Induced Illness], *Jahrbuch fur Kinderheilkunde* 14 (1906): 521–28.

7. Edgar A. Schuler and Vincent J. Parenton, "A Recent Epidemic of Hysteria in a Louisiana High School," *Journal of Social Psychology* 17 (1943): 221–35.

8. James A. Knight, Theodore I. Friedman, and Julie Sulianti, "Epidemic Hysteria: A Field Study," *American Journal of Public Health* 55 (1965): 858–65.

9. Silvio Benaim, John Horder, and Jennifer Anderson, "Hysterical Epidemic in a Classroom," *Psychological Medicine* 3 (1973): 366–73.

10. Manohar Dhadphale and S. P. Shaikh, "Epidemic Hysteria in a Zambian School: 'The Mysterious Madness' of Mwinilunga," *British Journal of Psychiatry* 142 (1983): 85–88. See p. 87.

11. G. J. Ebrahim, "Mass Hysteria in School Children, Notes on Three Outbreaks in East Africa," *Clinical Pediatrics* 7 (1968): 437–38. See p. 438.

12. Harvey Armstrong and Paul Patterson, "Seizures in Canadian Indian Children," *Canadian Psychiatric Association Journal* 20 (1975): 247–55.

13. Harry D. Eastwell, "A Pica Epidemic: A Price for Sedentarism among Australian Ex-Hunter-Gatherers," *Psychiatry* 42 (1979): 264–73.

14. Henry E. Sigerist, *Civilization and Disease* (Ithaca, NY: Cornell University Press, 1943), pp. 218–19.

15. Martha Baldwin, "Dancing with Spiders: Tarantism Is Early Modern Europe," pp. 163–91, in *Experiencing Nature: Proceedings of a Conference in Honor of Allen G. Debus*, ed. Paul Theerman and Karen Parshall (Dordrecht, the Netherlands: Kluwer, 1997), pp. 163–64.

16. Jean Fogo Russell, "Tarantism," *Medical History* 23 (1979): 404–25; Harold F. Gloyne, "Tarantism: Mass Hysterical Reaction to Spider Bite in the Middle Ages," *American Imago* 7 (1950): 29–42.

17. Ioan M. Lewis, "The Spider and the Pangolin," *Man*, n.s., 12 (1991): 513–25.

18. George Mora, "A Historical and Social-Psychiatric Appraisal of Tarantism," *Bulletin of the History of Medicine* 37 (1963): 417–39.

19. Russell, "Tarantism," p. 413.

20. Robert E. Bartholomew, "Tarantism, Dancing Mania and Demonopathy: The Anthro-Political Aspects of Mass Psychogenic Illness," *Psychological Medicine* 24 (1994): 281–306. See p. 281.

21. Justus Friedrich Hecker, *Epidemics of the Middle Ages*, trans. B. Babington (London: Sydenham Society, 1844), p. 127.

22. Darnton, *Great Cat Massacre*.

23. Rossell Hope Robbins, *The Encyclopedia of Witchcraft and Demonology* (New York: Crown, 1966), p. 393.

24. Ibid.

25. Darnton, *Great Cat Massacre*, p. 83.

26. Ibid., pp. 83–84. During the carnival of Burgundy, youths would pass around cats, and each person would tear out a chunk of fur and relish in the howls of agony (p. 83). At the St. John the Baptist festival, there were "cats tied up in bags, cats suspended from ropes, or cats burned at the stake. Parisians liked to incinerate cats by the sackful. [Others] preferred to chase a flaming cat through the streets" (pp. 83–84).

27. Stanley Cohen, *Folk Devils and Moral Panic* (New York: Routledge, 2002).

28. Cotton Mather, *The Life of Sir William Phips* (New York: Covici Friede, 1929 [1697]), p. 130.

29. John Hale, *A Modest Enquiry into the Nature of Witchcraft, and How Persons Guilty of That Crime May Be Convicted: And the Means Used for Their Discovery Discussed, Both Negatively and Affirmatively, According to Scripture and Experience* (Boston: B. Green and J. Allen, for Benjamin Eliot under the Town House, 1702), pp. 132–33.

30. Frances Hill, "Witchcraft in Salem," *Spectator* 278 (February 15, 1997): 35–36.

31. Paul Boyer and Stephen Nissenbaum, *Salem Possessed: The Social Origins of Witchcraft* (Cambridge, MA: Harvard University Press, 2003), p. 3.

32. Hilary Evans and Robert E. Bartholomew, *The Encyclopedia of Extraordinary Social Behavior* (New York: Anomalist Books, 2009), pp. 561–66; Isaac Reed, "Why Salem Made Sense: Culture, Gender, and the Puritan Persecution of Witchcraft," *Cultural Sociology* 1, no. 2 (2007): 209–34. See p. 212.

33. Linnda Caporael, "Ergotism: The Satan Loosed in Salem?" *Science* 192 (1976): 21–26.

34. Alan Woolf, "Witchcraft or Mycotoxin? The Salem Witch Trials," *Clinical Toxicology* 38, no. 4 (2000): 457–60; Nicholas P. Spanos and Jack Gottlieb, "Ergotism and the Salem Village Witch Trials," *Science* 194 (1976): 1930–34.

35. Richard Werking, "'Reformation Is Our Only Preservation': Cotton Mather and Salem Witchcraft," *William and Mary Quarterly* 29 (April 1972): 281–90. See p. 283.

36. Boyer and Nissenbaum, *Salem Possessed*, p. 12.

37. Peni Jo Renner, *Puritan Witch: The Redemption of Rebecca Eames* (Bloomington, IN: iUniverse, 2013), p. 49.

38. Boyer and Nissenbaum, *Salem Possessed*, p. 15.

39. Ibid., p. 14.

40. Ibid., p. 17.

41. Ibid.

42. Gretchen A. Adams, *The Specter of Salem: Remembering the Witch Trials in Nineteenth-Century America* (Chicago: University of Chicago Press, 2008), p. 16.

43. Louis Florentin Calmeil, *De la Folie, Consideree Sous le Point de Vue Pathologique, Philosophique, Historique et Judiciaire* [On the Crowd, Considerations on the Point of Pathology, Philosophy, History and Justice], vol. 2 (Paris: Baillere, 1845), p. 73.

44. Robbins, *Encyclopedia of Witchcraft and Demonology*, p. 320.

45. Ibid., pp. 319–23.

46. Madden, *Phantasmata*, p. 377.

47. Ibid., pp. 377–79.

48. Balthasar Bekker, *Le Monde Enchanté* (Amsterdam: P. Rotterdam, 1694), pp. 523–28.

49. Ibid.

50. Ibid.

51. St. Clare, p. 268.

52. Paul Richer, *Etudes Cliniques de la Grande Hystérie* (Paris: Delahaye et Lecrossnier, 1885), p. 852.

53. Hippolyte Blanc, *Le Merveilleux dans le Jansenisme &c.* (Paris: Plon, 1865), p. 279.

54. Catherine-Laurence Maire, *Les Possédées de Morzine* (Lyon, France: Presses Universitaires de Lyon, 1981), p. 40.

55. Ibid., p. 41.

56. Richer, *Etudes Cliniques de la Grande Hystérie*, p. 854.

57. Tavernier, quoted in Maire, *Les Possédées de Morzine*, p. 51.

58. *Spiritual Magazine* (May 1, 1855), p. 214; Maire, *Les Possédées de Morzine*, pp. 85–86.

59. Fournier cited in Maire, *Les Possédées de Morzine*, p. 89.

60. *Le Monde* cited in Blanc, *Le Merveilleux dans le Jansenisme &c.*, p. 280.

61. William H. Burnham, "Suggestion in School Hygiene," *Pedagogical Seminary* 19 (1912): 228–49. See p. 229.

62. P. Schutte, "Eine neue form Hysterischer Zustande bei Schulkindern" [A New Form of Hysterical Conditions in Schoolchildren], *Muenchener Medizinische Wochenschrift* 53 (1906): 1763–64, cited in "A Recent Epidemic of Hysteria," trans. Edgar Schuler and Vincent Parenton. This quote appears on p. 222.

63. William H. Burnham, *The Normal Mind* (New York: D. Appleton, 1924), p. 327.

64. Schoedel, "Uber Induzierte Krankheiten," pp. 521–28.

65. Burnham, "Suggestion in School Hygiene," p. 234.

66. L. Hirt, "Eine Epidemie von Hysterischen Krampfen."

67. Burnham, "Suggestion in School Hygiene," p. 233.

68. Ibid., p. 229.

69. E. I. Thorndike and R. S. Woodworth, "The Influence of Improvement on One Mental Function upon the Efficiency of Other Functions," *Psychological Review* 8 (1901): 247–61.

70. Simon Wessely, "Mass Hysteria: Two Syndromes?" *Psychological Medicine* 17 (1987): 109–20.

71. L. Laquer, "Uber eine Chorea Epidemie" [An Epidemic of Chorea], *Deutsche Med-*

izinische Wochenschrift (Leipzig) 14 (1888): 1045–46; R. Wichmann, "Eine Sogenannte Veitstanzepidemie in Wildbad" [A So-called Epidemic of St. Vitus Dance in Wildbad], *Deutsche Medizinische Wochenschrift* (Leipzig) 16 (1890): 632–36, 659–63.

72. H. Johnson, "Moral Instruction and Training in France," in *Moral Instruction and Training in Schools: Report of an International Inquiry*, vol. 2, ed. Sir Michael Sadler (London: Longmans, Green, 1908), pp. 1–50. See p. 26.

73. Ibid.

74. Ibid., p. 27.

75. B. Dumville, "Should the French System of Moral Instruction Be Introduced into England," pp. 116–17, in Sadler, *Moral Instruction and Training*.

76. Joseph Lukas, *Der Schulmeister von Sadowa* (Mainz, Germany: Kirchheim, 1878), p. 475.

77. Steven R. Welch, *Subjects or Citizens? Elementary School Policy and Practice in Bavaria 1800–1918* (Melbourne, Australia: University of Melbourne, 1998).

78. The Swiss education system was similar to the Germans'. Refer to G. Spiller, "An Educational Democracy: Moral Instruction and Training in the Schools of Switzerland," pp. 196–206, in Sadler, *Moral Instruction and Training*, pp. 196, 199, 203.

79. Schuler and Parenton, "Recent Epidemic of Hysteria," p. 228.

80. Ibid., p. 229.

81 Ibid., p. 228.

82. Ibid., p. 230.

83. Ibid., p. 231.

84. Ibid., p. 233.

85. Ibid., p. 227.

86. Ibid., p. 233.

87. Eng-Seng Tan, "Epidemic Hysteria" (paper read at the Scientific Session of the Annual General Meeting of the Malaysian Medical Association held at the General Hospital, Johor Bahru, on April 12, 1963), published in *Medical Journal of Malaya* 18, no. 2 (December 1963): 72–76. See p. 72.

88. Ibid., p. 72.

89. Ibid., p. 73.

90. Ibid., p. 75.

91. Bob Peries, "A Vengeful Ghost Tried to Lure a Girl to Its Tree Lair," *Straits Times* (Singapore), October 9, 1962, p. 1.

92. "Jinns in a Tree Says Bomoh as Girls Scream at Ghosts," *Straits Times* (Singapore), September 28, 1962, p. 22.

93. Ibid.

94. Robert E. Bartholomew and Robert Rickard, *Mass Hysteria in Schools: A Worldwide History Since 1566* (Jefferson, NC: McFarland, 2014), p. 6.

95. Ibid.

96. Cal Harrison, "Mysterious Ailment Strikes Students at Welsh," *Lake Charles (LA) American Press*, March 28, 1962, p. 1.

97. J. Knight, Theodore I. Friedman, and J. Sulianti, "Epidemic Hysteria: A Field Study," *American Journal of Public Health* 55 (1965): 858–65.

98. Ibid., pp. 858–61.

99. Ibid., p. 861.

100. W. H. Phoon, "Outbreaks of Mass Hysteria at Workplaces in Singapore: Some Patterns and Modes of Presentation," in *Mass Psychogenic Illness: A Social Psychological Analysis*, ed. M. Colligan, J. Pennebaker, and L. Murphy (Hillsdale, NJ: Lawrence Erlbaum, 1982), pp. 21–32.

101. Ibid., p. 23; Michael J. Colligan and L. R. Murphy, "A Review of Mass Psychogenic Illness in Work Settings," in Colligan, Pennebaker, and Murphy, *Mass Psychogenic Illness*, pp. 33–52. See p. 36.

102. Phoon, "Outbreaks of Mass Hysteria," p. 23.

103. Ibid.

104. Susan E. Ackerman, "Cultural Process in Malaysian Industrialization: A Study of Malay Women Factory Workers" (PhD thesis, University of California at San Diego), (Ann Arbor, MI: University Microfilms, 1980).

105. Phoon, "Outbreaks of Mass Hysteria," p. 31.

106. Walter William Skeat, *Malay Magic* (London: Gimlette, 1900); John Desmond, *Malay Poisons and Charm Cures* (London: Oxford University Press, 1915); Kirk Michael Endicott, *An Analysis of Malay Magic* (Oxford, UK: Clarendon, 1970); P. C. Chen, "Indigenous Malay Psychotherapy," *Tropical and Geographical Medicine* 22 (1970): 409.

107. Aihwa Ong, "The Production of Possession: Spirits and the Multinational Corporation in Malaysia," *American Ethnologist* 15 (1988): 28–42. See p. 38.

108. Baruch Modan et al., "The Arjenyattah Epidemic," *Lancet* 2 (1983): 1472–74.

109. A. Hafez, "The Role of the Press and the Medical Community in an Epidemic of Mysterious Gas Poisoning in the Jordan West Bank," *American Journal of Psychiatry* 142 (1985): 833–37. See pp. 834–35.

110. Modan et al., "Arjenyattah Epidemic," p 1472.

111. Ibid.

112. Hafez, "Role of the Press," p. 834.

113. Modan et al., "Arjenyattah Epidemic," p. 1472.

114. Hafez, "Role of the Press," p. 834.

115. Ibid.

116. Modan et al., "Arjenyattah Epidemic," pp. 1472–73.

117. Ibid., p. 1473.

118. Philip Landrigan and Bess Miller, "The Arjenyattah Epidemic: Home Interview Data and Toxicological Aspects," *Lancet* 2 (1983): 1474–76. See p. 1475.

119. D. Bates, "Facebook to Blame for the Panic Surrounding Mysterious Tourettes-like Illness Spreading in Rural NY Town," *Daily Mail* (London), February 5, 2012, p. 1.

120. J. McVige, C. Fritz, and L. Mechtler, "Mass Psychogenic Illness in Leroy High School, New York," supplement, *Annals of Neurology* 72, no. 516 (2012): S192.

121. Melissa Holmes, "Dr. Speaks on NBC's *Today Show*," WGRZ.com, February 24, 2012, http://www.wgrz.com/news/article/151637/13/Parent-Disagrees-With-LeRoy-Illness-Diagnosis (accessed January 23, 2013).

122. "12 Girls at NY High School Develop Involuntary Tics; Doc Says It's Mass Psychogenic Illness," *Washington Post*, January 20, 2012.

123. "Thera Sanchez Develops Mysterious Tourettes-like Illness—Along with 11 Other Girls from School," HuffPost Healthy Living, January 19, 2012, http://www.huffingtonpost.com/2012/01/17/thera-sanchez-tourettes-like-illness-tics-leroy-high-school_n_1210681.html (accessed January 26, 2012).

124. E. Drantch, "Dr: LeRoy Girls have PANDAS-like Illness," report filed by WIVB-TV, Buffalo, NY (Channel 4), February 7, 2012; "Dr. Predicts PANDAS Syndrome in NY Medical Mystery," Fox TV News, USA, January 13, 2012.

125. Robert E. Bartholomew, Simon Wessely, and James Rubin, "Mass Psychogenic Illness and the Social Network: Is It Changing the Pattern of Outbreaks?" *Journal of the Royal Society of Medicine* 105 (2012): 509–12; Robert E. Bartholomew, "Mystery Illness in Western New York: Is Social Networking Spreading Mass Hysteria?" *Skeptical Inquirer* 36, no. 4 (July–August 2012): 26–29.

126. Ibid., p. 511.

CHAPTER 9: IMMEDIATE COMMUNITY THREATS

1. Norman Jacobs, "The Phantom Slasher of Taipei: Mass Hysteria in a Non-Western Society," *Social Problems* 12 (1965): 318–28.

2. Donald M. Johnson, "The 'Phantom Anesthetist' of Mattoon: A Field Study of Mass Hysteria," *Journal of Abnormal Psychology* 40 (1945): 175–86.

3. Robert E. Bartholomew, "Redefining Epidemic Hysteria: An Example from Sweden," *Acta Psychiatrica Scandinavica* 88 (1993): 178–82; Robert E. Bartholomew et al., "The Swedish Ghost Rocket Delusion of 1946: Anatomy of a Moral Panic," *Fortean Studies* 6 (1999): 64–74.

4. Jan Bondenson, *The London Monster* (Gloucestershire, UK: Tempus, 2005), pp. 275–77.

5. "Old Bailey Proceedings, 8th July 1790," Old Bailey Online, http://www.oldbaileyonline.org/browse.jsp?path=sessionsPapers%2F17900708.xml (accessed June 1, 2015).

6. Bondenson, *London Monster*, p. 212.

7. Ibid., p. 232.

8. Ibid., pp. 55–56.

9. Ibid., pp. 57–58, 69–70.

10. David G. Keyworth, "Was the Vampire of the Eighteenth Century a Unique Type of Undead-Corpse?" *Folklore* 117, no. 3 (2006): 241–60.

11. Thomas D'Agostino, *A History of Vampires in New England* (Charleston, SC: History, 2010), pp. 49–50, citing John S. Pettibone, *History of Manchester, Vermont*, pp. 9–10.

12. Ibid., p. 10.

13. Michael Bell, *Food for the Dead: On the Trail of New England's Vampires* (Middletown, CT: Wesleyan University Press, 2002).

14. D'Agostino, *History of Vampires*, pp. 49–50, citing Pettibone, *History of Manchester, Vermont*.

15. Gareth Henderson, "'History of Vampires' Recounts Woodstock Tale," *Vermont Standard*, November 18, 2010. See also: "Early New Englanders Ritually 'Killed' Corpses, Experts Say," *New York Times*, October 31, 1993, p. 1; "'Vampires' Vampirism in Woodstock," Woodstock History Center, citing Rockwell Stephens, "They Burned the Vampire's Heart to Ashes," *Vermont Life* (1966): 47–49.

16. Jeremiah Curtin, "European Folk-Lore in the United States," *Journal of American Folklore* 2, no. 4 (1889): 56–59. See pp. 58–59.

17. John Warner Barber, *Connecticut Historical Collections Containing a General Collection of Interesting Facts, Traditions, Biographical Sketches, Anecdotes, & c. Relating to History and Antiques of Every Town in Connecticut with Geographical Descriptions* (New Haven, CT: Durrie & Peck and John W. Barber, 1836), p. 558; D'Agostino, *History of Vampires*, pp. 39–40, incorrectly cites this account as written by John Warner "Barker."

18. Bell, *Food for the Dead*, p. 67.

19. Jeff Belanger, *World's Most Haunted Places* (New York: Rosen Publishing, 2009), p. 121.

20. Bell, *Food for the Dead*, pp. 21–22.

21. Figures were for 2002, obtained from the Seattle Biomedical Research Institute, 4 Nickerson Street, Suite 200, Seattle, WA, 98109. Refer to http://www.sbri.org/Mission/disease/Chagas.asp.

22. Ibid.

23. Leland O. Howard, "Spider Bites and 'Kissing Bugs,'" *Popular Science Monthly* 56 (November 1899): 31–42. See p. 34.

24. James F. McElhone, "Bite of a Strange Bug," *Washington Post*, June 20, 1899.

25. Howard, "Spider Bites," p. 34.

26. McElhone, "Bite of a Strange Bug."

27. "Kissing Bug Scare Reaches Alameda," *San Francisco (CA) Call*, July 11, 1899, p. 9.

28. *Salt Lake City (UT) Herald*, October 14, 1899, p. 1.

29. "Kissing Bug Club," *News-Herald* (Hillsboro, OH), July 27, 1899, p. 3.

30. "Cause of Death a Kissing Bug," *San Francisco (CA) Call*, July 19, 1899, p. 3.

31. "Died of a Kissing Bug's Bite," *Naugatuck (CT) Daily News*, July 19, 1899.

32. "Does It Presage the End of the World?" *North Platte (NE) Semi-Weekly Tribune*, August 15, 1899, p. 2.

33. Eugene Murray-Aaron, "The Kissing Bug Scare," *Scientific American*, n.s., 81(July 22, 1899), p. 54.

34. Howard, "Spider Bites," p. 34. Italics in original.

35. W. J. F, "Editorial," *Entomological News* 10 (September 1899): 205–206.

36. "Kissing Bugs Discussed," *Evening News* (New York), September 7, 1899.

37. "Kissing Bugs Harmless," *Pacific Commercial Advertiser* (Honolulu, HI), August 22, 1899, p. 4.

38. Murray-Aaron, "Kissing Bug Scare," p. 54.

39. "Weird Tales of Kissing Bug," *Chicago Daily Tribune*, July 11, 1899, p. 2.

40. Howard, "Spider Bites," p. 34.

41. "The Kissing Bug," *Chicago Tribune*, July 20, 1899, p. 7, cited in *Rockford (IL) Register-Gazette*.

42. John McNaught, "Editorial Variations," *San Francisco (CA) Call*, July 23, 1899, p. 6.

43. "Melanolestes Picipes," *News-Herald* (Hillsboro, OH), August 24, 1899, p. 1.

44. "Kissing Bug Gets Knocked Out," *Milwaukee (WI) Journal*, July 22, 1899, p. 2.

45. "Kissing Bug Cure," *Shenandoah Herald* (Woodstock, VA), September 8, 1899, p. 4.

46. James F. McCloy and Ray Miller, *The Jersey Devil* (Wallingford, PA: Middle Atlantic, 1976), p. 39; J. Sullivan and J. McCloy, "The Jersey Devil's Finest Hour," *New York Folklore Quarterly* 30, no. 3 (1974): 233–39.

47. Loren Coleman and Bruce Hallenbeck, *Monsters of New Jersey: Mysterious Creatures in the Garden State* (Mechanicsburg, PA: Stackpole, 2010), p. 98.

48. Janet Bord and Colin Bord, *Alien Animals* (Mechanicsburg, PA: Stackpole, 1981), pp. 118–19.

49. "'Jersey Devil' on Wrong Track; Frightens Inocuous [sic] Milk Driver," *Woodbridge (NJ) Independent*, March 28, 1924.

50. John Koesar, "Jersey Devil Is Still Scaring People, Even If It Is a Trifle Nonexistent," *Spokane (WA) Daily Chronicle*, November 18, 1960, p. 4.

51. Mike Mallowe, "The Enduring Reign of the Jersey Devil," *Bulletin* (Philadelphia), October 30, 2008.

52. Brian Regal, "The Jersey Devil: The Real Story," *Skeptical Inquirer* 27, no. 6 (2013): 50–53. See p. 50.

53. James F. McCloy and Ray Miller, *Phantom of the Pines: More Tales of the Jersey Devil* (Wallingford, PA: Middle Atlantic, 1998), p. 46.

54. Ibid., p. 110.

55. "Comet May Kill All Earth Life Says Scientist," *The Call* (San Francisco, CA), February 8, 1910, p. 1.

56. "Coming End of World," *Ogden (UT) Standard*, February 9, 1910, p. 1.

57. "Discuss Halley's Comet," *Washington Post*, February 6, 1910, p. 15.

58. Ibid.

59. "Comet's Poisonous Tail: Yerkes Observatory Finds Cyanogen in Spectrum of Halley's Comet," *New York Times*, February 7, 1910, p. 1.

60. Richard Flaste et al., *The New York Times Guide to the Return of Halley's Comet* (New York: Times Books, 1985), p. 68.

61. Carl Sagan and Ann Druyan, *Comet* (New York: Random House, 1985), p. 140.

62. "Southern Negroes in a Comet Frenzy," *New York Times*, February 19, 1910, p. 1.

63. "Comet Jerusalem's Omen," *Washington Post*, May 11, 1910, p. 1.

64. "Miners Refuse to Work," *New York Times*, February 19, 1910, p. 1.

65. "Fear Comet Gas May Suffocate Week-Old Kangaroo at Zoo," *Fort Worth (TX) Star-Telegram*, May 16, 1910.

66. Flaste et al., *New York Times Guide*, p. 80.

67. Sagan and Druyan, *Comet*, p. 140; "Pope Not Impressed by Halley's Comet," *New York Times*, May 29, 1910, p. 2.

68. "Parisians Feared Comet Would Kill," *New York Times*, May 22, 1910, p. 3.

69. "Alarm on the Rand," *New York Times*, February 19, 1910, p. 1.

70. "Fear of Comet Caused Attempt at Suicide," *Desert Evening News* (Great Salt Lake City, UT), May 20, 1910; "In Fear of Comet Rancher Suicides," *Daily Arizona Silver Belt* (Gila County, AZ), May 19, 1910.

71. "Comet Causes Suicide Attempt," *New York Tribune*, May 20, 1910.

72. "Gets Rich on Comet Pills," *New York Times*, May 17, 1910.

73. "Do Big Trade in 'Comet Pills,'" *Los Angeles Times*, May 20, 1910.

74. Michael Goss, *The Halifax Slasher: An Urban Terror in the North of England* (London: Fortean Times, 1987), p. 6.

75. Ibid., pp. 22–23.

76. Ibid., p. 23.

77. "Razor Slashers Sought in Five English Towns," *Evening Independent* (UK), November 30, 1938.

78. Goss, *Halifax Slasher*, p. 23.

79. Ibid., p. 12.

80. Ibid., p. 16.

81. "Razor Slashes Sought."

82. Goss, *Halifax Slasher*, pp. 19–20.

83. Ibid., p. 17.

84. Ibid., pp. 24, 28–31.

85. Ibid., pp. 15–16, 28–29.

86. Ibid., p. 30.

87. "A Town in Terror: Army of Police Seek Mythical 'Slasher,'" *Mirror* (Perth, Australia), February 25, 1939, p. 12.

88. Reconstruction of the initial "attack" on Mrs. Kearney is gleaned from the following sources which include firsthand interviews by Mattoon police and psychiatrist Harold S. Hulbert, "Anesthetic Prowler on Loose," *Daily Journal-Gazette* (Mattoon, IL), September 2, 1944, p. 1;"Show How They Were Gassed," *Chicago Herald-American*, September 10, 1944, p. 10; E. Alley, "Illness of First Gas 'Victim' Blamed for Wave of Hysteria in Mattoon," *Chicago Herald-American*, September 17, 1944, p. 3; "Chicago Psychiatrist Analyzes Mattoon Gas Hysteria," *Chicago Herald-American*, September 17, 1944, p. 3; Johnson, "'Phantom Anesthetist.'"

89. "'Mad Gasser' Adds Six Victims! 5 Women and Boy Latest Overcome," *Daily Journal-Gazette*, September 9, 1944, p. 1.

90. Robert Ladendorf and Robert E. Bartholomew, "The Mad Gasser of Mattoon: How the Press Created an Imaginary Chemical Weapons Attack," *Skeptical Inquirer* 26, no. 4 (July–August 2002): 50–53, 58. See p. 53.

91. Ladendorf and Bartholomew, "Mad Gasser of Mattoon," p. 53.

92. "Safety Agent to Aid Police in 'Gas' Case," *Daily Journal-Gazette*, September 6, 1944, p. 6.

93. "Chemists Trace Mattoon Mad Man's 'Gardenia Gas,'" *News-Gazette* (Champaign, IL), September 9, 1944, p. 3.

94. "'Mad Gasser' Adds Six Victims!" p. 1.

95. Ibid.

96. C. Ballenger, "Mattoon's Gas Fiend Attacks Girl, 11, in Home," *Chicago Daily Tribune*, September 9, 1944, p. 10.

97. "Mattoon Gets Jitters from Gas Attacks," *Chicago Herald-American*, September 10, 1944, p. 1.

98. "Mattoon Gets Jitters from Gas Attacks," p. 1; "'Chasers' to Be Arrested," *Daily Journal-Gazette*, September 11, 1944, p. 1; "Sidelights of 'Mad Gasser's' Strange Case," *Daily Journal-Gazette*, September 12, 1944, p. 4.

99. "'Chasers' to Be Arrested," p. 1.

100. "To All Citizens of Mattoon," *Daily Journal-Gazette*, September 11, 1944, p. 1.

101. "Sidelights of 'Mad Gasser's' Strange Case," p. 4.

102. G. Erickson, "Mad Gasser Called Myth," *Chicago Herald-American*, September 13, 1944, p. 1.

103. "'Gasser' Case 'Mistake,'" *Daily Journal-Gazette*, September 12, 1944, p. 4; "Police Chief Says Sprayer Tales Hoax," *Illinois State Journal*, September 13, 1944, p. 1; "Cole Amplifies Statement," *Daily Journal-Gazette*, September 13, 1944, p. 1.

104. E. K. Lindley, "Thoughts on the Use of Gas in Warfare," *Newsweek* 22 (December 20, 1943): 24; V. Sanders, "Our Army's Defense against Poison Gas," *Popular Science* 146 (February 1945): 106–11; E. W. Scott, "Role of the Public Health Laboratory in Gas Defense," *American Journal of Public Health* 34 (March 1944): 275–78.

105. J. Marshall, "We Are Ready with Gas If the Axis Turns on the Gas," *Collier's* 112 (August 7, 1943): 21.

106. "No Gas, Not Even Madman Seen during Night," *Daily Journal-Gazette*, September 15, 1944, p. 6.

107. Ibid.

108. Ralph Champion, "New Three R's Dancing Craze Worries Us," *Argus* (Melbourne, Australia), April 7, 1956, p. 14.

109. Ibid.

110. "Rock 'n Roll Hits Perth: Please, Teenagers, Take It Gently!" *Mirror* (Perth, Australia), April 21, 1956, p. 7.

111. Larry Foley, "Elvis with the Rotating Pelvis: Teenagers in Raptures, Adults Irate," *Mirror* (Perth, Australia), July 14, 1956, p. 4.

112. Ibid.

113. "Rock 'n Rollers Riot," *Argus* (Melbourne, Australia), September 4, 1956, p. 2.

114. "'Rockers' in a New Riot," *Argus* (Melbourne, Australia), September 13, 1956, p. 7.

115. Australian Associated Press and Reuters, "'Rock 'n Roll' Riot by Finns," *Canberra Times* (Australia), October 1, 1956, p. 1.

116. "'Rock 'n' Roll' Riot in Brisbane," *Central Queensland Herald* (Rockhampton, Australia), November 22, 1956, p. 4.

117. "Indict Deejay Freed in Rock-Roll Riot," *Milwaukee (WI) Sentinel*, May 9, 1958, p. 1.

118. "4 Boys Fined in Riots at Rock 'n' Roll," *Pittsburgh (PA) Post-Gazette*, May 5, 1961, p. 10.

119. "Rock 'n' Roll Riot Wrecks Paris Spot," *Ottawa Citizen* (Canada), November 1, 1961, p. 2.

120. "Gangs Wreck Home," *Argus* (Melbourne, Australia), September 4, 1956, p. 2.

121. Australian Associated Press, "Three Shot in Riot Over Rock 'n Roll," *Canberra Times* (Australia), September 24, 1956, p. 3.

122. New Zealand Press Association, "Incident in Singapore," *Evening Post* (Wellington, New Zealand), September 17, 1956.

123. "Rockers in a New Riot," *Argus* (Melbourne, Australia), September 13, 1956, p. 2.

124. Patricia Lewis, "The Tweest: Bigger Than Rock," *Evening Post* (Wellington, New Zealand), December 16, 1961.

125. Robert Lindsey, "'Jaws,' Setting Records Helps Revitalize Movies," *New York Times*, July 8, 1975.

126. Tom Cardy, "Damn You, Spielberg," *Dominion Post* (Wellington, New Zealand), January 6, 2004.

127. Associated Press, "Shark Sighting Reports Credited to Movie 'Jaws,'" *Lawrence (KS) Journal-World*, June 25, 1975, p. 20.

128. Robert E. Dallos, "Shark Wave—Americans Are in the Jaws of a Scare," *Milwaukee (WI) Journal*, July 12, 1975, p. 1.

129. Ibid.

130. United Press International, "Decline in Beach Trade Blamed on Shark Movie," *Dispatch* (Lexington, NC), August 4, 1975, p. 6.

131. "Try These Teeth for Size," *Rome (GA) News-Tribune*, April 17, 1975, p. 5.

132. Robert M. Press, "More Americans Eating Shark—Thanks to Movie, Cheap Price," *Christian Science Monitor*, December 18, 1975.

133. Peter Benchley, "Oceans in Peril," http://seawifs.gsfc.nasa.gov/OCEAN _PLANET/HTML/ocean_planet_book_peril_intro.html (accessed January 15, 2015).

134. Ibid.

135. "Moments after Shark Attack Recalled," *Free Lance-Star* (Fredericksburg, VA), July 13, 2001, p. A6; "Shark Victim's Aunt, Uncle Express Thanks," *Charlotte Herald-Tribune* (Port Charlotte, FL), August 22, 2001, p. 8B.

136. "A Comparison of Shark Attack and Bicycle-Related Fatalities 1990–2009," Florida Museum of Natural History, February 10, 2011, http://www.flmnh.ufl.edu/fish/ sharks/attacks/relariskbike.htm (accessed January 15, 2015).

137. Tanya Basu, "Feeling Lucky? How Lotto Odds Compare to Shark Attacks and Lightning Strikes," December 19, 2013, http://news.nationalgeographic.com/news/ 2013/12/131219-lottery-odds-winning-mega-million-lotto/ (accessed January 15, 2015).

138. "Relax: You're Not That Tempting," *New Scientist* 174, no. 2345 (June 1, 2002): 25.

139. Benjamin Radford, *Tracking the Chupacabra: The Vampire Beast in Fact, Fiction, and Folklore* (Albuquerque: University of New Mexico Press, 2011), p. 3.

140. Ibid.

141. Ibid., p. 40.

142. Ibid.

143. Rosalva Hernandez, "Mythical 'Chupacabra' Instills Fear," *Orange County Register* (Santa Ana, CA), June 4, 1996, p. 1.

144. Robert E. Bartholomew, "The Influence of Culture and Imagination Imagery on the Perception and Interpretation of Unexplained Phenomena" (master's thesis, State University of New York at Albany, 1984).

145. Radford, *Tracking the Chupacabra*, p. 179.

146. Rudolfo Anaya, *Curse of the Chupacabra* (Albuquerque: University of New Mexico Press, 2013).

147. Aristine Lowell, *El Chupacabra* (CreateSpace: printed by author, 2010).

148. T. H. Pine, *Night of the Chupacabra* (Vero Beach, FL: La Maison Publishing, 2013).

149. Katie Ayres, *Taken by the Chupacabra* (Moon Mountain, printed by author, 2013).

150. Radford, *Tracking the Chupacabra*, p. 124.

151. Lalit Kumar, "DIG Says 'Shoot at Monkeyman' as Panic Spreads," *Times of India*, May 14, 2001.

152. "'Monkey' Gives Delhi Claws for Alarm," *Australian* (Surry Hills, New South Wales), May 17, 2001.

153. "Analysis: Monkey Man Attacks in New Delhi," *Morning Edition*, American National Public Radio, May 17, 2001 (Michael Sullivan reporting from New Delhi).

154. Michael Fathers, "Monkey Man Attack! Simian Assailant Sweeps Parts of New Delhi—Anxious Populace Is Gripped by Terror," *Time Asia* 157, no. 201 (May 28, 2001), http://www.time.com/time/asia/news/magazine/0,9754,127298,00.html (accessed June 2, 2015).

155. Ibid.

156. S. K. Verma and D. K. Srivastava, "A Study on Mass Hysteria (Monkey Men?) Victims in East Delhi," *Indian Journal of Medical Sciences* 57, no. 8 (August 2003): 355–60.

157. Sydney Lupkin, "Ebola in America: Timeline of the Deadly Virus," ABC News, http://abcnews.go.com/Health/ebola-america-timeline/story?id=26159719 (accessed October 24, 2014).

158. "Ebola Response Roadmap Situation Report Update," World Health Organization, November 7, 2014, http://apps.who.int/iris/bitstream/10665/137592/1/roadmap sitrep_7Nov2014_eng.pdf?ua=1 (accessed January 25, 2015).

159. "Q & As on Transmission," Center for Disease Control and Prevention, October 30, 2014, http://www.cdc.gov/vhf/ebola/transmission/qas.html (accessed January 27, 2015).

160. Michael Brooks, "The Great Ebola Scare," *New Statesman* (October 17–23, 2014): 31–33. See p. 33.

161. Jeffrey Kluger, "Fear Factor," *Time* 184, no. 15, 2014, pp. 30–34. See p. 33.

162. Ibid., p. 33.

163. Hampton L. Carson, "The Trial of Animals and Insects," *Proceedings of the American Philosophical Society*, vol. 56 (Philadelphia: American Philosophical Society, 1917), pp. 410–15.

CHAPTER 10: MORAL PANICS

1. Jeffrey S. Victor, *Satanic Panic: The Creation of a Contemporary Legend* (Chicago: Open Court, 1993), p. 195.

2. Stanley Cohen, *Folk Devils and Moral Panics: The Creation of the Mods and the Rockers* (London: MacGibbon and Key, 1972), p. 9.

3. Jeffrey S. Victor, "Social Construction of Satanic Ritual Abuse and the Creation of False Memories," pp. 191–216, in *Believed-In Imaginings: The Narrative Construction of*

Reality, ed. Joseph de Rivera and Theodore Sarbin (Washington DC: American Psychological Association, 1998), pp. 192–93.

4. Stanley Cohen, *Folk Devils and Moral Panics*, 3rd ed. (New York: Routledge, 2011), p. 14.

5. Philip Jenkins, *Intimate Enemies: Moral Panics in Contemporary Great Britain* (New York: Aldine de Gruyter, 1992).

6. Ibid., p. 7; Erich Goode and Nachman Ben-Yehuda, *Moral Panics: The Social Construction of Deviance* (Oxford: Blackwell, 1994).

7. Michael Welch, *Flag Burning: Moral Panic and the Criminalization of Protest* (New York: Aldine de Gruyter, 2000).

8. Goode and Ben-Yehuda, *Moral Panics*, pp. 144–84; Erich Goode, *Deviant Behavior*, 6th ed. (Upper Saddle River, NJ: Prentice-Hall, 2001), p. 344.

9. Ibid.

10. Ibid., pp. 24–28.

11. James L. Gilbert, *World War I and the Origins of U.S. Military Intelligence* (Lanham, MD: Scarecrow, 2012), p. 34.

12. Ronald Schaffer, *America in the Great War* (New York: Oxford University Press, 1991), p. 20.

13. Howard S. Becker, *Outsiders: Studies in the Sociology of Deviance* (New York: Free Press, 1963).

14. Schaffer, *America in the Great War*, p. 21.

15. Robert Rickard and John Michell, *Unexplained Phenomena: A Rough Guide Special* (London: Rough Guides, 2001), p. 111; David G. Bromley and Anson Shupe, "Public Reaction against New Religious Movements," pp. 305–34, in *Cults and New Religious Movements: A Report of the American Psychiatric Association from the Committee on Psychiatry and Religion*, ed. Marc Galanter (Washington, DC: American Psychiatric Association, 1989).

16. Ray Allen Billington, "Tentative Bibliography of Anti-Catholic Propaganda in the United States (1800–1860)," *Catholic Historical Review* 18, no. 4 (1933): 492–513.

17. William Hogan, *Popery! As It Was and As It Is; Also, Auricular Confession; and Popish Nunneries* (Hartford, CT: Silas Andrus and Son, 1853).

18. Marie Anne Pagliarini, "The Pure American Woman and the Wicked Catholic Priest: An Analysis of Anti-Catholic Literature in Antebellum America," *Religion and American Culture: A Journal of Interpretation* 9, no. 1 (Winter 1999): 97–128.

19. D. J. Guy, *Sex and Danger in Buenos Aires: Prostitution, Family and Nation in Argentina* (Lincoln: University of Nebraska Press, 1991).

20. Jo Doezema, "Loose Women or Lost Women? The Re-emergence of the Myth of White Slavery in Contemporary Discourses of Trafficking in Women," *Gender Issues* 18, no. 1 (1999): 23–50. See p. 29.

21. Edgar Morin, *Rumour in Orleans* (New York: Pantheon Books, 1971).

22. D. Morton, "Sir William Otter and Internment Operations in Canada during the First World War," *Canadian Historical Review* 55, no. 1 (1974): 32–58. See p. 36.

23. Ibid., p. 33.

24. Paul R. Magocsi, ed., *Encyclopedia of Canada's Peoples* (Toronto: University of Toronto Press, 1999), p. 607.

25. F. MacDonnell, *Insidious Foes* (New York: Oxford University Press, 1995), p. 23.

26. Ibid., pp. 25–26.

27. Fraser Sherman, *Screen Enemies of the American Way: Political Paranoia about Nazis, Communists, Saboteurs, Terrorists and Body-Snatching Aliens in Film and Television* (Jefferson, NC: McFarland, 2010), p. 8.

28. Ibid.

29. James Davidson, Pedro Castillo, and Michael Stoff, *The American Nation* (Upper Saddle River, NJ: Prentice-Hall), p. 694.

30. Excerpt of 1950 speech made by McCarthy to the Woman's Club of Wheeling, West Virginia, citing the Congressional Record of the 81st Congress, 2 Sess., pp. 1952–57, http://www.turnerlearning.com/cnn/coldwar/reds/reds_re3.htm (accessed July 21, 2013).

31. Joel Best and Gerald Horiuchi, "The Razor Blade in the Apple: The Social Construction of Urban Legends," *Social Problems* 32, no. 5 (1985): 488–99. See p. 491.

32. Ibid., p. 494.

33. Ibid., p. 491.

34. Benjamin Radford, "Halloween Panics," pp. 162–69, in *The Martians Have Landed! A History of Media-Driven Panics and Hoaxes*, by Robert Bartholomew and Benjamin Radford (Jefferson, NC: McFarland, 2012). See p. 165.

35. Joel Best, "Halloween Sadism: The Evidence" (unpublished paper, 2007). Best is a professor of sociology and criminal justice at the University of Delaware.

36. "Nasty Videos 'Like Peddling Drugs,'" *Auckland Star* (New Zealand), January 3, 1984.

37. Peter Enos, "British MPs Want 'Video Nasties' Curbed," *Auckland Star* (New Zealand), January 12, 1984.

38. Graham Murdock, "Figuring out the Arguments," p. 64, in *The Video Nasties*, ed. Martin Barker (London: Pluto, 1984).

39. "Violent Videos on Agenda," *New Zealand Herald*, June 18, 1985.

40. "Move to Have Videos Censored," *New Zealand Herald*, June 28, 1985.

41. "Video Nasties: Loose in Your Living Room?" *Grapevine* (Auckland, New Zealand), August 1985, pp. 10–17.

42. Colin Hogg, "Driller Killer . . . The Horrible, Boring Truth," *Auckland Star* (New Zealand), October 12, 1985.

43. Marianne Nørgaard, "Driller Killer . . . The Horrible, Boring Truth," *Auckland Star* (New Zealand), October 12, 1985.

44. Geoffrey Pearson, "Falling Standards: A Short, Sharp History of Moral Decline," pp. 88–103, in Barker, *Video Nasties*.

45. Margaret Talbot, "The Devil in the Nursery," *New York Times Magazine*, January 7, 2001.

46. Edgar Butler et al., *Anatomy of the McMartin Child Molestation Case* (Lanham, MD: University Press of America, 2001), pp. 28–34.

47. Paul Eberle and Shirley Eberle, *The Abuse of Innocence: The McMartin Preschool Trial* (Amherst, NY: Prometheus Books, 1993), p. 21.

48. Butler et al., *McMartin Child Molestation Case*, pp. 14–15.

49. Ibid., pp. 13–14.

50. Ibid.

51. Ibid., p. 5.

52. Eberle and Eberle, *Abuse of Innocence*, pp. 380–81.

53. Daniel Wright et al., "When Eyewitnesses Talk," *Current Directions in Psychological Science* 18, no. 3 (2009): 174–78. See p. 175.

54. Ibid.

55. Ibid.

56. News reports appearing on WRGB, Schenectady, NY (Channel 6), and WAST, Menands, NY (Channel 13), airing on the day the Buckeys were acquitted.

57. Eberle and Eberle, *Abuse of Innocence*, p. 202.

58. Talbot, "Devil in the Nursery."

59. Tony Rogers, "MIT Student's Death Attributed to Violent 'Knockout' Game," *The Day* (New London, CT), September 23, 1992, p. 3A.

60. Ibid.

61. Ibid.

62. Associated Press, "MIT Student Killed after Robbery," *Tuscaloosa (AL) News*, September 19, 1992, p. 2A.

63. C. Buckley, "Police Unsure if Random Attacks Are Rising Threat or Urban Myth," *New York Times*, November 22, 2013, p. 19A.

64. Ibid.

65. "'Knockout Game' Is a Fabricated Trend, Victim James Addlespurger Says (VIDEO)," HuffPost Crime, December 8, 2013, http://www.huffingtonpost.com/2013/12/08/knockout-game-isnt-real-james-addlespurger_n_4408112.html (accessed December 8, 2013).

66. Buckley, "Police Unsure."

67. Morgan Winsor, "Police Keep Close Eye on Reports of Disturbing 'Knockout' Game," CNN, November 24, 2013, http://edition.cnn.com/2013/11/22/justice/knockout-game-teen-assaults/ (accessed January 20, 2015).

68. John H. Tucker, "Knockout King: Kids Call It a Game, Academics Call It a Bogus Trend, Cops Call It Murder," *Riverfront Times*, June 9, 2011, http://www.riverfront

times.com/2011-06-09/news/knockout-king-elex-murphy-hoang-nguyen-dutchtown
-murder/full/ (accessed January 20, 2015).

69. Mike Males, "Another Round of 'Knockout Game' Idiocy," Center of Juvenile and Criminal Justice, November 26, 2013, http://www.cjcj.org/news/6976 (accessed January 20, 2015).

70. Aisha Dow, "90 Killed in Single-Punch Assaults since 2000," *Sydney Morning Herald* (Australia), December 2, 2013, http://www.smh.com.au/national/90-killed-in-singlepunch-assaults-since-2000-20131201-2yjtr.html (accessed December 3, 2014).

71. Ibid.

72. "Crime in the United States 2013—Aggravated Assault," Federal Bureau of Investigation, http://www.fbi.gov/about-us/cjis/ucr/crime-in-the-u.s/2013/crime-in-the-u.s.-2013/violent-crime/aggravated-assault-topic-page (accessed January 15, 2015).

73. Thomas Tracy, "Brooklyn Tourist Attacked in Possible 'Knockout Game' Variation," *New York Daily News*, March 25, 2014, http://www.nydailynews.com/new-york/nyc-crime/nyc-tourist-attacked-knockout-game-article-1.1734312 (accessed January 15, 2015).

74. Ibid.

75. "'Knockout' Attack Victim Actually Just Fell Down," *Gothamist*, March 27, 2014, http://gothamist.com/2014/03/27/knockout_attack_victim_actually_jus.php (accessed January 16, 2015).

76. Ibid.

77. Brian Chapman, e-mail to the Forteana Group, November 28, 2013 (quoted with permission).

78. Gregor Bulc, "Kill the Cat Killers: Moral Panic and Juvenile Crime in Slovenia," *Journal of Communication Inquiry* 26, no. 3 (2002): 300–25. See pp. 307–308.

79. Ibid., p. 308.

80. Ibid.

81. Ibid., p. 309.

82. Ibid., pp. 309–10.

83. Ibid., pp. 311–12.

84. Ibid., p. 317.

85. Ibid.

86. Ian Marsh and Gaynor Melville, "Moral Panics and the British Media—A Look at Some Contemporary 'Folk Devils,'" *Internet Journal of Criminology* (2011): 1–21, published online at: www.internetjournalofcriminology.com.

87. P. Barkham, "How a Top Can Turn a Teen into a Hoodlum," *Guardian* (London), May 14, 2005, cited in Marsh and Melville, "Moral Panics," p. 12.

88. Jack Fawbert, "Boys N the Boodie," *Society Guardian*, March 3, 2008.

CHAPTER 11: RIOTS

1. Anthony Oberschall, "The Los Angeles Race Riot of August 1965," *Social Problems* 15 (1968): 322–41.

2. Kathy S. Stolley, *The Basics of Sociology* (Westport, CT: Greenwood, 2005), p. 185.

3. Curtis Tucker, *To Rebuild Is Not Enough: Final Report and Recommendations of the Assembly Special Committee on the Los Angeles Crisis* (Sacramento, CA: Assembly Publications Office, 1992); George Ritzer, *Introduction to Sociology* (Thousand Oaks, CA: Sage, 2013), p. 622.

4. Christopher T. Husbands, "Racial Attacks: The Persistence of Racial Vigilantism in British Cities," in *Traditions of Intolerance: Historical Perspectives on Fascism and Race Discourse in Britain*, by Tony Kushner and Kenneth Lunn (Manchester, UK: Manchester University Press, 1989), p. 97.

5. John Lofland, *Protest: Studies in Collective Behavior and Social Movements* (New Brunswick, NJ: Transaction, 2007), p. 85.

6. John Spiegel, "Hostility, Aggression and Violence," pp. 332–39, in *A Social History of Racial Violence*, ed. Allen D. Crimshaw (Brunswick, NJ: Transaction, 2009); Ralph W. Conant, "Phases of a Riot," pp. 108–10, in *Collective Behavior*, 2nd ed., ed. Ralph Turner and Lewis Killian (Englewood Cliffs, NJ: Prentice-Hall, 1972).

7. Reid Luhman, *The Sociological Outlook*, 2nd ed. (San Diego, CA: Collegiate, 1989), p. 435.

8. Stanley Lieberman and Arnold Silverman, "Precipitants and Conditions of Race Riots," *American Sociological Review* 30 (1965): 887–98.

9. George Rude, *The Crowd in History, 1730–1848* (New York: John Wiley, 1964), pp. 57–59.

10. Neil J. Smelser, *Theory of Collective Behavior* (New York: Free Press, 1962), pp. 230–31.

11. Ibid., p. 248, citing Gordon Allport and Leo Postman.

12. Jerry Rose, *Outbreaks: The Sociology of Collective Behavior* (New York: Free Press, 1982), p. 102.

13. Spiegel, "Hostility, Aggression and Violence."

14. Frederick Mish, ed., *Merriam-Webster Collegiate Dictionary*, 11th ed. (Springfield, MA: Merriam-Webster, 2004), p. 1081.

15. Charles F. Marden, Gladys Meyer, and Madeline H. Engel, *Minorities in American Society*, 6th ed. (New York: HarperCollins, 1992), pp. 272–73; David Wallechinsky and Irving Wallace, eds., *The People's Almanac* (Garden City, NY: Doubleday, 1975), p. 233.

16. Douglas Massey, "Origins of Economic Disparities: The Historical Role of Housing Segregation," pp. 39–80, in *Segregation: The Rising Costs for America*, ed. James Carr and Nandinee Kutty (New York: Routledge, 2008), p. 76.

17. James Davidson, Pedro Castillo, and Michael Stoff, *The American Nation* (Upper Saddle River, NJ: Prentice-Hall, 2000), p. 464; Wallechinsky and Wallace, *The People's Almanac*, p. 183.

18. David L. Miller, *Introduction to Collective Behavior and Collective Action*, 2nd ed. (Prospect Heights, IL: Waveland, 2000), p. 317.

19. Jeffrey Goldstein, ed., *Sports, Games, and Play: Social and Psychological Viewpoints* (Hillsdale, NJ: Lawrence Erlbaum, 2009), p. 322.

20. John S. DeMott, "Wreaking Havoc on Spring Break," *Time* 127, no. 14, April 7, 1986, p. 29.

21. Joel Tyler Headley, *The Great Riots of New York 1712–1873* (New York: Thunder's Mouth, 2004). Main text and bibliographic note briefly detailing riots not covered in the main text by Headley, pp. 265–69.

22. Willard A. Heaps, *Riots U.S.A. 1765–1965* (New York: Seabury, 1966), pp. 50–51.

23. Headley, *Great Riots*, pp. 110–11.

24. Ibid., p. 114.

25. Ibid., pp. 125–26.

26. Ibid., pp. 145–46.

27. Ibid., pp. 123–24.

28. Ibid., pp. 207–10. Some of these vicious events are re-created in the 2002 Martin Scorsese film *Gangs of New York*.

29. Iver Bernstein, *The New York City Draft Riots: Their Significance for American Society and Politics in the Age of the Civil War* (New York: Oxford University Press, 1990), p. 288.

30. Clio Francis, "The Battle of Manners St," *Dominion Post* (Wellington, New Zealand), August 13, 2011, p. 2A.

31. John Costello, *Love, Sex and War* (London: Guild Publishing, 1985), pp. 323–24.

32. "Manners Street Battle—A Return to the Fray," *Contact* (Wellington, New Zealand), June 25, 1992.

33. Clio Francis, "Paper Boy Wartime Witness to Battle of Manners St," *Dominion Post* (Wellington, New Zealand), August 17, 2011, p. 7A.

34. "Manners Street Battle—A Return to the Fray" *Contact* (Wellington, New Zealand), June 25, 1992.

35. Kathy Peiss, *Zoot Suit* (Philadelphia: University of Pennsylvania Press, 2011), pp. 24–25.

36. Ibid., pp. 88 –91.

37. "Troops Tear Suits off Youths in Los Angeles Riots," *News* (Adelaide, Australia), June 9, 1943, p. 3.

38. "'Glad Plaid' Youths Go Khaki-Wacky!" *Pittsburgh Press* (Pittsburgh, PA), June 9, 1943, p. 1.

39. "Rioting by Zoot Suit Gangs to Be Probed; Fighting Subsides," *Victoria Advocate* (Victoria, Texas), June 11, 1943, p. 8.

40. Ibid.

41. "Mexican Official Protests Attacks on Zoot Suiters," *Lewiston (ME) Daily Sun*, June 10, 1943, p. 11.

42. United Press International, "National Guard Called to Datonya Beach Riot," *Sarasota (FL) Herald Tribune*, February 27, 1956, p. 1.

43. Ibid., p. 2.

44. Ibid.

45. United Press International, "8,000 Rioting Florida Students Set Fires after Sports Wins," *Sarasota (FL) Herald-Tribune*, December 6, 1964, p. 9.

46. United Press International, "'Enticing' Coeds Touch off Riot in Gatorland," *Ocala (FL) Star-Banner*, December 7, 1964, p. 2.

47. Ibid.

48. United Press International, "1 UF Student Expelled, Nine Are Suspended," *St. Petersburg (FL) Times*, December 22, 1964, p. 4B.

49. David Carter, *Stonewall* (New York: St. Martin's Griffin, 2004), p. 160.

50. Ibid., pp. 150–51.

51. Ibid., p. 176.

52. Ibid., p. 185.

53. Ibid., pp. 190–91.

54. Ibid., p. 201.

55. Ibid., p. 204.

56. Martin Gottlieb and James Glanz, "The Blackout of 2003: The Past; The Blackouts of '65 and '77 Became Defining Moments in the City's History," *New York Times*, August 15, 2003, http://www.nytimes.com/2003/08/15/us/blackout-2003-past-blackouts-65-77-became-defining-moments-city-s-history.html (accessed January 10, 2015).

57. "Night of Terror," *Time*, July 25, 1977, pp. 12–26.

58. Ibid., p. 17.

59. Ibid., p. 18.

60. "Looking for a Reason," *Time*, July 25, 1977, p. 17.

61. The Rodney King beating video can be viewed at https://www.youtube.com/watch?v=xZDrZDEqeKk (accessed June 2, 2015).

62. Melissa Pamer, "Los Angeles 1992 Riots: By the Numbers," KNBC Los Angeles (Channel 4), April 20, 2012, http://www.nbclosangeles.com/news/local/Los-Angeles-1992-Riots-By-the-Numbers-148340405.html (accessed February 3, 2015).

63. Madison Gray, "The L.A. Riots: 15 Years after Rodney King—Reginald Denny," *Time*, October 28, 2008, http://content.time.com/time/specials/2007/la_riot/article/0,28804,1614117_1614084_1614511,00.html (accessed January 15, 2015).

64. Linda Deutsch, "Williams Sentenced to Ten Years," *Times Daily* (Florence, Alabama), December 8, 1993, p. 2.

65. Steve Lopez, "The Forgotten Victim from Florence and Normandie," *Los Angeles Times*, May 6, 2012, http://articles.latimes.com/2012/may/06/local/la-me-0506-lopez-riot-20120506 (accessed February 22, 2015).

66. "'We've Just Got to Stop,'" *St. Petersburg (FL) Times*, May 2, 1992, p. 1.

67. Daniel Briggs, "Introduction," pp. 9–25, in *The English Riots of 2011: A Summer of Discontent*, ed. Daniel Briggs (Hampshire, UK: Waterside, 2012), p. 10.

68. Daniel Briggs, "Frustrations, Urban Relations and Temptations: Contextualising the English Riots," pp. 27–41, in Briggs, *English Riots of 2011*, p. 10.

69. Ajmal Masroor et al., "The Citizen's Inquiry into the Tottenham Riots, 2012," Citizens UK, http://www.citizensuk.org/wp-content/uploads/2012/02/Citizens-Inquiry-into-the-Tottenham-Riots-REPORT.pdf (accessed October 6, 2014).

70. Bernard Hogan-Howe, *4 Days in August: The Strategic Review into the Disorder of August 2011, Final Report March 2012*, Metropolitan Police Service, p. 14.

71. Daniel Briggs, "Introduction," pp. 9–25, in Briggs, *English Riots of 2011*, p. 10.

72. Ferguson Police Dept. "Racial Profiling Data 2013," http://ago.mo.gov/Vehicle Stops/2013/reports/161.pdf (accessed May 15, 2015).

73. Tim Barker, "Ferguson-Area Businesses Cope with Aftermath of Weekend Riot," *St. Louis (MA) Post-Dispatch*, August 11, 2014.

74. Melanie Eversley, "Two Reporters Arrested in Ferguson, Mo," *USA Today*, August 19, 2014.

75. Wesley Lowery, "Federal Judges [*sic*] Tosses '5 Second Rule' Being Used to Police Ferguson Protests," *Washington Post*, October 6, 2014.

76. "Police Tactics Blamed after Race Riots," *Dominion Post* (Wellington, New Zealand), August 16, 2014, p. 1B.

77. "Review Ordered of Firepower at Police Officers' Disposal," *Dominion Post* (Wellington, New Zealand), August 26, 2014, p. 2B.

78. David von Drehle and Alex Altman, "The Tragedy of Ferguson," *Time*, September 1, 2014, p. 40.

79. Ferguson Police Dept. "Ferguson Crisis Arrest Data," http://i2.cdn.turner.com/cnn/2014/images/08/22/arrest.data.from.8-10.to.8-22.pdf (accessed June 2, 2015).

CHAPTER 12: SMALL-GROUP PANICS

1. Robert Buckhout, "Eyewitness Testimony," *Scientific American* 231 (1974): 23–31; Robert Buckhout, "Nearly 2000 Witnesses Can Be Wrong," *Bulletin of the Psychonomic Society* 16 (1980): 307–10.

2. Robert Sheaffer, *The UFO Verdict* (Amherst, NY: Prometheus Books, 1981).

3. C. M. Massad, M. Hubbard, and D. Newston, "Selective Perception of Events," *Journal of Experimental Social Psychology* 15 (1979): 513–32. See p. 531.

4. Leon Festinger, "Informal Social Communications," *Psychological Review* 57 (1950): 271–80. See p. 272.

5. Fred Tracy Stiles, *Old Days–Old Ways: More History and Tales of the Adirondack Foothills* (Hudson Falls, NY: Washington County Historical Society, 1984).

6. Ibid.

7. "Mirage at Sea," *Fulton (NY) Patriot*, March 4, 1937.

8. Hadley Cantril, *The Invasion From Mars* (Princeton, NJ: Princeton University Press, 1966), p. 181.

9. William J. Cromie, "False Memories" (an interview with psychologist Daniel Schacter), *Harvard University Gazette*, September 19, 1996, http://news.harvard.edu/gazette/legacy-gazette/# (accessed December 22, 2014).

10. Tony Jinks, *An Introduction to the Psychology of Paranormal Belief and Experience* (Jefferson, NC: McFarland, 2002), pp. 124–25.

11. Ibid., p. 126.

12. Ibid., pp. 128–29.

13. J. R. Hilgard, *Personality and Hypnosis: A Study of Imaginative Involvement* (Chicago: University of Chicago Press, 1970); J. R. Hilgard, *Personality and Hypnosis: A Study of Imaginative Involvement*, 2nd ed. (Chicago: University of Chicago Press, 1979).

14. Sheryl Wilson and Theodore Barber, "The Fantasy-Prone Personality: For Understanding Imagery, Hypnosis, and Parapsychological Phenomena," in *Imagery: Current Theory, Research, and Application*, ed. A. A. Sheikh (New York: Wiley, 1983).

15. Ibid., p. 351.

16. Ibid., p. 346.

17. M. Pines, "Invisible Playmates," *Psychology Today* 12 (1978): 38–42.

18. Wilson and Barber, "Fantasy-Prone Personality," p. 346.

19. Cotton Mather, *Magnalia Christi Americana* (Hartford, CT: Silas Andrus & Son, 1853), pp. 621–23.

20. Ibid., p. 621.

21. Ibid.

22. Ibid. Italics in original.

23. Ibid., p. 622.

24. John James Babson, *History of the Town of Gloucester, Cape Ann, Including the Town of Rockport* (Gloucester, MA: Procter Brothers, 1860), pp. 212–13.

25. Mather, *Magnalia Christi Americana*, p. 622.

26. Ibid., pp. 622–23.

27. Frances Hill, *The Salem Witchcraft Reader* (Cambridge, MA: DaCapo, 2009), p. 275.

28. Peter Muise, *Legends and Lore of the North Shore* (Charleston, NC: History, 2014), p. 118.

29. Mary Beth Norton, *In the Devil's Snare: The Salem Witch Crisis of 1692* (New York: Vintage, 2003), p. 232.

30. Mather, *Magnalia Christi Americana*, p. 623.

31. Emerson Baker, *A Storm of Witchcraft: The Salem Trials and the American Experience* (Oxford: Oxford University Press, 2015), p. 144.

32. John Warner Barber, *Connecticut Historical Collections, Containing a General Collection of Interesting Facts, Traditions, Biographical Sketches, Anecdotes, &c., Relating to the History and Antiquities of Every Town in Connecticut, with Geographical Descriptions* (New Haven, CT: John W. Barber, 1836), p. 446.

33. Ibid., p. 447.

34. Ron Robillard, *Windham and Williamantic* (Charleston, SC: Arcadia Publishing, 2005), p. 12.

35. Isabel Davis and Ted Bloecher, *Close Encounter at Kelly and Others of 1955* (Evanston, IL: Center for UFO Studies, 1978); Josef Allen Hynek and Jacques Vallee, *The Edge of Reality: A Progress Report on Unidentified Flying Objects* (Chicago: Henry Regnery, 1975); Robert J. M. Rickard, "More Phantom Sieges," *Fortean Times* (Winter 1985): 58–61.

36. Davis and Bloecher, *Close Encounter at Kelly*, p. 14.

37. Joe Nickell, interview with Lonnie Langford on August 20, 2005, then aged 62. Joe Nickell, "Siege of 'Little Green Men': The 1955 Kelly, Kentucky, Incident," *Skeptical Inquirer* 30, no. 6 (2006): 12–14.

38. Ibid., p. 14; Ronald Westrum, "Phantom Attackers," *Fortean Times* (Winter 1985): 54–58; Rickard, "More Phantom Sieges."

39. Experts can disagree. The "Space Goblins" case of Kelly, Kentucky, is an example. When Robert Bartholomew wrote this entry, Peter Hassall strongly objected. Peter asserts that if owls were to blame, why were there no traces of blood, and why would they walk toward bullets fired from the house instead of flying away? Peter considers the owl explanation weak. He views the statement that the Air Force placed this case in their "crackpot" file as demeaning to the witnesses. Robert accepts the owl explanation as the most viable. He says it shows how the Air Force dismissed the case without even investigating, and that this places the Air Force, not the witnesses, in a negative light.

40. Harold T. Wilkins, *Flying Saucers on the Attack* (New York: Citadel, 1954).

41. Edward J. Ruppelt, *The Report on Unidentified Flying Objects* (Nashville, TN: Source Books, 2002).

42. John G. Fuller, *The Interrupted Journey: Two Lost Hours aboard a Flying Saucer* (New York: Berkley Medallion, 1966), p. 12.

43. Ibid., p. 16.

44. The summary of this incident is based on the following sources: ibid.; James and

Coral Lorenzen, *Abducted! Confrontations with Beings from Outer Space* (Berkeley, CA: Medallion, 1977); Sheaffer, *UFO Verdict*; Ronald Story, *Sightings* (New York: Quill, 1982).

45. Ronald Story, *The Encyclopedia of UFOs* (New York: Doubleday, 1980), p. 176.

46. Walter N. Webb, *A Dramatic UFO Encounter in the White Mountains, New Hampshire—The Hill Case—Sept. 19–20, 1961*, report submitted to the National Investigations Committee on Aerial Phenomena, Washington, DC, August 30, 1965, 61 pp. See p. 15.

47. Buckhout, "Eyewitness Testimony," p. 25.

48. Don Donderi, "Essay Review: Three New England Abduction Stories and One New Reality," *Journal of Scientific Exploration* 28, no. 2 (2014): 361–72. See p. 362.

49. Edwin E. Moïse, *Tonkin Gulf and the Escalation of the Vietnam War* (Chapel Hill: University of North Carolina Press, 1996).

50. Donald E. Schmidt, *The Folly of War: American Foreign Policy, 1898–2005* (New York: Algora Publishing, 2005), p. 264.

51. Maurice Isserman, *Vietnam War* (New York: Facts on File, 2003), p. 53.

52. Ibid.

53. Moïse, *Tonkin Gulf*, p. 107.

54. Ibid., p. 108.

55. Isserman, *Vietnam War*, p. 53.

56. "Gulf of Tonkin 60 Minutes 1," YouTube video, 6:54, from an episode of *60 Minutes* televised by CBS in 1971, posted by "mrkhistory," April 17, 2011, https://www.youtube.com/watch?v=3Uy5RZ70Jkk (accessed December 26, 2014).

57. Fred Beck and Ronald A. Beck, *I Fought the Apemen of Mt. St. Helens, WA*, Bigfoot Classics, http://www.bigfootencounters.com/classics/beck.htm (accessed December 10, 2014).

58. Ibid.

59. "Fight with Big Apes Reported by Miners," *Portland Oregonian*, July 13, 1924, p. 1.

60. Beck and Beck, *I Fought the Apemen*.

61. Ibid.

62. Ibid.

63. Ibid.

64. "Party Discounts Apeman Story," *Lubbock (TX) Morning Avalanche*, July 18, 1924, p. 1.

65. Gregory L. Reece, *Weird Science and Bizarre Beliefs: Mysterious Creatures, Lost Worlds and Amazing Inventions* (New York: I. B. Tauris, 2009), p. 85.

66. Jerome Clark, *Unexplained! Strange Sightings, Incredible Occurrences & Puzzling Physical Phenomena* (Farmington Hills, MI: Visible Ink, 1999), p. 335.

67. Andrea Perron, *House of Darkness House of Light: The True Story*, vol. 1 (Bloomington, IN: AuthorHouse, Kindle Edition, 2011), p. 60.

68. Ibid., p. 382.

69. Ibid., pp. 53, 311, 313.

70. Andrea Perron, *House of Darkness House of Light: The True Story*, vol. 2 (Bloomington, IN: AuthorHouse, Kindle Edition 2013), p. 293.

71. Ibid., pp. 265–66.

72. "Cluster Flies, How to Gid Rid of Cluster Flies—EHS Pest Solutions," Environmental Health Services, Inc., http://ehspest.com/cluster-flies.htm (accessed January 22, 2014).

73. Perron, *House of Darkness*, vol. 2, pp. 260–62.

74. Perron, *House of Darkness*, vol. 1, p. 156.

75. Ibid., p. 157.

76. Joe Nickell, *The Science of Ghosts: Searching for Spirits of the Dead* (Amherst, NY: Prometheus Books, 2012), pp. 41–43, 109.

77. Perron, *House of Darkness*, vol. 1, p. 185.

78. David J. Hufford, "Sleep Paralysis as Spiritual Experience," *Transcultural Psychiatry* 42, no. 1 (2005): 11–45. See p. 20.

79. Perron, *House of Darkness*, vol. 2, pp. 70–72.

80. D. Pearson et al., "Prevalence of Imaginary Companions in a Normal Child Population," *Child: Care, Health and Development* 27, no. 1 (2001): 13–22.

81. Karen Majors, "Children's Perceptions of their Imaginary Companions and the Purposes They Serve: An Exploratory Study in the United Kingdom," *Childhood* 20, no. 4 (2013): 550–65.

82. Perron, *House of Darkness*, vol. 1, pp. 431, 438.

83. Ibid., p. 445.

84. Ibid.

85. "The Conjuring . . . The Truth behind the Movie . . . Harrisville Haunting," YouTube video, 1:06:26, interview with Andrea Perron by Rite Scott from Westport Radio (Ireland), WRFM 98.2, posted by "ritascott1," June 8, 2013, http://www.youtube.com/watch?v=8y8CKlE7ntY.

86. Westrum, "Phantom Attackers."

87. Ibid., p. 55.

88. Ibid., p. 54.

89. Ibid., p. 55. Italics in original.

90. Ibid. Italics in original.

91. Ibid.

92. Dennis Pilichis, *Night Siege: The Northern Ohio UFO-Creature Invasion* (Rome, OH: printed by author).

93. Ronald Schaffner, "Retrospective: Rome, Ohio Incidents," report filed for Don Keating, head of the Eastern Ohio Bigfoot Investigation Center in Newcomerstown, Ohio,

http://web.archive.org/web/20081208172714/http://www.angelfire.com/oh/ohiobigfoot/romeohio.html (accessed January 21, 2015).

94. Pilichis, *Night Siege*, p. 5.

95. Ibid., pp. 7–10; Schaffner, "Retrospective."

96. Schaffner, "Retrospective."

97. Pilichis, *Night Siege*, p. 13.

98. Ibid.

99. Ronald Schaffner, "Rome, Ohio, Part II," http://web.archive.org/web/20050708074153/http://www.angelfire.com/oh/ohiobigfoot/romeohio2.html (accessed January 15, 2015).

100. Ibid.

101. Pilichis, *Night Siege*, pp. 14–16.

102. Ibid., p. 21.

103. Associated Press, "Scourge from Outer Space? Australians Report Seeing UFOs," *Ocala (FL) Star-Banner*, January 22, 1988, p. 6.

104. Mike Smithson, Channel 7 news report, Adelaide, South Australia, aired January 20, 1988.

105. Keith Basterfield and Ray Brooke, "The Mundrabilla Incident—An Update," p. 6, report filed for UFO Research South Australia, circa 1988),

106. Ibid., p. 7.

107. Ibid.

108. Basterfield and Brooke, "Mundrabilla Incident," p. 9.

109. Anthony M. Luke, "Report M4375/88," issued January 29, 1988 by the Applied Sciences Group of Amdel Technology and Enterprise, 31 Flemington Street, Frewville, South Australia 5063, p. 3.

110. Ibid., pp. 1–2.

111. Basterfield and Brooke, "Mundrabilla Incident," p. 7.

112. Lynton Grace, "South Australia's X Files: Part 1—Family Car Attacked by UFO," *Adelaide Advertiser*, June 7, 2014, http://www.adelaidenow.com.au/news/special-features/south-australias-x-files-part-1-the-day-a-ufo-attacked-a-car-on-the-nullarbor/story-fnknbqfx-1226937054540 (accessed January 1, 2015).

113. Ibid.

114. Richard Hall, *The UFO Evidence: A Thirty Year Report*, vol. 2 (Lanham, MD: Scarecrow, 2000), pp. 232–36.

CHAPTER 13: POSTSCRIPT

1. Elizabeth Knowles, ed., *The Oxford Dictionary of Quotations* (Oxford: Oxford University Press, 2001), p. 44.

INDEX